POLITICAL LEADERSHIP IN SIERRA LEONE

In an age when men have come to believe that their destinies can be determined by human actions rather than by fate, the question looms large of what a leader can do to fulfil the aspirations of those looking for guidance. Since the political arena is one involving the use of power, the position of the political leader in particular has become the focus for men's hopes and fears.

This book is a case study of the effect that different forms of political leadership can have upon the shaping of a single state. It focuses upon two successive Prime Ministers of the Small West African state of Sierra Leone: Sir Milton Margai and his younger brother Sir Albert Margai, By examining their dealings with local political units, their handling of ethnic and regional conflicts, their attitude to change and their relations with major economic forces, the author assesses why both leaders had such different measures of success with their divergent political policies.

The major findings of this study are that the method that a leader chooses to accomplish his goals can be as important to their realization as the choice of goals themselves and that a leader may find himself committed to a particular course through simply pursuing a line of least resistance.

JOHN R. CARTWRIGHT Associate Professor of Political Science at the University of Western Ontario, London, Canada.

Political Leadership in Sierra Leone

JOHN R. CARTWRIGHT

UNIVERSITY OF TORONTO PRESS / TORONTO AND BUFFALO

First published 1978 in Canada and the United States of America by
University of Toronto Press
Toronto and Buffalo
Reprinted in paperback 2015

ISBN 978-0-8020-5404-3 (cloth)
ISBN 978-1-4426-3897-6 (paper)

Canadian Cataloguing in Publication Data

Cartwright, John R., 1937-
Political leadership in Sierra Leone

ISBN 978-0-8020-5404-3 (bound) ISBN 978-1-4426-3897-6 (pbk.)

1. Sierra Leone – Politics and government.
2. Prime ministers – Sierra Leone. 3. Leadership –
Case studies. I. Title.

DT516.8.C37 320.9'66'4 C77-001449-6

CONTENTS

Acknowledgements

1. Introduction: Settings for Political Leadership 9

2. Sierra Leone at the Start of Deconolonisation: A Brief Overview 32

3. Major Political Events in Sierra Leone, 1951-67 59

4. Milton and Albert Margai: A Portrait of Two Leaders 89

5. National Leaders and Local Politics 116

6. Leadership and Ethnic Conflict 159

7. The Pace of Social Change as a Source of Conflict 212

8. Economic Development and Political Leadership 238

9. Conclusions 274

Methodological Appendix: The 1968 Questionnaire Regarding Leadership in Sierra Leone 303

Index 305

ACKNOWLEDGEMENTS

This study grew out of a proposed joint study originally worked out by Professor Robert S. Jordan, who had been Littauer Visiting Professor at Fourah Bay College, the University College of Sierra Leone, during my final year of teaching there in 1965-6. In 1967 I completed the manuscript for my *Politics in Sierra Leone,* and in 1968 I was able to return to Sierra Leone for a few weeks to complete field research for the leadership study. However, pressure of other commitments stopped both of us from writing, and finally in 1971 Bob Jordan decided to withdraw from the project. In 1972-3 I fortunately had a sabbatical, and was able to complete the manuscript; apart from clarifying arguments and providing more up-to-date footnote references on a few points, I have not changed it since then.

At this point I would like to thank both my academic co-workers whose co-operation and stimulation make research such a pleasurable activity, and the political actors without whom political scientists would have to be re-employed in far less interesting work; I would like to think that the latter group may occasionally find in the writings of academics some interesting ideas which can serve as a small recompense for their willingness to help us. Since much of the material for this study was obtained in the same discussions that furnished the information for my previous book, I would first repeat my thanks to the large number of Sierra Leonean political activists who shared their time and thoughts so generously with me during my years at Fourah Bay. Without wishing to slight others who have given me illuminating comments, I would like to thank particularly Salia Jusu-Sheriff, Peter Tucker, Bankole Timothy, Sir Banja Tejan-Sie, M.O. Bash-Taqi, C.A. Kamara-Taylor, and (although I am afraid he may not like the judgements I have rendered on his career) Sir Albert Margai. I am also grateful to a number of former British civil servants and others who spent much time in Sierra Leone, particularly Dennis Kirby, Sir George Beresford-Stooke, Sir Foley Newns, Sir Maurice Dorman, John Morten of Sierra Leone Selection Trust, and David Williams, editor of *West Africa.*

My debts to academic colleagues are almost as numerous. Besides Bob Jordan for conceiving the idea of the book, I owe my usual debt of gratitude to Mary Hrabik Samal for her judicious blend of encouragement and sharp criticism of ambiguities and confusions in my arguments, and to Fred Barnard for a number of suggestions on the nature of leadership. Among the large number of 'Sierra Leoneanists' whose comments have been most helpful I would thank particularly Laurens van der Laan, James Littlejohn and Tom Cox, and also Walter Barrows, Christopher Clapham, Milton Harvey, Carol Hoffer, Kenneth Little, Peter Mitchell, Ken Rothman and Ken Swindell, as well as the readers for the Social Science Research Council of Canada and for the University of Sierra Leone Press.

I also would like to praise a number of very able and dedicated research assistants who contributed greatly to different stages of this long-drawn-out process: James Sanpha Koroma, who did excellent work in helping me organise a survey in 1968, Betsy Gryzb, Mike Kacaba, J'Anne Winton, Jean Bradshaw, and Christine Troughton, whose ability to find and interpret the significance of comparative works went far beyond my own. I was also aided greatly during my sabbatical in England by the courteous and helpful staffs of several libraries, especially Margaret Clark of the Foreign and Commonwealth Office Library, and also the Foreign Office Legal Library, the Institute of Commonwealth Studies, University of London, and the Centre of West African Studies, Birmingham University. Finally, I should like to thank our departmental typists Margaret Lott, Faye Murphy and Jill MacDonald, for accepting all the unthinking demands placed on them by academics preoccupied with getting their work out.

Like most Canadian scholars, I have benefited greatly from the Canada Council's assistance, in the form of a Research Grant in 1968 and a Leave Fellowship in 1972-3. Also, this book has been published with the help of a grant from the Social Science Research Council of Canada, using funds provided by the Canada Council. None of these agencies, of course, any more than the individuals thanked earlier, are responsible for the views expressed here, or for errors which may remain.

John Cartwright

University of Western Ontario
November 1976

Map 1

SIERRA LEONE
KOINADUGU
Kabala
Kamakwie
BOMBALI
NORTHERN
PROVINCE
Kambia
KAMBIA
Makeni
Port Loko
PORT
LOKO
Lunsar
Marampa
Magburaka
Lungi Airport
Pepel
TONKOLILI
Freetown
WESTERN AREA
KONO
EASTERN
Yengema
Sefadu
Jaiama
PROVINCE
Kailahun
Moyamba
MOYAMBA
Mano
BO
Pendembu
Segbwema
SOUTHERN
Bo
Kenema
KAILAHUN
Gbanbatoke
Bumpe
Sumbuya
KENEMA
Gbangbama
Mattru
Bonthe
BONTHE
PROVINCE
Pujehun
PUJEHUN
PROVINCIAL BOUNDARY
PROVINCIAL HEADQUARTERS
DISTRICT BOUNDARY
DISTRICT HEADQUARTERS
MAIN ROADS
RAILROADS
0 10 20 30 40 50
MILES

Map 2: Ethnic Distribution: Major Tribes

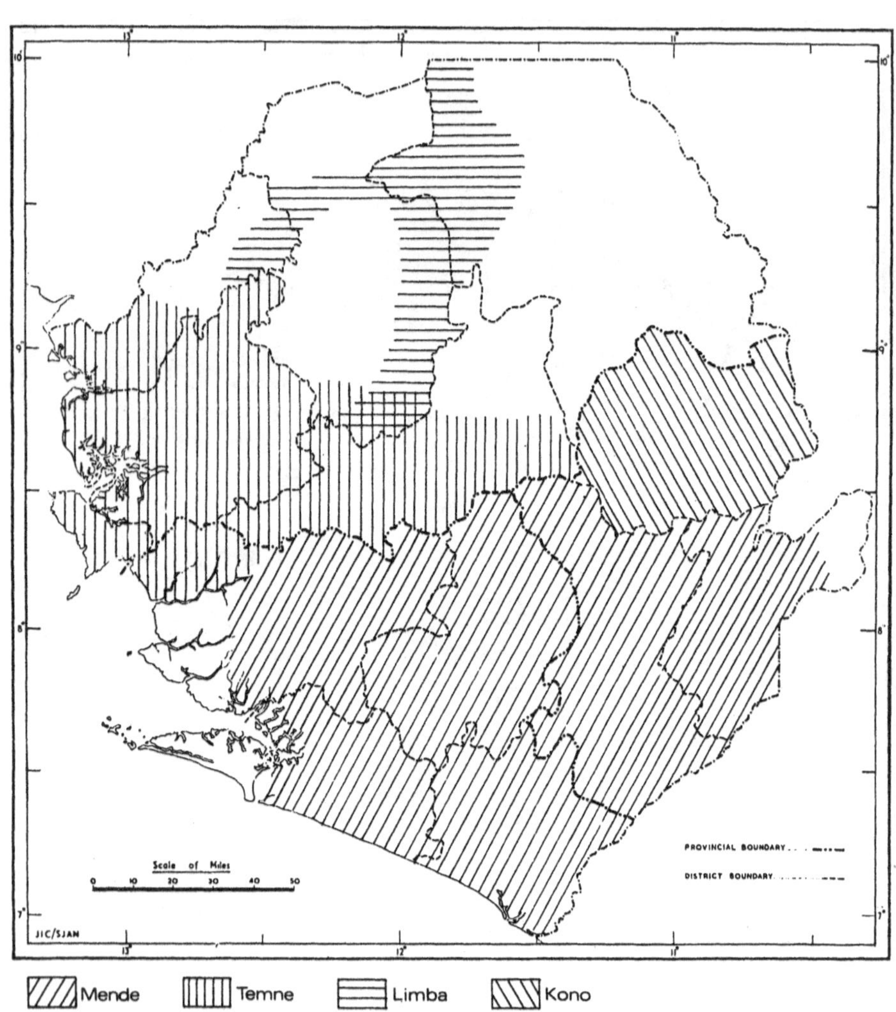

Source: *Sierra Leone in Maps* ed. John I. Clarke

1 INTRODUCTION: SETTINGS FOR POLITICAL LEADERSHIP

This is a study of the effect that different types of political leadership can have upon the shaping of a single state. It focuses upon two successive Prime Ministers of the small West African state of Sierra Leone, examining how the different elements comprising their political 'leadership' interacted with the range of constraints that put limits on what they could do. Since the major constraints upon them – entrenched local interests, ethnic rivalries, disputes over the desirability of new ways, and economic dependence – were characteristic of most African states and many other 'underdeveloped' countries as well, the study also draws some explicit comparisons with these other states. More broadly, its consideration of the components of leadership, of the interactions of various constraints, and of the implications of various courses of action, all have relevance to the study of leadership in any state, not just the special categories of 'African' or 'underdeveloped' countries. Finally, by pointing out the problems arising from different approaches taken by political leaders, this work may have a certain prescriptive value in indicating to other leaders at least some of the pitfalls awaiting them.

The study of political leadership is in a paradoxical position. On the one hand, it has been among the more neglected areas of political science in recent decades, for reasons that will be noted below. On the other hand, study of this area has become increasingly desirable as political leadership itself assumes increasing importance. In an age when more men than ever before have come to believe that their destinies can be determined by human actions rather than being left in the hands of fate, and yet at the same time the very organisations that men have created seem to have acquired lives of their own beyond the power of their creators to control, the question of what a leader can do to fulfil the aspirations of those looking for guidance looms large. And since the political arena is the one involving the use of power, and also the one whose participants are most widely felt to be accountable for their actions, the position of the political leader in particular has become the focus for men's hopes and fears. It is to individual leaders rather than to social movements that most men look to produce paradise, and whom they condemn when their hopes are dashed. Whether there is some element of realism in this appraisal, whether an individual leader can exercise some influence on the course followed by a polity, would seem to be not only a legitimate but a desirable object of scholarly enquiry.

Yet the question of what a political leader can do is one on which the literature is surprisingly sparse. Certain general features of contemporary social sciences seem to have encouraged this situation. The tendency to examine societies in terms of social movements rather than in terms of individual choices, an increasingly prominent feature of social science since the time of Marx, calls attention away from the role of leadership, even if it does not lead to a determinism which obviates the need for leadership entirely. A more recent and specific tendency among more 'scientifically' inclined students of society, the desire to provide rigour and 'precision' in studies of human relationships, has also pulled scholarly attention away from the necessarily imprecise study of what leaders do and how they do it to the apparently more 'precise' (or at least more readily quantifiable) area of leaders' attributes or at least the attributes of the elites from which leaders are presumed to spring. Then too, the study of leadership does take us into some of the most nebulous and least clearly resolved areas in the social sciences, involving as it does 'a process of complex mediation between the leader's personality, the followers' expectations, the circumstances and a set of goals'.[1]

The result of these trends has been a concentration in more theoretically-oriented works upon political elites rather than upon leaders as such, upon the 'who' rather than the 'how', the 'what' or (perhaps wisely) the 'why' of leadership. We have a fairly good collection of elite studies, both of single countries and at the cross-national level,[2] but we do not have more than a handful of theoretically-oriented studies of the person or persons at the top who have the greatest influence in making the key choices for a polity.[3] Unless we can make the dubious assumption that studies of elites provide us with sufficient information to understand leaders' actions, we must accept that most information on leaders has been provided by political biographers who generally have not used any explicit framework for analysing the range of interactions between leaders and led.[4] The other major source of material on leaders, studies of polities which incidentally are dominated by a single individual, again normally do not raise explicitly the question of what effect a leader has on the polity.[5] But there have been few attempts to provide any general examination of the ways in which leaders can deal with the constraints imposed on them by their polities, and most of these have made little advance beyond the precepts advanced by

Machiavelli in *The Prince.*[6]

There has not, then, been a great deal of work done on how leaders perceive their choices, or on the effects that changes of leadership in a given situation might have. Yet particularly in Africa and elsewhere where the institutions comprising the new state have not yet become firmly established, Stanley Hoffman's warning seems apt: 'At a time when so many regimes are nothing but a leader writ large, general and abstract frameworks and models run the risk of collapsing like sand castles whenever the leader falls.'[7] The dramatic shifts in internal relationships that have taken place with a change in leaders in such states as Congo-Brazzaville, Uganda and Libya underline his point. While not all polities undergo such dramatic transformations with a change in leadership, nearly all bear some imprint of the individual who leads them in their formative years. The questions we shall be concerned with here are, how much of an imprint does a leader leave, and how can we analyse his leadership in such a way that comparisons may be made between polities?

More specifically, this study will consider: the nature of the constraints within which a leader must operate, and how the various features of his environment interact with each other; of what the various elements of his 'leadership' consist, and how these affect his ability to deal with the constraints which he encounters; and how the attitudes of the leader, and his ways of handling problems, affect the outcome of these problems. Beyond this, it will be concerned with the questions of how 'decisions' are taken and the extent to which 'rationality' is possible for political leaders. While I do not claim that I can produce a 'theory of leadership', I do think that by providing a simple but universally applicable framework for the study of leadership I can at least allow others to collect comparable data which can then be used to build theories.

The Elements of Leadership

While the notion of 'leadership' may seem to be something we all intuitively understand without the need for elaborate discussion and definition, it is actually a rather complex concept, since it can be taken at both a structural and a behavioural level, and draws in such concepts as power, legitimacy and hierarchy. In order to provide a reasonably clear but simple usage of the terms 'leaders' and 'leadership' which is in accord with commonsense understandings of their meanings, I am going to use the term 'leader' to describe the structural role whose occupant is permitted to take decisions which commit the group of which he is a member, and the term 'leadership' to describe the (behavioural) ability of an individual to get others to do what he wants, for their own or for society's good rather than for his own.[8]

To illustrate these rather terse and abstract definitions, let us consider a troop of scouts accompanied by a scoutmaster who have just settled down for a picnic lunch. Now there is little doubt that in most situations – for example, deciding where to stop for the lunch – the scoutmaster's approval is necessary in order to have the troop fully accept an action. Individual scouts may attempt to get the action they want by imploring the scoutmaster or the other scouts to stop, and at times the scoutmaster may feel that he has no choice but must acquiesce in their wishes, but it is not until *he* announces the halt for lunch that the troop will feel that a 'proper' decision has been made.

Even the scoutmaster's decision may not be fully accepted. In order to make the leadership situation in our group of scouts resemble more closely that of a multi-ethnic 'new state', let us assume that our scouts consist of two distinct and long-established troops which have just been brought together under one scoutmaster. The troop which has lost its own scoutmaster in such circumstances might well be reluctant to accept the authority of a 'stranger', and might undertake petty acts of disobedience as challenges to his authority. If the scoutmaster employed coercion to compel obedience, the dissident troop might well regard this as illegitimate and unwarranted, and might even attempt to remove the scoutmaster, or to secede. In any case, his role as leader would be somewhat circumscribed.

While we could conclude that the role of 'leader' appears to entail a 'right' to take decisions committing the group, a number of unresolved questions remain, namely: Who initiates proposals for a new course of action? What roles does the leader play in shaping the choices before selecting among them? To what extent do various members of the group regard a particular role as that of 'leader', and over what areas of decision-making? We can sidestep the problems surrounding the initiation and formulation of proposals by taking the position that the role of 'leader' is required only at the point where a choice is to be made which commits the group to one or other of a set of alternatives, and not in these 'preliminary' stages. The question of the range of matters over which people accept an individual as a 'leader' is one involving the boundaries of the role, and one which we can determine empirically in each case, without affecting the concept.

The behavioural approach helps to tell us how well in fact the role of leader is being filled. To return to our picnicking scouts, let us suppose that they have just discovered they are seated under a wasps nest. Numerous initiatives may be proposed by the scouts – packing up and moving, burning the nest, and so on. Whatever is proposed, however, (other than panic flight) will almost certainly require ratification from the scoutmaster before action is taken. This would probably be true even of a proposal from a forceful scout in the dissident troop, and would certainly be true of a proposal coming from a scout who does not make much of an impression on his fellows. Now supposing the scoutmaster simply sits paralysed by fear (or by wasp stings) and fails to ratify any course of action (in the manner of Captain Queeg in *The Caine Mutiny*). It is possible that one of the scouts will 'take charge' and issue orders as though he were the scoutmaster, orders which under the circumstances his fellows will feel it well to obey. In such a situation the person occupying the role of leader has signally failed to exercise 'leadership'; on the other hand, a person with no claim to a leader's role has succeeded in providing 'leadership', despite the handicap that his position does not give him the right to issue orders to his fellows.

This illustration shows how the structural and behavioural concepts are separate yet interrelated. A leader who acts as our scoutmaster did will not retain the role of 'leader' long; conversely a person who shows such signs of leadership as our scout will probably be chosen to fill a role as 'leader'. The behavioural perspective allows us to look at the question of who accepts the leader and to what extent, or more broadly, how far and in what directions can a leader lead? On the other hand, it gives us no help in ascertaining the basis of legitimacy from which he works, nor does it tell us what powers if any he has available to reinforce his leadership. The structural approach guides us to the person occupying the role from which we expect leadership to be exercised, and tells us what powers inhere in that role to enable him to carry out his tasks as leader; but it does not tell us how effectively the occupant fills the role. Both approaches will be necessary in order to examine the position of a leader in relation to other individuals; our task now will be to consider just how the role and the behaviour within the role can each be broken down for analysis.

Since any role necessarily implies a structure within which it is performed, we need to consider the structures within which a leader operates. We first need to establish the boundaries of the 'political community' or *arena* based on shared rules within which the political leader operates.[9] Since our concern here is with *national* political leaders, that is persons occupying the role of leader of a politically sovereign state, our task is a relatively easy one, since the boundaries of the national political arena are more precisely defined and better protected than those of any other political community, and in fact than those of any other social group. Not only do they have precisely defined, universally recognised membership[10] but they enjoy a relatively high degree of freedom from overt interference from outside their boundaries and a relatively free hand in dealing with members of subnational units within those boundaries.

This is not to say that a national state can maintain complete autonomy from forces beyond its boundaries. While an overt attempt to impose direct control over a state by either another state or by an international body will generally be condemned by 'world opinion',[11] more powerful states clearly do sometimes compel less powerful ones to do their bidding, and international organisations can interfere in the policy-making of even relatively strong states.[12] Yet in relation to any international organisation, a state generally has some advantage in power, and in any case there is no international arena with a shared set of rules and an accepted means of enforcing them. Ultimately the exercise of supranational power depends upon the exercise of power by the stronger among the individual states.[13]

Below the level of the national state, we find a range of subnational political arenas, such as local governments, ethno-regional groups and so on. While generally subnational groups' members also possess some commitment to the national arena, we cannot take this for granted, as such cases as the successful secession of the Bengalis from Pakistan to form Bangladesh, and the resistance by force to the claims of the national government by the Nagas in India and by the Anyanya movement in Southern Sudan have shown. Non-acceptance of the national arena need not be underlined by the use of force; a passive withdrawal in the form of, say, withholding crops from national markets, an action not challenging enough to bring reprisals from the central government, may indicate a secession in spirit if not in legal form. But although such behaviour suggests the weakness of the hold the national political community possesses over its putative members, still the range of resources available to the national political leader is such that he usually can in time overcome resistance to incorporation into the national arena, and in doing so can generally count on a degree of acquiescence from outsiders far greater than is the case when an attempt is made to interfere with the autonomy of a national state.

While we can say that all persons living within the boundaries of the national state can be considered as participants in the national arena, there are significant differences in the ways in which various participants' roles interact with that of the political leader. The two significant elements here seem to be the degree of *autonomy* which individuals' roles possess in relation to the role of the leader, and the degree of *legitimacy* which the leader's role enjoys in the eyes of various individuals. We can categorise members of the national political arena into three groups,[14] as follows:

(1) Members of the set of political structures forming hierarchies for which the leader's role is at the peak (for example, in a Parliamentary system, the House of Commons, the civil service, the governing political party). Within these structures, and provided he operates within the framework of rules that circumscribe his role, the leader enjoys not only the generalised legitimacy inhering in his role as leader of the polity, but also the expectation that those subordinate to him in each hierarchy will obey his orders because his role entitles him to set the goals for each of these hierarchies. Those subordinate to him, in other words, possess no autonomy in that they have no independent right to set their own goals. In practice, of course, the extent to which the occupants of these subordinate roles will in fact obey the leader's wishes will depend upon his 'leadership'.

(2) Members of other structures within the political arena, who grant the leader legitimacy as head of the polity of which they are members, but whose structures have their own bases of support and set their own goals. These more or less autonomous institutions (for example, a local government, or a retail merchants' group) share a commitment to the continuation of the polity, though not necessarily a commitment to the retention of power by the leader. But the fact that they possess their own independent bases of power and other resources means that their goals will almost invariably diverge from those sought by the leader, and thus they can be expected to offer more resistance to him than those institutions which are directly subordinated to him. Yet at the same time the fact that they accept the maintenance of the polity puts limits on how far they will go in seeking their own way.

(3) Members of institutions which intervene in the national political arena possess autonomy from the national leader, and at the same time lack any commitment to either his or the polity's survival. While in most cases an organisation operating within a state has at least the minimal commitment to the survival of that state occasioned by its own self-interest, if its focus of decision-making is outside the state and it is in a position to cut its losses and pull out if the situation is not to its liking, then there is no necessity for it to show any commitment to the survival of the state.[15] Similarly, a group determined to secede from the state

will show no commitment to it, let alone to the leader. Clearly the potential for resistance to the leader's wishes in such circumstances is even higher than that of category (2) above.

Within an individual state the various participants within the national arena can show great variation both in the degree to which they can possess autonomy from the national political leader, and in the legitimacy which they accord that leader. The autonomy of different participants is affected by (among other factors) the resources under their control, the degree to which they are involved in interdependent relationships with others, and the values embodied in the political culture, while the legitimacy of the leader's role is affected by the extent to which different elements have come to accept common membership in a single state.

More specifically, in the 'new states' of Africa and elsewhere in the 'Third World' we find substantial numbers of individuals who live in what Aristide Zolberg terms the 'residual sector',[16] that is to say persons having a minimal involvement with political or economic institutions operating at the state level, and with a primary political commitment to institutions operating at the micropolitical scale of the village or chiefdom. Such persons enjoy a form of 'autonomy by default', coming about essentially because the national government finds it too difficult to reach them. This form of autonomy is quite different from the autonomy enjoyed by nonpolitical institutions in a 'pluralist' society[17] where the cultural value of 'freedom from political control' offers a substantial barrier to infringements on such institutions' autonomy, and where these institutions often possess sufficient control over resources that they can bargain on a more or less equal footing with the political leader over matters affecting the whole state. The autonomy of members of the residual sector, by contrast, rests almost entirely on a lack of power in the hands of the political leader, rather than on restraints imposed by the values of the political culture. This autonomy does not provide countervailing power in the residual sector, capable of influencing the national government; it merely prevents the national government reaching far enough to do anything to the residual sector that that sector does not want.

The obverse side to this autonomy, the inability of the residual sector to influence the national government, is reinforced by the nature of 'underdeveloped' countries' political structures. Any political structure produces disparities in influence, based upon differential access to key decision-making points; but in the industrialised states this disparity is limited by universal literacy and the diffusion of the skills needed to organise on behalf of one's interests throughout the society.[18] In an 'underdeveloped' country, by contrast, the skills required to operate modern administrative structures, which give by far the most effective access to political leaders, are highly concentrated, and vastly different from any skills available in the residual sector; and while family ties may help to bridge this gulf for a fortunate few, most members of the residual sector lack any means of organising in ways that will give them countervailing power against the administrators. In an ultimate sense, the residual sector exercises power over the central government through its ability to embark on passive resistance which will cut off the government's resources; but until the point is reached where such passive resistance spontaneously envelopes much of the populace, the political leaders can ignore this sector and concentrate upon satisfying the more vigorously pressed claims of the 'modern' elite.[19]

The gap between a 'residual' and a 'modern' sector raises even more significant problems with respect to the legitimacy of the leader. Given their overriding commitment to their own micropolities, we can expect that most persons in the 'residual' sector lack any strong belief in the legitimacy of the national leader. They may not characterise his role as illegitimate; it is simply that they do not perceive him as a figure with whom they have any relationship, if indeed they perceive him at all. While in such a situation a leader may be able to obtain acquiescence to his wishes through his command of superior force, he is unlikely to obtain that acceptance of his right to rule which would buttress his position against forcible usurpation. From persons in the 'residual' sector, a national leader will have difficulty in eliciting any direct commitment of support for his role as leader; his only hope for obtaining legitimacy in this sector is to represent himself as being linked to the local political hierarchies which they already obey.

But a further obstacle to the legitimacy of the leader arises here, not just in the new African states but in any single political arena in which are juxtaposed different cultural or linguistic groups each possessing its own distinct set of political values. The problem basically is one of which values will prevail, or more crudely, 'Whose state is this to be?' Since it is difficult for a leader to dissociate himself from his membership in one of the conflicting groups, the prospect arises that members of other groups will not accept him as *their* leader, or in other words will regard his occupancy of the role of national leader as illegitimate. Even if the leader should take extra measures to conciliate members of other groups, to try to establish that the state exists for all persons comprising it, his actions are still likely to be viewed through the lens of ethnic group membership, and assessed on the basis of whether they favour 'us' or 'them'.[20]

In real life, few individuals are likely to be so completely in the residual sector that they are totally unaware of any relationship between themselves and the leader, or so completely committed to their own group within the polity that they accord no legitimacy whatsoever to a leader from another group. Yet leaders in Africa and elsewhere do have to deal with substantial numbers of individuals whose attitudes approximate to those of these 'ideal' types, which puts rather more severe limits on their potential strength than is the case with leaders of more mobilised and integrated polities.

A further variation among states stems from the degree to which the forces for change working on them, particularly economic change, are exogenous. In the 'underdeveloped' countries, these forces take several forms: a desire within the country to emulate the way of life of the 'more developed' countries, offers of 'aid' and trade relationships by other states, and most commonly, requests by corporations based in the industrialised states that they be allowed to undertake economic activities, generally of an extractive nature, in the 'underdeveloped' host country. Foreign governments and foreign corporations, needless to say, have a high degree of autonomy from the host country, limited only by the extent that they have 'hostages' in the form of investment and personnel located in it. At the same time, there is no reason for them to accept the legitimacy of the 'host' state's political institutions except in so far as this suits their interests. When, as is the case in many 'underdeveloped' countries, a substantial portion of the economy is under the control of foreign corporations, the political leader's ability to get his way in economic matters is subject to considerable limitations.

The institutional relationships outlined above provide the framework of constraints within which any leader has to work. Both the arenas and the relationships of various structures to the leader can be changed, either by the leader's efforts (for example, the leader can abolish local governments, or nationalise a foreign-owned company) or by the efforts of other participants (for example, a region can secede, or a professional group can obtain the power of self-regulation of its membership). But to bring such changes requires the use of existing resources, and it is to an analysis of the nature and range of the resources a leader possesses or can create that we now turn.

The most fundamental resource for a leader when seeking to obtain active support for his objectives is widespread legitimacy among members of the polity. Now a leader can survive without this legitimacy;

in most polities there is a broad middle ground between legitimacy and illegitimacy, with many members of the polity acquiescing in the exercise of power by persons occupying particular roles without necessarily accepting their right to exercise that power. The person exercising power does at a minimum need to be accepted as a legitimate ruler by those acting as his agents of coercion; and it is hard to imagine any leader of a modern 'positive state' operating for long purely on the basis of his ability to coerce the bulk of the population. A leader who wishes to accomplish anything involving participation by a substantial portion of the populace must achieve more than passive acquiescence; he must manage to bind people to him in such a way that they will comply with his wishes voluntarily. Legitimacy in its different manifestations underpins such support, although different types of legitimacy each entail a need for further specific resources in the hands of the leader.

In his writings on legitimacy, Max Weber commented that his classification of three types of legitimacy according to the ties that bound followers to the leader 'can only be justified by results'.[21] Unfortunately, most persons employing his concept or modifying it have continued to treat it as a unidimensional concept, even where this has created considerable ambiguities.[22] I prefer to break 'legitimacy' down into two dimensions, which can be combined to give us four 'ideal types' of relationship between leaders and other actors. One of these dimensions is the extent to which legitimacy adheres to the leader as an individual or to the leader as occupant of a specific institutional role. The other is the extent to which acceptance of the leader is based upon expectation of some personal benefit or deprivation (e.g. patronage, liquidation) or upon more selfless considerations, which might be described as broadly as 'acceptance-for-its-own-sake', or perhaps, using the term very loosely, 'spiritual' considerations. This gives us the following 'ideal types' of linkage between a leader and those subject to his authority:

		Commitment to leader is as: Individual	Institution
Nature of reward for supporters is:	Spiritual	(charismatic)	(rational-legal, theocratic)
	Material	('boss', caudillo)	(patrimonial)

Clearly no one of these 'ideal-type' relationships predominates for long in the relations between a leader and all the members of his polity. But at any given time, the ties between a leader and a given section of the polity will approximate to one of these types, and will require the deployment of specific types of resources by the leader. The charismatic relationship will require a high degree of self-abnegation on the part of the leader, but no great deployment of material resources nor adherence to established patterns of leadership behaviour. The 'boss' relationship will require little beyond a plentiful supply of whatever material resources the followers desire. (However, this is undoubtedly the most unstable of all the four types of leadership, lacking as it does any basis for commitment by the followers beyond a continuing stream of material payoffs.[23]) The rational-legal and the theocratic relationships, besides requiring a show of willingness by the leader to put the general good above his own, require him to adhere carefully to established conventions; on the other hand, they can survive an absence of personal 'payoff' for the followers. The patrimonial relationship, while it can appear arbitrary and capricious in its treatment of individuals, also operates within a broad framework of established conventions, and additionally requires a considerable outlay of material rewards.[24] To some extent a leader can seek a middle ground between these conflicting demands for resources, or shift from one type of relationship to another, but the further he goes towards one type, the more difficult it becomes to change to another; the convention-breaking entailed in charismatic leadership, for example, will make many people sceptical of a subsequent claim to restore the rational-legal legitimacy which he has departed from,[25] while the control and distribution of largesse entailed by patrimonial leadership will work against a leader's claims to be endowed with a self-denying 'gift of grace'. A 'boss' building a following through the judicious distribution of material favours similarly makes an unlikely convert to the role of selfless charismatic leader, while both the rational-legal and the patrimonial leader who seek the freedom from established rules enjoyed by the 'boss' or by the charismatic leader can expect to find many of their followers turning against them for such 'lawless' behaviour.

If we were to summarise the advantages and disadvantages of the different types of legitimacy from the leader's perspective, we could note these points:

On the dimension of adherence to the individual or to the institution, the argument for seeking support for oneself as an individual would be that this allows the leader to transcend the limitations imposed by party and governmental organisations, and thus gives him freedom to innovate. On the other hand, support for the leader as individual means that he personally has to maintain the links of his patronage organisation or keep his personal charismatic appeal. Support for the institution rather than the individual offers the advantage that should the leader's personal appeal wane, he still retains the legitimacy adhering to the role. On the other hand, it means that the leader must remain within acceptable conventions for the role, which limits his opportunities for innovation.

On the dimension of material versus 'spiritual' rewards for followers, or to use F.G. Bailey's terms, 'mercenary' and 'moral' supporters, again there are strong arguments on both sides.[26] The 'moral' supporter can be counted on to remain faithful even though the leader can offer him nothing beyond spiritual comfort, and may even support the leader for reasons which render him impervious to the lures of the leader's rivals. But this commitment has its costs. To keep his moral followers, the leader may have to take an unbending position in his dealings with others; for example, a nationalist leader may be unable to compromise with colonial officials for fear of being charged with 'selling out'. Then too, such a commitment may be based on shared membership in an exclusive 'solidarity group' – a clan or ethnic group, for example – the effect of which is to call up a negative reaction on the part of competing solidarity groups. The 'mercenary' follower, whose support has to be bargained for on an issue-to-issue basis, and who requires a substantial level of material payoffs, nevertheless has his advantages. He is less likely than the moral follower to be shaken by the leader's tactical zigzags, and does not insist that the leader share with him a broad vision of the good society. Moreover his adherence to the leader is unlikely to drive away other potential supporters, except in so far as the total supply of rewards is limited.

In real life, except in those rare instances where a charismatic leader sweeps away all established political institutions,[27] some legitimacy inheres in the role of leader regardless of the occupant. Such legitimacy can neither be created nor destroyed overnight. In the short run, we can take the leader's legitimacy as a given factor and concern ourselves with a different level of behaviour, the policies the leader puts foward, the means by which he does this, or what I shall term his 'style', and the nature of the 'world view' or ideology within which he anchors his policies and style.

In considering these features, I shall make two simplifying assumptions. One is that the leader wishes to maintain his position as leader.

While this is not an entirely realistic assumption, since some leaders have chosen to lose office in order to maintain an ideal,[28] still it does seem generally true and allows us to evaluate his actions against a consistent standard. In making this evaluation, we should note that the leader does not have to concern himself constantly with maximising the difference between his support and opposition, but can be content simply to remain above the critical threshold at which he loses his position.[29] He has, in other words, some leeway in which to sacrifice a degree of popularity to principle on specific issues, provided his overall support remains sufficiently high.

The other assumption is that the leader seeks some kind of 'public good' rather than his own self-interest alone, and is perceived by some to be seeking that good. This does put some restraint upon the means to be used by leaders to retain their power. For example, the late François Duvalier of Haiti and General Idi Amin of Uganda have been among recent practitioners of terror as a means of keeping themselves in power; the fact that Duvalier, under whose government Haitians' standard of living steadily declined, died peacefully in bed,[30] certainly suggests that this method of self-preservation is not ineffective. That more leaders have not adopted a similar approach is attributable in part, I suggest, to a belief that the long-term effects of such policies would be far too destructive to the polity to be acceptable, both to the leader and to his supporters. Clearly many leaders use some intimidation to protect their own position, and a good many more act in ways that suggest a predominant concern with their personal benefits rather than the good of the society. But I think we can view these as shortfalls from the ideal-type leader as one who *persuades* others to follow his path in pursuit of a *public* good; or we might make a distinction in terms of Aristotle's 'good' and 'bad' governments, considering leadership as present only in so far as leaders approximate to the 'good' form.

The range of policies that a leader may bring forward to maintain his position is nearly infinite, depending as it does upon his own inclinations, his assessment of what different elements in the society want or oppose, and the resources available for the implementation of different policies. Analytically, however, we can represent the range of policy choices in a rather simple fashion, by imagining the range of choices as resembling a sea urchin, with varying degrees of change represented by spines running outwards from a central point of 'things as they are'. We may term the leader who maintains the *status quo* in all his policies an (ideal-type) 'conservative'; a leader who makes a change in any policy in any direction we may term an 'innovator'.[31] Different 'innovators' may make policy changes of different degree and in different directions (for example, one may make a small change towards greater equality of income distribution, whereas another may make a much larger change towards greater inequality), or may make changes along quite different planes (for example, one may innovate in social welfare policies, another in foreign alliances). But all 'innovators' have in common the consideration that some members of their polity will gain and others will lose from their innovation. The innovative leader's problem is to decide whether his margin of support will be improved or worsened by his innovation.

'Conservative' and 'innovative' policies are clearly appropriate in opposed situations. A 'conservative' policy will be most acceptable when there is general contentment with the *status quo*, or when such discontents as exist cancel each other out. An 'innovative' policy, by contrast, will be most acceptable when there is a strong body of opinion inclined in favour of the innovation, either through a shift of attitude on the part of persons already participating in the polity, or through the entry into active participation of a new segment of the polity. At the same time, to be successful the innovator needs either the acquiescence of supporters of the *status quo* in his innovation, or else the means to override them.

How successful either a 'conservative' or an 'innovative' policy is depends to a considerable extent upon how the leader goes about trying to implement it. While a given policy will automatically attract or repel some members of the polity, regardless of what the leader does to bring it about, there is generally a good deal of scope for him to build support for it. We may again contrast two ideal types of what I termed the leader's 'style', the 'brokerage' and the 'creative'. The 'brokerage' style takes as given the constellation of overt interests in the polity, and tries to put together those combinations of existing interests that seem most likely to provide the leader with the support he needs. The 'creative' style, by contrast, seeks to bypass or override opposition from existing interests by calling into being new groupings, either through attracting new participants into the national political arena or by inducing some present participants to look at events in new ways.[32] I would note here that there is no *necessary* connection between a leader's style and his policy; it is quite possible for two leaders, one employing a brokerage style and the other a creative style, each to be pursuing the same policy, either conservative or innovative, although as I shall argue shortly, certain policies and styles tend to cluster together.

Once again, the brokerage and creative styles are most likely to be successful in opposite situations. The broker functions best where role expectations both for himself and for others are clearly established, where most of the potential interests in the polity are articulated, and where the range of policies sought by different interests is not too divergent. In such a situation the broker's approach of balancing and conciliating different groups, of seeking a 'general interest' which represents an equilibrium among articulated demands, is most likely to provide him with the support he needs. In a situation where role expectations are not clearly established, where many interests are not articulated to a degree commensurate with their potential strength in the society, or where the goals being sought by different interests are strongly opposed, the mediator's tendency to follow a 'path of least resistance' can lead to policies which appear one-sided and unfair to a significant part of the polity, and to the entrenchment of those segments benefiting from the unfairness. Such a situation is likely over the long run to be as disastrous to the leader as to his country, since uncorrected grievances will tend to accumulate, and the leader will lack the power to correct them.

The creative leader, by contrast, is likely to be most effective when both role expectations and the alignments of interests are at their most fluid. In such a situation he can most readily shape his own role to suit his needs, and call into being those new alignments he needs to support this new role, either by appealing to hitherto non-participant members of the polity or by making politically salient those areas in which participants are most likely to reach a consensus supporting his position. But where structures and expectations are firmly fixed, the creative leader's latitude is sharply curtailed. If he persists in his attempts to build new alignments, he may well succeed only in pushing together against him enough of the existing interests that his support drops below the critical theshold needed to keep him in office. Even in a relatively fluid situation, such as a society in the throes of discontent and searching for new directions, a creative leader may fail simply because there are too many centres of resistance to overcome, because his policies contain serious flaws,or because circumstances beyond his control prevent the new alignment he seeks. An inescapable element of luck inevitably makes the final determination of whether a creative leader succeeds or fails.

In developing his policies, and to some extent in selecting his style of operation, a leader will normally allow his selection to be simplified by his philosophy of life. There are, however, significant differences between leaders both in the extent to which they have worked through their philosophies into a coherent form, and in the extent to which they are prepared to struggle to achieve the implementation of such a philosophy. If we combine these two variables of coherence and commitment, we can say that some leaders possess and others lack an 'ideology';[33] and we can go further and divide the 'ideologues' into those whose ideology is based on maintenance of the *status quo* and those who desire major social changes. This variable of the leader's ideology allows us to cluster the other variables we have used, legitimacy, policies and style, into 'ideal types' of leadership which offer some useful models for analysis.

The absence of such a set of beliefs does not rule out either innovative policies or a creative style, but it does seem more compatible with conservative policies and a brokerage style. A leader lacking any clear ideology lacks the guidelines to indicate what innovations might be beneficial to the polity or to himself, and also lacks an important source of motivation to attempt to go beyond the existing alignments of interests. Such a leader may well innovate in response to shifts in demand, or attempt to bring together new political alignments in order to protect his personal position, but basically he is not going to carry out any major policy changes nor (at least by design) reshape the patterns of the polity. Generally, too, his legitimacy will be essentially that of his office rather than accruing to him personally, and can equally well depend upon material or spiritual rewards.

This non-ideological type of leadership will have its own special strengths and weaknesses. Its strengths include its relative adaptability to changing conditions, unhampered by any strong commitment to outmoded values, its responsiveness to the whole range of articulated demands in the polity, and quite possibly its avoidance of major economic and social disasters through the fact that it is unlikely to plunge dogmatically towards some major goal. Its greatest weakness is likely to be its penchant for responding on an *ad hoc* and short-run basis to specific problems, an approach which can lead both to opening up new problems in other areas, and to a long-run worsening of problems.

A leader possessing comprehensive beliefs in the maintenance of the *status quo* or a 'conservative ideology' shares with the 'non-ideological' leader a liking for conservative policies and a 'brokerage' style, although he is quite likely to use a creative style if he considers it necessary to bring new elements into participation in the polity to offset shifts which threaten the *status quo.* His legitimacy as the champion of the 'old order' may have a more personal (possibly even a charismatic) basis than that of the non-ideologue, although he will also reap whatever legitimacy may accrue to the office he occupies in his capacity as a guardian of established values. His strengths include a sense of purpose in his actions, coming from a knowledge of what it is he is trying to preserve, and thus leading to a likelihood that he will take a long-range view of the potential solutions to problems. His major weakness, particularly in a situation where change is being thrust on the polity by forces beyond his control, is that he will fail to give sufficient recognition to new participants and their demands, thus accumulating frustrations and antagonisms.

A leader possessing a comprehensive commitment to social change (a 'radical ideology') is by definition going to introduce predominantly innovative policies, and will almost be forced to adopt a largely creative style.[34] His legitimacy will also tend to rest relatively heavily on his personal appeal, and upon spiritual rather than material rewards for his followers, the latter for the good reason that he will rarely have access to a great deal of material goods for his supporters. The strengths of his approach are also its weaknesses. The fact that he possess a comprehensive understanding of the goals he seeks for the polity provides guidelines by which he can assess the long-run effects of specific innovations, both in their own sphere and in their ramifications elsewhere. He may thus manage to avoid measures which demonstrate 'short-run adequacy and long-run inadequacy', to use Richard Fagen's apt phrase.[35] But this very commitment to comprehensive goals may lead him to press forward with measures containing unperceived flaws that can prove disastrous either for himself or for the polity. It can also lead him, out of conviction that what he is doing is for the best, into forcing his wishes on the country, again with potentially disastrous results.

This study focuses upon two African political leaders who differed significantly in their approaches to leadership, while operating within a largely comparable setting.

Leadership Approaches of Two Leaders

Dimension	Sir Milton Margai	Sir Albert Margai
World view	conservative ideologue	non-ideological
Policies	conservative	somewhat innovative
Style	brokerage	creative
Legitimacy	institutional, 'spiritual'	individual, material

The two enjoyed markedly different degrees of success, for reasons which will be developed below. But beyond the possibilities for comparison of different leaders' approaches along the dimensions indicated, the theme that will emerge most clearly in this study is the extent to which any leader is a prisoner of the past, and the limitations on his possible avenues of escape from this past. The 'choices' which have been made in one set of conditions, when alternative courses were perceived in a particular way, in retrospect turn out to have foreclosed subsequent courses of action even in apparently quite unrelated fields. The 'choices' in fact may not even have been perceived as choices at the point where alternatives were open; at best they may simply have appeared as the 'line of least resistance'. Yet unless a leader possesses a rather startling degree of prescience – one might even say clairvoyance – it is unlikely that he can anticipate the consequences of a given course of action. This is not to say that we must accept Oakeshott's vision of political activity as sailing on 'a boundless and bottomless sea, . . . [without] destination [and with] the enterprise [being] to keep the ship afloat'.[36] But it does suggest that the span of time over which we should expect a leader to make his imprint on the polity must be a rather lengthy one. We may also suggest that only a rather limited number of combinations of the variables constituting a leader's approach to politics will give him the necessary time, and that even if he succeeds in gaining sufficient time, his approach may not work. But these are at this stage merely tentative hypotheses, awaiting the examination of supporting evidence.

Notes

1. Dankwart Rustow, 'The Study of Leadership', in Dankwart Rustow (ed.), *Philosophers and Kings: Studies in Leadership,* New York, Braziller, 1970, p.20. Rustow sees essentially the factors I have cited as being responsible for the lack of interest in leadership studies. Ibid., pp.3-4.
2. Typical of this genre would be such single-country studies as Frederick Frey, *The Turkish Political Elite,* Cambridge, Mass., MIT Press, 1965; W.L. Guttsman, *The British Political Elite,* London, MacGibbon & Kee, 1963; Raymond F. Hopkins, *Political Roles in a New State* (Tanzania), New Haven, Yale University Press, 1971; John Porter, *The Vertical Mosaic* (Canada), Toronto, University of Toronto Press, 1965; Marshall Singer, *The Emerging Elite: A Study of Political Leadership in Ceylon,* Cambridge, Mass., MIT Press, 1964; John Waterbury, *The Commander of the Faithful: The Moroccan Political Elite,* New York, Columbia University Press, 1970. There are also a number of cross-national studies, such as Harold Lasswell, Daniel Lerner and Easton Rothwell, *The Comparative Study of Elites,* Stanford, Standford University Press, 1952, and William Quandt, *The*

Comparative Study of Political Elites, Los Angeles, Sage, 1970. The latter contains a comprehensive bibliography in this area.

3. Stanley Hoffman's study of De Gaulle, 'Heroic Leadership: The Case of Modern France', in Lewis Edinger (ed.), *Political Leadership in Industrialised Societies,* New York, Wiley, 1967, is one of the few studies of a single leader which attempts to provide a framework within which comparisons can be made with other leaders.
4. Basil Davidson's *Black Star: An Account of the Life and Times of Kwame Nkrumah,* London, Allen Lane, 1973, is one of the few biographies which does attempt to assess alternative possibilities open to a leader in a given situation.
5. A few studies, such as Dennis Austin, *Politics in Ghana,* London, Oxford University Press, 1964, Carolyn McMaster, *Malawi: Foreign Policy and Development,* London, Julian Friedmann, 1974, Jan Pettman, *Zambia: Security and Conflict,* New York, St Martin's Press, 1974, and R. Cranford Pratt, *The Critical Phase in Tanzania, 1945-1968,* London, Cambridge University Press, 1976, deal explicitly with a particular leader's impact on the choices made within his country, but as single-country studies they are not concerned with offering a framework for comparative analysis.
6. Richard Neustadt's *Presidential Power,* New York, Wiley, 1962, and Howard Wriggins' *The Ruler's Imperative,* New York, Columbia University Press, 1969, are two such attempts to provide guidance for a ruler uncertain about what he can and cannot hope to do. A more ambitious attempt to provide a framework for the analysis of leadership is that of Warren Ilchman and Norman Uphoff, *The Political Economy of Change,* Berkeley and Los Angeles, University of California Press, 1969, which attempts to offer an analysis of the techniques for increasing the leader's 'productivity' in political outputs. For a discussion of what is needed for a 'theory of leadership', see Lewis Edinger, 'The Comparative Analysis of Political Leadership', *Comparative Politics,* 7, 2, Jan. 1975, pp. 253-70.
7. In Edinger, *Political Leadership,* p. 108.
8. This latter definition is taken from Neustadt, *Presidential Power,* p. 46.
9. I have taken this term from F.G. Bailey's *Stratagems and Spoils,* Toronto, Copp Clark, 1969, pp. 23-4.
10. Conflicts over 'stateless' persons and over dual citizenship are conflicts between states over which shall have jurisdiction; and with these rare exceptions, we can find scarcely any persons over whom a dispute may arise concerning the state to which they belong.
11. Since 'world opinion' generally means the opinions of leaders of other national political communities, it might be suggested that their views are not entirely disinterested. However, a belief that national communities' autonomy has greater sanctity than does the autonomy of subnational communities seems to be fairly generally accepted by other articulate members of the world community.
12. The power of multinational corporations to bring about exchange crisis in the industrial states through their movement of liquid assets from weak to strong currencies is a particularly dramatic illustration of this point. For some instances, see Hugh Stephenson, *The Coming Clash,* London, Weidenfeld & Nicolson, 1972, pp. 122-37.
13. Thus, the success of the Organisation of American States' sanctions against Cuba rested almost entirely upon the predominant power of the United States in that organisation, while the relative futility of United Nations sanctions against Rhodesia is attributable to the unwillingness of a few powerful states to enforce the international organisation's rules.

14. It might be argued that we have four cells based upon our two dimensions of autonomy versus non-autonomy and leader's legitimacy versus non-legitimacy. A foreign interest and a would-be secessionist would differ in that the former would possess autonomy as well as lacking any regard for the leader's legitimacy, while the secessionist, although he would have an equally scant regard for the leader's legitimacy, would not enjoy autonomy. For purposes of considering reactions to the leader's wishes, however, this difference need not concern us here.
15. The willingness of International Telephone and Telegraph to embroil Chile in a civil war to prevent Salvador Allende becoming President is (one hopes) an extreme illustration of this. See Anthony Sampson, *The Soveriegn State*, London, Hodder & Stoughton, 1973, pp. 244-56, for a brief summary of this episode.
16. See Aristide Zolberg, *Creating Political Order: The Party-States of West Africa*, Chicago, Rand McNally, 1966, esp. pp. 131-34.
17. In the sense the term is used by Robert Dahl and other political scientists. See his *Pluralist Democracy in the United States*, Chicago, Rand McNally, 1966, esp. pp.22-4.
18. The range within which divergences of interest may be promoted by organised groups is clearly much narrower in the industrialised Communist states than within the Western democracies: but within the limits set by an overarching ideology, there is some room for differences to be pressed, and there will almost certainly be persons capable of articulating these differences in ways that can be understood by others in the political arena.
19. While over the long run I would accept Huntington's claim that 'the stability of a government depends upon the support which it can mobilise in the countryside' *(Political Order in Changing Societies*, p. 433). I would suggest that it takes a great accumulation of rural discontents before these threaten a government's hold on office. Even small-scale urban protests, by contrast, are taken seriously by most governments.
20. Such divisions between groups may be based on an 'encompassing principle' other than ethnicity, as Northern Ireland shows. But ethnic differentiation, that is to say differentiation based upon race and culture, seems far and away the most frequent basis for calling into question the legitimacy of the state's leader.
21. See his essay 'The Types of Authority and Imperative Co-ordination' in *The Theory of Economic and Social Organisation*, trans. A.M. Henderson and Talcott Parsons, Glencoe, Illinois, Free Press, 1947, p. 325.
22. This is particuarly notable in the otherwise very useful attempts to revive Weber's 'patrimonial' sub-type of 'traditional' legitimacy. (See ibid., p. 347, for Weber's discussion of the term.) Zolberg, in *Creating Political Order*, pp. 141-5, attempts to utilise the concept of 'patrimonial' rule to analyse the personal rulership of contemporary African leaders, but weakens his case by claiming that their legitimacy derives from the fact that people have simply become accustomed to the new state structures. If this were the case, it would be hard to find any legitimacy that was not 'traditional'. Guenther Roth, 'Personal Rulership, Patrimonialism and Empire-Building in the New States', *World Politics*, XX, 2, Jan. 1968, pp. 194-206, maintains that 'patrimonialism' is a separate category from either 'traditional' or 'charismatic' leadership, and in its 'non-traditional' manifestation is 'inextricably linked to material incentives and rewards' (p. 196), but he does not make explicit the fact that he is dealing with two separate dimensions of legitimacy, material v. non-material attachment by the follower, and attachment to the leader's person v. attachment to the institution of leader.

23. Weber seemed to regard attachments for personal advantage as so unstable that they should not be regarded as a basis for legitimacy at all. See *Theory of Economic and Social Organisation,* p.325.
24. Weber's discussion of the 'patrimonial' type of ruler does not make it clear just how far the ruler is bound by established conventions, though by treating it as a sub-type of 'traditional' ruler he seems to imply that the ruler is fairly strictly bound. (See ibid. pp. 341, 347.) Roth, on the other hand, seems to regard his 'patrimonial' type of ruler as being fairly free from any institutional constraints; his 'patrimonial' type approximates to what I have termed the 'boss'.
25. While Weber regarded charisma as unstable and tending towards being 'routinised' into a rational-legal type of legitimacy, what he was referring to was the acceptance on a continuing basis of the *new* norms established by the charismatic leader.
26. See Bailey, *Stratagems and Spoils,* ch. 3.
27. Most revolutionary leaders, such as Sekou Touré of Guinea or the late Ho Chi Minh of North Vietnam, built up a party or administrative structure which to some extent provided an institutionalised base for their legitimacy. Those such as Fidel Castro who have continued to rely upon their personal appeal are very rare exceptions.
28. An extreme case was that of Governor John Altgeld of Illinois, who insisted on pardoning the Haymarket anarchists even though he knew full well he was committing political suicide, because, as he snapped back at an adviser, 'It is right!' It should be added that Altgeld lost the next election, and never again held elective office. See Harry Barnard, *Eagle Forgotten: The Life of John Peter Altgeld,* Indianapolis, Bobbs-Merrill, 1938, p. 214.
29. Calculating this threshold is not such a simple matter, however; a leader has to consider how strongly different elements feel about a matter and what their resources are. Where there is a likelihood of military intervention, he clearly has to assess military susceptibilities, and know what their 'intervention threshold' is regardless of the attitudes of other segments of the populace.
30. See Robert D. Crassweller, 'Darkness in Haiti', *Foreign Affairs,* XLIX, 2, Jan. 1971, pp. 315-29, for a discussion of Duvalier's techniques.
31. A rather similar set of categories has been proposed by Taketsugu Tsurutani, who suggests 'innovative', 'consolidative' and 'mediative' types of leadership. However, while his 'innovative' and 'consolidative' categories refer to policies on essentially the same basis as my 'innovative' and 'conservative' classification, his 'mediative' category seems rather to be referring to a style or method of leadership rather than to its policy content. See his 'Political Leadership: Some Tentative Thoughts from Early Meiji Japan', *Journal of Political and Military Sociology,* 1, 2, 1973, pp. 201-14.
32. Illustrations of the 'creative' style might include Benjamin Disraeli's 'leap in the dark' in 1867 in enfranchising part of the British working class as a counterweight to the pro-Liberal urban middle-class electorate, or Juan Peron of Argentina's appeal to the 'shirtless ones' in the 1940s.
33. I am using the term 'ideology' here to denote both a comprehensive and coherent set of beliefs and a commitment by the holder of these beliefs to act on them, while the term 'ideologue' here simply denotes someones who acts on the basis of an ideology.
34. It is possible that such a leader may be able to find a sufficient constituency simply by appealing to groups that have participated but been left under-represented by previous regimes. However, in most cases underrepresented groups are also non-participating groups, and thus need to be brought into

active participation. Black Americans in the southern United States, and the Chilean poor whom Allende tried to draw into full participation are cases in point.

35. Richard Fagen, *Politics and Communication*, Boston and Toronto, Little, Brown, 1966, p. 90. Fagen actually uses the phrase in the rather narrower context of communications; a usage more closely approximating mine is that of Taketsugu Tsurutani, *Political Leadership in Transitional Societies*, New York, Chandler, 1973, pp. 154-7.
36. Michael Oakeshott, *Rationalism in Politics*, New York, Basic Books, 1962, p. 127.

2 SIERRA LEONE AT THE START OF DECOLONISATION: A BRIEF OVERVIEW

The focus for this study is the choices that were open to men occupying the role of political leader within a state and the factors that bore upon their selection among those choices. Specifically, the study examines the choices made by the first two Prime Ministers of Sierra Leone, Dr Milton Margai and his brother Albert Margai, from the early 1950s until Albert Margai's fall from power in 1967. Now for a good part of this period, until 1961, Sierra Leone was a British colony, with ultimate legal responsibility for its governance resting in the hands of the British Governor who was responsible not to Sierra Leoneans but to the British government. But from 1951 to 1961 power was gradually devolved from British officials to Sierra Leonean elected representatives, with Sierra Leoneans taking 'Ministerial' responsibility for some government departments in 1953, and for all but external affairs and defence after 1958, while Dr Margai became Chief Minister in 1954, Premier in 1958 and Prime Minister in 1961. While the presence of British officials and the Governor's reserve powers acted as checks on Dr Margai until 1961, still in matters concerning internal politics he clearly bore the major responsibility for several critical choices made before this time. Since some of the most significant consequences for the Margais' regimes flowed from the constitutional conflict arising out of the first constitutional step towards self-government in 1948, I will deal with this struggle briefly. Also, since a number of events had consequences reaching far beyond 1967, I will also consider some of the actions taken by the civilian regime of Siaka Stevens, which regained power from the military in 1968. But the main focus will be upon events from the major social upheavals of 1954 and 1955 to 1967. Since this is an analysis of leadership rather than a political history of this period, I am not providing a comprehensive account of Sierra Leone politics during the period, but simply enough information to permit an analysis of the leaders' actions.[1]

The Field for the Contest: Some Constraints Upon Political Action

Before examining the political scene itself, we should consider both physical and human features lying outside the scope of political action but imposing constraints on it. Some physical features of a state are for practical purposes permanently fixed, such as the amount of fresh water or of specific minerals available, while others, such as the quality of harbours or the amount of arable land, can be altered, though often only at a cost which forecloses other actions. Similarly, some human features are relatively slow to change, such as child-rearing patterns or linguistically based identities. We shall consider first those features of Sierra Leone which can be taken as given for much more than the decade which is our primary focus of interest, and second those features which were undergoing change during this period, but at rates and in quantities largely beyond the control of any political leaders.

The first feature of Sierra Leone worth noting is that it is a relatively compact state. With just over 2.1 million people in 28,000 square miles, it ranked in 1962 28th out of 40 countries in Africa, and 96th out of 135 in the world in population, and 37th in Africa and 106th in the world in size.[2] Very roughly circular in shape, its diameter at its widest point is just over 200 miles in a straight line, while its population density of 78 to the square mile means that people are generally close enough to allow fairly easy word-of-mouth dissemination of information. Its small size eliminates one physical barrier to the creation of a unified national elite, and also reduces the opportunities for elites to isolate themselves from the populace.

The second key feature of Sierra Leone is its location within 10° of the equator on the west coast of Africa, just at the point where the rain forest begins to give way to tree savanna. The resulting hot, damp climate has both positive and negative effects. On the positive side, it has enabled men to enjoy a considerable margin for error or disaster in a subsistence economy; if the staple crop, rice, fails, there are alternative sources of food, and the need for clothing and shelter is minimal. On the negative side, the same climate nurtures a particularly wide variety of organisms debilitating to man or destructive of his crops. While superficially the struggle for survival may seem easier than in a more temperate zone, the effects of disease on top of widespread malnutrition put limits on the extent to which people will make extra efforts to bring about social and economic change.

Certain further features flow from Sierra Leone's location. Being on the coast meant that it was subjected to relatively intense European pressure both from business and missionaries during the period of European expansion, and later participated in the flow of nationalist ideas both from within the Gold Coast and Nigeria, and from Africans returning from Britain. Its neighbours, the French colony of Guinea and American-influenced Liberia, had little impact upon Sierra Leone up to independence, and have lacked the power to intervene significantly as states in Sierra Leone's affairs.[3] But the weakness of their control over their inhabitants helped allow a tremendous influx of illicit diamond miners in the 1950s,[4] and Liberia did nothing to hamper the tremendous flow of smuggled diamonds which for the entire period under review was a continuing problem for the Sierra Leone economy.

Sierra Leone's physical environment affected the range of possibilities open to political leaders in a number of further ways. Reclaimable swamplands along the coast and in the Kenema and Bombali districts provide a substantial reservoir of further arable land to replace the increasingly-eroded hill rice farms, but only at the cost of a heavy investment in machinery and organisational skills. Sierra Leone is no more and no less favoured than several other African states for growing its principal cash crops for export, namely palm kernels, coffee, cocoa and piassava.[5] In short, the agricultural sector could be improved to provide both a surplus of foodstuffs for domestic use and renewable export resources, but only at considerable cost and at some risk.[6]

Sierra Leone's minerals have since the 1930s overshadowed agriculture as her chief source of export earnings, with one resource, diamonds, providing 60 per cent of the value of Sierra Leone's exports by 1960. Since Sierra Leone's diamonds were alluvial, their production, unlike most mineral extraction, could be undertaken either by the usual capital intensive, highly sophisticated methods usually available only through entrepreneurs from industrialised states, or by the much less sophisticated hand digging of native Sierra Leoneans, which from 1954 onwards co-existed alongside the more efficient but foreign-owned and operated Sierra Leone Selection Trust (SLST).[7] Since at least 30,000 men, 6 per cent of the entire adult male population of Sierra Leone, were annually involved in diamond digging during the 1950s and 1960s, the impact of this industry on Sierra Leone societies was considerable, involving as it did labour migration, entry into a money economy, removal from chiefdom controls and exposure to a wide range of new sights and ideas. While diamond mining was certainly a force for change, rather than a constant quantity, it was just as certainly a force beyond the control of any political authority, as will be argued below.[8]

Other minerals, while important to the economy and the government's revenues, had nowhere near the impact of the diamond rush. Iron mining was started at Marampa in 1933 by the Sierra Leone Development Company, a subsidiary of William Baird of Glasgow, and by the 1960s was exporting 1.5 million tons of ore concentrated to 64.5

per cent iron and valued at some £5 million a year down its private railway to its company port at Pepel and thence to Britain. But its labour force of about 2,500 Sierra Leoneans not only was far smaller than that involved in diamond mining, but tended to become a more stabilised urban population, with consequently less flow of ideas and attitudes back from the workplace to the home village. It was much more characteristic of mineral extraction enterprises in underdeveloped countries, in that it provided relatively little employment for Sierra Leoneans, was largely a self-contained enclave providing few linkages either backwards or forwards with the Sierra Leone economy, and possessed as an ultimate sanction the fact that if it abandoned operations, Sierra Leoneans would be unable to take over the enterprise. The same was true of Sierra Leone's other much less important mining enterprises, the chrome mine which closed in 1963 and the bauxite and rutile mining operations which began in 1963 and 1967 respectively.

Apart from these raw materials, which shared the common characteristic that only countries already possessing a fairly sophisticated industrial plant could utilise their end products in economically viable quantities, Sierra Leone is not plentifully endowed with natural resources. Most important, it lacks fossil fuels; there is no coal and no prospect of oil. Nor do its rivers have sufficient volume and sufficient drops to offer the alternative energy source of cheap hydro-electric power on a large scale although small projects were possible in the Freetown peninsula and in the interior.[9]

The rivers complicate Sierra Leone's life in other ways. No less than seven different river systems cross Sierra Leone from north-east to south-west but with seasonal fluctuations of up to 60 feet in their level, and with heads of navigation only a few miles from the sea, they provide little basis for an inland transportation system. Yet they contributed substantially to the difficulties of road and rail building, with the result that Sierra Leone's district capitals were not fully linked by roads until the late 1940s.

Even more important than the physical resources of a country in determining the constraints and possibilities for its politics are its human resources. Physical resources do not have memories; those that exist at a given time can be used in the future without regard for the past. The human material with which a politican must work is far less amenable to his manipulation; men act as much on the basis of recollections from the past as of aspirations for the future. And the relationships which Sierra Leoneans had developed with one another held rather more difficulties than promises for a leader.

Like Northern and Southern Nigeria, or the nineteenth-century union of the two Canadas, colonial Sierra Leone comprised two quite separate political units held together by little more than a common name. The Colony of Sierra Leone, the mountainous peninsula around Freetown, had come under the British Crown in 1808, following private attempts dating back to 1787 to establish it as a settlement for liberated slaves and other Africans whom Europeans felt would be better off in their 'ancestral homelands'. It followed the usual pattern of Crown Colony government, with 'unofficial' representation of the inhabitants in the advisory legislative council, British judicial practices (including trial by local jury), and British subject status for its inhabitants. The standard-setting groups among these inhabitants were black settlers removed from Britain, Nova Scotia and Jamaica, who gradually fused with a far greater number of Africans rescued from slaving ships to form the 50,000-strong group known as the Creoles, of whom more below.[10]

A Protectorate was declared over the bulk of the territory and its inhabitants in 1896. Unlike the Colony, its government was purely an administrative one,[11] and its inhabitants were only British protected persons. The terms which were used to describe the Protectorate, 'up-country' and later 'the Provinces', and the term 'countrymen' for its inhabitants (not to mention the Creoles' references to 'aborigines') suggest its decidedly hinterland status in relation to the Colony. Its administrative structure consisted of a variable number of Districts (finally stabilised in 1949 at twelve), each administered by a District Commissioner, and under each of these a number of chiefdoms, in most cases roughly corresponding to what were believed to be the boundaries and personnel of the pre-colonial units.[12] Supervising the District Commissioners was a Chief Commisioner for the Protectorate, reporting directly to the Governor, who had responsibility for both territories.

Within the Colony and Protectorate were found the homelands of people of a total of sixteen different language groups,[13] if we include the Creoles, who had developed their own language, Krio, largely out of English and the commonest African language of their ancestors, Yoruba. Among the indigenous groups, the largest were the Mendes of the south and the Temnes of the north-central area, each comprising about a third of Sierra Leone's two million people.[14] Most of the people of these various 'tribes' of Sierra Leone were probably aware during the colonial era of their identities as Mendes, Temnes and so on; the Mende, for example, had a strong unifying agency in their principal male secret society, the Poro, which in serving to ensure uniformity of social customs throughout Mendeland, undoubtedly also instilled a Mende identity into its members.[15] The Temne believed that they had common ancestors who came from the Fouta Jallon[16] and other tribes had similar unifying beliefs and customs. But the 'tribe' was not the most salient political unit for most Sierra Leoneans. The focus of most was on the much smaller chiefdom, a unit which in 1963 contained an average population of 13,600.[17]

The chiefdom in Sierra Leone had two political functions, which tended to be mutually supporting but could easily conflict. One function was as a social unit of solidarity, with the Paramount Chief as its political head or 'the father of his people', but with numerous checks to ensure that he acted in the interests of his people. A Mende chief, for example, could be deposed by the Poro Society, while the Temne chief could under certain circumstances be killed by his councillors.[18] Less drastic, but still highly effective, was the shame that would accrue to a chief who 'spoiled the country' by abusing his position.[19] In any case, the chief did not rule alone, but was generally advised by a body of elders, whose advice and contacts with different sections of chiefdom opinion carried considerable weight.

The other function of the chiefdom, as the lowest unit of the British administration, threatened considerable conflict with its internal socio-political function, particularly for the chief, who was expected to take the responsibility for acting for the administration. That this conflict did not undermine the position of chiefs in Sierra Leone as much as it seems to have elsewhere in Africa[20] can be attributed, I think, to the relatively low level of demands placed on them by the British administration. Apart from the relatively small tax demanded from each household head,[21] the British made few demands; they did not, for example, require forced labour as did the French[22] and did not open up the country to the same degree as in the Gold Coast Colony or southern Nigeria.[23] Some 'developmental' actions undertaken by the District Commissioners served to strengthen the chiefs; the latter could point to new roads and other signs of change as improvements brought by their standing, provided of course that these were not outweighed by the unpopular side of development, increased taxes. But for the most part, the potential conflict was muted rather than reconciled by administrative inaction.

For many people in the Protectorate, however, the chiefdom did not form the horizon of their political, economic or social worlds, and for some it was no longer even the principal focus of that world. The war had uprooted a considerable number of men in Sierra Leone, as elsewhere in the colonies; the 1946 Annual Report stated

> In the middle of 1943 it was estimated that 23 per cent of the adult male population of the Protectorate had left agriculture and was employed either in the Services or on works for the Services or Government.[24]

This would mean somewhat over 100,000 men, as substantial a body as later were to be involved in the diamond rush. Some 12,000 men were demobilised in 1946[25] though these were reabsorbed into civilian life without much difficulty, and did not give rise to militant veterans' organisations as their counterparts did in the Gold Coast and elsewhere. By 1948 there were some 36,786 persons reported as working for businesses employing six or more persons,[26] which on the basis of later years we can assume represented roughly half the total body of wage-earners. Somewhat more than half these wage-earners, 20,621, were employed in the Protectorate, with the mining companies employing some 6,000-7,000.[27]

A large proportion of farmers were also drawn into the money economy, though in a rather limited way. The Chief Commissioner for the Protectorate observed that:

> in 1948 producers received about £1,880,000 for their export crops [i.e. just over £1 per capita]. Almost certainly it would be to err on the high side to do more than double these figures to arrive at a very approximate estimate of the average *cash* income of the primary producers of the territory.[28]

But he went on to observe that this cash flow was fairly widely diffused; apart from the Koinadugu and Kono districts, 'most farmers are *not* engaged purely in subsistence farming'. This picture of widely dispersed cash-crop farming as a supplementary activity was strengthened by the observations of District Commissioners collecting 'house tax'[29] who noted that whereas before the war most farmers had grudgingly produced handfuls of pennies, now most paid in shillings or larger coins, and a third presented currency notes.[30]

A somewhat different indicator of the broadening of horizons is provided by the extent of literacy and of schooling in varius parts of the country. The 1948 Census[31] gave a figure of 33,729 literate persons in the Colony, though unfortunately no figures for the Protectorate. Little had cited a figure of 30,000-35,000 persons in the Protectorate who were literate around 1950,[32] although it is not clear whether these included his broader 'literate' group of persons able to speak and understand English but not read or write it, nor whether they included persons literate in Arabic. An extrapolation backward from the 1963 Census suggests a figure of 24,000-30,000 literate in English in 1950.[33] Whatever the precise figure, there was certainly not a substantial body of persons socially mobilised.

A similar picture is obtained from the school enrolment figures. In 1948 there were 12,311 children enrolled in primary school in the Colony, or about 55-60 per cent of the six to thirteen-year-old age group,[34] and 14,737 in the Protectorate, or about 4-5 per cent of the school-age group.[35] Taking the country as a whole, the proportion of primary school-age children actually in school would have been about 8 per cent. For secondary school, the drop-off was extremely sharp; there were 1,714 students in the Colony, including 149 from the Protectorate, and 186 in Protectorate secondary schools.

The numbers of those uprooted from chiefdom life, and even of that broader group who might look for political leadership beyond the chiefdom, did not appear to be large, although they were not much less as a proportion of Sierra Leone's population than were their counterparts in other British colonies,[36] and the country's size meant that there was a much greater opportunity for an elite embracing the whole country to develop than in, say, the Gold Coast or Kenya with their distant northern frontier regions. But the critical factor in deciding how these 'mobilised' individuals would help shape Sierra Leone's future was the identities into which they were mobilised. If all the educated, literate and wage-earning groups came to identify themselves as Sierra Leonean nationalists, their impact would be quite different than if they mobilised into conflicting communities.

The crucial development which set the stage for the emergence of Dr Margai and the Sierra Leone Peoples Party was the fact that Sierra Leoneans in the 1940s were mobilised into two antagonistic groups: the Creoles and the 'countrymen'. A combination of specific historial events and the values which developed in their community served to set the Creoles apart from the indigenous inhabitants of Sierra Leone, and made it difficult for them to enter into wholehearted co-operation. While I will reserve a full discussion of their differences for a later chapter,[37] we can note for now that the Creoles differentiated themselves from the 'countrymen' or 'aborigines' by their use of European surnames[38] and dress, their adherence to Christianity, their use of English or Krio, and less frequently their descent from the

Settlers or the Recaptives who had populated the peninsula before 1850. They were also 'Europeanised' in their values in so far as they placed great stress on individual achievement, tempered by a continuing commitment to one's family, but sufficient to lead many families along the path from petty trader in one generation, through prosperous merchant or white-collar worker in the next, to those ultimate pinnacles of respectability, the medical and the legal professions. A vital means to this end was the acquisition of formal education, and in Creole society considerable emphasis was placed on schooling for both boys and girls,[39] with results that we shall see below.

Despite their distinct value patterns, the Creoles did not form a closed caste. A considerable number of up-country persons 'went Creole', sometimes through being brought up as wards of Creole families or being taken in as the children of their Creole fathers, but also sometimes simply by identifying themselves as Creoles and cutting off their non-Creole past. Over a generation or two Creole society was generally prepared to accept such assimilation, but it did insist on such persons taking on the attributes of a Creole.

The combination of their own values, the encouragement of missionaries, and the accessibility of facilities meant that the Creoles held a considerable lead over the up-country people in the acquisition of those skills which were necessary to administer a Western-style state, and more generally in training for all the higher levels of Western roles. Of the seventy Sierra Leoneans who had qualified as medical doctors by 1950, all but three were Creoles;[40] of the equally large group of lawyers, the first from up-country to qualify was Albert Margai in 1948. In the intermediate ranks of the civil service which were shortly to provide recruits for the Africanisation programme, and in the teaching profession, Creoles predominated.[41] More broadly, of all those classified as 'literate', Creoles comprised some 40-35 per cent.[42] For the future their position would be less secure, since probably less than half the children in school in the Colony were Creole[43] and these were outnumbered by the children in school in the Protectorate, but given the greater encouragement from their families, and their generally higher aspirations, even this numerical weakness might not be as serious as it seemed.

Given this background of uneasy relationships, the prospects for Creole-countrymen co-operation were not rosy. Under certain conditions (for example, harsh oppression by the British of both groups on an equal basis) they might have come together in a common front, but in the circumstances of Sierra Leone, where it became clear at an early stage that Britain was going to devolve some power willy-nilly to one or other indigenous group, mutual suspicions and fears that the other side might gain a permanent advantage quickly swamped such prospects of co-operation. Since most of the personnel whose understanding of the European government structure would enable them to take over the Europeans' roles were Creoles, it seemed likely that a stalemate between Creole skills and Protectorate numbers would retard decolonisation.

A quite different disparity, at the time overshadowed by the more dramatic disputes between the Creoles and all the Protectorate peoples, lurked in the background. This was the difference in exposure to social change between the southern and northern halves of the Protectorate, a line which coincided with the boundary between Mendes and Temnes. For several reasons, the southern area was more 'developed' than the north. The railway line ran mostly through the Southern and Eastern Provinces, with only a small spur line to Makeni, and the network of feeder roads was somewhat denser in the south, with a mile of road to every 14.8 square miles in the Eastern Province, to 17.3 square miles in the Southern Province, and 18.6 square miles in the Northern Province.[44] It is significant, in the light of later northern feelings, that the central government was neglecting their area, that in the next ten years the ratio of miles of road to square miles of territory in the Northern Province increased only to 1:11.7, while in both the southern provinces in 1957 it stood at 1:9.0. But the difference lay almost entirely in the fact that Tribal Authorities in the south constructed roads at almost twice the rate of the northern Tribal Authorities, building 522 miles of roads over the 13,609 square miles of the two southern provinces from 1948 to 1957, against 263 miles in the Northern Province's 13,875 square miles.[45] This disparity suggested either poverty or indifference on the part of the north's own local rulers, and in the light of the misappropriation of funds later revealed, more likely the latter.[46]

Economically, the south also seemed to have a slight edge. While palm kernels, the main agricultural export, seemed to be drawn nearly as much from the north as from the south[47] other crops, including those which were to prosper most greatly in the next decade, were concentrated in the south.[48] There were 85 commercial vehicles registered in the south, against 29 in the north, in 1948;[49] and ferry crossings, another indirect indicator of trade, were twice as frequent on the main Southern Province road as on the main Northern Province one.[50]

In another area which bore directly on the future prospects for persons from the two regions, education, the north was even further behind, with 3,291 children in primary schools against 11,446 in the southern provinces.[51] In part this disparity could be attributed to the fact that the southern province had been penetrated earlier by missionaries, but it appears also that the Mendes tended to be more receptive to Western education, possibly because Islam was less widespread.[52] In any case, the Protectorate's first lawyers, first doctors, and many others whose qualifications include a high degree of formal Western education, came from the Mende and Sherbro areas. The southern lead was not insurmountable, and in any case both south and north were far behind the Creoles in levels of education, but initial advantages could be built into permanent ones, and were at the same time particularly visible.

I do not wish to leave the impression that these ethnic and regional divisions were fixed and immutable, nor that they precluded any cross-cutting alignments along other dimensions; as will be shown at a number of points in this study, these identities were essentially situational, shifting in accordance with changing circumstances, and even the most cohesive regional and ethnic identities were never strong enough to achieve complete solidarity among their membership even at the times of sharpest polarisation. Nevertheless, provided we bear in mind that other claims such as class, kinship or personal friendship may exert conflicting pulls on many individuals, we can safely take regionalism and ethnicity as the strongest bases for political cohesion during this period.

Elite Groups in the Sierra Leone Polity

I have suggested that the focus of identity for most Sierra Leoneans at the beginning of the 1950s was the chiefdom, in which the key figure was the Paramount Chief. The chief and those associated with him in the Tribal Authority could generally be considered an elite by S.F. Nadel's definition, which I find most useful for this study:

> Elites . . . must have some degree of corporateness, group character and exclusiveness. There must be barriers to admission. The . . . elite must be aware of their pre-eminent position . . . as something which they enjoy jointly and which sets them off from other people . . . Above all, the pre-eminent position must be regarded . .. as belonging to the [elite] not fortuitously . . . but by right – by a corporate right which is not within the reach of everyone.[53]

These characteristics of high status, corporate identity and exclusiveness, and recognition and acceptance of their standards by the society, were certainly applicable within each chiefdom. But we might also suggest that they were in large measure applicable to provincial Sierra Leone taken as a whole. The British had done a good deal to foster this sense of corporate identity; in 1905 they had set up the Bo School exclusively for the sons and nominees of Paramount Chiefs, and in their development of the principle of a hereditary right to rule on the part of certain families they had less directly furthered the same sense of exclusiveness. One could also argue that by using the chiefs as exclusive spokesmen for their people in the interwar period, and continuing to structure new institutions in the postwar period so that chiefs continued to predominate, the British were further aiding the recognition of chiefs as leaders by their people, although this could certainly be a double-edged weapon if the people perceived the chiefs acting in the interests of the British rather than of their subjects.[54] The informal chiefs' assemblies begun during the war and the formally constituted district councils and Protectorate Assembly in 1946 provided forums in which the chiefs could meet, as did the chief-dominated Protectorate Educational Progressive Union (PEPU).[55]

But the chiefs were not the only group which could plausibly claim elite status in Sierra Leone. The Western-educated men, by virtue of their education and life styles, formed an equally identifiable group, and one moreover which not only came closest to emulating the 'superior' European status group, but also alone possessed the skills which would entitle them to challenge the Europeans for the right to rule Sierra Leone. Since their occupations were essentially urban, they congregated in Freetown and the provincial capitals, where most of their social relationships would be with each other, and where the more local claims of kin and chiefdom would be less insistent.[56] This proximity brought the Western elite, both Creoles and countrymen, into close personal contact; most of the group who formed the SLPP and the opposition parties had come to know each other well during their years of service in the various provincial capitals. But on the other hand, this urban orientation put them at a disadvantage vis-à-vis the chiefs; their local roots had often atrophied too far for them to appeal successfully to the majority of their countrymen.

The educated men, we have noted, were quite deeply divided along Creole-countrymen lines. Equally important was the fact that the up-country educated men were nearly all sons or close relatives of chiefs, largely because the chiefs alone had possessed the resources to send their children to primary and secondary schools. On the chiefs' side, from the 1940s onwards Tribal Authorities tended to elect new chiefs from the ranks of the educated men, with the result that these two groups were closely linked. They were more than a single elite, in that they derived their status from different roots; but they were not quite two separate elites, in that there was a considerable interchange of personnel between these two roles and because the persons occupying these roles were generally members of the same families. Furthermore, neither group was united in its attitudes to change.

Each of these elites – the Creole intelligentsia,[57] the Protectorate intelligentsia, and the chiefs – was to some extent restricted in its ability to co-operate with the others by its base of support. The Creoles, as spokesmen for a compact and highly mobilised society, had the least freedom for manoeuvre of the three, and the social separation and widespread fear for the Creole position found in Creoledom made it difficult for them to go far in accepting the Protectorate demands for majority rule. The elite's own predilections varied considerably, from Bankole-Bright's passionate denunciations of the Mende 'murderers of our ancestors',[58] to the action of H.E.B. John, Harry Sawyerr and others who at the outset joined the 'countryman's party', the SLPP. One of the tragedies of Creoledom was that the moderates were out-shouted by the Bankole-Brights whose intransigence reinforced the legacy of suspicion between Creoles and countrymen for many years. But it would have taken a strong leadership with far less extremist pressure on it to put successfully this 'best possible' approach of subordination and infiltration, and there are few cases in history of a beleaguered privileged minority accepting such leadership.

The chiefs had far fewer problems to contend with from their base of support, the ordinary farmer of the Protectorate who still generally looked to chieftaincy as the source of leadership in all relations with the outside world. Their people would not have created trouble if they had attepted to conciliate the Creoles. But they did face one danger as the British handed over national control to an African elite. Their own power depended on their sticking closely to their people's local affairs; a chief could hardly afford to spend half his working time in Freetown. But it was patently clear that national office-holders would maintain the full power of the British over individual chiefs, and only slightly less clear that they could also undermine the institution of chieftaincy itself, both through introducing competing structures and through cutting away such vital powers as the chief's control over land. The land issue was a particular point of friction between Creoles and countrymen; the Creoles had pressed for years to be allowed to buy land freehold in the Protectorate, while Protectorate, people were united in their desire to maintain the existing prohibition on any alienation beyond long-term leasing. Because they were vulnerable to changes in the national rules, the chiefs needed to be able to trust whoever took power at the national level; and the Creoles' views on land tenure, among other matters, were not conducive to this kind of trust.

The third group, the Protectorate intelligentsia, had a less certain base than either the Creoles or the chiefs. To the extent that they had any 'natural' constituency, it comprised all those who had become attracted to the idea of social change, and could perceive those possessing a Western education as being in the forefront of such change. But part of this constituency was pulled away by the fact of its being Creole; and the remaining portion, the up-country youths who had been exposed to wage labour, schooling or other stimuli for change, were spread among a number of provincial towns, each of which was heavily outnumbered by a hinterland still firmly adhering to its chiefs. This did not necessarily leave them helpless; they could have used their supporters as a spearhead for change fanning out into the hinterlands and exploiting intra-chiefdom quarrels to develop a mass political movement, as was shortly to be done in Ghana.[59] But this was not to be done, for two reasons. One reason, to be discussed below, was that as a preliminary to a mass movement undercutting the chiefs, the intelligentsia would have had to force the British to introduce a political structure allowing more direct popular participation than the constitutional change the British were proposing at the time. But to do this would have required a united front of all the intelligentsia, Creole as well as up-country; and mass popular participation, in which the Protectorate's numbers would enjoy their greatest advantage, was precisely what the Creoles could least afford to support. The second reason, already noted, was the fact that the up-country intelligentsia were closely linked with the chiefs. While their interest as rival claimants for national power, and possibly their predilections for social change and for popular participation, would lead them into conflict with the chiefs, their personal ties would tend to offset this by making them sympathetic to the chiefs' position. While they could have joined forces with either Creoles or chiefs, the nature of their bargain with the Creoles would have been an improbable one: Creole support to introduce a mass franchise, followed by an alliance in which the magnitude of the countrymen's base would always have been a threat to the Creoles' superiority in talents. The bargain with the chiefs would be somewhat more plausible; the chiefs would retain local control and provide the necessary support at elections, while the intelligentsia would refrain from actions at the national level which would hurt the chiefs, but otherwise would have a free hand. From the chiefs' viewpoint, such a bargain was more plausible than one with the Creoles, both because of the close relations and consequent trust they enjoyed with the up-country intelligentsia, and because the intelligentsia would be almost totally dependent on the goodwill of the chiefs to retain their electoral base.

Such bargains depended upon a number of factors beyond the control of the three groups cited. Above all, they assumed the existence of particular political structures, which would provide advantages and disadvantages for each participating group, and might even keep some elements of the polity completely removed from participation. The participating groups of course played roles in altering the structures, increasingly so as the British devolved more and more power to them, but at each stage the formal political framework provided constraints upon the action of all the groups concerned. Before proceeding further in our examination of political interactions, it would be well to outline the changes that took place in the formal framework, while leaving discussion of who played what part in bringing these changes for later sections.

Constitutional Advances in Sierra Leone, 1951-61

Constitutional proposals to start Sierra Leone on the road to national self-government were first formally put forward by the then Governor, Sir Hubert Stevenson, in 1947. Preliminary steps had already been taken in the Protectorate a year previously with the introduction of District Councils and a Protectorate Assembly, which both rested, as we have already noted, on an electoral base of Tribal Authorities themselves not popularly elected but largely controlled by the Paramount Chief. The national organs of government at that time were the Legislative Council, comprising eleven British officials, four nominated members from business and the missions, three appointed Paramount Chiefs to represent Protectorate interests, and three Colony representatives elected on a franchise with high property and educational qualifications.[60] The Executive Council had included since 1943 two unofficial members of the Legislative Council, while the basic running of both Colony and Protectorate was under the Governor and his officials organised into functional departments.

The new proposals contemplated a Legislative Council containing an unofficial majority comprising ten representatives from the Protectorate, four from the Colony, and two nominated members, against seven officials.[61] While Africans could thus have a majority over the British officials, a snag lay in the fact that the mode of selection for the Protectorate representatives was through the Protectorate Assembly, a body solidly controlled by the chiefs. Both Creoles and the Protectorate intelligentsia feared that the chiefs were too firmly under the control of British District Commissioners to act independently, a fear with a certain amount of justification.[62] The first attack on the constitutional proposals thus developed along lines similar to those employed by the nationalists in Nigeria and the Gold Coast, where similar proposals had been implemented a year earlier.[63] But unlike the other two colonies where all indigenous pressure was directed towards hastening broader participation, in Sierra Leone the Creole representatives soon back-tracked from acceptance of the Protectorate's dominance to a demand for equal representation for the Colony. A two-year stalemate ensued and was broken only when a new Governor, after unsuccessful attempts to mediate a compromise, imposed a slightly modified form of the original proposals with the critical addition (earlier accepted by the Creoles) that unofficials should have a majority in the Executive Council as well as in the legislature.

The constitution brought into being in 1951 ensured, then, three things: that the Protectorate representatives would outnumber those of the Colony (there was to be one elected by each of the twelve District Councils, and two by the Protectorate Assembly, against seven elected from Colony constituencies); that the chiefs, through their control of the District Councils and Protectorate Assembly, would play the key role in selecting the members from the Protectorate[64] and that whoever controlled a majority in the Legislative Council would also be able to participate in the exercise of executive powers. Of the three contending elites, the chiefs came out best from the British decision to impose the Stevenson constitution; it guaranteed them a preponderant position. The Creoles were assured of a minority power base as long as the franchise in the Colony remained restricted on criteria of education and property; but saving the highly improbable eventuality that they could combine with the British officials to form a majority against the Protectorate unofficials, they would have to come to terms with the chiefs or be a permanent minority. The Protectorate intelligentsia were left without any independent electoral base; their choice would be to ally themselves with the chiefs and hope that the chiefs would accept their claim to be better qualified to manage national affairs, or to seek to persuade the Creoles to offer them a share of their minority of directly elective seats. It was hardly surprising to find that the ultimate outcome of this situation was that the Protectorate intelligentsia took national office on the basis of the chiefs' Legislative Council votes, with the Creoles relegated to an opposition role. The main point at issue between the two Protectorate groups was how large a role the chiefs should play at the national level, and conversely how far the intelligentsia should go in controlling the chiefs' behaviour, which forms the subject matter of a later chapter.[65]

Those key changes which shifted the balance of power between different groups in the polity up to Independence should be noted briefly. In 1955 the power to depose a Paramount Chief was shifted from the Governor alone to the Governor-in-Council, that is to say from British officialdom to the embryonic Cabinet in which the national Sierra Leone politicians were soon to predominate.[66] In 1955 a Commission[67] recommended a two-step extension of the franchise, the first stage to be taxpayer (universal male) suffrage and the second to be universal adult suffrage. Although many Creoles and some chiefs opposed the proposed extension, it was implemented for the 1957 election. This election therefore offered the first opportunity for politicians to build a base independent of the chiefs, although only a few younger SLPP supporters and two opposition parties made any attempt of this sort. The chiefs, meanwhile, remained members of the single legislative chamber, but were elected separately from the ordinary members, one from each District Council. (In 1962 this was changed to election by the Tribal Authorities – between one and three thousand – of each district).

In 1958 came full internal self-government, with the British officials (except the Governor and his newly appointed Deputy) withdrawing from the Executive Council and Sierra Leoneans taking over Ministerial responsibility for all government matters except external affairs, the police and the military. In practice, while British officials now had to persuade their own Minister rather than speaking directly to the whole Cabinet, their influence remained strong. A British official was Secretary to the Prime Minister until 1962; the last British Provincial Secretary did not leave until 1966; and the British heads of the police and the army did not leave until 1963 and 1964 respectively. But the decisive political power, particularly as regards struggles for power within Sierra Leone, now lay almost completely with Sierra Leoneans.

The Independence Constitution brought into being on 27 April

1961[68] was essentially the British Parliamentary system committed to writing. It provided for a Governor-General to appoint as Prime Minister a person 'likely to command the support of a majority of the members of the House [of Representatives]' (Section 48, 2) and to dissolve the House on the request of the Prime Minister, unless some other government could be formed. In relation to his Ministers, the Prime Minister's power to appoint and the power to dismiss[69] were enough by themselves, in view of the desirability of Ministerial office vis-à-vis other employments, to ensure the Cabinet's acquiescence in his views. Ministerial control of patronage, in turn, was a powerful lever for controlling backbenchers, while advancement in the public service could be indirectly controlled by the Prime Minister through his power to appoint the Public Service Commissioners.

The formal checks on the power of a Prime Minister in the Sierra Leone Parliamentary system were few. Unlike most former British colonies, Sierra Leone lacked an Upper House; Paramount Chief representatives, one to a district, were included in the unicameral legislature.

The main formal checks lay in the fact that key parts of the Constitution, including a Bill of Rights, were protected by a simple but demanding amendment procedure, and the upholding of this procedure was in the hands of a judiciary whose Sierra Leonean members were to some extent insulated from direct political control and whose final court of appeal was the Judicial Committee of the Prvy Council in Britain (Section 84). The amendment procedure for 'entrenched' clauses required passage of the amendment by a two-thirds majority of *all* members of the House, followed by a dissolution and passage of the amendment again by a two-thirds majority of the new House (Section 43, 1 and 3). Sections entrenched included safeguards for freedom from arbitrary detention and for freedom of assembly and association, as well as certain insulating procedures for the appointment and removal of judges.[70] Unfortunately, under a state of public emergency the protection against arbitrary detention only applied after a person had been detained for six months[71] while freedom of assembly and association was not contravened by any law 'reasonably required in the interests of defence, public safety, public order, public morality or public health . . .' or 'reasonably justifiable in a democratic society'.[72] While it would be up to the judiciary to determine 'reasonableness', there was clearly a fairly strong presumption of legality with respect to most actions a government would be likely to take against opponents. A Prime Minister determined to remove all opponents from political activity would find no serious obstacles imposed by the Constitution, either through the Bill of Rights or through the Parliamentary structure.

There were, however, two obstacles to a leader's dominance which deserve mention. One was the use of the single-member constituency as the basis for representation in the legislature. Making the basis of election for each legislator a separate chiefdom or small cluster of chiefdoms, rather than using a province or the whole country as the basis for multi-member constituencies, enhanced the ordinary member of Parliament's power vis-à-vis the Prime Minister in two ways. First, it encouraged legislators to look towards the local needs of their constituents and to respond to those needs as the most effective way of winning elections. Conversely, it discounted commitment to a central party organisation; since most of the electorate received little encouragement to vote by party, and a great deal to vote according to their concept of local interest, a legislator would have little to gain by accepting party discipline, and a great deal to lose by ignoring local demands, which helped to ensure that party organisation remained relatively weak.[73]

The other major source of local autonomy was the position of the Paramount Chiefs, and more generally, of the chiefdom governments. Formally, the Chiefdom Councils (known as Tribal Authorities until 1963) were creatures of the national legislature, with the only constitutional protection for them being an entrenched constitutional prohibition on 'the abolition of the office of Paramount Chief as existing by customary law and usage'.[74] But in reality, as we shall see, the institution of chieftaincy was strongly supported, particularly by those who were prominent in the governing Sierra Leone Peoples Party. While a Prime Minister could without much difficulty remove an individual chief for violation of customary standards of behaviour or for backing an opposition party, it would be almost suicidal for him to attack the institution of chieftaincy.

We could summarise the features of the independence constitution as follows: it put tremendous power into the hands of the Prime Minister vis-à-vis his Ministers, backbenchers who aspired to be Ministers, and civil servants. But it made the growth of disciplined, nationally-oriented parties difficult, whether as creatures of the Prime Minister or as autonomous entities, and it offered considerable difficulties to any leader who sought to change it, as Albert Margai was to discover when attempting to introduce first a one-party state and then a Republic. The constitution also helped safeguard the Paramount Chiefs, both by the entrenchment of a clause protecting the office of Paramount Chief (Section 44) and by the inclusion of Paramount Chief members in the House of Representatives.

Sierra Leone's inheritance at the start of decolonisation was not startlingly different from that of other African states. It shared essentially the same physical environment and natural resources as such neighbours as Guinea, Liberia, Senegal and the Gold Coast, with the rather important exception that its alluvial diamonds provided widespread opportunities for indigenous entrepreneurs to acquire wealth in a way that existed nowhere else in Africa except perhaps in the Central African Republic. Ethnically, its diversity was also comparable to that of its neighbours, with again one important exception. The exception was the Creole community, whose establishment of what they regarded as a 'superior' culture made their position somewhat analogous to the white settlers of Kenya and Northern Rhodesia, the Arabs of Zanzibar, and the Americo-Liberians. Unlike the Liberian settlers, however, the Creoles were themselves subject to the rule of a colonial power, and unlike the white settlers in East Africa they could not claim affinities of 'kith and kin' to mitigate this subordination. Their position, therefore, was a uniquely ambivalent one, on the one hand asserting their role as the bearers of Western civilisation, on the other being pushed by British slights into a recognition of their ties with their 'brother Africans'.[75] While they did not form a caste in the way that whites and Indians both did in East Africa, they were far more set apart from other Sierra Leoneans than were the coastal elites of other West African states, with the result that the Sierra Leone 'nationalist' movement was left critically short of Western-educated men to push for social change.

Sierra Leone's political framework was also essentially similar to those of other decolonising British territories. Political activity in all the British African territories focused on gaining control of the territorial government through legislative representation, thus giving considerable support to pluralist tendencies, particularly of a regional or local nature; in this it contrasted markedly with the French Assembly, an approach which tended to smother intra-territorial divisions. The pluralism inherent in the British system of electing local representatives to a territorial legislature could be offset by the perceived need to unite all the 'nationalist' forces against colonial rule, but substantial resistance to such unification persisted in every territory except Tanganyika.[76] In Sierra Leone, where a substantial portion of the educated men who formed the organising cadres of the nationalist movements elsewhere has isolated themselves from any such movement, the prospect of a pan-territorial orientation was particularly unpromising. To create a mass movement like the Convention Peoples Party in the Gold Coast, or the Tanganyika African National Union, would not have been an easy task. But there were some choices open as to the form a political movement might take at the start of decolonisation, and it is to these choices that we now turn.

Notes

1. For political histories at the national level, see my *Politics in Sierra Leone, 1947-1967*, Toronto, University of Toronto Press, 1970, and Martin Kilson, *Political Change in a West African State,* Cambridge, Mass., Harvard University Press, 1966. For an excellent analysis of the local level politics which underpin these national events, see Walter L. Barrows, *Grassroots Politics in an African State,* New York, Africana, 1976, and see also Victor Minikin, *Local Politics in Kono District, Sierra Leone, 1945-1970,* unpublished Ph.D thesis, University of Birmingham, 1971.
2. Calculated from Bruce Russett et al., *World Handbook of Political and Social Indicators,* New Haven, Yale University Press, 1964, Tables I and 40. I have divided the late Central African Federation into its three components, but otherwise have used only those countries listed in Russett's tables.
3. Following an attempted coup in 1971, Siaka Stevens called in Guinean army units to help protect him against possible disloyalty by the Sierra Leone Military Force, but this was certainly not a case of Guinea interfering against the wishes of the Sierra Leone government.
4. See below, p. 63.
5. Piassava, a heavy palm fibre used in street sweeping brushes, is the one crop of which Sierra Leone is a nearly exclusive supplier, but it faces increasing competition from artificial fibres. Minor crops such as ginger or potential ones such as citrus fruits are equally at the mercy of fluctuations in supply elsewhere as well as to the vagaries of transport for small quantities of goods.
6. This will be discussed further in Chapter 8.
7. See below, pp. 61-3, 245-6, 250.
8. See below, pp. 64-6.
9. The Guma Dam near Freetown, completed in 1966, is primarily a reservoir for the city, but also is used to provide 2400 kw of electricity during the rainy season. A project to harness the Sewa was dropped because it would flood diamond areas, while a plan to utilise a fall on the Rokell was not pressed forward until 1973.
10. The standard historical work on the Colony is Christopher Fyfe, *A History of Sierra Leone,* London, Oxford University Press, 1962. Other useful works on the Creoles are Arthur T. Porter, *Creoledom,* London, Oxford University Press, 1962; John Peterson, *Province of Freedom,* London, Faber, 1969; and Leo Spitzer, *The Creoles of Sierra Leone: Responses to Colonialism, 1870-1945,* Madison, University of Wisconsin Press, 1974.
11. Under the 1924 Constitution, three chiefs from the Protectorate were appointed to the Legislative Council as spokesmen for Protectorate interests. But this was the only legislative opening for political participation

for Protectorate people until the setting up of District Councils and the Protectorate Assembly in 1946. The Colony, by contrast, had had Creoles in the legislature since 1863 and Freetown had had its own Mayor and Council since 1893.

12. The pre-colonial chiefdoms had in fact been rather fluid in their membership, due to constant splitting away of disaffected groups, successful impositions of hegemony by strong chiefs over their neighbours, and similar factors. Their territorial limits were even more fluid; between the shifting strength of chiefs, shifting agriculture, and lack of pressure on the land, boundaries were not of vital concern. See below, pp. 123-6 for a fuller discussion of the chiefdoms. The number of chiefdoms was finally stabilised in the 1950s at just under 150, having been amalgamated down from well over 200 since the mid-1930s.
13. This does not include one further rather important group, the Lebanese, who in Sierra Leone as in the rest of West Africa, occupied a commercial niche between the large-scale European enterprises and the petty African entrepreneurs. Although they numbered only a few thousand (the 1963 census listed only 3,300 citizens of Lebanon and Syria) the Lebanese in Sierra Leone enjoyed considerable opportunities for political influence through their wealth. For a further discussion of their role see pp. 182-4.
14. The complete list of 'tribes' and their numbers, according to the 1963 Census, is as follows:

Mende	672,831	Fula	66,824
Temne	648,931	Mandingo	51,024
Limba	183,496	Kissi	48,954
Kono	104,573	Creole	41,783
Sherbro	74,674	Yalunka	15,005
Koranko	80,732	Krim	8,733
Susu	67,288	Vai	5,786
Loko	64,459	Gola	4,854
		Gallinas	2,200

1963 Population Census of Sierra Leone, Freetown, Central Statistics Office, 1965, Vol. II, Table 3.

15. See Kenneth Little, *The Mende of Sierra Leone,* rev. edn. London, Routledge & Kegan Paul, 1967, p. 183; also his 'The Political Function of the Poro', *Africa XXXV,* 1965, pp. 349-65, and *XXXVI,* 1966, pp.62-72.
16. Vernon R. Dorjahn, 'The Changing Political System of the Temne', *Africa XXX,* 2, Apr. 1960, p. 119.
17. The largest chiefdom in 1963 had 49,000 people, the smallest 1,200. See *1963 Census,* Vol. I, Table 5.
18. See Little, *The Mende,* pp. 183-5, 202; Dorjahn, 'Changing Political System of the Temne', p. 114. Little, in 'The Political Function of the Poro', Part II, comments that political power was balanced between the Poro and chieftainship (p. 69).
19. See Ruth Finnegan, *Survey of the Limba People of Sierra Leone,* London, HMSO, 1965, p. 39.
20. For a specific study which shows a sharp contrast with the treatment of chiefs in Sierra Leone, see Jean Suret-Canale, La Fin de la Chefferie en Guinee', *Journal of African History,* VII, 3, 1966, pp. 459-93.
21. Up to the Second World War, this tax was about five shillings per head of household.
22. For a comment on the depth of feeling forced labour aroused, and its political significance,see Aristide Zolberg, *One-Party Government in the*

Ivory Coast, Princeton, NJ., Princeton University Press, 1964, pp. 55-7.

23. As one indication of agricultural development, in 1950 agricultural exports per capita had a value of £13 in the Gold Coast, £4 10s in Eastern and Western Nigeria, and £1 16s in Sierra Leone. (Calculated from *Blue Books* for 1950).
24. Great Britain. Colonial Office, *Annual Report on Sierra Leone for the Year 1946*, London, HMSO, 1947, p. 52.
25. Ibid., p. 3.
26. Hubert Childs, *A Plan of Economic Development for Sierra Leone*, Freetowns, Government Printer, 1949, p. 6 (hereafter *Childs Report*).
27. Ibid.
28. Ibid.
29. This tax was levied on every male head of household in the Protectorate for central government revenue. By 1950 it had crept from the prewar rate of 5s a head to about 11s 6d. See *Cox Report*, p. 127.
30. Sierra Leone, *Annual Report on the Provincial Administration for the Year 1952*, Freetown, Government Printer, 1953, p. 3.
31. This *Census of the Colony and Protectorate of Sierra Leone*, 1948, Freetown, Government Printer, 1949, was a rather brief document of two pages, using sampling techniques for the Protectorate, and providing only population figures, and for the Colony, literacy and some ethnic data.
32. See Kenneth Little, 'Structural Change in the Sierra Leone Protectorate', *Africa*, XXV, 3, July 1955, p. 220.
33. The 1963 Census asked 'Can this person read and write English [or Arabic]?' A total of 117,090 persons were recorded as literate in English, and 19,225 in Arabic, for the entire country. But while less than a tenth of the Arabic literates were in the Western Area (the former Colony), nearly half the English-speaking literates lived there. This left the ratio of Arabic to English literates in the provinces at more than 1 to 4 in 1963. But the 1963 Census also revealed that while the literacy rate for ten to twenty year-olds in English was nearly double that for adults, for Arabic the proportion of literates had not increased. In other words, it seems likely that since English literacy had doubled in the previous decade, while Arabic literacy had remained constant, those literate in Arabic in 1950 might have comprised about 40 per cent of the total literate group, and it would be quite likely that the overlap between Arabic and English literates would be small, since they followed quite different schooling patterns. This could give us a figure of from 18,000 to 21,000 persons literate in English in the Protectorate around 1950. However, if we extrapolate backward from the 1963 Census, we get a somewhat higher figure. There were about 24,000 persons twenty-five years or older in the Protectorate who were literate in English in 1963. Assuming none of these learned to read and write after 1950, we have only to account for those literates who died between 1950 and 1963. If we can assume these had the literacy rate of 1963's over forty-fives, 1.7 per cent, and that the age group died at the rate of 20,000 to 25,000 a year, we can add a figure of between 4,400 and 5,500 to the 24,000 surviving literates, for an approximate total of 28,000 to 30,000 persons literate in English in 1950.
34. I am assuming that the percentage of those in the six to thirteen-year-old group as a proportion of total population was the same in 1948 as it was in 1963, i.e. 17 per cent (calculated from *1963 Census*, Vol. I, Table 10.) Data on school enrolments is from the *Annual Report of the Education Department for the Year 1948*.
35. Ibid.

36. Data from Lord Hailey's *An African Survey* rev. edn., London, Oxford University Press, 1957, suggests that Sierra Leone's proportion of wage workers to total population was about the same as for the Gold Coast, Uganda, and French Equatorial Africa (about 5 per cent in each) but substantially lower than the Belgian Congo, Tanganyika or Kenya (calculated from pp. 143, 1350-1). In education Sierra Leone had already begun to lag by 1947, having a lower proportion of children in primary school than any other British West or East African territory (p. 1258). However, the differences were hardly of such an order of magnitude as to 'explain' the relatively greater hold of traditional ways.
37. See below, Chapter 6.
38. Though many Creoles also used a Yoruba name along with their Christian ones. There was also a considerable minority group, the Aku Creoles, who were differentiated not only by their use of Yoruba surnames, but also by their adherence to the Muslim religion.
39. For discussions of Creole culture, see Arthur Porter, *Creoledom,* esp. pp. 89-94, 109-18, and Gaynor Cohen, 'Recruitment to the Professional Class in Sierra Leone', paper presented to the Sierra Leone Symposium, University of Western Ontario, May 1971. One outstanding example of upward mobility is given in John Hargreaves, *A Life of Sir Samuel Lewis,* London, Oxford University Press, 1958.
40. See Dr M.C.F. Easmon, 'Sierra Leone Doctors', *Sierra Leone Studies,* New Series 6, June 1956, pp. 81-96.
41. An examination of the 1950 *Staff List,* Part I: Senior Service, reveals forty-one Creoles against no more than five up-country Africans. Particularly striking was the fact that all five Sierra Leoneans in trainee District Commissioner posts were Creoles. But we should also note that the total number of Senior Staff was just under 500.
42. If we assume that three-quarters of the 28,000 Creoles recorded in the 1948 Census (i.e. all those over ten years old) were literate, this leaves us with about 12,000 up-country people in the Colony who were literate, plus an additional 30,000 up-country.
43. While we have no breakdown for the whole Colony, we do have the interesting study by two British social scientists of the Western Rural Area, which noted that nearly all Creoles sent their children to school, but only about a fifth of the people of up-country origin did so. E.M. Richardson and G.R. Collins, *Economic and Social Survey of the Rural Areas of the Colony of Sierra Leone,* London, Colonial Office Research Department, 1954, p. 441. Even if this ratio applied to Freetown as well, the Creoles should have had some 4,800 children in primary school, against some 3,200 of up-country origin. In fact, since we know that there were some 12,300 children in primary schools, it seems likely that this 'excess' was attributable largely to additional children of up-country parents.
44. *Childs Report,* p.34.
45. See D.T. Jack, *An Economic Survey of Sierra Leone,* Freetown, Government Printer, 1958, p. 49 (*Jack Report*).
46. See below, pp. 67-68.
47. *Childs Report,* p. 17, indicated that 29,000 tons of kernels came from the southern and eastern provinces along the railway lines, 7,095 tons came from the Northern Province by rail, and 30,254 tons came from 'the Colony and adjacent areas'. Since considerable stands of oil palms are found in Port Loko district within easy road or water journeys from Freetown, it is likely that at least half this tonnage came from the Northern Province.
48. Cocoa, ginger and piassava were already well established, with coffee

developing slowly. Kola and groundnuts were grown in the north, but had not nearly the export potential of the southern crops.

49. Cited in *Jack Report*, p. 50.
50. *Childs Report*, p. 55.
51. *Annual Report of the Education Department for 1948.*
52. Richardson and Collins note that in the Western Rural Area, where all ethnic groups had approximately equal access to schools, 40 per cent of school age Mende children attended schools, but only 12 per cent of the Temne children did so. *Survey of the Rural Area*, p. 441.
53. S.F. Nadel, 'The Concept of Social Elites', *International Social Science Bulletin*, VIII, 1956, p. 415.
54. As an illustration of the British view of the chiefs' role, consider these remarks of Governor Slater: 'If . . . direct African representation was to be conceded . . . the representatives must, at present at least, be Paramount Chiefs; under the tribal system no others would have adequate title to speak with authority.' *Legislative Council Debates*, Session 1924-5, p. 221. When District Councils were introduced in 1946, the chiefs were made *ex-officio* members, and the second member from each chiefdom was chosen by the Tribal Authority, in which the chief's voice generally predominated.
55. See Cartwright, *Politics in Sierra Leone*, p. 38 for a discussion of PEPU.
56. See Little, 'Structural Change', for a good discussion of the development of this elite.
57. I am using the term 'intelligentsia' very loosely here to cover those persons who formed an elite by virtue of their pre-eminence in the amount of Western-type education they had received.
58. See his letter in *Sierra Leone Weekly News*, 26 August 1950. Ironically, Bankole-Bright twenty years earlier had promoted the claims of Dr Margai, the first Protectorate medical doctor, to a government appointment against the claims of a Creole doctor, and at other times in his career had supported Protectorate interests.
59. For a discussion of the spread of the Convention Peoples Party in Ghana before the 1951 election, see Dennis Austin, *Politics in Ghana, 1946-1960*, London, Oxford University Press, 1964, pp. 114-34.
60. To quality as voters, Colony residents needed to be male British subjects or natives of the Protectorate domiciled in the Colony, age twenty-one, literate in English or Arabic, and either own or rent property rated at £10 in Freetown (£6 in the Rural Area) or have a salary of £100 (£60 in the Rural Area) per annum. Sierra Leone (Legislative Council) Order-in-Council, 1924, Sections 23 and 24.
61. Sierra Leone. *Proposals for the Reconstruction of the Legislative Council in Sierra Leone*, Seasonal Paper No. 2 of 1948, Freetown, Government Printer, 1948, p. 1.
62. 'Trouble-making' chiefs could always be subjected to tribunals of enquiry, and sacked by the administration for 'conduct unbecoming a Paramount Chief'. Since this could cover behaviour which caused trouble with chiefdom residents, as well as the more normal levying of illegal taxes and tributes, few chiefs could escape censure from an enquiry into their conduct. On the other hand, the Chiefs in the Protectorate Assembly did on occasion take quite forceful stands in defence of their own interests against the wishes of the administration. For one such instance, see Cartwright, *Politics in Sierra Leone*, pp. 44-5.
63. For the Gold Coast, see Austin, pp. 50-8. For Nigeria, see James S. Coleman, *Nigeria: Background to Nationalism*, Berkeley, University of California Press, 1958, pp. 275-381.

64. The only major handicap for the chiefs was the requirement that members of the new Legislative Council had to be literate in English, a requirement which eliminated many of them from contention, and in one district guaranteed the selection of a non-chief.
65. See below, Chapter 5.
66. The Protectorate (Amendment) Ordinance 1955, No. 13 of 1955, Section 4.
67. *Report of the Commission for Electoral Reform* (Keith-Lucas Commission), Freetown, 1954.
68. The Sierra Leone (Constitution) Order-in-Council 1961, Statutory Instrument, West Africa, No. 741 of 1961.
69. Although technically it was the Governor, and later the Governor-General, who possessed the formal powers of appointment and dismissal, even in 1951 Dr Margai's recommendations seem to have been accepted. See *Legislative Council Debates,* 1951-2, p. 271, where Dr Margai stated that the Governor had suggested names and he had 'approved or disapproved of them'.
70. Section 76 provided that a Judicial Service Commission, two of whose four members were to be judges, was to make appointments to the Sierra Leone Supreme Court, while Section 77 provided for the establishment of a tribunal of three judges to determine if a judge's misbehaviour warranted his removal from the bench. Section 84 entrenched the right of appeal to the Judicial Committee of the Privy Council in London.
71. Section 13 (5), (6) provided that a person detained under emergency regulations could, after six months, appeal to a tribunal whose presiding officer must be appointed by the Chief Justice.
72. Section 22 (2).
73. Against this decentralising tendency of the single-member constituency has to be put the centralising tendency inherent in a Parliamentary system because of the need to maintain continuous support for the leader in the legislature. I would only observe here that until late in the nineteenth century, Parliamentary systems such as those of Britain and Canada contained a considerable number of 'loose fish' whom a leader had to cajole and induce to support him after they had been elected to the legislature. It was the socio-economic changes creating a national electorate which made it possible for leaders to develop a substantial degree of centralised control over their party followers, rather than qualities inherent in the Parliamentary structure *per se.*
74. Section 44.
75. Africans in Senegal (both the *originaires,* or French citizens of the four communes, and the subject Africans assimilated through the French educational system) were another group in a similar position, nominally granted equal treatment with Frenchmen, but in practice frequently discriminated against on racial grounds. For a discussion of race relations in Senegal in theory and practice, see Michael Crowder, *Senegal: A Study in French Assimilation Policy,* London, Oxford University Press for the Institute of Race Relations, 1962, esp. Chapter 5, and Rita Cruise O'Brien, *White Society in Black Africa: The French of Senegal,* Evanston, Northwestern University Press, 1972, esp. ch. 2.
76. I would suggest that this contrast between the British focus upon locally elected members to a territorial assembly and the French focus upon a territory-wide election for a representative had as much to do with the greater pluralism in the British colonies as did the British tenderness towards minorities as compared with the French concern with obtaining an African leadership with which they could deal. It is certainly striking that all the

British East and West African colonies at the time of independence (with the single exception of Tanganyika) had significant viable organised opposition groups, whereas of the eighteen French colonies only Senegal, Togo, Dahomey, Cameroon, Congo-Brazzaville and the Malagasy Republic had organised opposition groups which lastedmore than a few months after independence.

3 MAJOR POLITICAL EVENTS IN SIERRA LEONE, 1951-67

This chapter attempts to provide a brief synopsis of what I consider to be the key political events in the period under review. Its purposes are twofold: to give the reader an overall picture of the pattern of major events, and to set out in broad terms the possibilities opened and foreclosed by each key event. This latter examination will require a brief consideration of the implications of each event in each of the arenas where political activity was taking place: the international, the national and the numerous local arenas, about which I shall try to make such general observations as seem appropriate.

The 1951 Constitution: The Estrangement of the Creoles

We have already considered the main elements of this key turning point in Sierra Leone's political history when examining the principal elites of the country. To recapitulate briefly, the British Governor introduced proposals for constitutional reform in 1947, the effects of which were to give the Protectorate a stronger position than the Colony in the Legislative Council, and to ensure that Paramount Chiefs would control the elections to the Protectorate seats. The combined Colony and Protectorate representation would comprise a majority of the chamber, but neither alone would have a majority. Two interpretations of this proposed arrangement were thus plausible: either the British sought to force the Colony and Protectorate to work together for self-government, or they were seeking to avoid the reality of Sierra Leonean control by devolving power to the chiefs, whose subjection to British administrative control left them, in the words of one educated Protectorate spokesman, 'reduced to a status worse than civil servants'.[1]

Both Creoles and the up-country intelligentsia at first attacked these proposals on the grounds that the chiefs should not be the sole spokesmen for the Protectorate people.[2] But Creole attacks soon developed this argument into a demand for equal representation for the Colony, comparing their position with that of the white settlers of Kenya and other groups wishing to preserve a 'superior' way of life.[3] The Protectorate intelligentsia meanwhile were demanding an opening up of the Tribal Authorities and District Councils so that they would be able to participate[4] but were completely opposed to the idea of parity of seats for the Colony. The bridges between these two groups gradually crumbled; Dr Herbert Bankole-Bright, who in 1948 had announced the formation of a new party embracing both Colony and Protectorate, in 1950 denounced the Mendes as 'murderers of our ancestors'[5] while I.T.A. Wallace-Johnson, who as Sierra Leone's most militant nationalist in the 1930s had already attracted many of the educated Protectorate youths to his Youth League,[6] now spurned an offer from the Protectorate intelligentsia to head a new party embracing all the 'progressive' elements from both camps,[7] and shortly afterwards joined with Bankole-Bright in the National Council of the Colony of Sierra Leone, a party dedicated exclusively to the protection of the Creole position.

The Protectorate intelligentsia were left at this point with the choice of allying with the chiefs or being rendered electorally impotent, since the new constitution was not to be imposed with or without the agreement of all the groups concerned. For some, notably Dr Margai, who had already acted as an adviser to the chiefs for a number of years, an alliance of this type held no obstacles; but for more militant individuals such as Albert Margai and Siaka Stevens, it meant a considerable curtailment of their dreams for change. None the less, aided by a few dissident Creoles and with behind-the-scenes encouragement from several chiefs, the Protectorate intelligentsia in late 1951 launched the Sierra Leone Peoples Party.

The new 'party' won no overwhelming successes in Sierra Leone's first national elections. In the Colony even a solid line-up of Creole candidates was of little avail against the NC's appeals to Creole solidarity; the SLPP's only victories came in the two seats where special factors cut away Creole strength.[8] In the Protectorate, where the electorates were the District Councils, SLPP-backed commoners lost all the elections in which they competed with chiefs; only Dr Margai himself, Dr William Fitzjohn from Moyamba, and Paul Dunbar from Kono could be considered as SLPP victors.[9] Chiefs held eight of the fourteen Protectorate seats in the Legislative Council, and their support had been necessary for the election of the other six Protectorate members.[10] While there was little danger that the chiefs would ally with the National Council, or that they would attempt to gain exclusive power as a group, their position was still a strong one.

Two major consequences flowed from the 1951 constitutional battle. The first was that the division between Creoles and countrymen was strongly enough reinforced that for a decade it remained the fundamental line of cleavage in the polity, at least among the national elites. The SLPP's leaders could both isolate Creole-led opposition movements, and patch over both regional and class divisions within the Protectorate, by appealing to Protectorate solidarity, and identifying theirs as 'the countryman's party'. Since the majority was automatically on the 'countryman's' side, the more so as the franchise was extended, such an appeal had great attractions for the SLPP.

The second consequence of the 1951 crisis was attributable to a combination of the British approach to representation and the weakness of the Protectorate intelligentsia. The use of a system of indirect elections resting ultimately on the base of the chief-controlled Tribal Authorities was understandable, given the British assumption that the chiefs were better able to speak for their people than anyone else; and the Protectorate intelligentsia could expect no support from chiefs or Creoles, and did not have the strength themselves to bypass the chiefly structure and create a mass movement demanding direct participation. The result of this system was that the chiefs secured a sufficiently strong power base in the national government that their desires had to be heeded, both in the question of who was to lead the government and in matters affecting their own rights and privileges. These two areas were to be of vital importance within a very few years.

The Diamond Rush: The Old Order is Loosened

Alluvial diamonds had first been discovered in Sierra Leone in 1930 by the Government Geologist, and in 1935 the colonial administration concluded an agreement with the Sierra Leone Selection Trust giving SLST exclusive mining and prospecting rights over nearly the whole of Sierra Leone. In return SLST was to pay income tax at a rate of 27 per cent,[11] (later increased to 45 per cent) on its profits, plus a negligible sum to a special development fund. This agreement began to attract criticism after the war from Sierra Leonean representatives in the Protectorate Assembly, particularly Siaka Stevens and Albert Margai, both on the grounds that Sierra Leoneans were excluded from the opportunity to win the mineral wealth of their own country and that there was no certainty that SLST, as a wholly owned subsidiary of CAST, was being completely honest in the value of its production and consequently in its reported profits. It was not surprising that when Stevens took Ministerial responsibility for the mining industry of Sierra Leone, he began to seek a greater share of revenue for Sierra Leone through taxes on SLST.

When considering these negotiations and the great Sierra Leone diamond rush, we should bear in mind two key characteristics of alluvial diamonds. One feature is that unlike most commercial minerals, they can be obtained not only by massive mechanical earth-moving and gravel-sifting operations, but also by the far less capital-intensive method of hand digging. In other words, any Sierra Leonean armed with a shovel and pan could compete with the massive draglines, wash houses and separator of the SLST, and find it economically rewarding work. The second feature is that diamonds' size-value ratio makes them ideal for stealing and smuggling. As long as there is a market somewhere in the world for them, diamonds can fairly readily be moved across security lines and frontiers without effective checks or taxes on their movement. These two features were to figure prominently in diamonds' role in Sierra Leone.

An agreement negotiated during 1953 with SLST by Stevens and Sierra Leone's Financial Secretary left the company's exclusive rights unchanged. In return for a higher tax rate of 60 per cent and some additional benefits for the Kono district, SLST was promised additional protection of the diamond-bearing deposits, which were already coming under severe pressure from illicit diggers.[12] Although in 1952 and 1953 it is believed that these diggers were largely local men inspired by the SLST's success, by 1954 belief in the possibilities of vast wealth had drawn an estimated 30,000 men to the Kono and Kenema area, and the flood had not reached its peak.

Table 3.1 Estimated number of diamond diggers, 1952-8

1952	5,000
1953	5,000
1954	30,000
1955	40,000
1956	50,000–75,000
1957	50,000–70,000
1958	25,000

Source: Van der Laan, p. 65.

Although it could easily be argued that the Sierra Leone Government would receive more tax by protecting SLST's monopoly and suppressing illicit mining, this course of action was simply not feasible. Accordingly, a year after the first renegotiation was concluded, the government sought new and more far-reaching revisions which ran almost directly counter to the existing terms.

By this time it was becoming clear that SLST's exclusive mining rights would have to be curtailed and the illicit diggers given some legalised place, even though Dr Margai was contending publicly as late as May 1954 that licensing of individual miners on the pattern of the existing Alluvial Gold Mining Scheme[13] was not possible. Apart from the fact that such a licensing scheme would break the agreement with SLST, he argued, mining required expensive techniques, government would lose revenue through illicit sales, and the policy would be expensive to administer.[14] Against this stand a powerful lobby spearheaded by the Bo District SLPP branch demanded that in the Bo and Kenema districts, which SLST was not working, licensed mining should be permitted,[15] and this view seems to have had the tacit support of Albert Margai and Siaka Stevens.[16] Since by this time the flood of illicit diggers was swelling beyond the government's capability to control them, Dr Margai had to reverse his position and join his brother and Stevens in putting forward proposals for opening up most of the country to licensed mining. The questions that had to be settled were the amount of compensation due to SLST for giving up its rights and the amount of leased lands it would be able to retain. After hard bargaining, SLST agreed in September 1955 to give up its rights to all but 450 square miles in Kono and Kenema districts in exchange for compensation of £1,570,000, thus freeing most of the alluvial deposits for licensed mining. A licensing scheme for diggers was implemented in 1956, whereby a Sierra Leonean could employ up to twenty men to work a claim, on payment of a fee for the licence and a small surface rent to the Tribal Authority of the chiefdom.

Two further problems remained. Many of those involved in the illicit mining had been foreigners, largely from Guinea, and were ineligible for the new licences, although they could – and did – work for Sierra Leonean licence-holders. Many in Kono continued to mine illicitly, and in October 1956, after considerable consultation with the French officials, Governor Maurice Dorman issued an order expelling the foreigners from the Kono district within the next three weeks. Much to everyone's relief and surprise, an estimated 45,000 left.[17] The other problem concerned buying the diamonds from the licensed diggers. The world's major buyer of stones, de Beers, had hastily established the Diamond Corporation of Sierra Leone to purchase all stones mined, in order to channel them into the London market where prices could be controlled. But the prices paid by DCSL were less attractive than those in Monrovia because of the imposition of a 7½ per cent export duty and the fact that Monrovia buyers paid in sought-after American dollars, with the result that the government was forced to undertake further measures to curb smuggling, which it estimated as having a value of £10 million a year. A Government Diamond Office opened in 1959 met the problem by the straightforward expedient of paying higher prices than the buyers in Monrovia, while the government cut the export duty to 4 per cent. The diamond problem was at last substantially under control, although there were still many opportunities for illicit diggers to raid the SLST's rich reserves, and illegal diamond dealing continued to infect many political relationships in Sierra Leone.

The diamond rush and the negotiations with SLST were significant at a number of levels. At the international level, both sets of negotiatons showed the weakness of a small country's government in dealing with a large corporation, although some of the terms may well have been decided by British officials with an ideological bias in favour of SLST's property rights. While the government's inability to contain the illicit diggers eventually led it to take away a substantial part of SLST's rights, it did provide fairly generous compensation, probably out of concern about the effect failure to provide such compensation would have had on the international business community.[18] The more extreme approach of a complete government takeover, though suggested by some Sierra Leoneans, was apparently not seriously considered by the government.

At the national level, perhaps the most serious effect of the diamond problems was the time they consumed of both the most capable Sierra Leonean Ministers and of the senior British officials. While both these groups might have been just as oblivious to the rumblings of grassroots discontent if they had had no such problems before them, it does seem plausible to argue that their preoccupation with the 'law and order' aspects of the diamond rush helped distract their attention from deeper social problems, in part aggravated by the inflation brought by the rush, in the last crucial months before Freetown and the North exploded in 1955-6. A further development from the diamond crisis was its bringing into sharp focus the deep differences of opinion between Dr Margai on the one side, and Albert Margai and Siaka Stevens on the other. Writing in 1957 (after being dropped from Dr Margai's government), Stevens claimed that Dr Margai had maintained in negotiations with SLST that 'the chiefs and people of Kono ... preferred that all diamond mining in Kono should be done by the SLST', a view with which Stevens 'violently' disagreed,[19] preferring to open up the area to licensed Sierra Leoneans. Dr Margai was undoubtedly right that the *chiefs* preferred the SLST, even though when the licensing scheme was developed, they became its chief financial beneficiaries.[20] But it is far less certain that the ordinary farmers of Kono did not want an opportunity of their own to dig for the wealth beneath their land.

A further facet of the diamond rush was that it showed the tenuousness of government's authority. By 1956 illicit miners were forming armed bands, and even their own 'governments' which safeguarded claims temporarily.[21] The government was able to exercise some power; most notably, it did remove the foreign Africans successfully in 1956. But for the most part, it had to come to terms with the diamond rush, and merely channel rather than curtail it.

It was at the grassroots level, however, that the diamond rush had its greatest effects. Its magnitude alone ensured that it would have a significant impact; at its peak there were more men involved than were employed in all forms of wage labour in the Protectorate, nearly as many 'strangers' in Kono as native Konos, and about six out of every hundred adult males in the country involved at any one time.[22] This does not take into account either the probability that most diggers would go for a year or two, and then their places would be taken by others, nor that the diggers seemed to be drawn disproportionately from the Northern Province. Assuming a turnover factor of three in the years 1954 to 1961, and an over-representation of northerners by a factor of two, we may have found some 30-40 per cent of all northern men taking part in the digging at some point. The numbers involved in this mobilisation were certainly substantial, and it was doubtful that such men would go back unchanged to their village and chiefdom way of life.

This mobilisation also kindled a number of broader identities than the chiefdom. Among Konos it encouraged a strong ethnic identity; it was Kono land that was being overrun by strangers, and Konos who were being shoved aside to provide mining space. This was coupled, particularly among Konos but also elsewhere, with a stirring of political radicalism; why should a foreign company be able to continue taking the diamonds that rightfully belonged to Sierra Leone and could be won by Sierra Leoneans? Radicalism was also encouraged in another way; if men had lived successfully in a society without chiefs, they might want a more egalitarian society in their home regions as well.

A less egalitarian, though more serious attack on chieftaincy was developed from a different quarter. The diamond boom provided a great deal of new wealth for Sierra Leoneans and allowed substantial numbers of diamond dealers and other entrepreneurs in the provinces to become quite rich.[23] This new wealth contributed greatly to the growth of patronage networks which rivalled those of the chiefs, but which being built upon the cash nexus both were less inhibited by traditional boundaries and at the same time tied men less firmly to their patrons.[24] The upshot was that chieftaincy was weakened in two ways: rival structures of patronage developed, and the comprehensive nature of men's bonds of obligation was undermined.

A final contribution of the diamond boom to Sierra Leone politics was the boost it gave the provinces in relation to the Colony. By stimulating the hinterland's economy, it helped give the up-country leaders additional self-confidence as well as a more credible economic base for their claims to self-government, and by the same token undermined possible Creole efforts to slow down the coming of self-government by leaving them relatively weakened. Through changing the nature of the countrymen's economic activity in a way that increased their likelihood of involving themselves in politics, it stimulated a broader base of political participation in the provinces, and this in turn by creating new alignments helped to reduce the importance of the bi-polar division of Sierra Leone into Creoles and countrymen.

The Country Erupts: The Freetown and Northern Riots, 1955-6

Since the end of the Second World War, Sierra Leone had been comparatively free of large-scale civil disturbances.[25] Not since the anti-Lebanese riots in 1919 and the Railway Workers' strike of 1926 had there been serious disturbances in Freetown, and up-country no disturbances had involved more than one or two chiefdoms since the Haidara Rebellion of 1931.[26] Now that Sierra Leoneans were beginning to share the decision-making power of the national government, and to bring their own independent lines of information to this government, it was to be expected that the government would be increasingly aware of Sierra Leoneans' views and thus more capable of controlling problems before they reached the point of large-scale violence. But this was not to be. The Sierra Leonean Ministers appeared at least as surprised as the British officials when in 1955 three days of serious rioting raged in Freetown, and then ten months later thousands rioted against the chiefs in the Northern Province.

The Freetown riots developed out of strike calls by the Artisans' Union and the Transport and General Workers Union, based on a pay claim following the rapid increase in basic food costs consequent on the diamond rush.[27] Despite the fact that the union leader, Marcus Grant, had called for a 'General Strike' on 9 February, the Governor embarked on a tour of the Protectorate and had to return in haste when rioting began.[28] Mobs of several hundred rioters roamed the city until the evening of 12 February, partly engaged in sporadic, aimless looting and confrontations with the police and army, but also directing some of their violence against the homes of three Ministers, M.S. Mustapha, Siaka Stevens and Albert Margai. In Mustapha's house 'nearly every pane of glass was destroyed', furniture was smashed, and smaller objects looted. Much of Stevens' furniture was also damaged.[29] A few months later, commenting on the report of the inevitable Commission of Enquiry, *West Africa* observed:[30]

> To the strikers, the Government was the enemy – but it was not officials but the Ministers who had to be protected from their wrath. The commission does not mention the attacks made by rioters on anybody wearing a collar and tie, though these are a subject of general conversation in Freetown . . . Were we seeing the first signs in West Africa of a revolt of manual workers against domination by clerks, or against the comfortable classes in government service who do not have to strike for more pay?

While evidence that the rioters possessed this conscious 'revolutionary' intent is lacking, we can at least infer on the other side that there was no great degree of empathy between the SLPP leaders and urban workers. Certainly the SLPP paper's description of the rioters as 'hooligans . . . unemployed . . . and dregs of the working class'[31] suggest a considerable gulf between the party and urban people.

More startling, because they involved men who were believed to be still tied to their chiefs and chiefdoms by a great range of social commitments, were the northern riots from November 1955 to March 1956. Again, the government was taken by surprise; a month before the first riots,

> a spokesman of the Ministry of Local Government yesterday denied allegations of excessive taxation in the Protectorate . . . He said that the Minister [Albert Margai] was conscious that there was a limit to the size of local taxes, and would not impose heavy taxes which would bring hardships to the people.[32]

Since taxes had risen from around 11s 6d per annum in 1950 to 25s 0d in 1955, and were due to rise again in 1956, this view seems optimistic. But it was not just the legal taxes, heavy though these had become, that incited disaffection; there was a whole range of fees, 'gifts' and straight extortion levied not just by the chiefs, but also by the Tribal Authorities and the NA clerks, all of which went, of course, not to public purposes but to the enrichment of these individuals.[33] These levies had been going on for years; the government's annual reports on the Protectorate rarely lacked accounts of anti-chief protests, with the protesters citing grounds such as these for their outbursts.[34] The grievances were intensified in 1955 by the fact that the tax rules had been reinterpreted to include large numbers of young men hitherto untaxed, and also probably by the fact that many men had taken part in the diamond rush, with its weakening effect on respect for 'the law' whether of British colonial rulers or of the chiefdoms. The triggering event was a demand by a particularly avaricious chief for an additional five shillings per taxpayer to build him a new concrete house.[35] A protest by more than 7,000 people in Port Loko seemed to inspire others, and within a few weeks attacks on chiefs' and TAs' property had erupted in most of the northern chiefdoms, ultimately causing damage to their property estimated at £750,000 (and leading to the deaths by police attacks of twenty-three rioters, as well as three policemen).[36]

Far more than in Freetown, a striking feature of the riots was their selectivity.[37] Europeans and Lebanese traders were carefully spared, as were the possessions of non-TAs. In one case rioters helped a Lebanese pack his trading goods into a launch before burning his shop, which was owned by a notoriously exploitative chief;[38] in another case rioters systematically drove nails through the metal sheets of roofing on a chief's house, rendering the roofing useless;[39] while in a third instance, rioters encountering the police explained that they did not wish to fight the police, but only to kill their chief and burn his property.[40]

Once again, a Commission of Enquiry was set up, and after hearing evidence throughout the riot areas, produced a devastating critique of the chiefs' rule:

> We have found . . . a degree of demoralisation among the people in their customary institutions . . . which has shocked us. Dishonesty has become accepted as a normal ingredient of life to such an extent that no one has been concerned to fight it or even complain about it. The ordinary peasant or fisherman seems originally to have accepted a degree of corruption which was tolerable; at a later stage he has been cowed into accepting it; finally he rebelled.[41]

The enquiry, however, could see no alternative to relying on the chiefdom as the basic unit of administration; it reported that while individual chiefs were bitterly condemned, no one had advocated abolishing either chieftaincy or the chiefdom as the basic unit of administration, and it felt that these were the only local institutions which could command support from the populace.[42]

The chiefs' reaction to the riots was reminiscent of the Bourbons. Giving evidence before the Commission, one subchief angrily shouted at a heckler:

> How dare you have the cheek to be shouting insults at me. You who were one of those who burnt my houses. If I had not remembered God and the law, you would not have been here talking to me today. I would have shot the whole lot of you.[43]

In the Legislative Council, the Paramount Chief members, and to a lesser extent Albert Margai and Stevens, suggested that the riots were instigated by the District Commissioners, with possibly some help from opposition parties. Not one chief acknowledged that the behaviour of the TAs might even have contributed to the outburst. Dr Margai's reply clearly showed the way he was being squeezed from the other direction by British officials wanting some action taken:

> . . . if we are running the country as a Government there are certain recommendations which would be doing more harm to the country by not implementing them . . . if . . . a Commission . . . comes all out and says that an enquiry should be held in certain number of chiefdoms, we shall be doing more harm to ourselves as a country and even to chiefs, if we say no . . .[44]

The upshot was hearings by outside Commissioners into the conduct of fourteen chiefs.[45] As a result of their enquiries, three chiefs were exonerated of the charges against them; five resigned their offices, two were suspended, and four were deposed.[46] However, three of those deposed or resigning as well as the two suspended had been restored within three years.[47] Some efforts were also made by the government to tighten up the controls over illegal levies, but these too fell into disuse in succeeding years.

The riots in the north showed both the SLPP and British officialdom that the former's authority was rather more precarious than either had believed. But the British had little choice at this point but to back Dr Margai, unless they wanted to reverse their entire colonial policy of withdrawing from political control and reinstate the full authority of the colonial administration. They could hardly allay the discontents revealed by the riots without imposing administrative controls more rigid than at the height of colonial rule (in so far as much of the discontent was attributable to the erosion of the chiefs' own authority), and imposing this degree of control would require displacing the SLPP Ministers. The best the British could do to redress the situation was to press strongly on Dr Margai the need for stricter surveillance of the chiefs' behaviour, which in turn would bring him into difficulties with his key supporters.

But besides the chiefs, Dr Margai did have to consider the possibility that opposition political movements might be organised to take advantage of an apparent body of potential support. The riots suggested that electorally the chiefs, at least in the north, might be less of an asset than an alternative party structure. At the same time, there was no other party for whom the chiefs could desert the SLPP. The aftermath of the 1955-6 riots appeared, then, to offer a chance for the SLPP to reorganise in a fashion less dependent on the chiefs, but this chance was not taken.

The Articulation of Protest: From Conservative Elite to Populist Radicalism

Seen in conjunction with the forthcoming extension of the franchise, the explosion in the North suggested an alluring prospect for rival elites wishing to challenge the SLPP. Evidently the SLPP's attempt to align all political conflict along a Creole-countryman basis in which it would have an assured majority might be undermined among the new electorate by some form of appeal to the 'common man' or to a desire for change. But at the same time as the franchise was being extended, power was increasingly devolved to the SLPP leaders, who were prepared to use both their own central government positions and the powers of the chiefs and TAs to make organised opposition an unrewarding task.

The first political party to attempt a serious challenge to the SLPP in the Protectorate was the United Sierra Leone Progressive Party, formed in 1954 by Cyril Rogers-Wright, a Creole lawyer whose brilliance was matched only by his lack of professional ethics.[48] Although the UPP's leadership was largely Creole, it made serious efforts to appeal to the spokesmen of discontent in the Protectorate, demanding controls on the chiefs' abuses and offering legal and moral support to the rioters.[49] Its tactics achieved some success following the 1957 elections, when a series of election petitions launched by Rogers-Wright brought about four by-elections which UPP candidates won, to add to the five seats they had won in the general election.[50] Unfortunately for the UPP, two of its three non-Creole members quickly crossed to the government side, one being rewarded shortly afterwards with the post of Ministerial Secretary. The UPP's concern in Parliament was largely focused on 'Creole' problems such as questions of land tenure, and in 1959 came a series of personal quarrels between Rogers-Wright and his followers, which resulted in Rogers-Wright remaining as the lone UPP representative in Parliament, and his followers styling themselves the Independent Progressive Party. After the United Front in 1960, only a small rump of the UPP remained outside the SLPP, and eventually joined the All Peoples Congress.

Meanwhile, a new party with a genuine up-country leadership had arisen in 1958 out of a split in the SLPP. Since at least 1953 sharp differences between on the one side Dr Margai, most of the chiefs, and other more conservative elements, and on the other side Albert Margai, Siaka Stevens, and a number of younger men who wanted more nationalistic policies and more rapid social change, had been apparent.[51] Following the 1957 election, a caucus of SLPP MPs had by a margin of one vote decided to replace Dr Margai with Albert as leader, but intense backstage pressure then induced Albert to step down in favour of his brother.[52] Stevens shortly afterwards lost his seat on an election petition, and more than a year went by with Albert Margai remaining a backbencher, although Chairman of the SLPP. In September 1958 Margai, joined by Stevens, launched a new party, the Peoples National Party, which was to press for more rapid progress towards independence, and African control of the civil service and of industry. The PNP's position on chiefs was ambivalent; while it proffered respect for 'our Natural Rulers' it also suggested curtailing their power in national politics by removing them to a separate House.[53]

The social base of the PNP provided its most enduring legacy. While its leaders, largely Mende and Creole professional men,[54] were of as high status and as closely linked with traditional ruling families as were the leaders of the SLPP, its demands for more rapid change attracted as a secondary echelon many of the less well-connected and less well-educated young men in the towns, the group Little described as the 'literate class'.[55] These young men, who had been largely excluded from participation in the chief-based SLPP, thus were given their first opportunity to participate in electoral politics as organisers and propagandists for the PNP.

But the PNP's appeal was not enough to overcome the powers at the SLPP's disposal. It did surprise the SLPP leaders by winning all three seats in the Bo Town Council elections in early 1959; but away from the major towns, the chief's considerable powers of intimidation against would-be organisers of opposition were too strong, and in the 1959 District Council elections it won only a handful of seats, largely in Albert Margai's home area. Interestingly, it did particularly poorly in the North, where it was alleged to have more members, and where its proselytising should have been most effective.[56] It continued to press for national elections before independence, suspecting that its chances of a fair contest would diminish rapidly after the British left, but it just could not show the sort of support which might have led the British to listen seriously to its claims.

A third party provided a more clearcut opposition to the SLPP, though only in a local area. At the height of the diamond rush, with the influx of 'strangers' awakening many Konos for the first time to the wealth that lay beneath their soil, a group of young Kono educated men met under the leadership of Tamba S. Mbriwa, a druggist, to form the Kono Progressive Movement.[57] This movement, although allying itself with all the major 'national' opposition parties, focused almost exclusively upon the need for providing a larger share of Kono's wealth for the ordinary Kono man. While its leaders were drawn from the same ruling family stratum as the SLPP and PNP elites, its base of support was much more the ordinary farmer who felt himself victimised by his chief as well as by the national government and the 'strangers'. Its combination of regional and radical 'class' appeals proved potent; at the national level it won all Kono seats in both 1957 and 1962,[58] and won control of the District Council in both 1960 and 1963. However, as a purely regional party it had to find allies; and after Chief Mbriwa (he had become a chief in 1961) was deposed and banished in 1963, its MPs were susceptible to the argument that Kono's interests would be better served from the Government side of the House. A partial cessation of SLPIM-SLPP conflict was achieved in 1963, and the SLPIM was formally dissolved and merged into the SLPP in 1965 by Chief Mbriwa after Albert Margai had ended his banishment and allowed him to stand again for the chieftaincy.

This first group of opposition parties was effectively eliminated as challengers for power in 1960 by one of the most masterful strokes of Sir Milton (as he had become in 1959) Margai's career. Before the final pre-independence constitutional conference, the opposition parties had been demanding not only further elections before independence, but also a separate House for the chiefs, and the replacement of Sir Milton with a more vigorous leader. But on 25 March 1960 the Prime Minister announced that a United Front Government would be formed,[59] providing Ministerial appointments for the leaders in Parliament of the opposition parties (except the SLPIM), but yielding none of the concessions they sought.

While this move effectively decapitated existing organised opposition groups, the discontents and fears they had articulated remained. Most important was the growing suspicion of many Northerners, as they looked at the new allocation of Cabinet posts, that Mendes were getting a disproportionate share.[60] Then, too, the deal by which opposition leaders gained some of the sweets of office provided not even a taste for their supporters, including the newly mobilised cadres of the PNP.

Within a few months, Siaka Stevens, who had created a small sensation at the London constitutional conference by refusing to sign the agreements (and who, being out of Parliament, could not claim Ministerial office), launched a further political party, the All Peoples Congress. With its emphasis on socialism and the need to curb the chiefs, the APC appeared to be a more extreme variant of the PNP. But although its leaders had for the most part gained political experience in the PNP, they were from somewhat lower status backgrounds and more significantly, were initially all Northerners.

The APC's relations with the SLPP got off to a poor start when before Independence their increasingly vehement demands for elections seem to have instigated violent actions by their followers. As a result, forty-four APC leaders and supporters spent a month before and after Independence in detention.[61] However, relations gradually improved, and in general elections not much more marked by intimidation than previous ones under the British the APC in 1962 carried twelve out of eighteen seats in the North, as well as four in the Western Area, to provide the strongest organised opposition to the SLPP since its inception. This almost solidly northern block of MPs helped confirm the APC's image as 'the Northern man's party', although its overt appeals continued to be directed at the common man's class interest, regardless of tribe. Although weakened by a few defections over the next five years, the APC withstood the threats and the blandishments of the government quite well.

The pattern of opposition, then, had gone in less than ten years from one where a beleaguered elitist minority, the upper-class Creoles, provided the principal opposition to a party supposedly based on the Protectorate masses, through a pattern of high-status opposition leaders calling 'the masses' into political participation, and then being replaced by lower-status leaders offering a more 'radical' appeal in the form of demands for a more egalitarian society. Cross-cutting the 'radical-conservative' continuum, however, was regionalism, and it was the combination of regional and radical appeals by both APC and SLPIM leader that gave their parties their staying power.

The action of successive opposition parties in appealing to mass discontent on one or both of 'class' and regional grounds put increasing pressure on Dr Margai as leader of the SLPP to expand the governing party's own range of supporters in one of two ways. Either he had to take steps to alleviate the various discontents that fuelled the opposition parties, or he had to build broader support for the SLPP by appealing to new identities which would override those giving support to the opposition. In either case he had to take into account the wishes of increased numbers of individuals, drawn from a wider range of strata than the chiefs and their families alone.

The 'Open Door' Development Policy

The 'Open Door' economic policy which Sir Milton Margai enunciated just before Independence did not represent a turning point in any way, but rather a confirmation of an approach to economic relationships which had already been firmly established. Investment from any source would be welcomed, provided only that the investors obeyed the laws and tried to employ Sierra Leoneans. Government would allow unlimited repatriation of profits by investors, and pledged that even if it were to change its existing policy of no nationalisation, it would pay 'fair compensation'.[62] It was, in short, a policy of *laissez-faire* in economic development, a willingness to accept whatever kind of investment might be offered, regardless of its effect on the overall economic position of Sierra Leone.

Such a policy was well in line with the approach already laid down by the British colonial officials and accepted by Sierra Leoneans with respect to the two major mining industries. The decision not to take over all SLST's holdings at the time the government bought out its monopoly was defended by Sir Milton on the grounds that any court of arbitration would have awarded the company 'from ten to twenty times' the £1.5 million compensation paid to SLST for the loss of its 'rights' and future profits,[63] although more important, perhaps, was his argument that 'if we want investment . . . we must regard agreements . . . as more than a scrap of paper'.[64] As for the iron mines, and later the bauxite and rutile operations, there was no threat to give government a stake in their operations under either Sir Milton or Sir Albert.[65]

The 'Open Door' welcome to all in practice meant a welcome to Western private investors. Partly this was because there were no real alternatives; although Albert Margai did try to attract the Russians, and did succeed in 1965 in obtaining a barter deal with them whereby the Soviet Union was to provide £1 million of agricultural machinery to be repaid in agricultural produce,[66] all other deals were with Western companies, and generally were either for purely extractive operations, as with the bauxite and rutile, or for rather dubious enterprises, as in the case of the Sierra Leone Cement Company and a diamond cutting plant.[67]

We might note at this point that towards the end of Sir Milton's regime and markedly more so under Sir Albert's, there was a spate of symbolic economic nationalism, directed largely against the retail trade control exercised by the Lebanese. Beginning with a ban on non-Africans trading in rice in 1963, a number of retail trade acts were passed, restricting certain areas such as transport and petty trade commodities to Sierra Leone nationals. None of these measures was very successful, for reasons to be considered below.[68]

The 'Open Door' policy not surprisingly left Sierra Leone still dependent for its international trade on the vagaries of tropical agricultural products and the non-job-producing mining of its diminishing mineral resources.[69] We will consider later whether there might have been some better policies for Sierra Leone's economic development, or whether for a small, marginal territory there is no way to develop. For now we should simply note that the hope of attracting more investment limited the range of pressures the government could bring against the established firms, and also note that their size and wealth relative to the Sierra Leone economy meant that they had the potential to exercise considerable influence in Sierra Leone politics.

Domestically, the 'Open Door' left Sierra Leoneans in a state of economic dependence on the industrialised states for most of the satisfactions to which they aspired. By eschewing policies of 'self-reliance' in favour of attempts to obtain some of the material artifacts of Western societies, Dr Margai incidentally ensured that the sort of rewards that would attract Sierra Leoneans to one set of political leaders rather than another would be material ones, with the implication that a leader who failed to provide a continuing stream of material benefits would experience serious loss of support. Such a basis of support, in view of the vulnerability of Sierra Leone's economy to world trends beyond its control, was one which at some point must give a leader trouble, particularly as other policies such as increasing education helped to create a growing body of individuals who wished to participate directly in the national political arena.

Albert Margai Takes Over

When Sir Milton Margai died on the night of 29 April 1964, he left no clearly designated successor. His brother, because of his forceful personality and the fact that he had already once been chosen leader of the SLPP, was clearly the strongest contender. But Dr John Karefa-Smart, the urbane Minister of External Affairs, had the advantage of being a Northerner and also of being more acceptable to the 'traditionalists' in the SLPP. There were also other possibilities, and if Dr Margai preferred one of them over the others, he certainly had not made his preference clear.

Certain key steps had been taken, however, which eased the way for Albert Margai, most notably his appointment to the powerful Finance Ministry in 1962 and the appointment of a strong PNP man, Berthan Macauley, to the post of Attorney-General in November 1963. Margai had done more in the way of infiltrating his supporters into key positions and establishing his presence both in the country and among the Parliamentarians than had any of his rivals for the succession, and while Dr Margai had done nothing to encourage him, neither had he taken steps to ward off the probability that his brother would succeed him. When Dr Margai died, the Governor General seems initially to have intended to select Karefa-Smart as the new Prime Minister. But under intense pressure from the Attorney-General, he soon swung round to the view that the most appropriate action would be to appoint Margai, and on the afternoon of 30 April, called on Margai to form a government.

The speed of the announcement took a number of Ministers and other MPs, who had expected to be consulted, by surprise. That night several Ministers and SLPP backbenchers, along with Stevens and his APC followers, met at a Minister's house to concert a protest against what they regarded as an undesirable appointment. Most of those involved were Northerners, but two or three Mende MPs were present. The next morning some of the MPs met the Governor-General to protest what they had misled themselves to think was an 'unconstitutional' appointment procedure, but by this time two or three of those present had told Albert what had happened. Retribution was swift; despite abject apologies for having erred in thinking his appointment unconstitutional, four Ministers found themselves dropped when Albert announced his new Cabinet. Two, including Karefa-Smart, were Northerners.[70]

It was in one way an inauspicious start to Albert Margai's regime. Sir Milton before his death had managed to contain the APC and SLPIM, but the regional discontents that had largely fuelled them were still strong. An opening purge which removed most representatives of the disaffected regions from his Cabinet could scarcely be expected to strengthen Albert Margai's support.[71]

But initially this difficulty was offset by several strong points. Albert's greater militancy had always won him much more sympathy than Milton among the younger literate elements, and there was at least a strong possibility that even some of the Northerners among them might be won over from the APC. The Creoles generally regarded Albert more favourably than his brother, and those in civil service positions were impressed by the greater concern he showed for good administration.[72] Even the initial suspicions of the chiefs were partially dispelled when among his first acts Albert announced the ending of the banishments of Bai Koblo and T.S. Mbriwa.[73] On balance, Albert Margai seemed to have built himself a fairly strong position in his first few months in office.

The Drive for a One-Party State

Despite the initial appearance of a vigorous new Prime Minister winning widespread popular support, there were serious weaknesses in Albert Margai's position. The regional and class discontents which nourished the APC and SLPIM still persisted, while the chiefs whose behaviour contributed to this discontent were still the only means by which an SLPP leader could reach the electorate. At the same time the chiefs' ability to influence the electorate was declining as other 'big men', in many cases business entrepreneurs made wealthy through the diamond trade, came to compete with them as patrons, and increasing numbers of individuals developed their own political ideas. All this meant that any national leader would be increasingly forced into relying on an ever more costly series of cash links with his would-be supporters. Since Albert Margai was not in any case as close to the chiefs as his brother, and wished to undertake social changes which would require the building of alternative support, he needed to break the SLPP away from its dependence on the chiefs as its main local intermediaries, and to do this he needed access to considerably greater material resources than his brother had bothered to command.

The problems inherent in the SLPP's reliance on the chiefs were made clear a few months after Margai took power, when he attempted to centralise and strengthen the party organisation. The chiefs and their allies were able to block this effort, and the net result was simply that the chiefs made greater efforts to suppress opposition parties, despite the fact that in the North this simply reinforced anti-chief feelings by making the chiefs appear to be doing a Mende government's bidding. Margai could not outflank the chiefs by making a 'populist' appeal to commoners, however, because the APC's regional appeal still served to keep northerners committed to it, and this appeal gradually gained in strength as various actions of the Prime Minister suggested that he was pursuing a policy of giving benefits to Mendeland first. Looming in the background, although it did not produce a crisis until 1966, was the fact that while the Prime Minister needed a great deal more money both for governmental projects and for personal and party use than had ever been available before, available revenues were not increasing. It may well have been the need for substantial additional revenues to finance his party-building efforts that led the Prime Minister into a number of costly ventures, such as contractor-financed construction projects,[74] which were to leave him open to severe attacks by the oppositon on the grounds of personal corruption. In any case, the shortage of funds imposed an additional constraint on the ability of the Prime Minister to move his party out of its increasingly disadvantageous symbiosis with the chiefs.

Against this background, the idea of a one-party state grew increasingly attractive to many of Sir Albert's[75] supporters. The Prime Minister's own views shifted slowly. Before becoming Prime Minister he had stressed the need for opposition;[76] by June 1965 he was still saying that if a one-party state were to come it would be by agreement and not by compulsion.[77] In October, on an exchange of visits with Nkrumah, he commented in Ghana that, like the CPP, the SLPP believed that government was not above the party.[78] In December at Port Loko he proclaimed that because of 'the suffering of our people . . . we want [the one-party state] and we shall proceed with it'.[79] Meanwhile a Paramount Chief member of Parliament had brought in a motion that 'government give serious consideration to the introduction of a unitary (One Party) system of government in this country',[80] The debate, on 20 and 21 December 1965, suggested that the government had not yet decided what form the one-party state should take, and further, that the justification for it was basically that they were tired of public criticism of their actions.[81] The APC for its part was rather hesitant in its opposition. Stevens had earlier argued that it was the weakness of the SLPP's support rather than any intrinsic weaknesses in the system which made a one-party state undesirable,[82] and the APC MPs still did not seem opposed to the system on principle. It turned out, in fact, that in private negotiations the APC leaders came very close to agreeing to enter a grand coalition with Margai's party.

But if the official Opposition wavered, strong extra-Parliamentary opposition soon stiffened it. Severe heckling of the Prime Minister at a rally in Freetown was not surprising,[83] nor was a demonstration in Tonkolili.[84] But when a crowd in Bo, in the heart of Mendeland, heckled the Prime Minister, he was evidently shaken.[85] Then came the fall of Nkrumah's regime, which Sir Albert had held up as a model of the progress a one-party state could bring. After 24 February official pronouncements on the one-party state, while not ceasing, took a much less emphatic tone. By this time it was becoming clear that not just the Creole community in Freetown, but also large numbers of Northerners who saw the one-party state as consolidating the position of unpopular chiefs (as well as entrenching 'Mende dominance'), and even a considerable number of Mendes, were turning against the idea. Within the SLPP, many MPs were sceptical, particularly as they saw Albert working to replace them with persons more in accord with his views.[86] Finally a number of civil servants were busily leaking damaging revelations about government decisions to the Opposition newspaper, *We Yone,* which kept up a steady drumfire of criticism of the government's pecuniary misbehaviour, and its alleged bias against non-Mendes.

The District Council elections of May 1966 gave the *coup de grace* to Albert Margai's attempt at creating a one-party state. Despite a massive effort by the SLPP to secure unopposed candidates, the APC managed to contest all but forty of the 135 seats in the Northern Province, winning seventy-two of them and capturing 67 per cent of the popular vote. It also made inroads in the Southern Province, winning seats in Moyamba and Bo districts. While the SLPP could claim to have won more seats overall, still there was no denying the fact that the most populous province was almost solidly behind the APC, and that without a considerable shift in popular sentiment a one-party state would not be a feasible proposition for the near future. Sir Albert quickly backed away, claiming in June that the one-party state had not been his idea, but that of his supporters, and that if the people did not wish it, he would abide by that wish.[87]

The one-party state drive, while failing to achieve the Prime Minister's objective, nevertheless made major changes in the Sierra Leone polity. Most obviously, it exacerbated regional conflict, with both northerners and Creoles seeing in it a plot to entrench Mende supremacy for all time, and Mendes by 1967 fearing the vengeance of northerners should their own party lose power. But alongside this regional conflict ran another attitude which partly mitigated the effect of politicians trying to stir regional sentiments, but which also served to undermine the links between any leader and the populace. This was the growth of suspicion about the *bona fides* of all politicians, an attitude present among most Sierra Leoneans at the best of times, but heightened considerably as it became apparent that the politicians' support for the one-party state was largely because it offered them some protection against the electorate. The APC's strong fight against the coercion of the government helped moderate this suspicion, but did not allay it completely. Finally, Sir Albert's and the chiefs' free use of violence against their opponents (free, that is, by previous Sierra Leone standards), helped accustom both the public and the opposition to a degree of open physical force which the APC in turn were later to apply against their opponents with great enthusiasm.

The 1967 Election: The Fall of Albert Margai

Despite his disavowal of the one-party state scheme, it was to be expected that few people now trusted Sir Albert not to try again to introduce the idea. These suspicions were heightened during the latter half of 1966 as the government proposed to bring in a constitution to make Sierra Leone a republic, which many opponents automatically equated with an executive Presidency. When the proposed constitution was in fact published in December 1966,[88] it did not make as great changes as expected; in fact, it did little beyond changing the Governor-General's title to 'President'. None the less, as an amendment to an entrenched part of the constitution, it would have to be passed by a further Parliament after a general election before it could take effect. The APC found itself in the ironical position of opposing the proposed change to a republic, despite its well-publicised support for ending the monarchical connection.[89]

As preparations for what both Sir Albert's supporters and his opponents regarded as the most critical election in Sierra Leone's history went forward, an ominous note was injected when in February 1967 the Prime Minister broadcast that a plot to stage a military coup had been revealed. The officers alleged to be behind the plot were all detained, but no trials were ever held. Whether in fact there was a plot or not, it was a convenient coincidence that all those alleged to be involved were either Northerners (including the second-in-command of the Army) or Creoles, thus leaving the officer corps almost entirely Mende.

While this purge seemed to establish the control of the Prime Minister and his ally, Brigadier David Lansana (who had taken over from a British commanding officer only in 1964, after Sir Albert came to power), the army officer corps had by this time become a turmoil of warring factions.[90] In part this reflected the deepening cleavage within the whole polity along the coinciding lines of political party commitment, ethnicity and regionalism, with the minority of northern and Creole officers growing restive over what they perceived as a Mende hegemony. But at least as serious were the frictions engendered by the inability of the CO, Brigadier Lansana, to get along with most of his officers, including Mendes, and his apparent readiness to allow the army to be subordinated to Albert Margai's personal ambitions. Dissension had started a year earlier with the dismissal of Lt.-Col. Ambrose Genda, a popular, able and apolitical Mende officer who firmly opposed the army's involvement in politics. From that time on a number of officers, Mende as well as Northerners and Creoles, began to consider ways of removing, if not the civilian government, at least Brigadier Lansana.

Again, the economic situation of Sierra Leone contributed to the army's dissatisfaction, by precluding any expansion of its ranks beyond its existing 1,500 men, or renewal of its equipment. Yet against this had to be put the non-material factors of Sierra Leone's deep-rooted adherence to constitutional procedures, the relatively high legitimacy of its civilian institutions, and the fact that most people still saw an election as the most appropriate means of replacing an unwanted regime. These widespread beliefs not only restrained the army, but also helped to restrain the attempts of the Margai regime to perpetuate itself in office through rigging the elections.

There were a number of points at which the official conduct of an election could affect its outcome: the ground rules under which it was fought, the way in which voters were registered, the process of nominating candidates, the conduct of voting and the counting of the ballots. While the SLPP gained some advantages at each of these stages, these were sufficiently minor to suggest either a considerable degree of self-restraint or sabotage from within. Thus the only ground rules which significantly increased the handicaps on the APC were the raising of deposits from 200 to 500 Leones,[91] and a requirement that candidates be available to answer questions by the Returning Officer the whole of Nomination Day, which tied up several of the APC's most experienced leaders.[92] Registration in some constituencies did seem to miss a number of Northerners, but on the whole the APC leaders regarded it as having been fairly conducted.

The nomination of candidates offered one opportunity for the SLPP to secure a substantial advantage; a total of ten APC candidates' nominations were rejected, either by the Returning Officers or later by the Electoral Commission (which had been purged of suspected APC sympathisers a year earlier) on such grounds as a candidate's omitting his middle initial from his signature, or misspelling the name of his constituency.[93] But despite the government's efforts to get as many unopposed returns as possible they obtained only six out of a total of sixty-six seats.[94]

Voting too was ineptly handled by the government. While extra ballots were available for the SLPP's supporters, they were not available in sufficient numbers to help the SLPP cause; in Port Loko, for example, only 2,000 extra ballots were available in a seat that the APC carried by 7,000 votes.[95] SLPP officials showed a lamentable lack of discretion in handing out these extra ballots; some fell into the hands of APC supporters who took them back to party headquarters, and it is likely that some found their way into the APC's boxes. The counting of the ballots also was conducted reasonably fairly; apart from a few incidents such as a mysterious power failure in Bo Town after the boxes had been opened, the APC felt they had not been cheated in this area.

The campaign was noteworthy for the extent to which the Prime Minister and his supporters appealed to Mende self-preservation, while the APC stressed the corruption of Margai's regime, and the need for equity among regions (a thinly disguised appeal to Northerners). Money flowed freely, with the APC seeming to have enough to meet deposits and afford some vans, while the SLPP was collecting substantial sums from Lebanese and various foreign firms.[96] It was equally noteworthy for the convergence of the two parties as organisations, with the SLPP succeeding in reducing the number of its supporters running as Independents from 117 in 1962 to 56 while the APC relaxed its formerly rigid tests of party loyalty to include among its candidates a number of SLPP defectors whose main virtue was that they might win.[97]

Voting took place on 17 March, with the twelve Paramount Chiefs' elections on 21 March. As the results trickled in (with the Sierra Leone Broadcasting Service taking care to announce results so that the SLPP appeared to be leading) it was apparent that the APC was carrying most seats outside Mende country, and that the final results would be very close. By 21 March it had become known unofficially that the APC had won thirty-two seats, the SLPP had won twenty-eight, and six were held by Independents, four of whom at this point sent a letter to the Governor-General saying that they would support Stevens, but not Albert Margai, as Prime Minister.[98] Sir Henry Lightfoot-Boston had tried to persuade Stevens and Margai to form a coalition, but when this attempt proved futile, he called upon Stevens to form a government.

However, at this point came an unexpected turn, when Brigadier David Lansana, the Army commander, declared martial law and arrested the Governor-General and Stevens, accusing the former of having acted unconstitutionally by not waiting for the Paramount Chiefs' election results. Three days later, when it became increasingly obvious that Lansana's intervention was intended to restore Albert Margai,[99] his subordinate officers arrested him, but instead of restoring civilian rule, they instituted a military regime styled the National Reformation Council.

Postscript

The NRC ruled for just over a year, during which time it held a series of spectacular hearings into the Margai regime's accumulation of wealth, before it in turn was overthrown by a revolt of the enlisted men.[100] These quickly restored Siaka Stevens to power, initially at the head of a 'National' government, but soon as head of an all-APC government with the SLPP (whose numbers were decimated by election petitions) in opposition. This government undertook some bold actions, most notably cutting itself in for a 51 per cent share of ownership in SLST's diamond-mining concession, but politically fell gradually into the SLPP pattern of relying on the chiefs for its local organisation. Though the North-South split remained the fundamental political division in the country, the APC gradually made some headway in Mende country, while at the same time a breakaway group of Temnes tried to form a new opposition party, which was promptly banned. In early 1971 some soldiers attempted a coup following which Stevens called in Guinean troops to help protect himself, and had Brigadier John Bangura, who had played a key role in restoring him to power, courtmartialled and with three others shot for mutiny, the first time any soldiers had been executed for the various coups. Stevens also passed the Albert Margai Republic Bill, and then promptly amended it to make himself an executive-style President. The APC also showed itself much more effective in the use of government powers of coercion than the SLPP had been, managing in 1972 to prevent the SLPP nominating candidates for a series of by-elections in former SLPP strongholds, and repeating the same tactic so successfully in the 1973 general elections that the SLPP was unable to contest a single seat. Sierra Leone thus became a *de facto* one-party state, with the APC accomplishing what Albert Margai had failed to achieve, the replacement of open opposition to the regime by covert attempts at its overthrow and conspiracies within the ruling group. The prospect of struggles within the APC were enhanced by the failing health of its unifying symbol, President Stevens, and two deep rifts, first between the long-time APC loyalists who had withstood SLPP persecution to bring the party to power and the more intellectual newcomers who had joined at the time of victory[101] and second, between the more 'moderate' and the 'revolutionary' elements among the loyalists, with the latter holding a slight edge through the fact that their leader, S.I. Koroma, had gained the posts of Vice-President and Prime Minister.

Notes

1. Albert Margai, 'The New Constitution of Sierra Leone is a Farce', *Sierra Leone Weekly News*, 27 Mar. 1948.
2. See 'Critique of the Governor's Constitution Proposals', *Sierra Leone Weekly News*, 13 Sept. 1947, for a Creole view: 'Memorandum of the Sierra Leone Organisation Society', ibid., 18 Oct. 1947, for a Protectorate view.
3. See, for example, N.A. Cox-George, 'Crucifixion of Sierra Leone?' (pamphlet), Freetown (1948).
4. See the 'Memorandum of the Sierra Leone Organisation Society', *Sierra Leone Weekly News*, 18 Oct. 1947.
5. Letter in ibid., 26 Aug. 1950.
6. For an outside observer's comments on the Youth League in the 1930s, see W.M. McMillan, 'African Development: Negative Example of Sierra Leone', in C.K. Meek et al., *Europe and West Africa: Some Problems and Adjustments* London, Oxford University Press, 1940, p. 76.
7. I was told by both A.B. Cotay and Doyle Sumner, who were involved in the early Protectorate political movements, that they had made approaches to Wallace-Johnson, offering him the chance to lead a countrywide movement, but he rejected this overture.
8. In Freetown East, M.S. Mustapha was probably able to appeal to his fellow Aku Creoles against the Christian Creole candidates Akinola Wright and M.A. Cole. In Bonthe, heavily influenced by the surrounding Protectorate, Dr Margai's friend A.G. Randle was able to secure an unopposed return, but does not appear to have declared himself for the SLPP until after his nomination.
9. Dr Margai and Dunbar were both unopposed. Another commoner, Lansana Kamara, was able to secure an unopposed return from Koinadugu, as one of the few literate men available; he sided with the SLPP after his election. Among the SLPP activists, A.J. Momoh lost in Bo, Arthur Massally lost in Pujehun, and G.F. Keitell, a Creole, lost in Kenema.
10. Albert Margai and Siaka Stevens, probably the two most 'nationally-oriented' as well as most capable SLPP members, were returned by the Protectorate Assembly on the urging of Dr Margai. It seems unlikely that either of them would have fared much better than Massally or Momoh if they had had to contest in the more local arena of a particular district, although Margai did take care to cultivate a base in Moyamba.
11. The Diamond Agreement and Licence (Ratification) Act 1935.
12. See Laurens van der Laan, *The Sierra Leone Diamonds*, London, Oxford University Press, 1965, pp. 3-4. I have drawn heavily on van der Laan's work

both for factual materials and for ideas for this section, although I take full responsibility for the interpretations offered.

13. This was a scheme begun in 1946 after the European companies had decided that for them dredging gold was no longer an economic operation. Africans were licensed to undertake small-scale hand operations on claims allocated to them, a pattern which provided the model for the later diamond scheme.
14. See the script of his party broadcast in the (Bo) *Observer,* 15 May 1954.
15. See ibid., 8 May 1954. Kono, which would benefit far less from licensed mining because SLST was working many of its prime areas, was far less favourably disposed towards the scheme. See Minikin, *Local Politicis in Kono,* p. 214.
16. At any rate, Bo District was also in the forefront of moves to replace Dr Margai with his brother at this time. See also Stevens's later claim, below, p. 64.
17. Van der Laan, p. 22.
18. SLST originally asked for £10 million compensation, which was a generous estimate of the profits they could have expected from the diamond-bearing beds they were giving up, if these were left alone. Since the beds would for the most part have been rendered worthless by illicit digging, the compensation the company received was undoubtedly more than they would have realised if they had retained the assets.
19. *Daily Mail,* 13 Sept. 1957.
20. When a digger leased land from the Tribal Authority, compensation was supposed to be given to the TA both for its own use and to reimburse the farmer who had lost his land. In practice, the chief frequently retained the farmer's share of the lease proceeds as well as the TA's share.
21. Van der Laan, p. 9.
22. Taking the total figure of 75,000 diggers at the peak of the rush, and deducting the 45,000 foreigners expelled the next year, we still have about 30,000 Sierra Leoneans out of a total adult male group of about half a million.
23. See below, p. 249.
24. See below, pp. 125-26.
25. Elsewhere, Nigeria had seen the Enugu coal miners' strike, the Gold Coast had had its ex-servicemen's demonstration which led to the Coussey Commission and Nkrumah's first trip to prison, and Senegal had seen the major strike on the Dakar-Bamako railway.
26. This was a religiously-inspired protest against both the chiefs and colonial authorities. See Kilson, pp. 113-16, and B.M. Jusu, 'The Haidara Rebellion of 1931', *Sierra Leone Studies,* (NS) 3, Dec. 1954, pp. 143-53, for details. Most disturbances up country, however, were confined to single chiefdoms, and while they took the form of 'grassroots' protests against oppressive taxation and abuses of authority by the chief and other officials, seem generally to have been inspired by rivals to the chief seeking office for themselves. See Kilson, pp. 179-92, and Barrows, pp. 316-33, for differing interpretations.
27. Van der Laan, p. 10. For details on the events of the strike, see the *Report of the Commission of Enquiry into the Strike and Riots in Freetown, Sierra Leone,* during February 1955 Freetown, Government Printer, 1955, otherwise known as the *Shaw Report.*
28. See *Daily Mail,* 10 Feb. 1955.
29. Ibid., 25 Feb. 1955; also *Shaw Report,* p. 31.
30. *West Africa,* No. 1998, 11 June 1955, pp. 529-30.
31. *Vanguard,* 18 Feb. 1955.

32. *Daily Mail*, 21 Oct. 1955.
33. For example, even though the chiefs now visited many villages by car, they still demanded the gift of rice and poultry which had traditionally been provided to feed the chief and his retinue during an overnight visit to the village. Now the gift would be taken back to the chief's home uneaten, and sometimes sold by him for cash. The clerks when they came to collect taxes would demand similar gifts, and also might demand a fee only slightly less than the tax to keep a tax-exempt person off the rolls. See the *Report of the Commission of Enquiry into Disturbances in the Provinces* (Nov. 1955 to Mar. 1956), London, Crown Agents for the Colonies, 1956 (hereafter *Cox Report*), *Passim.*
34. See, for example, the *Annual Reports on the Sierra Leone Protectorate for 1947*, pp. 7-8, and ibid., 1948, pp. 6-7.
35. See *Daily Mail*, 21 Nov. 1955. While it was traditional for the chiefdom to provide a mud and thatch house for the chief, a permanent structure which would become part of his family's inheritance was a rather different matter.
36. *Cox Report*, pp. 13, 83.
37. This was remarked on by the Acting Provincial Commissioner, Northern Province in his testimony before the commission to consider compensation to 'victims' of the riots. See *Riot Damages (Provinces) Commission 1958, First Report* (mimeo), p. 12.
38. *Cox Report*, p. 63.
39. Ibid., p. 125.
40. Ibid., p. 57. The sentiment of wishing to 'kill their Chief' may not have been meant to be taken seriously; and the destruction of a chief's property could be interpreted as a warning and a sufficient punishment. See note 42.
41. Ibid., p. 8.
42. Ibid., p. 151. James Littlejohn, who was in the Northern Province shortly afterwards, suggests that the whole uprising was merely a warning to the chiefs to mend their ways, rather than a serious desire to be rid of them, a 'rebellion' rather than a 'revolution' (Personal communication).
43. Reported in *Daily Mail*, 7 May 1956.
44. Legislative Council Debates, 1956-7, 25 Oct. 1956, p. 477.
45. *Reports of the Commissioners of Enquiry into the Conduct of Certain Chiefs and the Government Statement Thereon*, Freetown, Government Printer, 1957, and *Further Reports ... into the Conduct of Certain Chiefs*, Freetown, Government Printer, 1957.
46. Ibid.
47. As far as I can determine, only one of the deposed chiefs who was still living in 1960 (Bai Banta of Buya Romande) was *not* restored.
48. He was disbarred in 1950 for several months, and again in 1959 for nine years.
49. For example, Rogers-Wright acted as legal counsel for many of the complainants when the Commissioners enquiring into the misconduct of chiefs held hearings.
50. I exclude from these figures the two seats won by the Kono Progressive Movement, nominally in alliance with the UPP.
51. See the interview with Albert Margai in the Bo *Observer*, 11 Apr. 1953.
52. See below, pp. 217-9, for an analysis of this event.
53. See *Liberty* (the PNP newspaper) 8 Aug. 1959.
54. The sixteen members of the Executive included seven lawyers and two other university graduates. Six were Mende and five were Creoles.
55. See 'Structural Change', p. 220.
56. The PNP won only three seats in the North, against twenty-six in the Southern and Eastern Provinces, out of 111 and 197 seats.

57. For details of the KPM, see Fred M. Hayward, 'The Development of a Radical Political Organisation in the Bush: A Case Study in Sierra Leone', *Canadian Journal of African Studies,* VI, I, 1972, pp. 1-28. After the 1957 election, it changed its name to the Sierra Leone Progressive Independence Movement (SLPIM), but remained a Kono party.
58. Taking the 1957 by-election rather than the general election as the more accurate expression of public sentiment.
59. See *Vanguard,* 26 Mar. 1960.
60. Including Ministerial Secretaries, the total allocations for each major group were: Mendes, eight; Creoles, six; Northerners, six. But from a northern perspective, what looked suspicious about the United Front was that all the portfolios which were cut down to make room for new Ministers were held by Northerners while no new Northerners were made Ministers.
61. See *Daily Mail,* 19 Apr. and 17, 18 and 19 May 1961, for the lists of those jailed and released.
62. The full text is in *Daily Mail,* 11 Mar. 1961.
63. Cited in ibid., 4 May 1959.
64. Ibid.
65. In 1969 the APC government of Siaka Stevens announced it would take a majority shareholding in all mining companies in Sierra Leone. But in 1973, after gaining its objective with SLST, it dropped this plan for the remaining companies.
66. See *Daily Mail,* 23 Dec. 1965, for the announcement.
67. See below, pp. 256-7 for details.
68. See below, p. 255 for a discussion of this topic.
69. By 1970, estimates of the remaining life of the SLST's diamond reserves ranged from five to fifteen years and for Delco's Marampa iron ore, from five to ten years.
70. We should note that Karefa-Smart did not join in making the abject apologies, although he did promise to serve Albert loyally.
71. The only Northerners remaining with Ministerial status were Amadu Wurie and Kande Bureh – and Bureh's base was in Freetown.
72. One of Albert's first actions was to hold a meeting with the civil service, at which he stressed both his sympathy for their needs and the duty they owed the country to work hard. This meeting appears to have been generally well received by those concerned.
73. Though he did not allow either chief to return to his own chiefdom until later. See *Daily Mail,* 18 May 1964.
74. See below, pp. 262-4.
75. His 'radical' image was somewhat tarnished by his accepting a knighthood in January 1965.
76. See *Daily Mail,* 8 Apr. 1964. His words were: 'When the time comes in Sierra Leone that Government lacks opposition, that will be the time that some of us will pack up our bags and baggage and quit politics.'
77. *Daily Mail,* 15 June 1965.
78. Ibid., 25 Oct. 1965.
79. Ibid., 18 Dec. 1965.
80. Second Parliament of Sierra Leone, Fourth Session 1965-6, Third Meeting, *Notice Paper,* p. 16.
81. *Parliamentary Debates,* Session 1965-6, 20 and 21 Dec. 1965, *passim.*
82. See *House of Representatives Debates,* Session 1965-6, Vol. I, 29 Mar. 1965, cols. 201-2.
83. His major Freetown rally on 28 Jan. 1966, had a turnout of about 3,000, of whom 400-500 were actively hostile, and many others merely curious.

One large group of hecklers was attacked by a squad of riot police and driven out of the stadium with clubs.

84. See *We Yone,* 15 Jan. 1966.
85. I was told this by an observer who was present at the Bo rally, and spoke with the Prime Minister afterwards.
86. Persons close to Albert or holding senior civil service posts were working to secure SLPP nominations in at least six seats. One of these was Sir Albert's personal secretary, who was seeking the nomination in a seat held by one of Sir Albert's Ministers, while another was the Secretary to the Prime Minister and Head of the Civil Service, George S. Panda.
87. See *Unity,* 11 June 1966, for a report of this Bonthe speech.
88. *Supplement to the Sierra Leone Gazette Extraordinary,* Vol. XCVII, 22 Dec. 1966.
89. To compound the irony, it was Albert Margai's constitutional amendments that the APC eventually used when it did make Sierra Leone a republic, since this was the only way it could avoid yet another dissolution and election.
90. For a detailed discussion, see Thomas S. Cox, *Civil-Military Relations in Sierra Leone,* Cambridge, Mass., Harvard University Press, 1976, pp. 82-104.
91. 'The Electoral Provisions (Amendment) Act 1967, Section 4. A Leone, the currency adopted in 1964, was worth ten shillings.
92. Section 5.
93. See testimony of Dr S.H. Pratt before the Dove-Edwin Commission, *Daily Mail,* 11 July 1967; and the *Report of the Dove-Edwin Commission of Enquiry into the Conduct of the 1967 General Elections in Sierra Leone,* Freetown, Government Printer, 1967.
94. Three of these unopposed returns were in safe seats in any case.
95. *Dove-Edwin Report,* p. 11.
96. Some of this money seems to have been spent on intra-party fights, with Margai's supporters using it to back opponents of Ministers who were not considered sufficiently loyal to him.
97. The most notable of these were Cyril Rogers-Wright, whose presence in the Cabinet had occasioned an APC protest in 1962, and Solomon Pratt, until 1966 the head of the Sierra Leone Railway.
98. See *Dove-Edwin Report,* p. 24.
99. In fact, I would hesitate to call Lansana's action a *military* coup, in that it seems most likely that he was acting at the behest of Sir Albert or more probably of some of the ousted Prime Minister's hardline supporters. Certainly there was no hint that he was trying to establish a military regime.
100. For two contrasting views of the military regime and the reasons for the enlisted men's coup, see Walter Barrows, 'La Politique de l'armée en Sierra Leone', *Le Mois en Afrique,* Dec. 1968, pp. 54-64, and my 'Shifting Forces in Sierra Leone', *Africa Report,* 13 Dec. 1968, pp. 26-30.
101. For this struggle, see John Cartwright and Tom Cox, 'Left Turn for Sierra Leone?' *Africa Report,* Jan. 1972, pp. 16-18.

4 MILTON AND ALBERT MARGAI: A PORTRAIT OF TWO LEADERS

Up to this point we have focused largely upon those features of Sierra Leone society which we can regard as external constraints upon the range of choices open to its political leaders. But before attempting to analyse particular policy decisions, we need to consider another type of constraint, that internal to the actors themselves. Two obstacles prevent a leader from fully exercising the freedom of choice the range of external constraints appear to leave him: what we may loosely term his desire for a 'best available' solution, and his predispositions or 'prejudices' (the latter in the non-pejorative sense Burke and others attached to it).

Even if we assume that a political leader wants the 'best possible' solution to every political problem he confronts, most of these problems are far too complex for him to canvass all possible approaches and solutions. As Herbert Simon has observed,

> The capacity of the human mind for formulating and solving complex problems is very small compared with the size of the problems whose solution is required for objectively rational behaviour in the real world – or even for a reasonable approximation to such objective rationality.'[1]

However the leader chooses to meet this problem, whether by following Simon's recommendation that he choose any course that is 'good enough' by his own criteria,[2] or by using some form of cost-benefit analysis,[3] he will inevitably employ some form of internal screening process to select what he considers to be the significant factors and to assign weights to these various factors. In some cases this internal screening may have been elaborated into a sufficiently comprehensive and coherent set of beliefs that we may consider it an 'ideology', but in most cases it tends to be a rather looser, more heterogeneous and even conflicting collection of beliefs which is better covered by the wider term 'prejudices'.[4] These prejudices may be more or less internally consistent, they may be more or less capable of standing up to rational scrutiny, and they may be more or less relevant to the problem at hand; but they will probably simplify considerably the leader's task of selecting his course of action in a given situation.

In considering the effect of these internal constraints upon leaders, we face even more difficulties than in assessing the external constraints. Many leaders may not even be aware of all their own predispositions; and even if they are, there are numerous reasons why they may not reveal them publicly. Even private revelations to friends may not be entirely free from the distortions self-justification will introduce. While actions may be more revealing than words, still they are not an infallible guide, since the leader may be operating under external constraints observers may be unaware of or have undervalued. The best the observer can do is to speculate cautiously on the most plausible interpretations of both words and deeds, bearing in mind how provisional his assessment must needs be.

There are certain key questions we may ask about any leader in order to winkle out something of his predispositions. We can ask first of all what is his view of the 'good society', what goals he will work for or against, what desires drive him? We can also ask how he sees himself in relation to others: what is his self-perception of the bases of his legitimacy as a leader, what are the weights he gives to different values in transactional relationships, and what sort of behaviour does he see as appropriate for himself as a leader? We should also consider his style of operation, becaue this will affect the effort he will be able to put into decision-making, and thus the relationship between his sub-optimal decisions and an optimal one. Most obviously it will affect the quality and the quantity of information he has available, but it also affects the nature of his priorities and his ability to realise them. For example, a leader who is unwilling to delegate details will be able to remain more satisfactorily informed about many areas, but only at the cost of not being able to concentrate his energies on major decisions.

In trying to determine a leader's basic goals and values, there are several hazards in trying to work backwards from his publicly known actions to draw inferences regarding his values. In the first place, he may not have worked out his own beliefs clearly enough in his own mind for them to serve as a guide to action, or there may be conflicts and contradictions in his beliefs that prevent his taking action. Second, even if he has a clear underlying philosophy, this may change in course of time in the light of new experiences. The 'radicalisation' of Julius Nyerere and of Milton Obote, the disillusionment of Sekou Touré with the Soviet Union, or the increased 'conservatism' of the regimes of Jomo Kenyatta and Eric Williams of Trinidad, are cases in point. Third, a leader may perceive constraints (whether real or not) as preventing the realisation of his beliefs, and thus may not even try to act in a way consistent with his beliefs; for example, after Iran's experience in 1953 even the most radical nationalist leader of an oil-producing state (or any mineral producer, for that matter) would have hesitated to challenge the major international corporations. Finally, even where a leader's values and his actions coincide, the values may not have directly led to the actions; at most, we can argue that they set limits to a leader's vision of what kinds of action were possible. For example, I shall argue that Dr Margai strongly upheld the idea of a stratified society with chiefs receiving deference because of their position; but I think it would be wrong to suggest that this underlying value was what led him to take a very cautious approach to developmental projects, when a more 'obvious' explanation was that the existing budget could not provide the necessary funds. It is only when we ask why he did not make moe effort to overcome this constraint (for example, by incurring larger debts) that we can come to his underlying values as a barrier against his considering such expedients.

In considering the two Margai brothers as political leaders, I will deal with each separately, offering first a brief sketch of their careers, secondly some comments on their general attitudes towards problems, and thirdly the style with which they sought to implement their attitudes. I will then attempt to summarise briefly what I see as the salient similarities and difference of the two as political leaders.

The Career and Character of Milton Margai

Milton Augustus Strieby Margai was born in Gbangbatoke, Moyamba district, in 1895, before the British annexed the Protectorate. His father, Milton Margai of Bonthe, was a wealthy merchant, who sent his eldest son through the EUB Mission School in Bonthe, the Albert Academy, and eventually to Fourah Bay College, where he was the first Protectorate student. At the same time, since his uncle was a Paramount Chief and the family had long been important in the southern Moyamba area, he was also thoroughly steeped in respect for traditional Mende customs and traditions, a respect which remained with him for his lifetime. After the First World War he was sent to Kings College Medical School, Newcastle, where he graduated in 1926. On his return to Freetown in 1928 as the first medical doctor from the Protectorate, he joined the Government medical service, and spent the next twenty years serving at various up-country stations. It was his experience up-country (and indirectly, in Freetown) that laid the basis for his later political career, for it was in this period that he not only provided cheap medical services for many Paramount Chiefs, but also acted as their own unofficial political adviser. The fact that he had worked 'in the bush' rather than in Freetown, where a number of the Creoles had taunted him as 'the Mende doctor', ensured that he would have a predominantly Protectorate base and orientation when he entered politics.

His political career formally began when he retired from the Medical Service in 1950 and was immediately elected to the Protectorate Assembly as one of the two representatives from Bonthe District (which he was to represent all the rest of his life in various legislative bodies). He had, however, already established his base through his contacts as a doctor and also through his role in the Protectorate Educational Progressive Union, a body of chiefs and other Protectorate leaders which attempted to stimulate social improvements in the Protectorate.

Perhaps his most significant work was in persuading leaders of the Mende women's secret societies to incorporate training courses in hygiene and child care offered by qualified instructors into their programme of initiation for young girls. While not accepted by all the chiefs, some of whom felt it represented a violation of the traditional rules, this work was widely regarded by women throughout the Protectorate.[5] This work illustrated clearly Dr Margai's willingness to utilise traditional channels to introduce innovative practices, but at the same time his concern to ensure that in innovating, the traditional customs were not violated.

In a sense, Dr Margai emerged as Sierra Leone's political leader by default. We noted earlier the relative positions in the period 1948-51 of the three groups contending for the power being devolved by the British on to Sierra Leoneans. The chiefs, enjoying the best strategic situations of these groups, none the less needed a person they could trust in control of the national government, since they were vulnerable to changes imposed from above. The Protectorate intelligentsia, lacking a base of their own, had to ally themselves either with the Creoles or with the chiefs, with the latter offering the prospect of a division between chiefly control at the local level and rule by the intelligentsia at the national level. The Creoles might attempt a similar bargain with the chiefs, or they might join the Protectorate intelligentsia in an effort to create a more popularly-based movement, but their exclusionary stand scuttled both these possibilities.

As Creole intransigence drove the two Protectorate groups together, it became clear that Dr Margai would be the only acceptable leader to the chiefs. Not only was he the eldest among the intelligentsia in a society which still respected age, but his years of work with and for the chiefs convinced them they could trust him to appreciate their point of view to a degree none of the younger educated men could match. A the same time, the educated men could respect his Western educational credentials, and could also look up to him as a father, or at least as an elder brother; while they might regard him as unduly cautious, they could still respect his education and his experience. The Creoles might have less grounds for respecting him, and might be uneasy about the vehemence of some of his comments on them; but it was hard to see them producing any more widely acceptable alternative.

Among the features which most sharply set Dr Margai apart from most of the African leaders who led their countries to independence were his self-effacement, his great concern to protect the position of the chiefs, and his close relations with the British.[6] These features can all be subsumed within a rather wider world view which I believe can help explain a good deal of the Doctor's behaviour, particularly with regard to his handling of political colleagues and opponents. The elements in this 'world view' which seem significant were the desirability of protecting Sierra Leone's traditional ways of life, and in particular the maintenance of a pattern of hierarchical relationships based upon ascriptive status; the belief that a ruler's legitimacy derived from his status and thus was secure against challenges from persons of lower status; and the belief that there were certain standards of conduct towards their people laid down by custom and tradition that rulers were expected to obey.

If we consider first his views on chieftaincy, we find a consistent pattern throughout his career, that of strongly supporting the authority of chiefs against all challenges, and only taking action against an individual chief under circumstances in which he felt the chief's own actions were undermining that authority. Thus we may consider his remarks following the Cox Report in 1956:

> I have often [said] that if we have to move towards progress we must move hand in hand with our chiefs, and I feel a little bit hurt when some of them get up and say they have a doubt in their minds. I think they are doubting the one who is their greatest friend. I do not ask that they should go on pressing their subjects but that they should continue ruling their people . . . My conscience would not allow me to uphold a chief who goes on oppressing his people. But a Chief who has not done any wrong, I am always here to uphold him.[7]

In the aftermath of the Northern riots, as noted earlier, eleven chiefs were removed from office, but five of those were later restored. Even the two major 'political' depositions and banishments of Paramount Chiefs after Independence, those of T.S. Mbriwa in 1962 and Bai Koblo Pathbana in 1963, could be partially interpreted in this light. Chief Mbriwa's leadership of the opposition SLPIM in Kono had certainly antagonised many of his fellow chiefs, who saw the party's programme as a direct threat to their personal wellbeing. The fact that Bai Koblo ran one of the more progressive chiefdom administrations in Sierra Leone, coupled with the suspicion that he might be pro-APC, could also be an embarrassment to chieftaincy, as well as a challenge to Dr Margai.[8]

Dr Margai's view of how a chief should behave towards his people without undermining the authority of the office was more lenient than his view of how they should behave towards superiors. Apart from his gentle handling of the chiefs after the Northern riots, he also took pains to reassure them, when the British Colonial Office finally forced Sierra Leone to prohibit forced labour for the chiefs' personal benefit, that 'we do not expect to really abolish communal labour'.[9] True to his word, the Prohibition of Forced Labour Ordinance[10] left the loophole that 'minor communal services' for 'public purposes' could continue, and through this loophole the chiefs continued to receive a considerable amount of free labour. In individual chiefdom disputes also he stood firmly behind the chiefs, until evidence of their violation of customary behaviour became overwhelming.

His position with regard to the chiefs and chiefdoms was not, however, one of complete adherence to the *status quo.* We have already noted his use of the Bundu society to introduce modern child-care techniques to Protectorate women. He also tried by persuasion (though not by legislation) to improve the status of women in marriage, warning that 'our daughters will have to choose for themselves whoever they may love and marry and parents must stop receiving large sums of money from the suitors'.[11] He also thought the chiefdoms ought to take on the financial responsibilities of local government; in 1951 he was almost alone in advocating that the chiefdoms should not transfer responsibility for schools to the District Councils, because 'we want to take the chiefdoms as separate units to be trained in local government'.[12]

Allied to this respect for the established position of chieftaincy was Dr Margai's insistence on the respect due to age. In part this was an argument based on self-interest; by the time he achieved a dominant position, he was the eldest among the Protectorate men. But both those who were his contemporaries and the younger men in his government concur that he seemed to hold the view that younger men should be kept in their place. He was once reported to have said, 'I am not going to build something up to see some young men destroy it',[13] and he tended to be wary of youthful impetuousness. Like his views on chieftaincy, his views on age suggest a picture of the ideal society as being a hierarchical one, with rank in the hierarchy being based largely on ascriptive status, and with some obligations concomitant with the prerequisites of high status.

The obverse side of respect for high ascriptive status is, of course, a tendency to keep inferiors 'in their place'. It seems plausible to argue that Dr Margai's conspicuous eschewing of attempts to speak directly with the populace, or to show any interest in building a party organisation independent of the chiefs, were at least partially attributable to a distaste for drawing 'the masses' into politics, or allowing openings for 'young men' without status to play political roles above their stations. Even before ill-health severely limited his public appearance, Dr Margai was far more likely to address the Tribal Authorities and chiefs on his up-country journeys than he was to appear at mass rallies, except when absolutely necessary. His reluctance to hurry the mostly young educated Africans into senior civil service positions may also have been partially attributable to this, since the intellectual arrogance of the young educated men was quite antithetical to his views of proper behaviour, especially towards elders.

In many ways Dr Margai seemed to model his role as Prime Minister upon that of a Paramount Chief, regarding himself as a 'father' to all Sierra Leoneans. Thus when his long-time opponent, Dr Herbert Bankole-Bright, died in poverty, Dr Margai contributed to his funeral expenses.[14] In the 1962 election, when five candidates were contesting a Mende constituency, and all sought his support, he publicly proclaimed that they were all 'his children'. This attitude of being a 'father' to all, of regarding himself more as the head of a household than the head of a state, had interesting implications for both accountability and legitimacy. The accountability of the head of a household is of quite a different nature from the accountability of the head of a state[15]; while a head of state is accountable in some sense to the people over whom he rules, either directly or through the fact that they too can interpret the laws of God or of tradition which bind him, the head of a household is accountable essentially to his own conscience. Dr Margai on a number of occasions did seem to take the view that he knew what was best for his people, and regardless of such ephemera as electoral majorities he was going to impose his view on them for their own good. While it is difficult to find conclusive evidence of his views, this interpretation of his notion of accountability is consistent with other aspects of his character. As for the legitimacy of his leadership, there could be no question of the right of a father to be the ultimate authority for his people; and again the high degree of self-confidence (as well as tolerance of opponents) displayed by Dr Margai may well have been reinforced by the certainty that his right to act was not subject to question.

At the same time, a 'father' cannot treat his 'children' as equals. When one adds to this Sir Milton's view that age was an important basis for deference, it is not surprising that none of his younger political colleagues was his intimate friend; that honour was reserved for a handful of persons whom he had known since the 1920s. It appeared that he expected the younger men to acquiesce to his wishes out of deference to his age as well as to his position,[16] and as Prime Minister he generally had the sanctions to back up this view.

Whether Sir Milton could have used the value of deference to impose his will on the 'young men' over a wide range of policies is an open question; in part, I suggest, he avoided a head-on conflict by insisting on his way in only a few areas. He was never terribly interested in administrative details, preferring brief chats to reading files and memoranda. As his illnesses became more severe, he became even more impatient with lengthy meetings or presentations of arguments, and tended to cut off discussion in Cabinet rather quickly. He also was prepared to rely upon others as his 'eyes and ears', notably the Resident Ministers appointed in 1961, who were designated the Prime Minister's 'personal Ministerial representatives in each Province'.[17] But while he did restrict the range of his interests, and even in these areas would make some effort to hear different points of view, once he made up his mind he would stick stubbornly to his position, no matter how untenable. This stubbornness was well shown during the 1955 Freetown riots, when it seemed clear to most advisers that a key step in ending the riots was to have the strike leader Marcus Grant call off the general strike. Dr Margai however, flatly refused to have anything to do with Grant, whereas Albert Margai was quite glad to have Sir Ernest Beoku-Betts act as an intermediary.[18] A public statement he made in 1960 seems to sum up fairly well his attitude:

> It would be awkward for a leader to say one thing at one time and then change later. I am not that type of man. I would like to be clearly understood, and no one should bring any suggestions to me . . .

> I have pledged my word to the United Front, and it is a thing I can never give up.[19]

Sir Milton possessed a great deal of self-confidence in the rightness of his judgements, a self-confidence which enabled him to be tolerant of opposition, but also to be tough enough to stick to his own position when he had made up his mind. He was not an articulate man, which often deceived people into thinking him stupid or unaware of what was going on, while his mild manner and lack of commanding presence led some to think he might be easily pushed around. But like Clement Attlee, who was once derided by Churchill as 'a sheep in sheep's clothing', he could be tough when he had to be. In all the major conciliatory acts of his career, the attempts at reaching a compromise in the leadership struggle in 1957, the United Front in 1960, and the release of the APC leaders from jail after independence, he got what he wanted. In 1957 he isolated and overcame his most militant critics; in 1960 he achieved a broadened base of support for his policies; and in 1961 he gained an opposition which promised to abide by the Parliamentary rules.

Furthermore, when he wanted something done, he was not prepared to let legal niceties or any other obstacles stand in his way, as the deportation of J.T. Refell showed. Refell, the Bassa Tribal Headman in Freetown, and a City Councillor, announced in October 1962 that he was standing as an APC candidate for the city council elections on 1 November. On 16 October the government revoked recognition of him as Tribal Headman[20] and then had him charged with perjury for declaring he was eligible for election when (the government claimed) he was a Liberian citizen. He was found guilty by three assessors on 30 October,[21] and sentenced to a fine or imprisonment. Immediately after sentence was passed, he was served with a deportation order, bundled on a plane and flown to Liberia[22] in defiance of a writ of *habeas corpus* which his counsel had immediately issued. It appears that Sir Milton simply refused to acknowledge receipt of the *habeas corpus* until Refell was safely removed from the country.[23]

In most cases he was far more tolerant of opponents. Not only were Siaka Stevens and his associates released from detention within a month of Independence, but Stevens a year later was included in Sierra Leone's United Nations delegation.[24] Oppostion members of Parliament received their share of trips and other personal perquisites, but also, more tellingly, they also received some patronage for their constituencies.[25] Shortly before the 1963 District Council elections, the Prime Minister sent this memorandum to Resident Ministers:

> In order to . . . permit the people freedom of thought and speech it is of vital importance that the Paramount Chiefs themselves afford all possible facilities within their means to each and every candidate, thus leaving no cause for any grievance or partiality . . .[26]

While the motivation was clearly prudential, the intention was certainly unequivocal, and probably contributed to the reasonable degree of fairness which marked the elections.

In another area too Sir Milton was conspicuous among African leaders: he made no lavish display of his status or power. When he travelled, the Prime Ministerial Rolls-Royce was unescorted. When he received customary gifts on visits up-country, he would normally arrange, in the customary manner, to give most of them back, and like a chief, would help anyone who was in need. He left few buildings or other signs of wealth around either Freetown or his home town. While several of his Ministers sought a considerable amount of worldly goods, Sir Milton's own hands stayed clean.[27]

At the same time, his 'Clean Hands' policy was not rigorously enforced against Ministers; there were only three cases of Ministers losing office under his leadership, and none after British influence had been diminished in 1958.[28] Even the Cole Report's public revelations of apparent self-enrichment on the part of several Ministers[29] did not cause him to dismiss anyone, although he did shift the Ministers concerned into other portfolios. There are two plausible interpretations of this unwillingness to dismiss Ministers for corruption. Sir Milton may have regarded Ministerial self-enrichment, like the chiefs' exploitation of their people, as an inevitable fact of life to be tolerated as long as it did not become too blatant. Another explanation is that since at that time (1963) there was considerable plotting to replace Sir Milton with his brother Albert, and the Ministers cited were among the stronger of the Prime Minister's supporters, he may well have felt it was too dangerous to sack these Ministers: they might have joined forces with Albert Margai, or at the very least Albert's supporters would have been able to fill the vacancies.

Sir Milton's inaction over the Cole Report illustrates another very important facet of his personality, his extreme caution. He inevitably preferred to let a problem wait rather than risk taking a false step. Such an attitude can be instinctual, but in Sir Milton's case it was reinforced by his philosophical conservatism, his awareness that there were going to be bad elements in any society, and that changes might make any situation worse as easily as better. His conscious attitude is well summed up by two stories. Shortly after Ghana's independence in 1957 he was being chided by a Ghanaian for Sierra Leone's tardiness in moving towards the same goal. He replied: 'Sir, in my country, on a journey, when we come to a big river, we send one man first and do not enter until he has reached the other side.' The other story is that in 1961 during the planning of the Independence ceremonies, Sir Milton insisted that the hymn 'Lead, Kindly Light' should be sung. After a moment's silence the Archbishop of Sierra Leone finally spoke. 'Mr Prime Minister, do you really think that's appropriate? Remember that the next line goes "Amidst encircling gloom".' Sir Milton looked around the table. 'I think there's quite a lot of encircling gloom.' The hymn was sung.[30]

His attitude towards the British also reflected this awareness that change might not make things better, as well as a considerable ambivalence. His use of a British official as Secretary to the Prime Minister for a year after Independence, his statement that even if a qualified Sierra Leonean was available for a post a European filling it 'would serve his normal term and the African step in afterwards'[31] and the high degree of trust he displayed in the integrity of British officials seem a little hard to reconcile with his comment in 1959 that if he were to indulge his personal feelings he would 'push all Europeans out of Sierra Leone today',[32] and the claim by one friend that his First World War sympathies earned him the nickname 'Von Margai'. He may also have hesitated to push Africanisation in part because the first Sierra Leonean claimants to such posts would have been Creoles, who would have become more entrenched than the British.[33]

But there was also a deeper ambivalence in his attitude towards the British, suggested by his relations with his English wife, whom he visited faithfully when in England on 'home' leave, yet refused to allow to visit Sierra Leone (although their two children did visit him there).

All the features we have noted about Sir Milton – his unwavering support for the values of the status and deference, his self-confidence, his lack of self-aggrandisement, and his lack of interest in such *minutiae* of politics as administration or building a political party – suggest someone with a strong commitment to an overarching set of beliefs, but at the same time a lack of zest for the political game. To use Payne and Woshinsky's interesting typology of motivations,[34] his dominant incentive seems to have been the desire to fulfil a 'mission', with a strong dash of 'obligation' thrown in.[35] With a strong commitment to certain goals, he could well afford to tolerate opposing voices, just so long as they posed no threat to him, and by tolerating them he could ensure that they did not become dangerous. When he felt it was important to get his way, as in the case of Bai Koblo's deposition, the deportation of Refell, or the question of keeping an expatriate as head of the armed forces, he would not hesitate to override anyone who stood in his way. At the same time, he gave the strong impression that he continued to rule the country not because he liked politics, but because he felt he could not trust anyone else to do the job better. His cautious approach (as the London *Times* observed, 'He drove with the brakes ready')[36] infuriated many; yet it was an essential part of his overall approach of tempering changes in such a way as to protect existing institutions.[37]

Albert Margai: The Vacillating Lion

Considering that the two men were brought up in the same milieu, the contrasts between Milton and Albert Margai could not have been much more startling. The wiry doctor was quiet and self-effacing, yet there was something decisive about his manner that made his colleagues hesitate to press him too far. Albert was able to dominate gatherings by his massive physical presence, was quick of tongue and insistent in manner; yet seeing him in action, one wondered how much of the imposing self-confidence was really a bluff. In their values too, the two men differed widely; if Milton epitomised a 'Tory' or aristoctratic tradition of belief in the value of fixed ranks in society, Albert in both statements and actions epitomised the drive for self-advancement of bourgeois man.

Albert Michael Margai was born in Bonthe in 1910, the sixth of seven sons of Milton Margai the merchant. Unlike his brothers, Albert was sent to the Roman Catholic primary school and educated as a Catholic, a religious commitment he maintained strongly over the years. After attending St Edward's Secondary School in Freetown, he entered the government medical service as a male nurse in 1932, and later qualified as a dispenser. In 1944, on a scholarship from PEPU, he left for the United Kingdom to study law. But interestingly, although he was involved in the West African Students Union and knew many of the other future African leaders such as Obafemi Awolowo, he does not appear to have used this period to develop a comprehensive critique of colonial rule or set of long-range political goals. The rhetoric of African nationalism certainly rubbed off on him far more than on his older brother, but behind the rhetoric it is hard to find any consistently worked out intellectual position in relation to such issues as colonial rule, the potential use of political power, or economic development.

In 1948 Albert Margai returned to Sierra Leone as the first Protectorate man to have qualified as a barrister, and quickly plunged into political activity. With the backing of Chief Julius Gulama, he became a member of the Moyamba District Council, and from there was elected to the Protectorate Assembly. To both these bodies he quickly brought a new tone, taking an aggressive and sharply critical approach to the British administrators' actions, something to which they were clearly unaccustomed.[38] His wide-ranging attacks on the colonial regime won him a considerable following among the younger educated men of both the Protectorate and Freetown, while his abilities as an orator were such that the SLPP regarded him as their key man for pre-election broadcasting in Freetown in 1951.[39] However, oratorical ability, a reputation as a 'nationalist', and even a considerable number of friends among the younger Creole intelligentsia were not enough to overcome Creole-Protectorate suspicions. When he decided to stand for Freetown Council in 1950, he was bitterly attacked by Wallace-Johnson's newspaper as a 'cradle baby' not intelligent or experienced enough to represent Freetown.[40]

He entered the Legislative Council in 1951 as one of the two members from the Protectorate Assembly, and became one of the most vigorous of the Sierra Leonean Ministers. However, policy differences between him and his brother, notably over the questions of abolishing the post of Chief Commissioner for the Protectorate (whom Albert distrusted for his influence over the chiefs, but whom Milton relied on), and over diamond policy[41] limited the extent to which his Ministerial talents were used, although he did play a major role in the diamond negotiations and in the 1956 constitutional revisions. In 1957 the conflict between the brothers came to a head at a post-election party caucus which by twenty-two votes to twenty-one chose Albert over his brother as party leader. After backing down under pressure a few hours later, Albert hesitated for a year while his brother consolidated his position, until finally in September 1958 he took the plunge into official opposition and formed the Peoples National Party.

The failure of the PNP to make electoral headway against the power of the chiefs helped to induce Albert Margai to join the United Front in 1960 (splitting with his old friend Stevens in the process) and in 1962 he brought the PNP back into the SLPP. Following the 1962 elections, he moved into the key Finance portfolio, which he held until his brother's death on 29 April 1964.

The changes which took place following Albert Margai's installation as Prime Minister were not so much in policies or personnel as in the political atmosphere. Within the SLPP a quiet struggle saw Albert trying to move PNP associates into key party offices, and to have them replace sitting MPs as candidates, while at the same time he tried to develop a more effective, centrally controlled party machine. (He also had himself elected 'Leader for Life' of the party). In the civil service, the authority of a few young Mendes increased sharply, while key administrators were pressed to a greater extent than ever before to play a clearly political role on behalf of the Prime Minister and the SLPP. Pressure on APC supporters was stepped up, largely through harassment by the chiefs, but at the higher levels through more frequent attempts to buy over individuals. The Prime Minister went to considerable lengths to make his presence known throughout Sierra Leone, and to arouse people to seek new directions and initiatives. In the area of policy, he proposed the opening of relations with the Communist states as well as with the West, a stronger interest in both regional and pan-African co-operation, and the development and indigenisation of Sierra Leone industries, as well as a more concerted effort to improve Sierra Leone's agricultural exports.

But in all these areas, many of his proposals came to seem largely empty rhetoric, and to be something of a cover for efforts to which he was devoting much more energy, efforts at property acquisition, business promotions and other materially rewarding enterprises. The apparent scale of this activity as much as his attempts to push through a one-party state seem to have contributed heavily to the widespread disillusionment with his regime that helped bring about his defeat in the 1967 election.

In the military coup following the 1967 election, Sir Albert was jailed briefly, and after his release by the NRC spent most of 1967-8 abroad, returning home only to testify before the Forster Commission of Enquiry into Ministerial assets. The commission's enquiry, which revealed a range of private economic activities by Sir Albert beyond even most of his enemies' allegations,[42] completed the blackening of his reputation. When the civilians were being brought back to power by the army rank-and-file revolt, Sir Albert appeared briefly in Freetown to resume leadership of the SLPP, but was firmly told that he was no longer wanted, despite his position as 'Life Leader'. He then retired to the United Kingdom and did not reappear on the Sierra Leone scene.

What motivated Albert Margai? Was there a consistent pattern, a vision of an ideal world, behind the mixture of 'radical' rhetoric and hesitant actions, the oscillation between appeals to self-sacrifice for Sierra Leone, and sordid greed? In judging Albert Margai's actions, we should bear in mind that a would-be 'innovator' invariably tends to appear less consistent than an upholder of the *status quo* like Sir Milton

Margai. The innovator, precisely because he is following an uncharted path, must necessarily take wrong turnings and go down blind alleys. Implementing a vision of what has not yet existed has to involve some readjusting and refocusing of the vision to accord with the limits of the possible. The conservative, by refusing to move out of his current surroundings, avoids the inconsistency of stepping forward and then retreating back to try another path, though he risks finding the ground crumbling underneath him. It is generally easier, in short, to appear consistent by continually doing very little than by embarking on first one course of action and then another, even if all of these have a single ultimate goal. I am not suggesting that Albert Margai had such an ultimate goal firmly in mind; in fact, I think he was considerably less clear in his own mind about what kind of society he wanted than was his brother, as well as being less inclined to think about this ultimate goal when contemplating any immediate action. All I am saying is that the considerable differences between the two brothers in their approach to political problems were magnified by the fact that one sought to promote, and the other to oppose, change.

One can pinpoint a number of specific sharp contrasts between Albert Margai and his brother. He had far less respect for 'traditional' institutions than did Sir Milton, despite his protestations of concern for chieftaincy. He was just as ready as his brother to discipline a chief whose behaviour threatened his personal position, as when he had Chief Gbwaru Mansaray of Wara Wara Yagala deposed in 1967 on the grounds that he was suspected of favouring the APC. But he went much further, placing the chiefs in an extremely self-destructive position by ending the time-honoured fiction that they were 'above politics', in order to force some slackers into more active pro-SLPP participation.[43] His lack of respect for customary institutions was also suggested by the fact that he left uncensured a Minister who slapped a Paramount Chief,[44] and in a different plane, by the famous 'Kabala cows' episode. In this episode, the Prime Minister on a visit to the country's poorest district had been presented with a large number of cattle as a traditional tribute. (It was alleged that the District Officer had put a good deal of pressure on the chiefs to make the tribute a particularly lavish one.)[45] Custom decreed that the recipient of such a gift would slaughter it and make a feast then and there for the givers, or contrive to return the gift or something of equal value. Instead, the cattle were trucked at government expense from Koinadugu to the Prime Minister's private cattle ranch in Mende country.[46] When asked in Parliament to justify the use of government funds for this private purpose, the Prime Minister replied:

> The legacy which we have inherited is that the person of the Prime Minister or for that matter Ministers of Government, is indivisible . . . for the time being I am Prime Minister of Sierra Leone, and if I go anywhere, whether to Timbucktu or to Russia or to Tokyo, if I am given the whole of Tokyo the Government shall be responsible for bringing my luggage home. . . When I cease to be Prime Minister the privilege will cease, but whilst I am here . . . it should be accepted and no words or any name will ever change my attitude towards that . . .[47]

The following year, Sir Albert's acquisitive tendencies again gained prominence when the editor of the APC newspaper *We Yone* ran a lengthy analysis of his known property purchases since becoming Prime Minister, including rather expensive houses in London and Washington.[48] An article in the SLPP paper purporting to justify Sir Albert's behaviour claimed he had stated in 1957, after stepping aside for his brother,

> If I have my way, politics will not be a business of money . . . but I have come to the conclusion from personal experience, that if you have no money to spend, then you have no business in politics.

But he also made the somewhat divergent argument that far from being a necessary evil, the acquisition of wealth was a positive virtue:

> As a private man, I have always been investment minded, *and this I preach to everybody.* (emphasis added)[49]

A few years later, he gave this writer a very clear statement on what he saw as motivating men:

> Human beings want advancement – everybody wants to improve himself. People want good roads they can travel on without being bitten by vipers, a little more food, a little more clothing . . .[50]

Such comments suggest fairly clearly that the Prime Minister's guiding vision was one of a bourgeois society, in which each person made the best use of the opportunities available to him for his personal self-enrichment. Ascribed status carried no great weight with him, except in so far as it provided an individual with opportunities for self-advancement. Not that the Prime Minister was miserly or hoarded his possessions; he did give lavish banquests at his sumptuous residence in the village of

Lumley. But conspicuous consumption is, as Veblen reminds us, quite compatible with bourgeois values.

A more positive side of this vision was Albert's keen interest in increasing equality of opportunity, an attitude manifested from the start of his political career. In 1949 he collided head-on with all the chiefs in the Protectorate Assembly by asking that school fees be reduced from one shilling to threepence monthly so that 'our less privileged brothers' could also afford schooling for their children.[51] The chiefs retorted that men who wanted their children educated should pay for it, and turned down the proposal. Albert not surprisingly was also pressing to have chiefs' participation in the legislature reduced in favour of non-chiefs.[52]

If the 'good society' towards which Sir Albert wished to move Sierra Leone was a bourgeois one, some opportunities would have to be provided for a bourgeoisie to develop. The most direct way of doing this would be to safeguard for Sierra Leoneans those areas into which they could easily move, both as entrepreneurial businessmen and as skilled personnel in large organisations. It would not be beneficial from this viewpoint to drive out major foreign firms, since their operations were as yet beyond the capabilities of Sierra Leoneans, but they could be pressed into providing both more revenue and more job opportunities for Sierra Leoneans. A much more promising target was those areas of retail trade dominated by Lebanese and Indians. From 1965 onwards a series of Retail Trade Acts attempted to confine a range of simple economic activities to Sierra Leone citizens.[53] For the same end, wholesale expulsions took place among the Ghanaian fishermen who dominated the onshore fishery. This last action occasioned considerable criticism of Sir Albert, since it appeared that a major beneficiary was Sea Products Limited, a fishery firm in which he held a substantial interest.[54] These actions will be examined more closely later; for now, the point to be made is that Sir Albert did appear to be trying to change the basis of Sierra Leone's economy in the direction of greater participation by Sierra Leoneans.

In the political sphere as well, Sir Albert moved to give his country a greater role in Africa and the world. He showed much more concern than his brother about pan-African and world affairs, taking his place among the more militant African leaders at the Commonwealth Conferences in discussions on Rhodesia[55] and ardently echoing the calls for unity of both Sekou Touré and Kwame Nkrumah, the leading apostles of an aggressively independent unified Africa.[56] One of his first acts in July 1964 was to stage a meeting with Sekou Touré, towards whom Sir Milton had been noticeably cool. In August 1964, Sierra Leone began serious talks on a regional free trade zone involving Guinea, Liberia and the Ivory Coast, and in February 1965 played host to the Defence Commission of the Organisation of African Unity.

Such moves on the international scene could be viewed by the sceptic as empty symbolism, as 'radical' gestures which would attract militants at home while not affecting the substance of Sierra Leone's internal relationships. But Sir Albert also tried to bring changes in the internal relationships of Sierra Leone, changes which played a large role in bringing him down. These changes could be summarised as attempts to concentrate power first, in his own hands, and secondarily, in the hands of individuals whose bases were in the 'modern' sector, who owed their positions to educational attainments and their hold on posts in the bureaucracy, the party and commercial enterprises. We have already noted that fact that he treated the chiefs as instruments to be used for the furtherance of the SLPP in ways which would undermine their standing with their people. Through his stress on increasing the availability of formal education, through attempts to increase the volume of cash-crop agriculture, and through his efforts to involve more youths and women directly in the SLPP, he provided more alternative channels to the chiefdom structures for participation in society than had been available under his brother. At the same time, his concern to utilise existing instruments for the consolidation of his own power led him to take advantage of the 1963 Local Courts Act to push some personal patronage appointments into Court Presidents' posts[57] and to become involved as a partisan in bitter local struggles over chieftaincy successions, rather than staying aloof as a mediator.[58]

All these actions aroused some antagonism, both on principle from 'traditionalists' who preferred Sir Milton's much more restrained approach both to forcing changes on chiefdom societies and to interference in the internal politics of chiefdoms, and on practical grounds from those who found the full weight of the Prime Minister's office turned against them in what had started as a local matter. Whether the Prime Minister's judgement on the costs and benefits of this course of action was sound will be considered later; the point to be made here is that Sir Albert's activities 'nationalised' far more political struggles than had been the case under his brother, and in so doing increased the opportunities for action of those whose power rested on their command of a Western-style 'rational' bureaucracy in which customary status counted for little.

Such changes clearly indicated a shift in the basis of legitimacy for

Sierra Leone's leaders. Much more than his brother, Sir Albert claimed to base his authority on the wishes of all the people of Sierra Leone, whose servant he claimed to be.[59] Many of his more ostentatious actions underlined this understanding of his legitimacy: the mass rallies, the press conferences carried live over the Sierra Leone Broadcasting Service (until mid-1965, when opposition newspapermen's questioning became too rough for his taste), and the policy whereby a day every week was set aside for any ordinary person to come to see him about any problem, all indicated attempts to convince the people that he was their Prime Minister, working for them. Conversely, those to whom he was shifting power were unlikely to accord him legitimacy on the basis of any 'right to rule', while those who still accepted this basis were being rendered less influential in politics.

Albert Margai's style of operation also had considerable effects on his performance as a Prime Minister. I have already cited his liking for ostentatious displays of his position[60] and his fondness for personal acquisitions, with their rather mixed effects on the degree of support he enjoyed. Another facet of his style was his keen interest in the details of government administration. Where Dr Margai could scarcely be persuaded to read documents more than a few lines long, Albert was prepared to work through the material necessary to keep a close eye on such complex and politically important Ministries as Interior and Development.[61] This readiness to concern himself with administrative detail did suggest an awareness by the Prime Minister that this was a necessary step in effectively controlling policies, especially as he became aware that the heavily Creole civil service might not be wholeheartedly in support of his goals. But it imposed as its cost a severe time constraint on the Prime Minister's opportunities to take long-range views, to consider the overall direction and consequences of his actions. Sir Albert Margai was not in any case inclined to look ahead; he tended to leap into a particular course of action without thought for the long-range effects, as the Kabala cows episode, the dissolution of the Freetown Council[62] and the unseating of four APC members of Parliament in 1965[63] all showed.

Coupled with his unwillingness or inability to take a long view was Margai's indecisiveness, or rather his tendency to be swayed back and forth in his views according to whoever was able to get to him at the right time. Now a person susceptible to the persuasion of others can still be swayed towards sound decisions if those who influence him have sound judgement. But here a further trait of Albert Margai's led him into difficulty. Despite his imposing manner and air of the self-confident party boss, Albert Margai seems to have been a rather shy and insecure man. He seemed unable or unwilling to develop close ties with older men or relatively recent acquaintances; not only were those who were generally regarded as his closest associates all comrades from the PNP days or earlier, but all were younger than he. He also seemed to want 'yes-men' in his Parliament; several of those whom he was supporting against his critics in the 1967 elections were conspicuous not only for their unquestioning devotion to him, but also for their lack of any strong personal base in the constituencies in which they decided to run.[64] This failure to develop close contacts with more experienced independent-minded individuals undoubtedly contributed to some of the costly blunders committed by Albert Margai during his brief years of leadership.

Albert Margai's enthusiasm for mass rallies, for contact with ordinary people (as long as they cheered him), and for ostentatious display of his 'big man' status, as well as his tendency to plunge into projects and to surround himself with younger men, all contrasted sharply with his brother's behaviour. They also suggested a very different basis for his emotional satisfaction from political life, the satisfaction that comes from the adulation of those with whom the leader is in contact.[65] This desire for adulation as the psychic basis for his political commitment dovetails neatly with the observable features of his political activity – the flamboyant gestures in policy, the choice of uncritical supporters, the sudden changes in approach and mood when things began to go badly,[66] and for that matter, the seeking after personal wealth, which was regarded as a symbolic indicator of high status. One danger with adulation as one's motive for undertaking the political struggle, however, is that one may lose sight of longer-range needs in seeking immediate praise; another danger is that one may be deceived into thinking that the people who praise one for their own motives are in agreement with one's overall goals; and a final danger is that the people whom one hears uttering praise may be a very small voice indeed. To all these dangers Albert Margai succumbed.

Sir Milton and Sir Albert: Some Implications of their Differences

In comparing the performance of the two Margai brothers as Prime Ministers, two facts must be kept firmly in mind: Dr Margai was Sierra Leone's first Prime Minister, and Albert followed him. Put crudely, this meant that Dr Margai could to a considerable extent shape the expectations of the Prime Ministerial role held by all those who worked with him (including even the British) whereas Albert had to take over a role in which the occupant's behaviour had been largely defined.[67] Dr Margai, for example, could choose to build an autonomous party organisation or to rely on the chiefs for electoral support; when Albert took over, the doctor's choice of the chiefs had become an entrenched part of the SLPP. Many of Albert Margai's problems as leader stemmed from the simple fact that when he took over, many of the expectations surrounding his new role had already been established in ways quite different from his own desires.

But having made this point, the effects of which will be more clearly seen when we examine specific cases, we must accept that the personalities of the two Prime Ministers had a considerable independent effect on their respective performances, regardless of the degree to which their roles were predefined. To summarise their differences briefly, Milton Margai leaned heavily towards those values and institutions which favoured the longer established power relationships and dominant persons in Sierra Leone societies, whereas Albert Margai tended to favour values and institutions more compatible with the ascendancy of persons whose status rested on their command of new techniques and resources. More specifically, Milton supported (as far as was compatible with a modern state) the institutions of chieftaincy and the associated complex of customary laws, secret societies and other elements of pre-colonial culture, and by and large sought to temper such exogenous pressures as economic change to enable these institutions to survive. Albert, by contrast, showed relatively less concern with the preservation of these 'traditional' institutions; his personal inclinations and his view of the ideal society combined to encourage the growth of a commercial society which allowed the rise of those with entrepreneurial and technological skills, and correspondingly downgraded men whose claim to superiority rested on heredity, knowledge of past customs, or other qualities irrelevant to a commercial economy.

The appearance of differences was heightened by the contrast in personal styles of the two men. Milton was abstemious in his living style, showing little interest in displays of either power or affluence; Albert showed a considerable appetite for all the earthly pleasures, and conspicuously enjoyed both the exercise of power and the display of his considerable wealth. Milton was slow and cautious in coming to a decision, but once he had made up his own mind, he would stick to his position regardless of how disastrously wrong it might be.[68] Albert was far less decisive in making up his mind, but would often plunge into an adventure with his mind only half made up, and then be forced into a humiliating retreat.[69] Quite independently of the policies he pursued, this style of Albert Margai's appeared to the more conservative elements in Sierra Leone society to threaten, and to the more impatient, to promise, wholesale social changes, an impression not always borne out by the reality of his policies.

More broadly, the two leaders' political appeals for support heightened the contrast between them. Dr Margai's style was almost pure 'brokerage'; he worked almost entirely with groups that had already thrust themselves into the political arena.[70] Albert, by contrast, attempted both as leader of the PNP and later as Prime Minister to mobilise the ordinary farmers by direct appeals, rather than relying on the chiefs to induce them to do the latter's bidding. This creative style, as was noted earlier, had its risks; those who already were participants in the political arena might resent invitations to newcomers, while the newcomers might not be drawn in a way that would be beneficial to the drawer. Yet even if he had seen these risks, Albert Margai's prejudices might well have led him to make this attempt, even if he had not seen it as the most promising way to bypass the chiefs.

Where Albert Margai, as a would-be policy innovator employing a creative style, ran into difficulties was in his lack of a clear ideology. I have indicated what appeared to be a 'bourgeois' set of values which inspired many of his actions; but it is not at all clear that these values formed a sufficiently coherent set of beliefs that they could direct his actions in a consistent pattern. Possibly the coherent set of beliefs was there without the will to implement them; but whatever the point at which the breakdown occurred, the beliefs were not translated into action. In fairness, we should recall the point I made earlier, that an innovator invariably appears less consistent than a conservative, and should note that Sir Milton's reluctance to take any action until forced to served to reduce his opportunities for inconsistency as well as the risks of making bad policies. Yet even making this allowance, Albert Margai seemed much less clearly guided by ideology than did his brother. I suggested earlier that the non-ideological leader could adapt most readily to new circumstances, but that he risked being unable to make fundamental changes because he lacked the vision to see when these were necessary, and the motivation to undertake a long-range effort to achieve them. A conservative ideologue like Sir Milton, by contrast, might be unable to adapt to new circumstances, but could fight more effectively to prevent a new situation from coming into being. It was the good fortune of Sir Milton, and the bad luck of Sir Albert, that changes building up under the former's regime did not come to a crisis point until the latter had taken power.

While the two brothers differed sharply in policies, in styles, in bases of legitimacy and in their ideological bearings, these differences were overshadowed by one common feature: both were Mendes, in a country where Mendes had a head start in filling 'modern' roles, but only comprised 30 per cent of the total population. Here Dr Margai's 'conservative' approach could only exacerbate ethnic conflict, while by the time his brother had a chance to try building new values and structures, he and his party were already suspect on ethnic grounds to a substantial part of the population. But before dealing with this problem (Chapter 6) we should explore the implications of their two approaches at the local level, since the chiefdoms provided a necessary political foundation for any elected leader.

Notes

1. *Models of Man,* New York, Wiley, 1957, p. 198.
2. Ibid., p. 205.
3. One proposal for a cost-benefit analysis, and a critique of Simon's 'satisficing' approach, is Alex Michalos, 'Rationality between the Maximisers and Satisficers', *Policy Science,* 4, 2, June 1973, pp. 229-44.
4. One could use a more 'scientific'-sounding term such as 'operational code', but the term 'prejudice' seems more apt because of its connotations of non-rationality.
5. See the article by Dr Margai, 'Welfare Work in a Secret Society', *African Affairs,* 48, 1948, pp. 227-30. We may also note as an indication of the chiefs' attitude that when he tried to have the Protectorate Assembly include funds for the scheme in the Development Estimates, all but two chiefs opposed him. *Proceedings of the Seventh Meeting,* 30 September 1950, pp. 61-5.
6. One of the African leaders with whom Dr Margai appeared to have the greatest rapport was Sir Abubaker Tafawa Balewa of Nigeria, who resembled Dr Margai in these respects probably more than any other African leader.
7. *Legislative Council Debates,* 1956-7, 25 Oct. 1956, p. 480.
8. See below, p. 156, note 82.
9. *Legislative Council Debates,* 16 Oct. 1956, p. 349.
10. Ordinance No. 33 of 1956.
11. From a speech in Kono District, reported in *Daily Mail,* 13 Feb. 1963.
12. *Proceedings of The Protectorate Assembly VIII,* 19 Oct. 1951, p. 41. The assembly voted 19-2 in favour of the transfer, preferring the argument that this expense should not be born by the chiefdoms, even though the District Councils derived their funds through precepts on the chiefdoms.
13. Quoted in his obituary, *Daily Mail,* 30 Apr. 1964.

14. This relationship went back to the time when Dr Margai first returned from his medical studies to Sierra Leone, when Dr Bankole-Bright fought for a suitable opening for him. In later years they still saw each other socially and played tennis together, and Dr Margai still referred to Bankole-Bright as 'my friend'.
15. This distinction goes back to Aristotle, although he considered rule by a monarch as that of a household head rather than that of the head of a state. See *The Politics,* trans. J.A. Sinclair, Harmondsworth, Penguin, 1962, Bk. I, Chs. 2 and 7.
16. One Minister claimed that Dr Margai would cut off dissidents in Cabinet with the comment, 'You're not as old as I am.' Interview with I.B. Taylor-Kamara, 8 July, 1968.
17. *Daily Mail,* 5 May 1961.
18. Testimony of Ernest Beoku-Betts before Shaw Commission, reported in *Daily Mail,* 26 Apr. 1955.
19. Quoted in ibid., 25 May 1960.
20. *Daily Mail,* 18 Oct. 1962.
21. Ibid., 31 Oct. 1962.
22. Ibid., 2 Nov. 1962.
23. For a summary of the case, see Sir Samuel Bankole-Jones, 'The Judiciary and the State: The West African Experience', paper presented at the Second Commonwealth Chief Justices' Conference, Port of Spain, Trinidad, April 1968, pp. 21-2.
24. *Daily Mail,* 6 Sept. 1962. This may have been a bit of sly mischief by 'Pa' Margai; several of Stevens's supporters sharply attacked him for taking part in a delegation which presented policies the APC did not accept.
25. Dr Margai not only would take up individual cases that opposition MPs brought to him, but also allowed these MPs to participate in the division of the Rural Development Grants within each constituency.
26. Memorandum from Prime Minister to Resident Ministers, 30 Jan. 1963. In Eastern Provinces File 13764/17.
27. His willingness to acknowledge a close relationship with J. Milhem, a Lebanese trader who was involved in several of the more questionable business deals in Sierra Leone, left some grounds for doubt. When Milhem's activities were attacked in the House of Representatives, Dr Margai commented that Milhem had lent him money to buy instruments for his nursing home, and 'wherever I am, he is my friend, but I would not like him to take advantage of government'. *House of Representatives Debates* (mimeo), 17 Jan. 1962, p. 146.
28. Chief Bai Farima Tass resigned as Minister without Portfolio in 1956 in consequence of his forced resignation from the chieftancy following the northern tax riots. Siaka Stevens and Albert Margai were not reappointed to the Cabinet following the 1957 election, partly in consequence of Albert's unsuccessful challenge for the SLPP leadership, partly, it is alleged, under pressure from the British Governor for their behaviour in allocating diamond licences.
29. *Report of the Commission . . . on . . . the Director of Audit's Report on the Accounts of Sierra Leone for the Year 1960/61.* Freetown, Government Printer, 1963 (hereafter *Cole Report*.)
30. Both stories were first told me by Sir Maurice Dorman, who had been Governor of Sierra Leone at that time, Personal interview, 20 Mar. 1973.
31. *Daily Mail,* 13 Feb. 1959.
32. Ibid., 11 Feb. 1959.
33. However, he also held back for several months from appointing his old

friend A.J. Momoh as Chairman of the Civil Service Commission, even though many Creoles as well as up-country people pressed for Momoh's appointment.

34. James L. Payne and Oliver H. Woshinsky, 'Incentives for Political Participation', *World Politics*, XXIV, 4 July 1972, pp. 518-46.
35. His widow commented ruefully that even when he was a student, he always had a very strong feeling that he must return home to work for his people's freedom. Interview with Lady Margai, 8 Apr. 1973.
36. *The Times*, London, 6 May 1964, p. 13.
37. That he possessed an innate reserve and caution regarding even those matters where his actions were unlikely to make any difference is suggested by his attitude towards African unity. While he claimed to support unity as an eventual goal he felt constrained to observe that 'even Europe has not succeeded in forming a political union after many years'. Quoted in *Daily Mail*, 18 May 1963.
38. The first heated argument to take place in the Protectorate Assembly arose in 1949, when Albert charged that the government's education policy was 'a deliberate attempt to lower the standard of education in the country'. The Director of Education retorted that Margai did not take 'a sufficiently serious view of his responsibilities as a member of this Assembly'. See *Protectorate Assembly Debates*, V, 5 May 1949, pp. 42 and 49.
39. The General Secretary of the SLPP wrote to Dr Margai concerning an election-eve broadcast in Freetown, 'I hope that Albert will deliver that one.' Letter from H.E.B. John to Dr M.A.S. Margai, 5 Nov. 1951.
40. See *African Standard*, 27 Jan. 1950.
41. See the interview with Albert Margai in the (Bo) *Observer* (then the SLPP paper), 11 Apr. 1953, for their differences over the Chief Commissioner and above, p. 64, for their differences over diamond policy.
42. The commission noted Sir Albert's involvement in, among other ventures, Strieby Poultry Farm, Sea Products Limited, and Construction and Design Company, the last named the holder of a number of government construction contacts. He also owned a considerable number of properties in Sierra Leone, England and the United States, as well as being the recipient of several thousand pounds from mysterious sources in his London bank account and unknown sums in his self-elected capacity as SLPP treasurer. The commission claimed that Sir Albert had received at least £200,000 beyond his lawful income during his thirty-five months as Prime Minister. See *Report of the Forster Commission of Enquiry on Assets of Ex-Ministers and Ex-Deputy Ministers*. Freetown, Government Printer, 1958, pp. 59-66.
43. This announcement came in response to a question at his monthly press conference broadcast live over the Sierra Leone Broadcasting Service. Notes by the writer, 12 Jan. 1965.
44. The fact that the minister was a Mende and the chief a northerner lent a further 'tribal' dimension to the affair.
45. See *We Yone* (the APC newspaper), 6 Mar. 1965, for an account of the episode.
46. M.A. Bash-Taqui charged in the House of Representatives that the bill had been Le 1,940, while the Forster Commission later cited a figure of Le 1,817.67 for the cattle not only from this trip but also from other visits up-country. See *House of Representatives Debates*, 1965-6, I, 29 Mar. 1965, col. 187, and *Forster Report*, p. 63, for their respective comments.
47. *House of Representatives Debates*, 1965-6, I, 30 Mar. 1965, col. 266.
48. See *We Yone*, 6 Aug. 1966.
49. See *Unity*, 13 Aug. 1966, interview with 'Frank Blunt'.

50. Personal interview, 22 Feb. 1973.
51. See *Protectorate Assembly*, V, 5 May 1949, pp. 51-4.
52. See his comments in ibid., VI, 5 Oct. 1959, and in the *Legislative Council Debates* 1951-2, 29 Nov. 1951, p. 10.
53. See below pp. 184, 255.
54. It is possible that Sea Products was not entirely a beneficiary of this move, since it depended for some of its own supplies on the catches of other fishermen, and the Ghanaians were the most efficient and reliable suppliers.
55. For example, in 1966 at Lagos he attacked Harold Wilson's arguments as 'vague, evasive and unconvincing' and demanded that Britain use force against the Smith regime. See *Daily Mail*, 13 Jan. 1966.
56. See the *Convention 1964 Report*, pp.26-7.
57. See below p. 144-5.
58. The Nongoaw dispute, below pp. 145-6 is a good illustration of the hazards of this approach.
59. See, for example, his argument for the introduction of a one-party state, *House of Representatives Debates*, 1965-6, 21 Dec. 1965, cols. 51-2; also the pamphlet *Albert Margai of Africa*, Freetown, Information Department, n.d., apparently by Bankole Timothy, which repeatedly stressed his accessibility to 'the people'.
60. We may also note the size of his delegations to the 1964 and 1965 Commonwealth Prime Ministers' Conferences, which numbered seventeen and thirty-three respectively, as well as his use of the Army Commanding Officer and the Commissioner of Police to accompany him on tours to both state and party rallies.
61. He was his own Minister of Development, and had all chiefdom disputes of any political significance channelled through Interior to his own desk.
62. In 1964 an APC Freetown councillor sought a Supreme Court judgement that the council was illegally constituted. The court accepted his contention, but left it to Council to remedy the illegality. The Prime Minister then leapt in with a Bill altering the Council drastically but cutting its nominated membership in half and providing for all councillors to be elected at the same time every three years. In a city where only a third of the seats had been consistently SLPP, such a move risked allowing the opposition to gain control of the capital's government, which it in fact did.
63. This last was a change in the rules of the House of Representatives which, by providing that any member who absented himself from the House for thirty days during an annual session 'without reasonable excuse' would lose his seat. Since the decision on what constituted 'a reasonable excuse' was to be made by a committee on which the SLPP would have a majority, and since four APC members were at the time beginning one-year prison sentences for riot and assault resulting from an election fight, the outcome was not hard to predict. But this method of unseating the APC members gave them the air of martyrs, and hardened northern resistance to Sir Albert.
64. A.B. Paila and James During, running in Moyamba North and Kenema Central, had spent much of their adult lives in Freetown, while in Bombali, three of the four SLPP nominees were Fulas, who generally were regarded as 'strangers' in the area, since they had no chiefdom of their own.
65. See Payne and Woshinsky, 'Incentives for Political Participation', pp. 521 4.
66. A striking illustration of the Prime Minister's changeability when things went badly was his behaviour at the Freetown rally in January 1966 when he was trying to win support for the one-party state. If ever there was a time when he should have been conciliatory and sweetly reasonable, this

was it. But when at the outset of his speech, he ran into strong heckling from a relatively small group, and widespread indifference from the rest of the audience, his tone became menacing, and eventually he warned 'the Freetown people' that he would impose the one-party state regardless of their wishes.

67. Montesquieu's observation is apt: 'At the birth of societies, it is the leaders of the commonwealth who create the institutions; afterwards it is the institutions that shape the leaders.' Cited in Rustow, *Philosophers and Kings*, p. 27.

68. For example, if Dr Margai had not been overruled by the British and his colleagues, his refusal to deal with Marcus Grant, the leader of the 1955 Freetown strikers, could have allowed the riots to get completely out of control. See above, p. 96.

69. The one-party state fiasco in 1965-6 is a case in point. See above, p. 77-9.

70. One possible case of Dr Margai appealing to a group which otherwise did not participate in politics was his work with the Bundu Society (see above, p. 92). But he does not seem to have used this activity to cultivate political support from women.

5 NATIONAL LEADERS AND LOCAL POLITICS

Political struggles at the local level in an African state may seem quite unimportant to an observer concerned with the actions of the national leadership. Such struggles tend to be largely personal or factional, not based on any broader social divisions. Since the participants tend to be largely in the 'residual' sector, their actions will have little if any impact upon the national arena. And even if their actions do affect the national arena, local leaders have to operate within both legal and financial frameworks set by the national leaders, and are open to fairly drastic coercion if they overtly oppose the national leadership.

Yet a national leader wishing to ensure his survival must pay some attention to local needs and problems in both urban and rural areas. He needs above all to assure himself of two things: sufficient popular acceptance of his rule to ensure its continuance, and sufficient economic resources to maintain the national political organisation.

It is possible, at least where governmental needs are modest, for a national government to obtain its economic resources from a very narrow base (for example, a rich mining enclave), and thus leave the bulk of the populace alone. But in most African states, as elsewhere in the world, any hope of expanding the resources available to meet the increasing range of perceived needs depends ultimately upon widespread productive economic activity by its citizens. There simply is not the revenue available to build dispensaries and roads, or even to pay the salaries of administrators and politicians, if the ordinary farmer decides to stop growing his coffee or sisal, or the miner decides to go back to a subsistence farm. The Sierra Leone government, with its two major mineral enclaves, was less dependent upon the revenues generated from the widespread dispersion of men into the money economy than were most other African states[1] but it nevertheless directly or indirectly derived perhaps a quarter of its revenue from the activities of the cash-crop sector.[2] Less direct, but equally important, was the fact that most of the staple foodstuffs that fed city-dwellers came from Sierra Leone's own farms.[3] If cash-crop farmers were to withdraw quietly back to more localised subsistence economies, the combination of a loss of tax revenue and of hunger in the cities would be devastating for any government.

In most African states, as the opportunities for a peaceful removal of the government were steadily curtailed, 'popular acceptance' came to mean increasingly 'acquiescence', an absence of such manifest indicators of discontent as riots, rebellions and attempted coups d'etat. Since such actions not only threatened the government's existence directly, but also undermined it indirectly both by impairing productivity and by scaring off prospective investors, most governments made some effort to respond to demand before they reached this stage. Somewhat greater responsiveness was required in those states where domestic rivals still could compete with the leader for the right to occupy his position.[4] In Sierra Leone's Parliamentary system, the Prime Minister needed to be sufficienty responsive to demands to obtain pluralities of votes for his supporters in a majority of the country's constituencies at elections.[5] While few other states required such a positive show of support for their existing leadership, any leader who wished to survive organised some form of communication with his people.

In any regime, communication between ruler and ruled is a two-way process. The leader must be able to transmit his wishes downwards, in order to implement his decisions, and (sometimes) to explain them. At the same time, he needs information transmitted upwards from the grass-roots, to know 'what he can get away with' and what the likely costs of alternative actions would be. Both types of communication require intermediaries between the leader and the populace, but both place conflicting demands upon any potential intermediaries. An intermediary willing to carry the leader's views and decisions downwards must necessarily have some commitment to the leader. But at the same time, if he is to be able to get those views or decisions accepted by his community, he must have some standing in that community. Similarly, to gather information and express local sentiments accurately, an intermediary must be an accepted member of the local community, but at the same time, if he is to be of any use to the leader, he must have sufficient commitment to the leader that the latter can rely on him to provide accurate information.

Clearly, these requirements can often conflict with each other, and the intermediary's commitment to one side must be at the expense of the other. What, for example, is he to do when from the leader's perspective a new road or factory is best located in another community, but by exercising his persuasive powers the intermediary may alter the decision in favour of his own community? What is he to do when his community comes to feel the leader is biased against them? It has even been suggested that in the case of communities heavily insulated against contact with the outside world, the very act of dealing with outsiders renders an individual suspect to his community, although I think this would be an exceptional situation in most of Africa.[6]

We can consider the relations between leaders, intermediaries and the populace from a number of perspectives: the nature of the intermediaries' response to the conflicting demands of their role; the type of links the intermediaries provide between the leader and the populace; and the way the leader's beliefs and style affect his selection of intermediaries.

Since the responses intermediaries may make to the demands placed on them pull them in either one of two directions, we may characterise intermediaries as either 'loyal' in the sense that they are committed to the leader, or 'strong' in the sense that they are influential in their local community. The 'loyal' intermediary (a civil servant or centrally-appointed party organiser, for example) is free to push hard for changes in the community, since he is not tied to the local 'Establishment'. He is also willing to do the leader's bidding not in hope of a quick material payoff, but out of the longer-term commitment which Bailey terms 'faith'.[7] But these advantages are balanced by a serious drawback; the 'loyal' intermediary's virtue of lacking ties to the local community also means that he is unlikely to be able to command much support within it, and thus will have considerable difficulty in implementing his leader's wishes, to the extent that these wishes require local co-operation.

The 'strong' intermediary, because of his standing in the local community, should be able to gather more accurate information, and if he wishes, to influence the community to do what the leader wishes. But because he has no other reason to work for the leader, he needs more short-run payoff to induce him to act as an intermediary. More serious is the fact that since the 'strong' intermediary is strong precisely because of his position as a local leader within the *status quo* (and this applies even if he is a member of a 'counter-elite') he is hardly going to do the leader's bidding in working for changes that might jeopardise his position.

In rural Africa, customary local leaders tended to be 'strong'.[8] Although subject to the coercive force of the central bureaucracy from above, and to the power of their people to refuse to co-operate as a force from below, the rural leaders generally were the only effective links between these two elements; the bureaucrats were powerless to impose changes from above without their co-operation. Bureaucracies were generally too thin on the ground to offer an alternative hierarchy of rewards. Where a party was well organised, it might offer such an alternative structure, but there was always the problem that it might be captured at the local level by the 'strong' intermediaries.[9] In countries such as Sierra Leone, where the bureacracy was thin and party structures non-existent, leaders had no choice but to rely on the available 'strong' intermediaries, who could act as links so long as no horizontal lines of cleavage divided them from their people.[10]

This brings us to a second perspective from which we can view the relations between the national leader and the various local arenas. Broadly speaking, a leader can link himself to the populace in two ways; he can make a direct appeal to them based on a perceived identity of interests, with intermediaries acting solely as transmission belts or cadres carrying orders and information, or he can confine his direct appeal to the intermediaries, leaving them to bind their followers to themselves by whatever means they think suitable, no matter how divergent their appeals may be from those of the leader. We may term these two models of relationships between the leader and the populace the 'direct contact' and the 'indirect contact' models respectively.

The appeal made by a leader in the 'direct contact' model will focus upon broad collective or group benefits, which can be either of a material or of an intangible nature. It can be to the entire membership of the state, or maybe to a lesser collectivity, such as a particular class or ethnic group, but it has to be cast in terms of group benefits rather than personal ones (e.g. 'Jobs for all' rather than 'A job for Joe'). It tends to be made in societies with a high level of internal communications, and with a sufficient level of affluence that individuals can respond to its relatively altruistic goal of benefits for a somewhat abstract collectivity, rather than benefits for the individual alone, although under certain conditions it can also be effective in societies with poor communications and low standards of living. In this latter case the key condition appears to be the perception that a group is being disadvantaged, and that there is no hope for the individual to avoid the disadvantages accruing to his group by individual action.[11] Such a situation, of course, implies a sufficient degree of pluralism within the polity that such a leader, who is in opposition to other leaders in the polity, would be permitted to survive. But it is also possible for a leader to appeal to the entire population of the state as an 'oppressed class'.[12]

Intermediaries in the 'direct contact' model are clearly expected to by 'loyal'; a leader probably will be pleased if they can command support in their own communities, but the essential feature is that they express the identity of interest between him and the populace. It is also unlikely that the intermediaries will be bound to the leader merely by personal material considerations; he needs the more enduring commitment of 'moral' followers, even with the concomitant limitations on his freedom of manoeuvre that this entails.

The 'indirect contact' model seems primarily applicable to those societies in which a form of clientage based primarily upon material pay-offs has supplanted (or at least found a significant place alongside) traditional collective loyalties, yet has not in its turn been supplanted by the growth of horizontal 'class' solidarities.[13] 'Traditional' political systems were, it is true, often built upon clientage, and sometimes, as in the Fulani-Hausa states, were of a scale comparable to contemporary states.[14] Yet holding the clientage system together there was usually a strong non-material (usually religious) bond providing an overarching unity of values throughout the length of the clientage chain. It is this unity based on a non-material bond that is weak or lacking in the 'indirect contact' model; the leader binds his intermediaries to him through some form of inducement that is relevant to their circumstances only, either individually or collectively, while they in turn make their own choice of inducements to bind their own followers to them. While both[15] levels can utilise non-material appeals (for example, a chief may keep his followers bound to him through their acceptance of traditional patterns of deference[16]) it seems more common to find material payoffs serving as the primary cement which holds each link together.[17]

Such payoffs will naturally be put in terms of individual benefits bestowed by the patron on his client. Lines of contact in this system run vertically, and persons in the same stratum are generally competing against each other as patrons or clients. It is of no concern to the patron how his client in turn obtains *his* following, so long as it is not used against the patron's interests. Such a system tends strongly towards pragmatic, personal and material appeals, rather than ideological and collective ones. It also requires each patron, including the national leader at the top of the chain, to spend time servicing each client individually; in this it is the antithesis of the 'direct contact' model, with its tendency to develop routines and impersonal rules to facilitate the handling of individual needs.

Since the leader is concerned only with the results obtained by his clients, he wants 'strong' intermediaries; their loyalty is useless to him if they lack sufficient standing among their own people to provide him with whatever resources he requires for them. Nor is it particularly important to him that the basis of their commitment is a relatively enduring one, so long as he maintains sufficient resources to keep them committed on 'mercenary' grounds.

We can suggest, then, that there are two probable patterns of contact between the leader and the populace: a direct appeal through loyal intermediaries, based to a substantial degree upon a notion of collective solidarity and upon non-material considerations; and a pattern of indirect links, through strong intermediaries, with the various links in the chain forged by appeals to personal self-interest, generally of a material nature. The pattern to which a leader will approximate depends in part upon his beliefs and style, but also upon the raw human resources available for him when he attempts to forge a pattern of contacts to his liking.

The non-ideological leader employing a brokerage style can work quite happily through indirect links and strong intermediaries. With no strong value commitments of his own, he suffers no hardship from the bias towards the *status quo* which is inherent in using strong intermediaries; and such intermediaries can not only represent what he can accept as the significant viewpoints in the polity, but provided he manages to find equitable compromises between their conflicting demands, they can maintain adequate support behind him, as long as they do in fact remain 'strong'. The main drawback to using this approach is the time required to service it, but the non-ideological leader may well find it a less costly alternative than relying on a direct appeal. The direct appeal entails working out policies which will produce a widespread commitment to the leader, developing channels through which such appeals can be made, and maintaining a degree of consistency in this approach, all of which entails as much effort on the leader's part as servicing personal patronage links. The need to develop consistency in his appeal is a major drawback for the non-ideological leader wishing to utilise a direct contact approach through loyal intermediaries. It may still be desirable for him to use it, at least in a society where such collective considerations have become paramount; but otherwise he will generally find the indirect contact approach less demanding.

The conservative ideologue can also work fairly happily through indirect contacts and strong intermediaries, although he is likely to have a rather stronger desire to have his beliefs accepted down all the links of the chain to the grassroots. He will be more inclined than the non-ideologue to attempt a direct appeal if he perceives either an external or internal threat to established values,[18] although against this must be weighed the likelihood that his view of 'proper' behaviour for the masses is that they should defer to the wishes of those above them in the hierarchy, without their capabilities being dignified by a direct appeal from the top of the hierarchy. Generally, then, he too will tend to the indirect approach, provided that those beneath him share his values on what constitute proper relationships.

The radical ideologue, by contrast, cannot work through an indirect appeal or strong intermediaries. If his mission is to change the values of society, it follows that he must be able to appeal directly to the mass of the people to support him, and that the intermediaries who carry his message must be loyal to him. If successful, his creative style will draw into the political arena participants who can become the 'loyal' cadres he needs to bypass the existing strong intermediaries. But if he cannot develop these loyal cadres, and make his direct appeal, his attempts to build a new order are likely to fail.

A leader's wishes may be thwarted, however, by a lack of suitable material for him to work with. The radical ideologue, as just noted, must be able to draw out the potential cadres to man a party or bureaucratic organisation, or his hopes of reaching the people with his plans for change will come to naught, since he will be forced back to a reliance on the 'strong' intermediaries who, we noted earlier, were unlikely instruments of change. The conservative ideologue, on the other hand, may be faced with an opposite problem: what to do with already mobilised persons wanting changes he is unwilling to provide.[19] He may be able to absorb or co-opt them into the system up to a point, but after a time, the pressure for change can easily become intolerable. The non-ideological leader has perhaps the easiest time; he can quite easily leave potential sources of demand for change quiescent, or if they have already been mobilised, can come to terms with them. His major problem is reaching an accommodation between the conflicting demands of those wishing change and those wishing to retain the *status quo*.

In Sierra Leone at the start of decolonisation, a leader seeking radical changes would have faced a difficult prospect because of the non-availability of loyal intermediaries. The civil service was too thin on the ground, with no more than four or five field men in each district[20] and furthermore, both the British and their Creole successors strongly upheld the idea that civil servants should not act as political agents of the government of the day. A political party might have been able to obtain sufficient cadres of 'young men' to organise a movement by-passing the Paramount Chiefs, but a combination of the latter's range of powers for harassment and a widespread preference for supporting only 'sons of the soil' offered formidable obstacles to this course. As time went on and a growing body of potential alternative intermediaries to the chiefs developed, the hold on local power established by the chiefs under the SLPP contributed to forcing these newcomers into opposition parties.[21] The position and powers of the chiefs, and the choices open to national leaders in dealing with the chiefs, form the subject matter of the remainder of this chapter.

The Distribution of Power in the Local Arena

Throughout the period of this study, the Paramount Chiefs remained the central actors in the most important local arenas, the chiefdoms.[22] While studies on chieftaincy in Sierra Leone as elsewhere discussed the evident weakening of the chief's position[23] under the threefold pressures of central government demands from above, popular shifts in attitude below, and rivalry from other potential intermediaries, still there is no denying the fact that no other single role in a chiefdom offered the range of potential powers open to a chief. From the establishment of the Protectorate onwards, the British administration sought to maintain the Paramount Chief as the central figure of authority in the chiefdom, responsible for dispensing justice (at least to natives of the Protectorate), collecting taxes and initiating such small developmental projects as the local revenue would support.

In 1937 a series of Ordinances sought to rationalise the rather loose legal and financial relationships existing between the chief, his elders and his people. The 'Tribal Authority' was officially proclaimed as the governing body of the chiefdom, though its composition and method of selection were left vaguely described as

> the Paramount Chief, the chiefs, the councillors and men of note elected by the people according to native law and custom, approved by the Governor and appointed...[24]

This vagueness facilitated the chief's ability to control the composition of the Tribal Authority, although a prudent chief would allow 'natural' spokesmen to emerge for all important sections of the chiefdom, and would only act to remove particularly dangerous individuals. Generally, however, he could be sure that the TA would do his bidding.[25] The only time the TA functioned free from chiefly dominance was when it had to elect a new chief.[26]

Financial controls in theory were more stringent. A Chiefdom Treasuries Ordinance was supposed to replace the hitherto unregulated and *ad hoc* collection of tributes and levies by a Chiefdom Tax (on top of the central government's House Tax), paid into a treasury where a proper accounting of income and expenditure could be maintained. In fact what generally happened was that the chief (and his subordinates, including the new chiefdom clerk) continued to collect such tributes as they wished, recording only that portion which was necessary to account for the officially sanctioned expenditures of the chiefdom. It was largely these unregulated and illegal collections which eventually led to the explosion in the North.[27] However, even though this 'rationalisation' made little practical difference it did leave the chief open to tighter supervision and censure from the central administration, and also introduced a further literate individual into the chiefdom's administration, the chiefdom clerk who was responsible for keeping the accounts as well as a written record of bylaws, court proceedings and other actions. Though the clerk because of his youth was frequently regarded as a 'small boy' by the Tribal Authorities, his control over the written records and the accounts gave him a powerful position within the chiefdom, a position hardly commensurate with the scanty salary he received as his only legal compensation.[28]

A further change also envisaged in the 1937 Ordinances was not brought into widespread use until after the 1955-6 riots. This was the replacement of the chief by another individual styled 'Court President' as head of the Native Administration court. Since much of a chief's prestige rested on his ability to judge disputes between his 'children' (the people of his chiefdom) his replacement as head of the court was the most severe blow of all. By the time of Independence, the chief faced several rival foci of power in his chiefdom – the Court President, the longer-standing Chiefdom Speaker[29] and even the chiefdom clerk. However, he was still recognised as head of the chiefdom, and his position was buttressed by the special position reserved for chiefs in the District Councils,[30] and in the national legislature.[31]

None of these changes came about with undue haste. The rationalisation of chiefdom administrations did not gain momentum until after the Second World War; in 1948, fifty-five of 191 chiefdoms were still 'unreformed',[32] and one remained unreformed up to Independence. The replacement of chiefs as heads of the NA courts was likewise a lengthy process, starting in the mid-1950s and not being completed until Independence. Some of the factors in this delay will be considered below.

The changes in chieftaincy were in part attributable to an influx of more broadly educated new chiefs. The percentage of literate chiefs rose from 24 per cent in 1948 to 56 per cent in 1962,[33] as men came to see chieftaincy as a worthwhile prize, both for political action and for personal aggrandisement.[34] While this frequently meant that the chiefs were the foremost agents for economic development in their chiefdoms,[35] it also meant that they often took rather lightly the traditional restraints on their behaviour.[36]

While the chiefs' conception of their role was thus changing, changes in their environment were setting up new poles of influence to challenge them. The most obvious of these changes took place within the chiefdoms as delayed results of the pre-war 'reform: ordinances. The introduction of regulations governing the chiefs' levies did not in practice greatly alter the flow of wealth to them, but it did leave them vulnerable to deposition or other disciplinary action by the central government. The educated members of rival ruling families were quick to make use of this weapon to bring the government down on their side against a ruling chief, at least in those societies such as the Mende which judged their chief on his instrumental performance. Barrows had made the important point that at least in Mende country, 'populist' protests against financial and other abuses by chiefs were almost invariably instigated by the 'big men' of rival factions,[37] with the goal being the replacement of the current chief rather than the toppling of the structure of chieftaincy. 'Populist' discontent also existed, as we shall see below, but undoubtedly it was often brought to the surface only to further the ascendancy of a rival to the chief.[38]

The most severe single blow to the chiefs during this period was the introduction of Court Presidents during the late 1950s. None of the existing members of the Tribal Authority, even the chiefdom speaker and the section chiefs, took roles which usurped that of the Paramount Chief. But the Court President's role of judging disputes was one which had been central to Paramount Chiefs throughout Sierra Leone. Even if, as often happened up to 1963, the chief through the TA was able to select as Court President an individual whom he could control, still this was another man taking over the chief's main function. Barrows states that in Kenema his informants 'were almost unanimous in pointing to the imposition of Court Presidents as a major cause' of the lowering of respect for chiefs.[39] My own country-wide survey produced similar results. In response to the question 'How do the chief's jobs differ from what they were in the past?' the only specific change cited (by 36 per cent of the respondents) was the loss of his power to judge local disputes.[40]

Economic changes beyond the control of the chiefs also made the boundaries of the local arena more porous, and allowed new linkages to develop across these boundaries. The increased wealth that had become available both through increased trade (particularly diamond dealing) and more directly through national politics, set up a number of new rivals to the chief. Part of the chief's power stemmed from his position as a patron, able to offer protection and sustenance to his people when they needed it. At the same time as the rationalisation of the local chiefdom administration attenuated the chief's personal ties with his people, through the interposition of a chiefdom treasury, a clerk and rules for using resources, other potential patrons appeared in the form of wealthy traders, who operated free of several of the restraints on the chief-as-patron. The 'big man' outside the chiefly structure was not under the chief's obligation to treat equitably all people in the chiefdom; he could select as clients those who provided the greatest 'payoff'. He was not limited, as was the chief, to operating in a single chiefdom, but was free to draw on the resources of the major town in the area, even if this was located in another chiefdom. Thus the wealthy commoner could become a formidable rival to the chief for influence.[41]

The incursion of national electoral politics into the chiefdoms created further poles of influence in competition with the chiefs. Though the candidates of the Sierra Leone Peoples Party were for the most part drawn from the chiefly milieu, and relied generally upon the chiefs to influence voters in their favour, still they competed with the chiefs in several ways. First, the successful politican would often be from a rival ruling family, or of a rival faction to the chief, who had managed to bring together a coalition of dissidents to the chief's rule, and might continue to work against the chief's powers. Second, the Member of Parliament's constituency generally comprised more than one chiefdom, and thus he would not be exclusively beholden to any one chief, even where he was not of a rival family. Third, the MP's arena involved a rather different set of contacts than the chief's; in particular, his greater proximity to Ministers gave him an edge in the discretionary allocation of small local amenities over the chief, whose dealings were more often with administrators.

Despite these assets, MPs as a group seem to have been regarded as considerably less useful than chiefs for patronage functions. In my 1968 survey 42 per cent of the respondents cited the Paramount Chief as the man who initiated local projects, as against 1 per cent citing the MP. Even in a function in which the MP had the greatest advantage over the Paramount Chief, contacting the national government, the survey results were rather surprising: forty-seven respondents (34 per cent) said they would contact the national government through the Paramount Chief, while only twelve (9 per cent) would go through their local MP.[42]

The process by which national and local politics became intertwined was not a simple one-way one. While national rivalries worked their way down into the chiefdom arena, chiefdom conflicts could also move up into the national arena, sometimes with costly results for the national leader. For example, a long-standing rivalry in Samu chiefdom, Kambia district, led to a polarisation of the chiefdom into 'SLPP' and 'APC' factions built around local ruling families. One investigation after the 1955-6 riots concluded that charges against Paramount Chief Bai Sherbro Yumkella III were unfounded and attributable to the hostility between him and the leader of the rival ruling family, Yolla Bangura.[43] Sir Milton Margai's attempts to mediate between the rivals failed[44] and since Yumkella was firmly aligned with the SLPP, Bangura turned to the APC upon its formation. In 1963 he, his son and several relatives were banished by the government from Samu chiefdom, and the APC henceforth used this banishment as an illustration of the oppressiveness of the SLPP government. This conflict illustrated well the costs to a national leader of being drawn into what started as a local quarrel; by acting at the request of a rather unpopular Northern chief, Sir Milton drew upon his 'Mende man's government' the odium of a harsh punishment meted out to a Temne dissenter, and thus helped increase northern concern over 'Mende dominance'.

While the proliferation of roles in direct competition with him were clearly the most likely to undermine the chief's position, we should also note the growth of a more indirect source of competition. In the 1950s and 1960s there was a steady increase in the number of national government specialists working in the field, beginning with the much appreciated medical personnel and teachers[45] and in course of time agriculturists, foresters, co-operative organisers, engineers and others who would propose a range of undertakings that they considered would benefit the people of the chiefdoms. Although they were not competing overtly with the chiefs for clientele, the very fact that the benefits they could offer were ones outside the chief's powers served to undermine the comprehensive nature of the chief's relationship with his people.

The challenges to the chiefs we have noted so far are all challenges presented by alternative roles fulfilling essentially the same function, that of bridging a discontinuity between statuses. Like the chief, the trader-patron, Member of Parliament, Court President and civil servant could each offer the benefits of their powers to other individuals whose status precluded them from such powers, and in return they could extract resources from those individuals. This 'factional' or 'clientage' model would set persons of a particular status against each other as competitors for the individualised benefits various patrons could bestow, and thus produce vertical alignments in the polity. But another model of relationships in the long run was even more menacing to the chiefs. If all persons dependent upon the chief as patron came to see his role as antagonistic to them, and united as a 'class' in opposition to the claims of the chief (and other patrons) then the chances were high that this class would support leaders who would seek to replace this entire relationship with a much more 'direct' form of contact between national leader and populace.[46]

Several groups in Sierra Leone seemed particularly likely to provide the basis for such a movement from a 'clientage' to a 'class' alignment. The 'sub-elite' of school leavers, whose aspirations often outran their training, would be hard put to see the chiefs' relevance to their needs, and could easily see them as oppressive. The labourers, artisans and other non-farm workers who had committed themselves to the insecurity of the money economy found themselves looking up from the bottom of a very long economic ladder. Their discontent would be directed more against the national elite, but they could easily see the chiefs as unnecessary. Finally, the small farmers forced into the money economy to meet their chief's cash levies would see him as positively oppressive in his demands for money, his control over land allocation and his standards of punishment for dissenters.

The first of these groups, the partially educated sub-elite, was too small in numbers to make a great direct impact on chieftaincy. If we take all those with primary education as a rough approximation of this group, in 1963 it numbered only 88,647 in all the provinces,[47] and most of these were in the larger towns. Their main threat would be their ability to furnish organising cadres for more numerous groups of the discontented.

The second group, the persons plunged abruptly into the bottom levels of the money economy, would include all those who left their villages to go diamond digging, as well as most persons in the larger towns, most petty traders, and in fact most non-farm workers and a good many persons working for hire on farms as well. While calculating the size of this group is a very hazardous business, we can get an extremely rough approximation, probably erring on the low side, by taking all persons who were not at the one end professional, managerial or clerical workers, and at the other end, self-employed farmers, fishermen and loggers and household help. In 1963 this group numbered some 175,509 persons.[48] Again, this group was concentrated in the towns, and would see chieftaincy more as an irrelevancy than as a positive evil. One could also consider many of the 170,000-odd farmers who relied primarily on cash crop sales[49] as being committed to the money economy, and again near the bottom. If this group also became disaffected with chieftaincy, the total body of potentially discontented would become fairly formidable in size.

The third group, the smaller farmers whose main contact with the money economy was forced sales of part of their crop to meet their chiefs' demands for taxes, was rather more likely to see the chief as an oppressive figure. Any attempt to calculate the size of this group is essentially guesswork; but to suggest that half of Sierra Leone's 700,000 farmers fell into this category might not be too far off the mark. The anti-chief riots which sometimes erupted in Sierra Leone chiefdoms might be taken as indicators of a latent discontent among this group: although as we noted earlier many of these uprisings were instigated by the chief's rivals, still the very fact that such mass risings could be stimulated fairly easily suggested something more than manipulation by members of the local elite, and certainly the spontaneity and extent of the 1955-6 northern riots suggested a widespread 'populist' discontent with the way many chiefs and TAs were running their chiefdoms.

Two factors, however, worked to hinder this potential discontent being incorporated into a 'populist' political movement aimed at curbing chieftaincy. The first was that while small farmers might grumble about the chiefdom government's impositions, they would find it hard to conceive of a universe in which a different system of rule existed.[50] To illustrate, the 1968 survey found that while small farmers[51] tended to be more discontented with local government structures than other groups (for example, 50 per cent saw the TA as doing only a 'fair' or 'poor' job, as against 38 per cent of the whole sample; 58 per cent saw the local court as showing biases, against 39 per cent for the whole sample[52]) at the same time they tended to favour special privileges for the chiefs (for example 87 per cent said the chief should have a 'big farm', against 73 per cent for the whole sample). The same point, that discontent with the functioning of an institution did not necessarily lead to a demand for change in that institution, had been made earlier by an anthropologist in a detailed study of the greed and mistreatment perpetrated by one chiefdom's successive Paramounts:

> Throughout the experience of misrule by three chiefs from the two ruling houses, the subjects never questioned or rejected the institution of chieftaincy and the right of the two ruling houses to rule.[53]

But even if the discontent felt by small farmers could be transmuted into a desire to end chieftaincy as an institution, a further obstacle faced them: the age-old conflict between the mass of men who would come to feel that an institution must be changed, and the leaders who would articulate their demands but when they came to occupy the seats of government would decide that the institution was too useful as a device for controlling their followers to give it up. Since most Sierra Leoneans did not desire the end of chieftaincy, this conflict did not arise, although the APC's policy of supporting the chiefs after 1968 must have seemed like just such a betrayal to its minority of 'radical' followers. However, there was certainly a conflict between what probably were the (unarticulated) aims of the small farmers who saw the chiefs as oppressors, and the groups, particularly the educated sub-elite, who saw them as irrelevant; the latter's approach, at least as epitomised by the APC, was to tighten central curbs on the chiefs' behaviour and to bypass them where possible through its party structure, whereas the small farmers were unlikely to wax enthusiastic about control by the central government, since they were more negative about it than about the chiefdom government.[54]

The general feeling among Sierra Leoneans throughout this period seemed to be that chiefs were still important, and not on the whole undesirable. Little in 1953 noted that educated men in provincial towns would treat the chief as *primus inter pares,* at least if he too were educated,[55] while Gamble's study of Lunsar in 1959 revealed that in this major town 'the general view was that at the top there is a "high class" consisting of the Chief, the court members, big traders, religious leaders, landowners . . .'.[56] My own survey in 1968 asked 'Who would you say is looked to by most people here to get projects started, or to settle disputes?' Of the 139 respondents, 58 (42 per cent) replied 'the Paramount Chief', while the next largest group, 44 (32 per cent) cited the section chief or town chief. Even on a question asking more specifically about innovations[57] the chief was still widely perceived as the source of innovation, with 48 (35 per cent) naming him. Other members of the TA, including the chiefdom speaker, section chiefs and so on, were cited by 54 (39 per cent), while the educated group, young men, and 'people generally' were cited by only 27 (19 per cent).[58]

When one considers that many Sierra Leone people saw their chiefs as essentially secular leaders and that in the case of the Mende and Limba at least, even the principles of hereditary succession only dated back to the beginning of British overrule[59] the chiefs' survival becomes even more impressive. With the consummatory values of their societies embodied in the secret societies, or in the case of the Mandingo and other peoples outside these societies, in Islam, the political structures had to be judged on the instrumental basis that they were ruling satisfactorily in the interests of all. Certain aspects of Sierra Leone's 'underdevelopment' aided them. They did not form a barrier to the upward climb of a large stratum of newly rich, as Owusu suggests occurred in Ghana;[60] for that matter, there were relatively few of the upwardly mobile white-collar workers who would find chieftaincy least relevant to their own needs, and could form their own alternative elites, and a substantial proportion of these new elites were related to the chiefs. Further, with four-fifths of the population tied to the land, the chief's control over the allocation of new land for farming gave him considerable leverage.

But beyond this there were more positive factors working for the chiefs. Chiefdom government was close to people, and more important, they seemed to feel they could control or influence it. Thus in the 1968 survey, in response to 'political efficacy' questions on the national and local arenas[61] only seven of the sixty-four farmers in the sample claimed they had a 'good' or 'fair' chance of changing an unjust national law, whereas fifty-one felt that they could change an unjust chiefdom law. While this is not a direct demonstration that local concerns were more important, it does indicate a greater likelihood of participation, particularly when taken in conjunction with the associated question 'What could you do?' to which nine of the twenty-seven farmers saying they would take action at the national level said they would work through a local intermediary and twelve others said they would contact their MP, whereas none proposed going to the Prime Minister or a Minister directly. At the local level, by contrast, thirty-six of the fifty-four farmers who said they could do something specified that they could go to the chief or the Chiefdom Committee directly.[62]

Then too, despite the numerous abuses against their people and the frequent displays of greed and self-seeking, the chiefs were subject to some internal restraint – some of them all of the time, nearly all of them some of the time. They did have to live among their own people, and so did their families; a chief, unlike a member of Parliament or civil servant, could not isolate himself in an exclusive compound. Their position did encompass the view that they were 'fathers' to their people, and though they might be bad fathers, stil. the belief in the ties persisted, and provided norms of conduct from which a chief could deviate only at the cost of some loss of self-esteem, as well as the esteem of others. Certainly their interpretation of the general welfare was heavily skewed in favour of themselves and other 'big men', but no more so than was the case with modern elites.

The chief, then, was the central figure in the arena which for the bulk of the population was the one which they could hope to influence, and which had the most direct effect on the lives of ordinary people. From the national elite's viewpoint, the chiefdoms were important both as the structures through which the countryside might be administered, and as the units in which electoral majorities had to be obtained. While an individual chief might be bypassed or his position undermined either by direct attacks from the centre or by building up a local rival to him, the only purpose in doing this would be to put a more desirable individual in his place. The range of strategies open to a Sierra Leonean national leader in his dealings with the chiefs was severely circumscribed, as we shall see now.

National Leaders and Chiefs

In dealing with the institution of chieftaincy and the individual chiefs, a national leader had three basic strategies open to him. He could accept both the institution and the individual role-holders as given, and offer them sufficient support to secure their reciprocal support for his position nationally. A second strategy would entail continuing support for the institution of chieftaincy, but a concerted effort to fill the chiefs' positions with individuals whose commitments ran upwards to the leader rather than down to their people. A third strategy, with several methods of implementation, was to bypass chieftaincy and render it superfluous by establishing other links between himself and the ordinary citizen. Broadly speaking, the first of these strategies was the one pursued by Sir Milton, the second by Sir Albert, while the third was pressed by the PNP and the APC when they were in opposition, although once in power Siaka Stevens moved quickly back to the second. Neither Sir Milton nor Sir Albert of course followed one of these strategies to the complete exclusion of the others, but each tended to lean rather heavily towards one approach, with only a few tactical departures. More important, because it influenced the response of other actors to their behaviour, was that each was perceived to be following a single dominant strategy.

The first strategy, offering the chiefs local autonomy in exchange for support nationally, had several advantages for the national leader, provided his aims did not differ too widely from those of the chiefs. First, it provided such popular support as the most influential figure in each chiefdom could muster, a consideration of great importance as long as competitive elections were maintained, and more generally useful in securing acceptance of government policies in taxation, agricultural development, education and many other areas. Second, by associating national institutions with chieftaincy, it helped provide legitimacy for the national government and its leaders. Third, it freed the leader from the demands on his time which would arise if he were maintaining detailed surveillance of the chiefdoms or were supervising an alternative structure, such as a party organisation, which was to perform the same functions. Fourth, by utilising men whose interests by virtue of their being local could not bring them into direct competition for his office, the leader limited the growth of potential rivals. Fifth, local autonomy for the chiefs as a collectivity did not preclude disciplining an individual chief, either for failing to carry out his side of the bargain, or for treatment of his subjects which would make him an electoral liability rather than an asset. Provided that the individual chief was not disciplined in a way which would bring other chiefs to his defence, the national leader's predominant position vis-à-vis any individual chief meant that the leader could have his way.

Against these advantages had to be set a number of disadvantages. From a 'national interest' point of view, the most serious was the fact that any innovative 'grassroots' programme, such as agricultural improvements or the spread of educational facilities, could be implemented only as far as the individual chiefs were willing to allow it. A related disadvantage was the fact that the national leader had also to leave selection of the personnel for the national political arena largely in the hands of the chiefs. Without the alternative of an autonomous party organisation, would-be members of Parliament had little choice but to look to the chiefs for electoral support.

A third disadvantage could potentially negate the time-saving advantage of chieftaincy for the leader. If they were left largely unchecked by the national government, the only curbs on the chiefs were intra-chiefdom ones, and as these became attenuated, there was a risk that many chiefs might use their powers in ways that created discontent, and thus electoral difficulties for the national leader. We will consider this problem closely in discussing the post-Cox Report actions of Dr Margai.

A leader seeking to consolidate his personal power would find that the bargain with the chiefs offered a fourth serious disadvantage. Reliance on the chiefs for selection of personnel and implementation of policies meant that a leader faced men with strong local power bases armed with little more than the weapon of persuasion. To change this would entail a Fabian strategy of nibbling away the chiefs' powers bit by bit, here curtailing one chief's collection of tribute, there installing a member of a rival ruling family as Court President. But to undercut the chiefs' power in this way required the steady erosion of time, and time in the twentieth century is one luxury few leaders have had.

Two other sets of persons would be affected by a leader's reliance on the chiefs, although the effect was indirect and limited. In every independent African state there had developed an 'educated elite', persons who had undergone relatively extended Western-type formal education and who owed their pre-eminence in the top of the civil service, teaching and other related hierarchies to this formal education. A number of chiefs in Sierra Leone (rightly) perceived Western education, along with the mass franchise, as a threat to their position, and tended to resist the intrusion of schools into their areas. The potential for conflict was here, in so far as senior civil servants were bound to feel frustrated by any policy which enabled chiefs to delay the spread of education, or for that matter of other development plans which the educated elite believed were good for people. The conflict was not serious, because many chiefs themselves formed part of the 'educated elite' and were as convinced as the civil servants of education's beneficial effects; but some basis for it existed.

The other set of persons affected by a leader's reliance on the chiefs was overseas investors, although here two partially contradictory tendencies were at work. We can assume that all investors wanted security for their investment and a good return. For the major investors in African states, the companies extracting raw materials for Western industries, these needs could be met by a host country which left their enclaves alone, provided the rather simple infrastructure they needed, and maintained sufficient control over the country that the companies were not bothered by guerilla movements, strikes or food shortages for their workers. The few companies hoping to develop a market for manufactured goods also needed sufficient wealth in the country to support their market, either as an urban bourgeoisie or as a wealthy farming stratum as in the Ivory Coast. It could be argued that to the extent that the dominance of chiefs worked against the development of a more urban bourgeoisie, the growth of such markets and thus of manufacturing investment might be inhibited, but this could be offset by the fact that the chiefs too showed a liking for the consumer society, and could also find the wealth to support it. A more important factor for most investors, in any case, was the likelihood that a chief-dominated polity was unlikely to follow a strong radical ideology, or to need symbolic issues such as taking over a foreign company to rally the populace around its leader. On balance, then, one could probably argue that reliance on the chiefs was more of an asset than a hindrance in attracting foreign investment.

The second strategy, of working through chieftaincy as an institution but making a considerable effort to control the selection of chiefs, eliminated some of the disadvantages of a *laissez-faire* policy towards the chiefs, but only at the cost of undercutting the advantages. To the extent that he was successful in selecting chiefs who shared or acquiesced in his programmatic views and his views on suitable personnel for national office, the leader could count on the chiefs' help in bringing about such changes as he desired, and in protecting his personal position, but the value of this help could be considerably reduced if a man appeared to have won the chief's office not through local support but by the grace of the Prime Minister. If the Prime Minister's chief represented a particularly weak or unpopular faction within the chiefdom, his selection could cost the Prime Minister considerably more support both from the electorate and from other 'big men' than he could bring. Local alignments drew in many individuals through the extended family system, and in slighting one claimant for a chieftaincy in order to install his favourite, a Prime Minister could easily antagonise half a dozen influential supporters.

A further disadvantage of involvement in local politics was simply the drain on a leader's time. Even though he would not involve himself in the internal politics of more than a handful of the 146 chiefdoms, to gather sufficient reliable information about even one chiefdom's alignments so that he could strike the best balance between each claimant's commitment to him and his standing in the chiefdom was a time-consuming procedure.

The third strategy, bypassing the chiefs by establishing other links from the grassroots to himself, was most likely to appeal to an 'innovative' leader, since it was the only way to alter the wealth distribution and stratification systems built around chieftaincy. This bypass strategy could be pursued directly through political means, or indirectly through encouraging certain types of economic development. The direct strategy involved setting up local poles of power which could offer benefits similar to those of the chief, but which were direct agents of the national leader. For example, political party organisers such as the local leaders in Tanzania may judge petty offences, settle disputes, do personal favours and offer help to individuals seeking contact with higher authority, and carry out most of the other manifold duties performed by Sierra Leone chiefs, yet remain directly accountable to the district party organisation above them.[63] Alternatively, it could be pursued through the bureaucratic hierarchy, each level of which explicitly owes obedience to the next higher level. However, to implement such an approach required sufficient resources under the control of the national leader, either in material rewards to or ideological commitment from the lower ranks of the party activists, to ensure that they did in fact offer more to the populace than the chiefs. The immediate problem in converting a political structure relying on the chiefs to one bypassing them, was that the chiefs and their supporters were installed in the national political process, and could hardly be expected to allow resources to be channelled to competitors.

From the point of view of enhancing his personal power, the national leader could also see considerable benefit from bypassing the chiefs. It was true that party or bureaucratic functionaries would also have sub-national loyalties which could impair their commitment to him, but they would not possess an institutional base with the degree of autonomy enjoyed by a chief.

If the chiefs and their allies were able to block the creation of structures bypassing them openly in the political sphere, they might be made irrelevant by economic growth in which major traders, manufacturers, and large-scale agriculturalists looked to the central government for specialised information on taxes, incentives, marketing opportunities, and supplies of competent manpower, while in turn orienting their employees to think nationally and to demand services which could only be provided by the national government. The major difficulty with this strategy, of course, was that no African government in the decade after independence had been able to obtain anything remotely approaching the amount of investment necessary to bring about this transformation. Even those countries such as the Ivory Coast, Ghana, Kenya and Nigeria that did relatively well in foreign investment found that the type of investment received was relatively limited in its 'nationalising' effect on the economy, very unevenly distributed regionally (with consequent problems of regional grievances) and largely beyond the control or direction of the national leader. This variant of the bypassing strategy, in short, was unlikely to be of much use to any Sierra Leonean leader in the foreseeable future.

We shall examine some instances where each of these strategies appear to have been followed, considering those cases which seemed to show the most typical behaviour of Sir Milton and Sir Albert. For Sir Milton, we shall consider his handling of the chiefs after the 1955-6 northern riots, and his reform of the local judicial system culminating in the Local Courts Act 1963. For Sir Albert, we shall consider his use of the Local Courts Act, his intervention in the Nongowa chieftaincy dispute, and his attempts to involve the chiefs actively in SLPP activities.

Dr Margai and the Chiefs

(a) Aftermath of the Northern Riots: The Chiefs Rise Again

The 1955-6 riots in the Northern Province highlighted a convergence of three shifts in the behaviour of key actors in the local arena. First, all those holding power in the NA system, from chiefs to clerks, were increasingly using their power for the personal acquisition of wealth. The chiefs in particular were tending less and less to distribute any wealth they acquired to their people, and more and more to concentrate on accumulating it through business enterprises and property for their own estate, a tendency most marked among younger literate chiefs who had often seen the chieftaincy as an opportunity for personal enrichment.[64] Second, the external checks on the Paramount Chief and the TAs had been sharply reduced as African self-government increased. The District Commissioner, the main channel for complaints against chiefly abuses, lost his principal source of information in 1954 when the Court Messengers were abolished.[65] Two further reductions of his prestige took place the next year, when first, collection of individual taxes was left entirely to the NA clerks without the DC's supervisory presence, and second, Paramount Chiefs began to replace DCs as Presidents of the District Councils. In such circumstances it was easy for chiefs to encourage among their people the idea that 'the District Commissioners were no longer in power in the Protectorate'.[66] But at the same time as this restraint was being removed from the chiefs, many 'young men' in the north were becoming conscious of the unfairness of their situation. The 'young men' had much to complain about: near-total exclusion from the TAs, the brunt of communal labour requirements, and of course the incessant demands for taxes and levies, largely illegal and for the personal benefit of the TAs. It seems likely, although I have no direct evidence for this, that the great diamond rush, which plunged men into an environment totally freed from traditional patterns of deference and restraint,[67] contributed heavily to awakening resentment towards this situation. It is possible that to some extent the riots were fomented, as were many in Mende chiefdoms, by members of rival ruling houses or other dispossessed members of 'the Establishment',[68] but their extent and severity seemed to reflect more profound grievances.

In the aftermath of the riots and the enquiries into them, the basic decision was how far the central government should go in punishing and curbing the powers of the chiefs. Both the British officials and the SLPP leaders concurred with the Cox Report's conclusion that chiefdoms and chieftaincy formed the only potentially viable unit for local government.[69] But it would be possible to follow the 'extreme' course of removing the chief from the local court, imposing strict supervision on all his collections and expenditures of revenue, ending such aggravations as forced labour, and making the TAs into 'rational' local councils firmly bound by rules and records. At the other extreme, the central government could make a few temporary gestures to popular feeling by suspending particular chiefs, and then when the situation had cooled somewhat, letting the *status quo* slip back.

Pressure for a 'tough' approach came essentially from the British, with some support from the younger educated elements in the SLPP. The Colonial Office allegedly told Dr Margai that the price of further constitutional progress was bringing the countryside back under control[70] and the new Governor, Maurice Dorman, warned on his first tour up-country:

> I strongly disapprove of 'big men' taking advantage of ordinary men . . . All these forms of extortion have got to stop. The Government will find ways and means to stop them.[71]

The chiefs were not slow to exert their own counterpressure. In October 1956 a rumour went around that the northern chiefs might form a 'Northern Peoples Party'[72] and a few weeks later the chiefs did form the Sierra Leone National Association 'to preserve the sovereign rights of Paramount Chiefs'.[73] While these organisational efforts came to nothing, the manifestation of concern by chiefs posed threats to both the SLPP and to Dr Margai's personal position. If the chiefs refused to help SLPP condidates, or worse, helped candidates opposed to the national SLPP leadership, it was quite likely that they retained enough influence with their people to have a decisive effect on the election. While the UPP as the only organised opposition party was too 'Creole' to pull all anti-SLPP elements together, some new alignment could easily emerge. And even if the chiefs did not oppose the SLPP, their passivity within the party could easily tip its internal balance against Dr Margai and in favour of the younger elements who would like to replace him.

On the other hand, if Dr Margai did not crack down on the chiefs, there was some risk that either the UPP or an indigenous northern group could use anti-chief feelings to develop a mass base which might pose a serious challenge to the SLPP. Two of the parties which had used anti-chief sentiments with some success, the Parti Democratique de Guinee and the Convention Peoples Party in the Gold Coast, were well enough known to the SLPP leaders that they could believe this threat.

Yet despite the pressures from the British and the threat of a mass-based northern party, Dr Margai's responses to the post-1955 situation were minimal. He did accept a series of enquiries into the conduct of particular chiefs, and also accepted the conclusions of these enquiries that the conduct of eleven chiefs had in varying degrees been 'subversive of good government', with the result that nine chiefs were deposed or resigned, and two were suspended.[74] At the same time, possibly in response to the widespread complaints before the Cox Commission that chiefs were both interested parties and final judges in many chiefdom disputes, he began replacing the chiefs with Court Presidents in the local chiefdom courts.[75] He also brought in a compromise with the Cox Report's recommendation that all forced labour under the 1932 Forced Labour Ordinance, whether for the chief's personal benefit or for chiefdom public works, be abolished. The compromise, the Prohibition of Forced Labour Ordinance 1956, prohibited forced labour for personal service, but allowed 'communal labour' to be continued 'for public purposes'. Dr Margai, defending this bill against cries from the chiefs that they were being made 'scapegoats',[76] implied that it was in part windowdressing for the benefit of international opinion, and that there would be considerable leeway for the chiefs to continue to utilise the labour of their subjects:

> At the International Labour Organisation there was some embarrassment to the Home Government that a certain amount of [forced labour] still exists in a Colony governed by the British Crown . . . But at the same time we do not expect to really abolish communal labour . . . If the Ordinance is passed . . . Tribal Authorities . . . could describe in their own way what they mean by communal labour . . . the Governor in Council would be able to bring that in as a schedule and say these are the forms of communal labour that would be allowed. . .[77]

In practice, communal labour did diminish in succeeding years, but this was attributable more to the growing awareness of their rights by the chiefs' subjects than to the government's willingness to enforce the law.

This initial flurry of activity all took place before the 1957 election had shown that despite some support for the UPP's appeal to anti-chief sentiments, its representatives could be co-opted into the SLPP,[78] and before the British officials withdrew from Ministerial posts in 1958.

From 1958 onwards Dr Margai kept direct control over the provincial administration, aided after 1960 by three Resident Ministers. Supervision over the chiefs, tightened after the Cox enquiry, began to slacken again. Despite the Cox Report's strong recommendation against paying compensation to the chiefs and Tribal Authorities since their misconduct and maladministration had been the main cause of the riots,[79] a Riot Damages Commission sitting from 1958 to 1960 recommended payments to chiefs and TAs totalling £394,360,[80] or more than half the estimated total damage. Finally, by 1961 all but one of the chiefs who had been deposed had been restored to office. It is likely true that in most cases the Temne belief that a chief once anointed remained chief for life was the key element in bringing their restoration, but even in the case of a chief whose conduct was described by the Commissioner of Enquiry as showing 'no extenuating circumstances' and being 'unworthy of a Paramount chief'[81] Dr Margai showed no hesitation in having him restored to office.

Concern for his own position coupled with a strong conservative ideology seems to have determined Dr Margai's relations with the chiefs. His unwillingness to institute any major changes in chiefdom government beyond the introduction of Court Presidents, and his restoration of the chiefs in 1960-1 may have been based in part upon prudential considerations, but seems also to be a part of his strong commitment to safeguarding the position of chieftaincy. If he had been less committed to the institution of chieftaincy, he might well have introduced more stringent central controls over the local arena, or used the Cox findings to justify stripping some powers away from the chiefs. While such a course would have entailed some risk of alienating the chiefs, the course he did choose alienated a substantial number of the younger educated men and also of the ordinary farmers in the north, with equally serious consequences. His resistance to the claims of these groups can, I think, best be explained not in terms of the relative pressure they were able to exert, but of his own predispositions, which committed him firmly to upholding the institution of chieftaincy.[82]

(b) The Reform of the Local Courts

We have noted earlier that the most important single function of a Paramount Chief was to judge disputes between his people. In precolonial times and well into the colonial period chiefs at all levels from the village head upwards were expected to perform this task of resolving conflicts, generally in a highly informal and unstructured manner. While to Europeans (or at least Anglo-Saxons) the sight of a chief executive also giving judgement in disputes seemed somehow contrary to 'natural justice', in Sierra Leonean society such an approach seemed quite natural. The object of justice in Sierra Leone was not so much to determine that one of the parties to a dispute was right and the other wrong, as to reconcile them and maintain the unity of the society. Who was more suitable for this task of reconciliation than the man who was 'father' to all the people of the community?[83]

The imposition of colonial rule brought a number of gradual changes in the native courts, and the chief's position in them. The courts' jurisdiction was restricted to civil and minor criminal matters, with the District Commissioner acting as a court of appeal, and they were denied any jurisdiction over 'non-natives' (i.e. Creoles and Lebanese).[84] Under a 1937 Ordinance, provision was made for a Court President and Vice-President appointed by the Provincial Commissioner to replace the Paramount Chief.[85] But in practice, the removal of the Paramount Chiefs from the courts had just begun at the outbreak of the 1955-6 riots. The riots did spur the process of replacing the chiefs, but the impact of the change was minimised by the fact that the provincial commissioners invariably left the selection of court presidents to the TA. Since the chief could normally control this body, it was not surprising to find that many Court Presidents were brothers or sons of the ruling chief.

However, even this minimal change bothered many chiefs. Not all of them were able to exercise sufficient control over their Tribal Authority to ensure that their wishes were met, and in any case a Court President necessarily represented an autonomous centre of power which could rival the chief. It was not surprising, therefore, to find the office of Court President coming to be regarded as the key post for a would-be challenger to the chief, nor to find the chiefs complaining:

> Why is it that Native Administration Presidents work directly under the District Commissioner and not the Paramount Chiefs? Will the Government see into this immediately?[86]

Albert Margai, by this time nearly ready to plunge into opposition, pinpointed the problem a few days later with the charge that Presidents 'attempt to usurp some of the powers of Paramount Chiefs', a charge which drew from the Premier the statement that Presidents 'are responsible only for the administration of justice. They have no powers or duties other than these.'[87]

But while the chiefs felt that in handling their role of judging cases to the Court Presidents, the government had gone too far, in another respect they too wanted reform. The exclusion of 'non-natives' from their jurisdiction had meant that while a Creole or Lebanese trader as plaintiff could hale a 'native' into the NA Court, if the tables were turned the 'native' would have to fight his case in the less friendly (and more expensive) surroundings of the magistrate's court. This interest coincided with that of the educated elite, particularly the Bar and Bench who were unhappy over the exclusion of lawyers from the NA courts' proceedings, and (as a matter of principal as well as money), over the lack of integration between these courts of native law and the courts following English law. Besides offering them the opportunity for additional fees (a consideration perhaps not of immediate importance, since most already had all the business they could handle), the lawyers felt that an integrated system with appeals lying from the NA courts right up to the Supreme Court would further the creation of 'One Country'. Finally, the senior civil service, both British and Sierra Leonean, generally shared the view that a greater separation of the chiefs from the judicial process, and integration of the various parts of that process, should be achieved.

Despite the range of pressures seeking a further change in the local courts, the Premier was apparently in no rush to act. In 1953 the Brooke Report had recommended a reorganisation of the local court structures but five years later the Premier replied to Albert Margai's query, 'How soon is it hoped to finalise the implementation of the recommendations?' with the statement that while 'many' had been accepted 'in principle',

> Before these can be implemented, however, new legislation is required and the Acting Judicial Adviser (Maurice Jones) has been studying the matter and is to make proposals for putting the accepted recommendations into effect.[88]

Four years later, when a permanent judicial adviser was appointed, he claims that he had to start drafting the bill which eventually appeared as the Local Courts Act 1963 – ten years after the Brooke Report.[89]

The 1963 Act offered one feature which pleased the chiefs, extension of the courts' jurisdiction over all persons living in their territory (section 13(2)). But against this it provided that Presidents and other members of the court should be appointed by the Minister for a three-year term, a central control mitigated only slightly by the practice of having the (Prime) Minister advised by a committee comprising the judicial adviser, the Provincial Secretary, and the District Officer, with the Paramount Chief also being consulted.[90] Although this central power of appointment did not help the Prime Minister politically as much as it was supposed to, largely because both disappointed aspirants and the public tended to blame him more than his appointees praised him, it had a much more adverse effect on the chiefs, who lost even the indirect control over cases they had retained, as well as losing their patronage power over the second most powerful post in the chiefdom.

The other major change introduced through the 1963 Act was that henceforth appeals lay through the 'English' judicial hierarchy, rather than to act in appeals, and since in all civil cases, even those involving customary law, the 'English law' judges had sole power, it was not hard to foresee that in the long run customary law would probably be brought into line with English law.[91] While I have found no publicly articulated protest against this, I suspect that many chiefs had some inkling that this would be the long-term result.

While it was under Dr Margai that these changes took place, I think the length of time they took to come about is an indication of his reluctance to undercut the chiefs.[92] Albert Margai, while still leading the PNP in opposition, claimed that as Minister of Local Government he had 'personally made a draft (bill) which would have made it possible for appeals to be made from a native court to higher courts, but the Government failed to implement it'.[93] A high British official commented that Dr Margai 'realised that it had to happen, and gave in to the more educated element who were demanding it',[94] a comment which suggests the degree to which the British also sought this change. Against these combined pressures both within the SLPP (intensified after the PNP lawyers were brought back into the fold, and S.T. Navo had become Judicial Adviser in 1962) and the British, he yielded in a way that probably preserved as much of the customary laws and the chiefs' powers as possible in a situation where most key central government posts were controlled by men who wanted to reform the system.

The Intrusion of National Politics: Albert Margai and the Chiefs

As was suggested earlier, Albert Margai took a considerably more active role in supervising chiefdom affairs than did his brother. Under him, the Ministry of the Interior became little more than a 'post-box', with all local political disputes going straight on to the Prime Minister's desk.[95] Albert was also much more prone than his brother to intervene in local disputes over such matters as illegal levies, and to press the chief concerned to mend his ways. His reason for doing this was prudential: he was quite aware that a local 'palaver' could produce enmities that would align people in rival national party camps. But in several instances his activism appears to have led him to underestimate the political costs involved, which were manifested in hostility being directed against the Prime Minister rather than against local figures.

(a) The Control of the Court Presidents

Albert Margai, as we have noted, was rather more enthusiastic than his brother to reform the local court system in Sierra Leone. His ascent to the Prime Minister's office followed closely upon the introduction of the Local Courts Act, with its power in the (Prime) Minister's hands to appoint Court Presidents. For some months he continued to use the system of having the Tribal Authority elect a President, with his own role solely one of ratification, but this perpetuated the existing weaknesses. As the Judicial Adviser, a close personal associate of Sir Albert, put it:

> . . . at least one-third of the Court Presidents are either brothers, sons or near relatives of Paramount Chiefs, the position (being) looked upon as another 'staff' in the chiefdom. On the other hand many Court Presidents challenge or flout the authority of Paramount Chiefs since they are voted for by the same Chiefdom Councillors who vote for the Paramount Chief.[96]

A change was swiftly introduced, with an advisory committee comprising the Judicial Adviser, the Provincial Secretary and the District Officer taking over the nominations with the Prime Minister still making the final decisions. Needless to say, this did not mean replacing the local political considerations of the TAs by a non-partisan approach; rather, it allowed the Prime Minister to control one more key source of patronage, and in several instances he used his power to install individuals whom he regarded as suitably loyal to himself and to the SLPP. Thus in the Limba chiefdom of Biriwa, a Mandingo man was appointed Court President; in Tonko Limba, another Limba chiefdom, Siaka Stevens complained in Parliament that the Court President 'cannot even speak the language of the people and has to work through an intepreter';[97] and in Yoni, a Temne chiefdom, an illiterate man was replaced ostensibly on the grounds that literacy was needed for the job, but in fact because the literate man who took his place was considered politically more reliable.

While this power of appointment offered the Prime Minister control over one of the most important local means of curbing political opposition, it also had heavy costs. When an appointment was unpopular, as some inevitably were, both the disappointed rivals and the populace could blame the Prime Minister rather than their own Tribal Authority. More fundamentally, many people were aware that a chance to choose had been taken away from them, and again their displeasure was directed against the Prime Minister. People were being forced into the national rather than the local political arena, but in a way which was as likely to align them against Albert as for him.

(b) Selecting a Chief: the Nongowa Case

While the power to select a Court President was a useful one for a Prime Minister, the power to select a Paramount Chief was considerably more alluring. Unfortunately for the Prime Minister, the obstacles to his controlling this key local office were formidable. Where a colonial innovation such as the Court President could easily have his tenure of office cut to a three-year renewable term without this action arousing any great protest, the feeling that a Paramount Chief was, saving misconduct, chief for life, immediately limited the opportunities for replacing him. While the Mbriwa case[98] showed that 'misconduct' could occasionally be stretched to cover political offences, deposing a chief for political offences left the nearly insuperable problem of finding a locally acceptable replacement. Even apart from the basic limitation that selecting a chief was a once-in-a-lifetime opportunity, there was the further need to find a candidate who would have sufficient support in the chiefdom to rule effectively. It would be a Pyrrhic victory for a Prime Minister to succeed in installing as a new chief a person who was widely unpopular with his people, since his unpopularity would reflect discredit on the Prime Minister. Thus the opportunities to intervene in the selection of a chief were few; they required, first, the death of, or a plausible reason for replacing, a ruling chief, and second, a candidate who combined local acceptability with an apparent willingness to support the Prime Minister.

Such an opportunity seemed to arise in Nongowa chiefdom, Kenema district, in 1966. In the ten years following the death of Chief Kai-Samba I, one of the outstanding chiefs in Sierra Leone's history, the chiefdom had been under the far weaker hand of his eldest son, Kai-Samba II. By 1965 he had become such a sick man that the Prime Minister was able to appoint as 'Deputy Paramount Chief' a man who had gradually been building for himself a powerful behind-the-scenes position, M.M. Koroma.[99] In 1966, Sir Albert took the further step of pensioning off Paramount Chief Kai-Samba II on the grounds that his illness made him incapable of performing his duties. The way was thus open for the selection of a new chief, and M.M. Koroma both wanted the post and seemed to have a good chance of winning it.

The Prime Minister had his own strong motive for intervening in Nongowa's affairs. The chiefdom comprised the major part of the constituency of Kutubu Kai-Samba, a brother of the pensioned chief and one of the most capable of the young Bo School graduates inside the SLPP who offered the most serious threat to Albert Margai's hold on office.[100] Undermining Kai-Samba (who at the time was Minister of Agriculture and Natural Resources in Margai's Cabinet) in his own constituency was the most effective way of removing him from the national political arena, the House of Representatives.[101]

But Sir Albert was stretching legality to make this attack. Neither the creation of a 'Deputy Paramount Chief' nor the removal of a chief for illness had any precedent in Mende country,[102] and Kutubu Kai-Samba and other supporters of the chief furiously attacked both Koroma and Albert Margai.[103] The bulk of the Kai-Samba family ultimately came to support the candidate of the rival ruling house, Foray Vangahun, rather than M.M. Koroma.

Two attempts were made in June and October 1966 to elect a chief, but the balance between the bulk of the two ruling houses on the one side, and the looming shadow of the Prime Minister on the other, were just sufficient to prevent either candidate gaining the 55 per cent majority of Tribal Authorities required to elect a chief.[104] The cost to the Prime Minister of getting so deeply involved in this local struggle was shown the following year in the national elections. Not only did Kutubu Kai-Samba, running as an Independent against the Prime Minister's private secretary, retain his seat, but one of his supporters, J.B. Francis, who had been trounced by the SLPP candidate in 1962, this time succeeded in winning the Kenema Town seat, also a part of Nongowa chiefdom.[105] The Prime Minister's strategy in this case had clearly backfired.

(c) 'Smoking out the Chiefs'

In one way, it would be quite misleading to suggest that Albert Margai's involvement of the chiefs in SLPP activities was something new. Under Sir Milton, chiefs had attended the SLPP's conventions, selected the candidates who were to receive the SLPP symbol, and been the main force in harassing opposition parties in the provinces. But some token gestures were made towards the myth of chiefly neutrality; a chief could tell his people that while he was SLPP, they were free to support whoever they chose, or he could remain neutral in a national election campaign, just as the law enjoined him.[106] While most chiefs were quite strongly in favour of Dr Margai and the SLPP (at least in preference to any of the available alternatives), their adherence was largely voluntary; there were no severe sanctions imposed against a chief who chose to remain above the battle. Even in the 1959 District Council election campaign against the PNP, and in the 1962 general election against the APC, not all chiefs campaigned for the SLPP.[107]

Albert Margai's innovation was one of degree only, but it had a considerable effect on chieftaincy. In his drive to turn the SLPP into an effective party organisation, and later in trying to gather support for the one-party state, he used several means to force the chiefs to become more active agents for the governing party. Following a 'Reorganisation Meeting' at Bo in January 1965 it was alleged that all chiefs were being taxed Le 6 per month, and Court Presidents Le 4, to support the SLPP.[108] The chiefs in turn stepped up their activity of 'recruiting' SLPP members in their chiefdoms, with one district claiming 16,000 membership by the time of the May 1965 convention. What had happened in fact was that a small group of 'big men' had raised the money, and the chiefs had had membership cards distributed to all who would take them.[109] Meanwhile Sir Albert announced at a news conference that henceforth chiefs would be free to take part in party politics,[110] a move whose purpose was confirmed by one Northern SLPP leader to be 'to smoke out those chiefs who sympathise with the APC'.[111]

The next few months saw a marked stepping-up in the campaign of harassment against the APC. In Port Loko, chiefdom seat of the unpopular Alikali Modu, the APC office was padlocked, and its leaders hauled before the Local Court for 'disrespect to the Paramount Chief'. In Bullom chiefdom, several suspect APC supporters were imprisoned in a pit for several days.[112] A few months later, at the height of the one-party state drive, it was reported that the Makari Gbanti chiefdom Council had 'unanimously' endorsed the proposal for a one-party state. An APC Councillor, D.M. Fornah, sent the *Daily Mail* a letter vigorously denying that the council had been unanimous.[113] He was immediately charged with holding the council up to ridicule, and sentenced by the Local Court to six months in jail.[114]

The hundreds of instances of this type of persecution did not always have the desired effect of frightening people away from the APC. Even some of the SLPP's local leaders expressed private concern that the actions of the chiefs and local authorities were simply driving a wedge between them and their people, and making most people more determined than before to vote for the APC at the next election.[115] Then, too, some chiefs were unwilling to work for Albert Margai, in some cases because they too could see the danger from their people, in others because they had no liking for what he was doing to the country. Chief Abu Baimba of Kakua, for example, who had been politically quiescent since he had signed the petition protesting against Albert's appointment as Prime Minister, took a studiously neutral role in the 1966 District Council elections, allowing the APC to convass freely in Bo and even offering police protection for their meetings if they requested it. An even more conspicuous deviant was Chief Bai Kafari of Tane, the brother of an APC MP, who made no secret of his own APC sympathies. Perhaps the Prime Minister felt that it was safer to isolate this somewhat undiginfied chief rather than make a martyr of him; at any rate, Bai Kafari survived to win the Tonkolili chief's seat in the 1967 election.[116] But these chiefs were the exceptions; most did undertake a good deal of activity, both in finding members and money for the SLPP and in hounding APC sympathisers and forcing them to operate covertly.

The full cost of this alignment to the chiefs was not revealed until after the APC had been restored to power in 1968. Almost immediately the local APC cadres began to pay off scores against the chiefs and their supporters, and in many cases to supplant the chiefs as arbiters, intermediaries and sources of authority. Stevens himself became rather alarmed by the implications of this, and the latter half of 1968 saw the ironic spectacle of an APC government trying to persuade people that the chiefs were still a necessary institution.[117]

For Albert Margai, the strategy of forcing the chiefs into working more intensively for the SLPP had been a 'second-best' alternative to having a strongly centralised party whose local workers were directly under his control. His efforts to move in this direction had been defeated at both the 1964 and 1965 SLPP meetings[118] so that realistically the best that could be achieved was to have more active though still autonomous local branches. The major gain from this strategy was that it kept the APC from organising too openly, and made it difficult for northern chiefs to support it covertly. But the cost of this strategy was born by the northern chiefs, who found themselves increasingly alienated from their people for supporting a Mende Prime Minister against 'dey yone' party.

Conclusions: The Strategies Compared

It could be argued that comparing the efficacies of Sir Milton's and Sir Albert's dominant strategies in dealing with the local arenas is a pointless exercise, in that neither could conceivably have followed the strategy of the other. Dr Margai's strong belief in the desirability of preserving chieftaincy and more broadly his commitment to a hierarchical society, were simply not compatible with a policy of actively forcing chiefs to do his bidding, even if his illness had not made it impossible for him to exercise the detailed supervision that such a policy entailed. Albert's desire for changing Sierra Leonean patterns of stratification was equally incompatible with a policy of non-intervention in chiefly affairs, quite apart from his desire to consolidate his personal position. In this respect, each seems to have chosen the strategy most appropriate to his own basic values, regardless of its suitability for his 'ruler's imperative' of retaining power.

However, we can make some general observations about the effects of the strategies pursued by the two leaders upon the Sierra Leone polity. Dr Margai's ideological conservatism, as noted earlier, pointed to a use of 'strong' intermediaries and indirect contacts, provided only that the intermediaries shared his general perspective. What would create difficulties for him would be either the growth of a body of men desiring change and possessing the resources to develop their own clienteles, or the growth of 'class' consciousness among those hitherto subordinated to his intermediaries. In the first situation, with his own predispositions and the local intermediaries upon whom he depended for his support opposing change, a new group of persons with the capability of building their own patronage structures would almost be forced to side with an opposition group. In the second situation, if the relationship between chiefs and their followers changed in ways that led the followers to question the very role of chieftaincy, then an ideologue committed to sustaining the former relationship would find his position irrelevant and without support.

To some extent, Dr Margai's approach led to both of these difficulties. His temporising over the reform of the local courts and more generally, his tendency to allow the chiefs a free hand in their relations with their people, irritated many of the educated men and the emerging traders; furthermore, the dominance of the chiefs as local intermediaries meant that these newer groups were frozen out of the SLPP except on terms acceptable to the chiefs. Thus a conflict between the chiefs' and the traders' rival patron-client chains tended to develop, particularly in the north, into a conflict between rival political parties.

At the same time, the tendency of the chiefs to seek their own enrichment produced some questioning of their role, and a feeling that their relations with their people were necessarily antagonistic. Despite the behaviour of the chiefs, persons holding such attitudes were still very much a minority by the time of Dr Margai's death; but the fact that they existed in any numbers at all was attributable in large measure to Dr Margai's continued insistence on supporting the chiefs without exerting pressure on them to mend their ways.

Despite these potentially serious conflicts, the chiefs did retain the support of most of their people, and this meant that Dr Margai's strategy contained several advantages. It offered a ready-made set of links with the populace, thus saving for other activities the time and effort which would otherwise be required to forge such links; and since these intermediaries were the foci of legitimacy for most of the populace, some of their legitimacy rubbed off on the national government they supported.

Against these advantages, however, had to be set certain costs. With each local unit free to pursue its parochial goals, and little educative effort being made by the national government to achieve national integration, there was the danger that any larger-scale identities achieved would be regional or tribal, with all the hazards of divisions that these entailed. More serious was the obstacle to even necessary changes already touched on. A party built upon local power-holders (even ones tempered by their own traditions of working for all their people) was scarcely going to propose the kind of changes that would undermine those local power-holders; yet it seemed highly probably that the kind of changes which would bring about a significant improvement in the daily lives of most men (a much broader cash economy, new roles to meet increased technological complexity, greater diversity of economic choices) would be precisely those that would threaten the chiefs. For example, the introduction of a large-scale agricultural improvement programme, including loans under certain government control would offer a considerable threat to the chiefs' hold on their people, unless the chiefs could capture control of the programme (as they did in Sierra Leone).[119]

Much of what Albert Margai tried to do in the field of local government was vitiated by his lack of a clear long-term set of goals. If his interventions in the selection of Court Presidents and of chiefs had been used to reform chiefdom government from within, by getting rid of those chiefs most resistant to change and advancing the claims of persons who would promote his ideas of 'progress', he might well have won a considerable following among the 'young men' in the chiefdoms.

As it was, his strategy was too patently aimed at getting chiefs who would be committed to Albert Margai personally; and unfortunately he was seeking to provide himself with 'loyal' intermediaries through an institution which was suitable only for 'strong' ones. His interventions did serve in some cases to protect his position by ensuring that challengers were deprived of a base, but only at the cost of attracting to the Prime Minister a great deal of antagonism that would otherwise have been concentrated on local-level leaders. More broadly, in trying to buttress his personal position, he undercut the position of the only intermediaries he had, with the result that they could not (and in some cases by 1967, would not) contain the growing opposition to his rule.

Yet while he undermined the chiefs, without a clear ideology he was quite unable to build up a cadre of loyal intermediaries to replace them. Although to some extent he did win sympathy from the 'young men' and other excluded groups by his show of readiness to curb the chiefs, he did not develop this into a sufficiently consistent approach to capture their loyalty. To a very large extent this was due to circumstances beyond his control; the resistance of the chiefs to his efforts at reorganising the SLPP and his consequent dependence upon them, coupled with the serious regional mistrust of his leadership, meant that he had to grab for whatever support he could find, without much thought for consistency. But it does seem possible that if he had had a clearer idea of what he was ultimately trying to accomplish with his power, he might have had more success in building up cadres who would have supported him in the realisation of these goals.

Notes

1. Roughly half Sierra Leone's export earnings came from its two major mining enclaves. Only seven other states had mining or oil enclaves that made a comparable or higher contribution to their Gross Domestic Product and/or their export earnings: Gabon, Guinea, Liberia, Libya, Mauritania, Zaire and Zambia.
2. We may make a *very* crude approximation of agriculture's contribution to government revenue by assuming that roughly half the revenue derived from import and export duties, and some from fees, were attributable to this sector, exclusive of the extra duties generated by the diamond rush. If we project the pre-diamond rush rates of increase in import duties on to 1960, we can attribute £3 million of the £4.7 million revenue of that year to activities other than diamond mining. We may thus attribute £1.5 million worth of import duties, £350,000 of export duties, and £0.5 million worth of fee revenues to the agricultural sector, or 21 per cent of the total revenue of £11.2 million. Data from *Quarterly Statistical Bulletin*, No. 1, 1963, Table 3.

3. Though we should note that thanks to the exodus of men from the farms to dig diamonds, from the mid-1950s onwards Sierra Leone annually imported up to 20,000 tons, or about a twelfth of her total requirements of her staple food, rice.
4. By 1967, when a rival in fact replaced the national leader of Sierra Leone in an election, there were only five other states in Africa where such a change might be considered a serious possibility: Botswana, Lesotho, Gambia, Somalia and Zambia. By 1973, the list had shrunk to Botswana and Gambia.
5. Given the weakness of party adherence and the consequent absence of 'safe seats' to which a Prime Minister who had lost his own seat might repair for another try, we might also suggest that in Sierra Leone he would also need to be sure of a plurality in his own constituency.
6. F.G. Bailey argues in *Politics and Social Change: Orissa in 1959,* Berkeley, University of California Press, 1963, p. 62, that the villagers in a relatively isolated village he studied regarded a member of the village who acted as a middleman between them and outside authorities as no longer completely trustworthy as 'one of them'. Minikin, in *Local Politics in Kono,* pp. 34-5, maintains that in Kono precisely the opposite occurred; a person with outside contacts *enhanced* his local standing. I am inclined to think Minikin's contention applies through most of Sierra Leone.
7. Bailey, *Stratagems and Spoils,* pp. 36ff.
8. See Norman Miller, 'The Political Survival of Traditional Leadership', *Journal of Modern African Studies,* VI, 2, 1968, pp. 183-7.
9. In Tanzania, the Tanganyika African National Union offered not only an alternative to the traditional chiefs, but also a structure which could extend the functions of the bureaucracy. See Jean O'Barr, 'Cell Leaders in Tanzania', *African Studies Review,* XV, 3, Dec. 1973, pp. 437-65; Norman N. Miller, 'The Rural African Party: Political Participation in Tanzania', *American Political Science Review,* LXIV, 2 June 1970, pp. 548-71. In other countries, however, such as the Ivory Coast, the local party cells soon came to be dominated by local notables, whose commitment was primarily downwards. See Aristide Zolberg, 'Ivory Coast', in James Coleman and Carl Rosberg (eds.), *Political Parties and National Integration in Tropical Africa,* Berkeley, University of California Press, 1964, p. 79.
10. See below, pp. 124-29 for a further discussion if 'class' and 'factional' models.
11. The Kabaka Yekka in Uganda, the Kono Progressive Movement in Sierra Leone and other 'defensive' ethnically-based movements are the best illustrations of what I have in mind here. Class movements have not as yet found the same degree of solidarity, although Peter Gutkind suggests that they are reaching this level of awareness; see his 'From the Energy of Despair to the Anger of Despair', *Canadian Journal of African Studies,* 7, 2, 1973, pp.179-98.
12. Sekou Touré has consistently made this case. For a more general statement regarding this situation, see Immanual Wallerstein, 'Class and Class-Conflict in Contemporary Africa', *Canadian Journal of African Studies,* 7, 3, 1973, pp. 375-80.
13. For a general outline of the dynamics of the transition, see James C. Scott, 'Corruption, Machine Politics and Political Change', *American Political Science Review,* LXIII, 4, Dec. 1969, esp. pp. 1146-9. See also René Lemarchand, 'Political Clientelism and Ethnicity in Tropical Africa', *American Political Science Review,* LXVI, 1, Mar. 1972, pp. 68-90.
14. See M.G. Smith, *Government in Zazzau,* London, Oxford University Press, 1960.

15. In real life there can clearly be many more than two levels of patrons and clients.
16. Lemarchand, 'Political Clientelism', p. 86.
17. Scott, 'Machine Politics', pp. 1151-4. See also Richard Sandbrook, 'Patrons, Clients and Factions: New Dimensions of Conflict Analysis in Africa', *Canadian Journal of Political Science,* VI, Mar. 1972, pp. 104-19.
18. The late Sir Amadu Bello's attempts to strengthen Islam among Northern Nigerians by 'conversion tours' illustrates this approach. See C.S. Whitaker, *The Politics of Tradition: Continuity and Change in Northern Nigeria 1946-1966,* Princeton, N.J., Princeton University Press, 1970, pp. 349-50.
19. The problems faced by Haile Selassie in Ethiopia culminating in the 1974 military takeover are a case in point. For a discussion of how the empire managed to contain these new elements, and the limitations on this 'containment' approach, see Christopher Chapham, 'Imperial Leadership in Ethiopia', *African Affairs,* 68, 1969, pp. 110-20.
20. In addition to a District Officer and one or two Assistant District Officers, the only other officials in the districts in 1951 were six Co-operative Inspectors, nineteen Agricultural Officers and seven senior police officers.
21. Cf. Angela Burger's study of the inability of newly emergent groups to find a satisfactory accommodation in the Congress Party in the Indian state of Uttar Pradesh, *Opposition in a Dominant Party System,* Berkeley and Los Angeles, University of California Press, 1969.
22. The other two possible local arenas, the District Council and the constituency, were simply not regarded by many people as having much significance in their daily lives. The District Councils, after collapsing in a welter of corruption and mismanagement, were finally abolished in 1972 with scarcely a murmur of protest, while the constituencies only acquired meaning every five years during election campaigns, and even then were regarded largely as extensions of the chiefdom arena.
23. See the interesting volume edited by Michael Crowder and Obaro Ikime, *West African Chiefs: Their Changing Status under Colonial Rule and Independence,* New York and Ife, Africana Publishing Corporation and University of Ife Press, 1970.
24. *Laws of Sierra Leone,* 1946, cap. 245, sec. 2. See also Lord Hailey, *Native Administration in the British African Territories,* part III, London, Colonial Office, 1951, pp. 300ff for a description of the situation in the late 1940s.
25. One chief with whom I was discussing the selection of TA members said he always allowed the people of a section of a village to choose their own section chief or village headman, so that he would not be blamed for a bad choice. When I asked him what would happen in the event of friction between himself and one of these sub-chiefs, he replied, 'I would have him removed immediately.' Pollock, *Influence, Authority and Economic Opportunity,* p. 55, notes that such actions were 'in no way unusual'.
26. We should also note the presence of the Poro and other secret societies among the Mende and several other tribes. The Poro could under certain conditions bind the chief and the Tribal Authority to abide by decisions reached in the Poro 'bush' and also initiate actions which would lead to a chief's deposition. See G.C. Bond, *The Contemporary Position of Chiefs in Sierra Leone with Special Reference to the Mende and Temne,* (unpublished M.A. thesis, University of London, 1962), p. 30; also Kenneth Little, 'The Political Function of the Poro', part I, *Africa,* XXXV, 4 Oct. 1965, pp. 349-65; part II, ibid., XXXVI, 1 Jan. 1966, pp. 62-71.
27. See *Cox Report,* pp. 121-56, for illustrations. An extreme example was the case of the chiefdom estimates which included £40 from canoe licences. The

canoes in the fishing villages of the chiefdom were licensed at a rate which would bring in at least £1,000 but by a miracle of precise accounting the amount recorded as coming into the chiefdom treasury was exactly the £40 provided for in the estimates. Ibid., p. 141.

28. Most clerks in the 1960s were paid in the range of £100-£200 per year.
29. The Chiefdom Speaker, or *lavali,* was historically only a Mende title, but was introduced by the British to designate a man acting as a deputy chief in most other chiefdoms.
30. Each Paramount Chief was an *ex-officio* member of his District Council.
31. Section 30 (1a), of the Independence Constitution provided that one Paramount Chief should be elected from each of the existing administrative districts. However, we might note that this clause was not entrenched.
32. Lord Hailey, *Native Administration,* part III, p. 303.
33. Figures for 1948 are found ibid., p. 305; for 1962 in the *Protectorate Handbook,* 1962. The latter, it should be noted, understates the number of literate chiefs.
34. See Dorjahn, 'Changing Political System of the Temne', pp. 129-36.
35. One young chief in the 1940s claimed that whenever he tried to get his TAs to discuss budgets and development expenditures, their response was 'Go away and don't bother us with white men's business'. Cited in Little, 'Mende Political Institutions in Transition', p. 18.
36. See, for example, in the *Reports of the Commissioners of Enquiry into the Conduct of Certain Chiefs,* the reports on Bai Kafari, pp. 17-20, on Bai Sebora Kamal, pp. 26 and 27 and on Bai Bairoh, pp. 67-8.
37. Barrows, *Grassroots Politics,* p. 104.
38. Luawa chiefdom in Kailahun district furnishes a neat illustration of this process. In 1950 an uprising instigated by the 'out' ruling house and involving some 5,000 protestors drove the then Paramount Chief, S.K. Banya, from office. He was succeeded by a member of the rival ruling house, Alpha Ngobeh. Fifteen years later the tables were turned and Chief Ngobeh in turn was driven from office by mass protests, this time led by the Banya family.
39. *Grassroots Politics,* p. 108.
40. Some 85 per cent of the respondents (N=132) saw the chief's power as diminished, though most did not cite specific illustrations.
41. See Pollock, *Influence, Authority and Economic Opportunity,* pp. 220-4.
42. Even if we include those who said they would go to the Prime Minister or another Minister, we still reach a total of only twenty-six (19 per cent) respondents using these elective channels. The question was 'When Sir Milton and Sir Albert were Prime Ministers, who did you go to when you wanted to let the national government know about a local matter (for example, a school, water supplies, a dispensary, a road, etc.) . . .?'
43. Findings of Special Commissioner Paul Storr, *Reports into the Conduct of Certain Chiefs,* pp. 7-8.
44. See his comments and those of Chief Yumkella in the debate on an opposition motion deploring the banishment, *House of Representatives Debates,* 1963-4, IV, 22 Nov. 1963, cols. 256-67, 266-7.
45. Although primary school teachers were employees of the District Councils, the money for their salaries came from the central government, and their orientation was usually towards the Ministry of Education.
46. The banned Sawaba Party in Niger and the Northern Elements Progressive Union (NEPU) in Nigeria epitomise this type of 'class' appeal.
47. *1963 Census,* Vol. II, Table 8.
48. Ibid., Vol. III, Table 6.

49. See R.J. Mutti et. al., *Marketing Staple Food Crops in Sierra Leone,* Njala, The University College, 1967, p. 52.
50. Cf. Donald S. Zagoria's finding that in India the *absence* of traditional non-material ties between peasants and landowners seemed a necessary pre-condition for support for Communist movements. 'The Ecology of Peasant Communism in India', *American Political Science Review,* LXV, 1 Mar. 1971, pp. 144-60.
51. I defined 'small farmers' as those who either had farms less than the average size for their section of the chiefdom, or sold less than half their crops. These two groups largely overlapped.
52. The Ns for these groups were: on the TA question, 30 farmers, 117 in whole sample; on the court question, 36 farmers, 127 in whole sample.
53. Bond, *The Contemporary Position of Chiefs in Sierra Leone,* p. 129.
54. On the question 'What kind of effect has the national government had?' 85 per cent (N=32) of the small farmers replied 'fair' or 'poor', while in their comments on national politicians, 64 per cent (N=28) gave negative evaluations.
55. 'Structural Change', p. 225.
56. David P. Gamble, 'Occupational Prestige in an Urban Community (Lunsar) in Sierra Leone', *Sierra Leone Studies,* N.S. 19, July 1966, p. 108.
57. The question was 'When a new barri (or market place, well, school or road) was built here, who proposed it?'
58. This is at variance with James Kingsland's claim, based on a study of District Councils' information-gathering activities, that the young men proposed projects and their elders followed along. 'Resource Allocation in the Bo and Bombali District Councils: a Decision-making Model', unpublished paper presented to Sierra Leone Symposium, UWO, p. 17. It may be, however, that the young men have to transmit their proposals through the chiefly structure to get action, and people subsequently come to attribute the initiation of the project to the Chief or TA.
59. For the Mende, see Barrows, *Grassroots Politics,* pp. 79-82; for the Limba, see Ruth Finnegan, *Survey of the Limba People of Northern Sierra Leone,* London, HMSO, 1965, p. 34.
60. Maxwell Owusu, *Uses and Abuses of Political Power,* Chicago, University of Chicago Press 1970, pp. 299-300; see also Lucy Mair, 'African Chiefs Today', *Africa,* XXVIII, 3, July 1958, pp. 198-9.
61. The questions were taken from Gabriel Almond and Sidney Verba, *The Civic Culture,* Boston and Toronto, Little, Brown, 1965, p. 141. The questions were: 'Suppose a law were being considered by the House of Representatives in Freetown that you considered to be unjust or harmful. What do you think you could do? . . . If you made an effort to change this law, how likely is it that you would succeed?' 'Suppose a regulation were being considered by the Chiefdom Committee that you considered unjust or harmful. What do you think you could do? If you made an effort to change this regulation, how likely is it that you would succeed?'
62. The difference was far less marked among white-collar and wage workers Of 38 white-collar workers, 13 thought they could change a national law, and 27 thought they could change a local law, while of 35 wage workers and traders, 5 thought they could change a national law and 20 thought they could change a local law. One interesting facet of this finding is the suggestion that these two groups may feel more remote from chiefdom government than do farmers.
63. See Henry Bienen, *Tanzania: Party Transformation and Economic Development,* Princeton, N.J., Princeton University Press, 1967, p. 356.

64. See *Cox Report*, pp. 160-1, *Reports . . . into the Conduct of Certain Chiefs*, pp. 27, 50; Dorjahn, 'Changing Political System of the Temne', pp. 133-6.
65. The Court Messengers were attached to the District Commissioner's office as a combination of messengers, policemen and general information-gatherers. They were abolished when the Sierra Leone Police were introduced into the Protectorate. See *Cox Report*, p. 220.
66. A comment from a witness during the Cox Commission's hearings, cited *Daily Mail*, 24, Oct. 1956. See also *Cox Report*, pp. 218-19, 222.
67. See above, pp. 62-65.
68. Some of the riot leaders, such as Peter Kamara of Port Loko, seem to have been absorbed later into the SLPP (see *Vanguard*, 29 July 1959), although others, such as Yolla Bangura of Samu chiefdom, later joined the APC. An undetermined number of the APC MPs elected in 1962 were members of ruling families which were rivals of the current chiefs.
69. *Cox Report*, p. 151. All senior British officials serving during the 1950s whom I interviewed claimed the chiefs were an essential and irreplaceable part of government.
70. Dr Margai noted that the Secretary of State for the Colonies had indicated that widespread public opinion in favour of the government's proposed constitutional changes was 'a prerequisite for his consideration' of the changes. One SLPP leader asserted more bluntly that Dr Margai was told he had to damp down the riots successfully in order to make any constitutional progress.
71. *Daily Mail*, 22 Sept. 1956.
72. *Daily Mail*, 2 Oct. 1956.
73. Ibid., 5 Dec. 1956.
74. See the *Reports of the Commissioners of Enquiry into the Conduct of Certain Chiefs and the Government Statement Thereon*, and *Further Reports*, etc.
75. The removal of chiefs had been recommended in 1953 in a report by N.J. Brooke, *Report on the Native Court System in Sierra Leone*, Freetown, Government Printer, 1953, pp. 24ff. (hereafter, *Brooke Report*).
76. See *Legislative Council Debates* 1956-7, 16 Oct. 1956, p. 340.
77. Ibid., p. 349.
78. All but one of the UPP's up-country representatives joined the SLPP within a few months of their election.
79. *Cox Report*, pp. 14-15.
80. Sierra Leone, *Riot Damages Commission. Final Report* (mimeo, 1960), p. 1528. The total damages claimed by persons appearing before the Commission had amounted to £1,162,311. Ibid., p. 1518.
81. Mr Justice Willan, *Reports into the Conduct of Certain Chiefs*, p. 60.
82. It seems significant that Dr Margai's only two depositions of chiefs after 1960 were of two of the more capable, progressive and honest chiefs in Sierra Leone, Tamba S. Mbriwa in Kono and Bai Koblo Pathbana in Port Loko. Mbriwa's suspension in 1962 followed by one day his announcement that his SLPIM was allying itself with the APC, while Bai Koblo's deposition, though arising out of alleged local offences against one section of his chiefdom, seems also to have involved suspicions that he leaned towards the opposition party.
83. See H.M. Joko-Smart, 'The Local Court System in Sierra Leone', *Sierra Leone Studies*, N.S. No. 22, Jan. 1968, pp. 33-4; also Ruth Finnegan, 'The Traditional Concept of Chiefship Among the Limba', ibid., No. 17, June 1963, pp. 246-7.
84. Joko-Smart, 'The Local Court System', pp. 34-41.
85. The Native Courts Ordinance 1933 (No. 40 of 1932), Section 8.

86. *House of Representatives Debates,* 1958-9, I, 20 Aug. 1958, p. 11.
87. Ibid., 25 Aug. 1958, p. 78.
88. Ibid., p. 77.
89. Interview with S.T. Navo, 17 July 1968.
90. Statement by the Prime Minister in Parliament, *House of Representatives Debates,* 1965-6, Vol. II, 18, 22 Sept. 1965, col. 308.
91. Section 31 provided that in all civil cases (the main area for customary law) an appeal would lie from District Appeals Courts to a Local Appeals Division of the Supreme Court, consisting of a Supreme Court Judge and two experts in customary law, with the decision vested exclusively in the judge. Beyond this point, appeals lay to the regular Supreme Court channels (Section 32).
92. Though it may have been more a responsiveness to pressure from the chiefs than his own convictions which produced the delay. The *Brooke Report,* in 1953, stated 'Dr Margai suggested that chiefs should divest themselves of their judicial functions' (p. 22), a comment which leaves the impression that he was not just being pushed into accepting this change.
93. *Daily Mail,* 18 Feb. 1960.
94. Interview with Sir Foley Newns, 15 Aug. 1968.
95. Interview with L.C. Greene, Permanent Secretary of the Ministry of the Interior, 11 Nov. 1965.
96. Letter from S.T. Navo to Provincial Secretaries, 2 Feb. 1965. Cited in Barrows, *Local-Level Politics,* p. 144.
97. *House of Representatives Debates,* 1965-6, III, 20, 17 Mar. 1966, col. 30. The Prime Minister's reply was a trifle indiscreet: 'Government is not aware of, nor does it attach much importance to it.'
98. See above, note 82.
99. This account of the episode is taken from Barrows, *Grassroots Politics,* pp. 183-92.
100. The Bo School, set up by the British in 1905 for the sons of chiefs, had produced among its graduates a transtribal cohesion rivalling that of French West Africa's Ecole William Ponty or the British public schools. Since nearly half the SLPP MPs had attended it, it provided a useful rallying point for internal opposition to Albert Margai, who had gone to a Freetown school.
101. Barrows, p. 185.
102. Ibid.
103. Ibid., pp. 185-96.
104. We might note that Vangahun emerged from the first vote with a slight majority, 388-358.
105. In 1962 Francis had finished third with 546 votes to B.S. Massaquoi's 3,595. In 1967, he won 2,464 votes to Massaquoi's 2,063, a change which informants attributed almost entirely to the Nongowa dispute, in which Massaquoi was aligned on the same side as Sir Albert.
106. The Electoral Provisions Act 1962 contained the usual prohibitions on exercising undue influence, treating and bribery, with the only special exemption for Paramount Chiefs being that 'a Paramount Chief may, if requested by any person . . . belonging to (his) chiefdom, advise such person on any matter concerning that election'. (Section 86.)
107. Or so I was assured by several PNP and APC candidates. One APC candidate claimed that a chief in his constituency had been restrained from working against him by the fact that the chief himself was standing for election, and feared to offend the pro-APC members among the TAs.
108. *We Yone,* 20 Feb. 1965.
109. This was explained quite openly at the convention. Notes by the writer, 21 May 1965.

110. Notes by the writer from the Sierra Leone Broadcasting System's live coverage of the press conference, 12 Jan. 1965.
111. Interview with G.A. Keister, Makeni, 13 Jan. 1965.
112. See *We Yone*, 20 Nov. 1965.
113. *Daily Mail*, 19 Feb. 1966.
114. *We Yone*, 19 Mar. 1966. His conviction was quashed, however, on appeal to the Supreme Court.
115. This view was particularly prevalent among the younger SLPP men, several of whom I spoke to in late 1965.
116. Bai Kafari had been seriously criticised and deposed after the 1955-6 riots. He was a rather heavy drinker, and perhaps not taken too seriously either in his own chiefdom or by other chiefs. Nevertheless, the police did keep an eye on his contacts; at least one Peace Corps worker was warned against associating with him.
117. See *West Africa*, 14 Dec. 1968, p. 1463, citing Stevens's remarks on a tour up-country. See also ibid., 25 Dec. 1972, p. 1717, for a reiteration of this point.
118. Cartwright, *Politics in Sierra Leone*, pp. 188-9, 192.
119. A classic study of this process of local notables gaining control of an innovative project and thus preventing it from realising its original intentions is Philip Selznick's *TVA and the Grassroots*, Berkeley and Los Angeles, University of California Press, 1949.

6 LEADERSHIP AND ETHNIC CONFLICT

Some Aspects of Ethnic Conflict

Our overview of Sierra Leone politics under the two Margais showed clearly the importance of conflict between ethnic or cultural groups as a basis for political action. From the first constitutional proposals, in which the Creole-countryman conflict quickly overshadowed the chief-commoner one, through the Kono regional party and a succession of opposition parties building on ethnic cores in opposition to the 'Mende domination' of the SLPP, these conflicts showed a persistence unmatched by any other basis of division. In this chapter we shall consider the characteristics of these identities that made them such a significant source of conflicts, and what range of policies political leaders could adopt to handle them.

In examining conflicts between cultural groups, we will find ourselves using a number of terms often confused with each other: 'ethnic group', 'ethnicity', 'regionalism', 'tribalism', 'nationalism', and some compounds from these. In defining these terms, I will treat them as having a common core of meaning in referring to a group of persons (or the attitudes held by such persons) sharing major elements of a common culture and the ability to maintain themselves as a self-sufficient social unit.[1] Beyond this, the terms differ in the extent to which they refer to a level of self-consciousness about the group's existence, in the basis of the group's identity, and in the ends sought by the group. Specifically, I use the term 'ethnic group' to refer to a group of individuals having a common race and common culture,[2] regardless of whether or not they are aware of this common feature, while 'ethnicity' refers to the possession of this feature. 'Ethnic identity' and 'tribalism' I use as synonyms to refer to a consciousness on the part of an ethnic group of their identity,[3] and an implied desire to preserve this identity, while 'regionalism' refers to a similar self-conscious identity based upon residence in a specific territory which forms part of a larger state. In all these cases, there is a potential willingness to create a separate state if necessary to protect this identity. 'Nationalism', finally, I use to refer to the conscious desire of any self-identified group to develop or maintain a politically sovereign unit. 'Nationalism' thus need not be based upon a single ethnic group or upon the whole of an ethnic group although for reasons that will be suggested below, many nationalisms are in fact based upon ethnic groups. 'Ethnic nationalism' seems to me to be an appropriate term for the desire of an ethnic or 'tribal' group to preserve its identity when it acknowledges explicitly the possibility of setting up its own sovereign state to achieve this end of self-preservation.

Since most of the world's states are multi-ethnic[4] most national political leaders have to deal at some time with the problem of reconciling different ethnic identities. The situations they have to deal with will vary with the extent to which different groups have become conscious of their own identities, the nature of their perceived needs for self-realisation, and their perceptions of the attitudes of other groups towards their desire for self-realisation. As ethnic groups become more concerned with the problem of preserving their identities, we find a steady narrowing of the limits within which leaders must work. When no group (other than possibly a dominant one) is conscious of its ethnic identity, a leader will clearly have no problem (for the time being) with ethnic conflict; members of different groups may interact with each other in a manner free of any consciousness of ethnic differences, or more likely they will exist in mutual ignorance of each other's presence.[5] When self-consciousness reaches the level at which we have 'tribalism' or regionalism, then the necessary desire for some autonomy may produce conflict, although this will depend upon the areas in which the group considers autonomy essential to the preservation of its identity, and the extent to which others are prepared to tolerate its autonomy in these areas. Finally, when a group becomes consciously nationalist and seeks political control of a state as the necessary means to its self-realisation, it faces a stark choice: either establish its dominance over the existing state, or secede and create its own. Fortunately, in this as in most other areas, most men are reluctant to carry their inclinations through to their logical conclusions.

By examining the ways in which ethnic identities develop, we can gain some inkling of how conflicts between them can be limited. We must start with the observation that defining an ethnic identity in terms of common racial and cultural attributes does not take us very far, since cultures often intergrade along their boundaries. For example, although 'Scots' and 'English' are generally considered to be two separate ethnic groups, there seems to be more similarity between the culture of lowland Scotland and that of Northumbria (or even Yorkshire) than there is between the latter and Sussex or Berkshire. What seems to set the boundary between groups in such situations is a particular set of historic circumstances. Thus there is no good 'objective' reason why the predominantly Catholic Bavarians should not think of themselves as ethnically distinct from the Lutheran Prussians, as do Austrians, nor why a person from Provence should see himself as sharing the same ethnic identity as a Normandy peasant; and conversely, the differences an outsider can discern between, say, Serbian and Montenegran cultures, or Norwegian and Swedish, seem scarcely enough for these groups to have developed separate identities.

The patterns and nature of contacts change in course of time, contributing to changes in ethnic identities. Thus it has been noted that Ibos in Nigeria living in a 'pedestrian society'[6] had until at least the 1940s very little understanding of their supposed common identity as Ibos; anyone living beyond a day's trip away was equally a 'stranger' and probably bad, whether he was Yoruba, Ijaw or another Ibo.[7] It was only when Ibos were thrown together in Lagos and other cities outside their own area that they became conscious of their 'Ibo' identity. Many other African 'tribes' similarly developed distinct identities when cast into such new situations.[8] Even those who did not travel to distant places could forge new ethnic identities over time. In Sierra Leone, the Banta and Vai were offshoots of the Temne and Kono respectively who had settled in Mende territory; within a few generations both considered themselves, and were considered by others, to be Mende.[9] The Temne were supposed to achieve ethnic cohesion through their belief in a common origin;[10] but Pollock has noted that the eastern Temne believe themselves to have been Koranko and the Yoni Temne start their history with a Fula warrior.[11] Yet in both these areas people most emphatically identified themselves as Temnes.

We can see two factors that work to prevent ethnic identities from becoming too rigid. One is that the boundaries between groups change in course of time, which implies that the cultural content for each group's identity will also change. The other factor is that even where boundaries are fixed, individuals may pass through them and take on new ethnic identities. In thus transforming his identity, however, an individual is unlikely to shed all his previous cultural equipment, and thus his acceptance as a member of his new ethnic group means that the group has accepted a certain amount of deviance from its previous cultural norms.

This rather fluid nature of ethnic identities should be borne in mind as we consider our original problem of how such identities develop, since for the sake of simplicity I will be using terms that imply that ethnic groups are fixed entities. I suggest that the starting point for the development of a group's identity must be contact with other groups in a way that allows each to perceive the other as comprising an ethnic group.[12] This contact will not of itself necessarily produce ethnic consciousness; groups could quite conceivably go through stages of increasingly close interaction until they have coalesced into one, as happened to the Congo River tribes lumped together as 'Bangala'.[13] A further step beyond intergroup contact seems to be necessary to produce ethnic consciousness; this further step is the perception by members of the group of a challenge to their identity.

A challenge will produce an assertion of a group's ethnic identity only within certain limits. At one extreme, the challenge can be so overwhelming that the group simply allows itself to be assimilated into the challenging culture. French-Canadians in Western Canada, for example, have largely vanished in an Anglophone sea,[14] and we may surmise that the Banta warriors in Sierra Leone's Mendeland were similarly swamped. At the other extreme, the 'challenge' may scarcely be perceived, and thus have no differentiating effect; few Frenchmen see the recent Breton revival as compelling them to assert their 'Frenchness', and I doubt whether we could find any Englishman who has become more conscious of his English culture as a result of a Cornish resurgence.

But between these extremes, there is a continuum of possible challenges that do produce ethnic self-assertion. Broadly we can break this continuum into three sectors. At one end of the continuum we find a politically predominant group wishing to ensure the continuation of its predominance, usually against the threat that a more numerous but non-participating group will enter the political arena. The Tutsi of Burundi and the Amhara of Ethiopia illustrate two ways in which such a group can seek to handle this situation.[15] In the middle of the continuum we find those states in which no one group is large enough or has sufficient advantages to dominate the polity, but where several groups are concerned lest others gain an advantage over them. The jockeying for position of the Ewe, Fanti and Ashanti in Ghana, or the Bemba, Lozi and Ngoni in Zambia illustrate this balance. Another variant of this balance occurs when different groups have power in different areas; the first Nigerian Republic, where the Hausa advantage in political representation was largely balanced by southerners' educational and economic superiority, was such a case, with all participants' ethnic consciousness inflamed by the fact that they could see the threats posed to their own position by the other side's advantages. Finally, the third section of the continuum comprises that numerous category of minority ethnic groups which perceive themselves as being at a disadvantage in relation to stronger ethnic groups, and which as a result assert an ethnic identity that overrides internal divisions. It is this situation that most commonly produces ethnic assertiveness; we find for example, the Scots and the

Welsh asserting ethnic identities distinct from the English, Basques and Catalonians distinguishing themselves from Castilian Spaniards, and Galla and other minority tribes declining to accept the equation of Amhara with the Ethiopian state.

But many of the challenges to a group from other groups grow out of a specific relationship, usually economic, and might thus be expected to give rise to 'class' rather than ethnic identities. For example, the Arab plantation owners in Zanzibar might equally well have been identified by Afro-Shirazi workers as either 'plantation owners' or as 'Arabs';[16] and if they had been identified as plantation-owners, conflicts between the two groups would have been much more likely to focus on limited and negotiable economic questions rather than growing into all-embracing polarisations between two communities.

The explanation for the ease with which conflicts over specific matters so easily turn into ethnic conflicts lies, I suggest, in the comprehensive nature of the ties binding together an ethnic group. An ethnic group normally will be defined by its own exclusive language (or dialect), and its members will share common assumptions and behaviour over most of the range of human interactions – family relations, bases for status, religion and so on.[17] While members of the group may disagree with each other within one segment of human relationships, still they will find that they share assumptions over most other segments, and that these shared assumptions set them apart from other ethnic groups. For example, a Swedish Communist and a Conservative will disagree deeply over desirable patterns for the state and the economy; but the Communist will probably find himself closer to his fellow Swede in his assumptions on marital relationships or child-rearing than to fellow Communists in Italy or Romania. It is this range of links, this ability to provide an all-embracing sense of 'belonging', that gives ethnicity its great hold on men.

The fact that an ethnic identity embraces an entire way of life, coupled with the activation of this identity through a threat perceived as challenging this way of life, tends to make the commitment to the identity a highly emotional one. While a conflict over a specific issue such as distribution of jobs or the position of retailers in the economy is fairly amenable to bargaining and compromise, a conflict over which way of life is to prevail is much more intractable. Group members tend to develop a 'suprarational' commitment, a belief that their way of life is a superior one[18] to be defended in its entirety and at all costs. At this stage political control over its own destiny becomes essential, with results that we have seen most recently in Bangladesh, Nigeria and Burundi.[19]

Fortunately certain factors work to counter this build-up of emotional commitment. If a threat to a group is generated along an ethnic dimension, it is often easier to perceive the source of the threat in precise terms than to so perceive its object. Thus in Sierra Leone, many people saw a threat in 'Mende domination', while in Nigeria various groups were concerned over 'Ibo domination' or over 'Hausa rule'. But who was threatened? In Sierra Leone, was it Temnes alone, or Konos, or Creoles? In Nigeria, did 'Hausa rule' threaten just Ibos, and 'Ibo dominance' in skilled jobs threaten only Northerners, or could each share the sense of being threatened with the Yorubas and with the 'minority' tribes? In other words, in most situations where a group was threatened, the counter to this threat was to ally with other groups similarly threatened, provided of course that group attitudes had not reached such a pitch of introverted emotionalism that co-operation was no longer possible.[20] But since there would be no comprehensive emotional base across ethnic boundaries, the allies in such a situation would have to focus their concerns upon those specific areas in which a threat existed, a situation much more conducive to rational negotiation.

Furthermore, an 'ethnic' perception of threats did not normally spring spontaneously from the grassroots; rather, it would be put forward by political leaders as a means of consolidating support. But to be effective, this tactic required considerable receptivity among the audience at whom such an appeal was aimed, and I think the comprehensiveness of ethnic identification goes a long way in explaining why such an appeal did succeed. But we can find another level of explanation as to why it succeeded, and also how it was partially contained, if we consider who received what benefits from emphasising an ethnic 'encompassing principle' as the primary line of political cleavage.

The interest of many members of the political elite in promoting ethnic solidarity was clear enough. Basically an ethnic appeal provided the politician with vertical links through which he could build a strong base of support, particularly important in those countries where elections still persisted, but also useful in strengthening his bargaining position in many non-elective systems. It also served to distract attention from the disproportionate share of resources accruing to the political elite, both by encouraging non-elite members of the group to enjoy vicariously the success of their champion,[21] and by attributing any perceived unfairness to the machinations of the 'tribalists' of other groups.[22] But ethnicity also provided some benefits for ordinary men as well. It gave a sense of solidarity with a larger grouping than one's immediate kin[23] and in particular it provided access to the power and protection afforded by a Minister or other prominent government figure,[24] as well as a comprehensible if not strictly 'rational' basis for allocating scarce resources among claimants.

There were naturally some costs associated with this ethnic appeal. For the ordinary man, the most serious was the stifling of the opportunity to have his 'class' interests articulated, although advocates of a more egalitarian society seem unrealistically optimistic about the chances of this being achieved under any form of democratic polity.[25] For the elite, the major hazard was that ethnic appeals would get out of hand, conceivably to the point where the state which was providing them with their present privileges would be broken up, a risk that only politicians with nothing to lose by a leap into the unknown would willingly take. Ethnic appeals thus incorporated their own strong inhibitor, provided only that some attempt was made within the elite not to exclude a particular segment from all privileges.

Ethnic consciousness could be summarised as an elusive yet powerful phenomenon. With the boundaries of an ethnic group both changeable and permeable, and varying degrees of emotional commitment, it was difficult to predict who would come together as a group, and what lengths they would go to to defend their identity. Yet if a threat were perceived by the self-identified members of an ethnic group (regardless of whether outsiders perceived it), it could conjure up a formidable commitment, even to the point of breaking up an existing state. Handling such a phenomenon would require a great deal of skill, and entail a great deal of risk, for any political leader.

There are three basic strategies open to a national political leader in dealing with ethnic conflicts, but the use of any one of these depends upon the proportions among different ethnic groups in the state, and the strength with which they hold their identities. The basic strategies are: a 'balancing' approach, taking individuals' commitments to their ethnic identities as fixed and overriding other commitments, and trying to offer a continuing series of adjustments and compromises between the claims of different groups; an 'assimilative' approach, taking the values of one ethnic group as suitable for all citizens of the state, and educating members of other groups into an acceptance of those values; and an 'overarching' approach, in which the leader attempts to create a commitment by citizens to a common set of values (for example, ideological or religious) which overrides their differing ethnic ones.

Each of these strategies only works under certain conditions (see Table 6:1), and each entails certain costs. The balancing strategy is most useful in a situation where no one group is dominant and where identities are already strongly held. In a multigroup situation where identities have not yet developed strong commitments, it can still work, but at the probable cost of strengthening these identities, while in a situation of strong identities and a dominant group, it is likely to be distorted beyond minorities' tolerance by the preponderant strength of the dominant group.[26] In the case of a dominant group and weak identities, a balancing strategy is clearly unnecessary.

The assimilative strategy will only work in the case of a dominant group and weak minority identities. Once minorities begin to sense their distinctiveness, attempts at assimilation are likely to backfire. And clearly, where no group is dominant, no one is in a position to pursue an assimilative strategy.

Table 6. 1 Strategies available under Different Conditions

		Degree to which ethnic groups are committed to their identities Strong commitment	Weak commitment
Relative position of ethnic groups in state	One group dominant	Overarching (possible; likely skewed) Balancing (if majority tolerant)	Assimilative Overarching
	No single group dominant	Balancing Overarching (possible; likely suspect)	Balancing (risks emphasizing identities) Overarching

The overarching strategy has its best chance of success where ethnic identities are weak; in particular, it is desirable where no one group can dominate and thus an assimilative strategy is ruled out, while a balancing strategy risks strengthening ethnic identities. Once identities become entrenched, it is difficult for leaders to persuade people to ignore them. In a situation where one group is dominant, either the 'overarching' appeal takes on strong assimilative overtones or the majority group may feel the leader is catering too much to the demands of minorities and ignoring their interests. Where no group is dominant, any one group can easily interpret an 'overarching' appeal as camouflage to give someone else an advantage.[27]

The leader's choice of strategies is also constrained by his ideology and style. While a non-ideological leader can happily pursue a balancing strategy, he will have a more difficult time consciously pursuing an assimilative strategy, or developing an overarching appeal, since to be successful these require the kind of consistency that only a general vision of society can give. The radical ideologue, by contrast, is unlikely to accept the 'mere tinkering' with the *status quo* implied in a balancing approach; his preference will almost invariably be for an overarching strategy, or just possibly if a dominant group is much more 'progressive' than the minorities, an assimilative one. The conservative ideologue can handle a balancing strategy somewhat more easily, although again the other two strategies will be more congenial to him.[28] The strategy he pursues also reflects a leader's style. An overarching policy to contain ethnic conflicts is a manifestation of a creative style, while a balancing policy in ethnic relations equally manifests a brokerage approach. The assimilative approach may grow out of either style, although if it is consciously pursued we would have to consider it again a manifestation of the creative style. A leader whose instincts incline towards a brokerage approach is thus unlikely to pursue an overarching strategy towards ethnic relations, while a creative leader will not be happy with a balancing approach.

The leader's position in the state will also be affected by the nature of the ethnic relations he inherits. Most fundamentally, if ethnic conflict has developed to the point where groups have become 'nations warring in the bosom of a single state' the leader's very legitimacy may exist only for members of his own group, and then because of his role within that group rather than in his capacity as head of the entire state.[29] There are of course many intermediate points between this extreme and the other more desirable one at which the leader enjoys equal legitimacy in the eyes of all the contending groups; most commonly he will be accepted most of the time as the leader of all, but occasionally will be perceived as a partisan of a particular group.[30] The degree to which he enjoys legitimacy will in turn affect his ability to pursue various strategies towards ethnic conflicts; a leader whose legitimacy in the eyes of certain groups is low will have a hard time convincing such groups of his sincerity in pursuing an overarching strategy.

The leader's pattern of contacts with the populace will also be affected by the nature of ethnic relations. Where ethnic identities are strongly held, the leader will normally have to bargain with 'strong' intermediaries representing various ethnic groups; individuals loyal to him simply will not have sufficient confidence among these groups to be able to carry out his wishes. Strong ethnic loyalties may also preclude transethnic patronage chains, thus forcing the co-ordination of different ethnic demands to the top levels of government.[31]

Rather than trying to present an exhaustive typology of interactions between ethnic conflict and leadership at this point, I would like to save further consideration of these interactions until we have dealt with our case study. But first, to conclude this general introduction, I will examine briefly some key features of ethnic conflict in Sierra Leone.

Among Sierra Leone's sixteen ethnic groups[32] there are some manifestations of 'ethnic nationalism' as I have defined the term, but these were held in check by a powerful combination of factors. The Creoles' assertion of their 'superior' identity led a number of them in the 1947-51 crisis to demand that the Colony be made a separate state,[33] while the 'Kono for the Konos' rallying cry of the SLPIM in the period 1956-65 also carried separatist implications.[34] Finally, in the 1967 election campaign Albert Margai's appeals to Mende fears that the northerners would take away their privileges was a fairly successful appeal to the emotional force of ethnic nationalism, although here its limits were clearly shown by the fact that while Mendeland held solid for the SLPP, his failure to carry non-Mende areas cost Margai the election.

Other appeals by members of the political elite were frequently directed *against* specific ethnic groups, from Dr Margai's denunciations of Creole misdeeds through to the APC's attacks on 'Mende domination'. But these appeals did not normally seek to exalt the superiority of a particular ethnic group, and for a very good reason: such an appeal would backfire against the person using it. Even the Mendes, whose electoral position was stronger than that of any other tribe, never controlled more than 43 per cent of the total legislative seats;[35] so unless Sierra Leone were to become a federal rather than a unitary state (a prospect never seriously considered after 1951), no group could hope to gain majority control through a purely ethnic appeal, and to use such an appeal was the surest way to unite all other groups against its users.

Other factors also contributed to reducing the emotional content of inter-ethnic conflicts. 'Tribal' identities were often situational, with an individual adjusting his 'tribe' to accord with his perception of his status. John Sinclair cites the case of a family in which one daughter who had gone to secondary school and worked as a teacher used her father's Christian surname, followed the Christian religion and although calling herself a Mende (her mother's tribe) was often taken for a Creole, while her half-brother, who had not attended school and worked as a lorry-boy, was a Muslim and used his maternal grandparents' Temne surname, regarding his father's name as appropriate only for educated people. Sinclair goes on to argue from this and numerous other cases that:

> tribes are not fixed natural groups, recruited solely on the basis of descent, but rather conceptual, cultural categories . . . (T)ribes have in fact been arranged into a culturally evaluated hierarchy, which for the participants may act as a proto-type model in their perception of social class. So an individual who has been socially mobile will attempt to crystallise his rise in status by taking the tribal identity of a group rated above his in the hierarchy.[36]

What is significant here is that where the situation called for an individual either to demand improved status for his 'tribal' identity, or to alter the tribal identity to fit an improved class status, he was likely to alter the tribal identity, a pattern of behaviour which certainly suggests a considerable degree of fluidity in these identities.

The widespread use of a *lingua franca,* Krio, which was neutral as between the various 'up-country' groups, also helped reduce feelings of intertribal dominance or subordination. By the 1960s Krio was firmly established as the language of both work and social situations involving intertribal contact, and even for a number of relationships between members of the same tribe.[37] Then too, the 'countrymen' in many work situations had been able throughout the 1940s and 1950s to see themselves as sharing a common subordination to Creoles and Europeans, and thus to transcend their specific ethnic consciousness. Later, as a belief in 'Mende domination' grew, all Northerners and other non-Mendes could share a similar feeling.[38] In both cases, the transtribal unity produced a focus on specific grievances rather than permitting a group the luxury of an all-embracing exaltation of its own superiority. Finally, we should recall that at least through the 1950s an elite of chiefs and Western-educated professional men largely transcended 'tribal' boundaries through their family relationships, their attendance at the same educational institutions, their use of English and Krio as their languages of communication, their similar occupations, and most of all their consciousness of their common elite position.[39] All these factors worked at both the elite and the grassroots levels to keep the emotional level of ethnic conflict low, at least by comparison with other African states.[40]

Ethnic Clashes in Sierra Leone Politics

(a) Creoles against Countrymen

It is one of the ironies of Sierra Leone's history that the bitterest and most long-lasting 'ethnic' conflict should involve on the one side the most permeable and least sharply defined 'ethnic' group, and on the other side a coalition of groups so broad as to be untenable as a basis for political agreement. Yet both Creoles and 'countrymen' were sustained in their antagonism by the threats they perceived from each other. The Creoles' long-standing awareness of themselves as a distinct and privileged minority turned to fear for their very survival as a group with the advent of the mass franchise, which left them seemingly dependent on the tolerance of the vastly superior numbers from the hinterland of Sierra Leone. The 'countrymen', whatever their differences between themselves, could agree that the Creoles, like the Europeans, were alien intruders whose values posed a threat to many aspects of their customary way of life, and who had the skills and economic resources to dominate the political and economic structures the Europeans had set up, and thus to impose their values on all Sierra Leone society. Throughout the period of decolonisation, both were given ample opportunity to find justification for their fears.

The Creole community was marked by the most comprehensive, yet at the same time the most permeable boundaries of any Sierra Leonean group. The original Settlers and the Recaptives who had come from outside Sierra Leone had by the late nineteenth century assimilated substantial numbers of 'up-country' Africans through wardship and adoption of children, marriage by traders up-country, and acceptance of successful entrepreneurs among the hinterland immigrants to the Colony.[41] A person could be accepted as Creole if he habitually spoke Krio, possessed formal education, professed a Christian religion, used a Creole rather than a 'tribal' name, and was engaged in white-collar or skilled work. Even if his own 'tribal' origins were remembered, his children's would almost certainly be forgotten.

Underlying these attributes was a basic value of Creole society which gave Creoles a considerable advantage over up-country people in maintaining control of the administrative, legal and educational structures bequeathed to Sierra Leone by the British. This value, most conspicuous in the Creole pursuit of education,[42] was the stress on individual achievement, which led to strong family pressure on Creole children to surpass other children in school, to go as far as possible in the educational system, to marry well, and to attain the highest-status career open.[43]

While the up-country man would often find that formal Western education and an ensuing professional or technical career set a great gulf between him and his family[44] the Creole's family would generally understand and appreciate his achievement.

The permeability of their boundaries did not prevent the Creoles from achhieving a high degree of ethnic solidarity. Their universal desire for achievement through education helped link rich and poor Creoles by inducing those too poor to afford primary education for their children to send them as wards to wealthier relatives.[45] The Creole death ceremonies, in which a deceased person's most successful relatives were put under an obligation to help meet his funeral expenses by being publicly named as his kin, also served to bridge the gap between rich and poor.[46] Among the more affluent, the Masonic Lodge performed much the same functions of building attachment to shared symbols and solidarity through social intercourse that the Poro Society did among the Mende.[47]

I have referred several times to the Creoles as 'Christian'. We should, however, note the existence of the Aku, or Muslim, Creoles, whose Yoruba surnames, Islamic religion, and pursuit of success through trade rather than professional or academic status, culminating in the pilgrimage to Mecca and the title of Alhaji, all served to set them apart, and in the eyes of the Christians, on a lower plane. Arthur Porter has observed that:

> until about the eve of the Second World War they were a community who did not share or contest a share in the status-reward-power system of Freetown,[48]

although since that time they have increasingly leaned towards the same educational goals as their Christian relatives. However, since a Western education for them was considerably less compatible with their family values than it was for the Christian Creoles, they can be considered as being under a similar handicap to the up-country youths in obtaining the basic passport to high-status positions in the national administrative and educational structures, while being sufficiently identified as 'Creole' that they could have little hope of success in the political structure.

The mutual suspicions between Creoles and countrymen which came to a head over the 1947 constitutional proposals had roots stretching back at least to the late nineteenth century, when 'the natives' first began to come in numbers to Freetown. The 1898 Hut Tax War massacres of Creoles by Mende surprise attacks had left a particular residue of suspicion towards the Mendes, and the introduction of chiefs into the Legislative Council in 1924 offered the first warning that a political system giving participatory rights to the vastly superior numbers of the Protectorate might some day be introduced by the British. But up to 1947, the Creole community continued to remain largely indifferent to the 'natives', both in the Colony and the Protectorate. Their role as 'Westernisers' outside Sierra Leone was being superseded,[49] they had been almost completely excluded from administrative positions in the Protectorate, and even in the Colony they were largely confined to professional and technical posts outside the mainstream of decision-making.[50] But as long as the franchise in the Colony was highly restrictive, they were safe from threats from below. While there was little political co-operation during the interwar period between Colony and Protectorate leaders, their relationships were generally based on indifference rather than hostility.

The 1947 constitutional proposals, with their implication that Creoledom would henceforth be a political minority at the mercy of Protectorate politicians, was a turning point in Creole-countryman relations. While a minority of Creoles saw the inevitability of this development, and sought to meet it by the only strategy which could be effective over the long run, the establishment of a political structure in which Creoles' inherent advantages could be maintained,[51] the majority reacted by opposing the proposed reforms so strongly that they brought about the polarisation they most feared. One could suggest that the intransigence of the Creoles, and the consequent alignment of all the Protectorate forces against them, was the result of bad leadership on the part of Bankole-Bright, Wallace-Johnson and others. But more moderate Creoles, such as Laminah Sankoh and H.E.B. John, did try to present the alternative strategy and failed to convince a majority of Creoles to follow them. While in retrospect the Creole community's behaviour was a mistake, it was the same mistake that has been made by nearly every privileged and distinctive community in the face of twentieth-century demands for broader political participation, from the Tutsi of Rwanda and the white settlers of Kenya to the Arabs of Zanzibar and the Protestants of Ulster.[52]

The Creoles' defeat in the battle over who was to control the legislature and executive did not end their efforts to exercise political power. Throughout the 1950s and 1960s the Creoles sought to entrench themselves at those points of influence in the polity where their educational and social advantages were greatest. A continuing struggle, covert under Dr Margai and more open under his brother, went on in many key government departments between Creoles seeking to maintain their position and provincial men working to oust them.

The key 'political' areas in which Creoles retained a strong position vis-à-vis the provincial men were the bureaucracy, particularly in the departments of education, finance, works, health and law, the legal profession, and the field of education, particularly at the secondary and post-secondary level. In the bureaucracy, in 1965 across the entire Administrative Class there were fifty-one Creoles against twenty-five men of up-country origin, and eleven of thirteen Permanent Secretaries were Creoles. Only in the District Officer group, with its up-country postings, did up-country men outnumber Creoles, there being twelve up-country DOs and ADOs against five Creoles.[53] In 1964, in the Department of Education, with its control over scholarships for advanced study, all but seven of the forty-two Sierra Leoneans who were principals, education officers or others who could make recommendations were Creoles, while in the legal arena, not only were all but two Supreme Court and Court of Appeal judges Creoles,[54] but the law officers with one exception were all Creoles.[55] In 1964-5, at Fourah Bay College, the training ground for both future civil servants and teachers, eighteen of the nineteen Sierra Leoneans on full-time teaching staff were Creoles.

Despite their strength in these key areas, the Creoles suffered some serious disadvantages. A major aggravation was the question of land ownership, since the belief of Creoles that a man should have his own house as a gathering place for all his family was freighted with as many suprarational attachments as was the possession of ancestral land for up-country people.[56] In the Colony land had always been available for freehold purchase, whereas up-country ownership had to remain vested in the chief and Tribal Authority.[57] Creoles found this doubly aggravating; on the one hand, they were unable to use their own wealth to acquire land up-country, while on the other hand they had to watch while first Lebanese and later wealthy individuals from up-country were able to purchase houses in 'dey yone' small peninsula.[58] In the long term it posed the threat that the Creoles would lose an important pillar of the economic foundation from which they were able to obtain the educational advantages which ensured their survival. The government decision in 1962 to permit land to be sold only to Sierra Leonean citizens was of some help to the Creoles (even though it could be seen as of even more benefit to the up-country people, since they could deal with the Creoles through political channels much more readily than they could deal with foreign nationals), but the SLPP flatly refused to accede to the continual Creole plea that the provinces should be opened to freehold ownership by any Sierra Leoneans.

A more immediate danger was the Creoles' lack of voting strength even in their Colony stronghold. The 1948 Census showed that even in Freetown itself, Creoles numbered only a quarter of the population.[59] Before the 1957 elections, the first with a broad franchise, a group of prominent SLPP Creoles felt compelled to write to Dr Margai and his brother (who was then party chairman) claiming that an agreement confining SLPP candidacies in the Colony to persons of Colony origin was being flouted by SLPP activists.[60] The flurry was soon smoothed over, and in both the 1957 and 1962 general elections nearly all SLPP candidates in the Colony were Creoles.[61] Creoles were also continuously represented in both Sir Milton and Sir Albert's Cabinets. But these political positions were held largely on the sufferance of the up-country element in the SLPP, and the Creoles were fully aware of this, from the time that Dr Margai first commented in 1952 that the Creoles were not essential to 'our majority'[62] to the tense period in 1966 when SLPP spokesmen claimed to see a 'Settler plot' driving a wedge between Mendes and Temnes.[63]

The up-country elite had their own fears about the Creoles, based for the most part on those factors we have noted as Creole strength. Up-country students at Fourah Bay claimed that Creole lecturers discriminated against them.[64] The lists of secondary school graduates granted awards for further study abroad consistently showed a preponderance of Creoles; even by 1969, fully seventeen years after up-country people had secured political power, 64 per cent of the award winners were Creoles.[65] The same predominance was shown in new appointments and promotions to the higher levels of the civil service. Of 98 appointments to superscale posts between 1 January 1963 and 31 August 1965, 68 were from the Western Area.[66] Even though a few particularly critical posts went to non-Creoles, as long as appointments were made on 'merit' (meaning formal educational qualifications), Creoles would gain a disproportionate share. While this irritated many up-country leaders, it was hard for them to attack 'merit' directly without seeming to demand a rather shameless favouring of 'their' people.

Politically the Creoles were in a position of considerable strength. While they would be totally defeated in a head-on electoral confrontation, they occupied sufficient key positions that for a government to arouse their collective antagonism would be a very costly move. They were a promising target against which to rally widespread support from both urban and rural masses, largely because of their privileged class position[67] but only if a government was prepared to accept a considerable worsening of its administrative capabilities.

(b) The Growth of Northern Self-Awareness

Up to the late 1950s few people in the Northern Province seem to have felt that either their identities as members of particular tribes or their collective identity as 'Northerners' were of great political significance. The largest tribe, the Temne, had begun in the 1940s to assert their claim to be the masters of Freetown under the leadership of their Tribal Headman, Kande Bureh,[68] but this was largely an urban phenomenon. For the most part, northern leaders had accepted as the most significant ethnic cleavage the Creole-countryman dispute, which saw them working side by side with the Mendes to establish 'the countryman's party', the SLPP, as the dominant political force. At the Ministerial level the SLPP seemed reasonably balanced. From 1951 to 1957 the six Ministers included Siaka Stevens, who although brought up largely in Mendeland also spoke his father's Limba tongue, and was generally regarded as a Limba, and Paramount Chief Bai Farima Tass, a Temne.[69] After the 1957 expansion of the legislature and Cabinet, although Stevens was no longer a Minister, Northerners still found places; Dr John Karefa-Smart, the first Temne doctor, I.B. Taylor-Kamara, the first Temne lawyer, as well as Kande Bureh, Paramount Chief Bai Koblo (from 1959) and Y.D. Sesay, a Loko school headmaster, all held Ministerial portfolios.

But while the Northern elite seemed to be receiving an equitable proportion of patronage, at the level of the ordinary farmer or worker the picture was less encouraging. We noted earlier[70] that at the start of decolonisation the north was considerably behind the southern and eastern provinces by most of the available indicators of economic and social development, and this situation continued up to and beyond Independence.[71] Thus we find in 1965-6 that northern farmers less often grew staple crops such as rice, groundnuts or cassava for cash than did farmers in either the southern or eastern province, either as their primary occupation[72] or as a supplementary activity.[73] Their farms were on the average smaller,[74] less often employed hired labour[75] and were less likely to be on newly cleared land,[76] indicating a more severe problem of population pressure. Those farmers who produced market crops suffered transportation handicaps relative to their southern competitors; more than a third (37 per cent) required more than three hours to ship their produce to market, whereas less than a fifth of southern farmers needed this length of time.[77]

But if farming in the north was less rewarding than in the south, the alternatives were even less promising. Only 11 per cent of the labour force worked at non-farm labour in the north, against 21 per cent in the six Mende districts.[78] Much of this difference could be attributed to the presence of alluvial diamonds in the south, but the fact remains that there was no equivalent opportunity in the north. It is scarcely surprising that while there were some 52,000 Temnes in the southern and eastern provinces outside their own areas, there were less than a tenth of this number of Mendes in the north.

Finally, the long-term prospects for northerners to join those parts of the elite requiring formal education were also limited. While from 1948 to 1963 the number of Northern children in primary school rose from 3,291 to 24,034,a rate of increase nearly twice that of the southern and eastern provinces, in absolute numbers the north still had less than half as many children in school as the two southern provinces.[79] Even excluding Koinadugu, the rest of the Northern Province had only 10 per cent of its five to nineteen year-olds in school, against 19 per cent for the six Mende districts.[80]

All these indicators of backwardness, however, would suggest that the northerners should simply continue quietly as junior partners in the SLPP hegemony. Men who were rural dwellers, subsistence farmers, limited in their contacts with the outside world, and with limited education and cash incomes, were not likely to spread their 'identity horizon' widely enough to encompass an entire tribe or region. What was it that seemed to have increased so substantially the number of individuals concerned with these identities, and to take political action on this basis?

It is easiest to start by hypothesising what seems to have happened among the northern elite and sub-elites. For these individuals the turning point seems to have been the United Front, in which additional Creoles and Mendes were taken into the Cabinet partly through the device of dividing Temne Ministers' portfolios.[81] At the sub-elite level, the leading opposition party, the PNP, split rather neatly along Mende-northern lines over the United Front, with most of its younger Mende cadres following Albert Margai and his associates back into the SLPP, while its northern activists joined Siaka Stevens in building the APC. At the same time, some of the SLPP northerners came to share the suspicion that Dr Margai was trying to entrench the Mendes in a position of permanent superiority, and gave tacit support to the new 'northern man's party'. At this level of political sophistication and activity, there was no problem of creating a broad enough identity to embrace all persons of an entire region; these men were already in frequent contact with each other, could see their situation in a national context, and could conceive of national political action as the appropriate means of dealing with perceived injustices – which injustices included the denial of their personal opportunities for advancement. All that was needed to encourage either a 'tribal' or a regional identity was an appropriate antagonistic group; and the advantages enjoyed by the Mendes, as well as the actions of the Mende Prime Minister, served this function well.

At the 'grassroots' level, the development of politically salient 'tribal' or regional identities was a somewhat more difficult matter, and requires a somewhat more complex explanation. I think that the diamond rush contributed greatly to this process, directly through the fact that great numbers of northerners saw for the first time the relative prosperity of the south, and were thrown together as 'strangers' in the diamond areas,[82] and indirectly through encouraging ordinary men to take responsibility for their own fate, rather than leaving all but the most routine activities in the hands of figures of authority. The northern riots probably also encouraged this self-reliance, sharpening it with the lesson that ordinary men could take actions that might have some effect in improving their political situation. While neither digging diamonds nor rioting had any necessary connection with *ethnic* expressions of political awareness (both were more likely to express a *class* orientation) the very fact that men would take these actions for the first time indicated a breadth of awareness which could later be translated into other forms of more specifically political activity.

Determining the extent to which ordinary men came to act politically upon a perception of themselves as an ethnic or a regional group is not easy. The mere fact that the APC leaders championed regional and class claims is no evidence that those who voted for them saw their situation in these relatively abstract terms. It is quite possible that a substantial proportion of 'APC voters', at least in 1962, chose their candidates on the same basis of personal and local factional considerations as did those who voted for SLPP and Independent candidates.[83] (By 1967, when the APC won 79 per cent of the votes in the Northern Province, it was clearly gaining substantial support on some basis wider than local grounds.) But while many APC supporters supported their candidate on these personal or local grounds,[84] nevertheless there were striking differences between their attitudes and those of Northern SLPP supporters in two areas. The APC supporters were much more critical of the chiefly 'Establishment', and they were also much more critical of a perceived pro-Mende bias on the part of Sir Milton as well as Sir Albert Margai.[85] We can suggest that at least for a considerable minority of Northern voters, ethnic or regional considerations seem to have played some part in their political choice at least as early as 1962.

I suggested earlier that an ethnic identity, because of the comprehensiveness of its links, was likely to develop intense emotional commitments which precluded rational bargaining.[86] A regional identity, by contrast, because it united disparate groups against a common antagonist, was likely to be more limited in its aims, and thus more amenable to the working out of compromises, assuming the will for compromise was present on the other side, and that a leader was prepared to seek an accommodation. At both the elite and the 'mass' level we can find powerful factors to encourage a Northern 'regional' rather than specific 'tribal' identities. For an elite to encourage 'tribalism' in its full supra-rational strength was counterproductive, since a coalition of tribes was necessary to control the polity, and a display of self-exaltation by one tribe would probably alienate others. At the mass level, some evidence suggests that 'class' discontent with their own chiefs and other notables was as powerful a factor as ethnic discontent in leading men to support the APC.[87] This 'class' discontent was a powerful antidote to 'tribalism', since 'tribalism' would entail a unifying of all members of the ethnic group, including the unpopular chiefs. While it seems plausible enough to suggest that men could simultaneously see themselves as being subject to mistreatment by their chiefs, and by an antagonistic region, it seems rather less plausible to suggest that they could simultaneously see themselves as mistreated by the chiefs and at the same time banded together with those same chiefs against all outsiders.

Once a regional identity had found political expression through an opposition political party, the constituency system and Parliamentary conventions worked to strengthen the region's differentation from the rest of the country. While the APC had tried in 1962 to appeal as much on 'class' as on regional grounds, it was a party led by Northerners and with most of its candidates in the north. Not surprisingly, the constituencies where its candidates gained pluralities were nearly all in the north (apart from four in the Western area), with the result that the Temne/Limba districts were represented by twelve opposition and only five government supporters. While this imbalance was quickly tempered by two APC members crossing to the government side and three of the northern SLPP members finding Cabinet posts,[88] their region was still heavily under-represented in the Cabinet by comparison with the Mende areas, which had a total of nine Cabinet posts. Short of forming a coalition government, or winning over individual defectors from the APC by offering them Cabinet posts, there was not much Dr Margai could do to right this imbalance, even though the effect was to further increase the northern sense of deprivation.

It was the succession of Albert Margai to the Premiership, however, that raised the level of northern discontent to the point where the APC became entrenched as 'our' party. One scholar has suggested that a factor in this resentment was the difference between Mende and Temne rules of chieftaincy succession; in Mende culture it was quite permissible for one ruling family to attempt to monopolise the chief's position, whereas in Temne culture rotation between different ruling families was the normatively approved practice.[89] More immediate was the fact that a region already feeling itself deprived now saw the country's top post remain in the hands of the group it perceived as better off, rather than going to one of its own strong contenders. Perhaps this grievance could have been partially smoothed over if Albert had taken immediate steps to placate the north; but instead, his first act was to drop from his Cabinet four Ministers who had opposed his succession, including two northerners.

Albert's poor relations with northerners were compounded, as we shall see, by a number of subsequent actions, not all within his control. For example, the appearance of Mende dominance in the civil service was not entirely through design; it happened that the most senior men for the posts being vacated by expatriates were Mendes. On the other hand, the taking of cows from the poor district of Koinadugu, the unpunished slapping of a northern chief by a Mende Minister, and the construction of airfields at Albert's home bases of Gbangbatoke and Bonthe while more distant Kabala continued to rely on a rough road, were all actions that suggested at least a lack of sensitivity on the Prime Minister's part towards northern feelings. Since he started with an initial handicap of suspicion, the new Prime Minister should have been aware that any actions appearing to discriminate against the north would have been noted and remembered much more carefully than actions to redress its disadvantages; but he almost completely ignored this maxim.

(c) The Konos: Ethnic Consciousness and Economic Radicalism

The Kono district was the first up-country area to maintain a sustained opposition to the SLPP, an opposition which like the APC in the north combined a strong regional consciousness with 'radical' economic proposals. In certain respects the roots of Kono discontent appeared to resemble those of the North: economic and social backwardness,[90] a conspicuous lack of spokesmen in the government,[91] and chiefs as exploitative of their people as any in Sierra Leone. But the basis for the chiefs' exploitation, as well as many of the other features which gave political conflict in Kono its special intensity, were the result of Kono's diamonds and the rush to mine them in the 1950s. When alluvial mining was licensed in 1956, the chiefs in the 'diamond chiefdoms' were able to tap their own mine in the form of land rents and extra-legal charges for residence permits, as well as high rents for accommodation for the hordes of 'strangers' who poured into the district. But these benefits of the diamond rush did not trickle down to the ordinary farmers, who often found the chief handing over their farm to 'strangers' for diamond digging and leaving them dispossessed. The sheer number of 'strangers' involved[92] would have created problems in any circumstances, but when the 'strangers' seemed to be getting preferred treatment from the Kono chiefs, it was not surprising to find a protect movement combining Kono nationalism with strong 'class' overtones against the chiefs' privileges.

Two further factors supported Kono ethnic self-consciousness. Kono's lack of educational facilities had meant that the better 'Africanised' jobs in the SLST labour force had been pre-empted by Creoles and Mendes, and even after 1956, when some 500 to 1,000 Kono school leavers a year began to come into the job market, their qualifications were still inferior to those of their 'stranger' competitors.[93] These Kono 'young men' eventually emerged as the leadership cadres of the Democratic Peoples Congress, after serving an apprenticeship in the earlier party, the Sierra Leone Progressive Independence Movement. The second factor was the pre-colonial resentment of Kono Poro society members against the domination of the somewhat different Mende Poro, a resentment which left Konos particularly sensitive to signs of 'Mende domination'.[94] The alluvial diamond mining agreement of 1956, which opened up all the Mende areas while leaving Kono's richest area in the hands of SLST, appeared to Konos 'a Mende plot, carried out with the connivance of the Mende-dominated SLPP'.[95] Kono suspicions of Mende dominance in the SLPP, then, had a much longer-standing basis than did the northerners' concern.

These grievances first cohered into the Kono Progressive Movement (later, as an aspiring 'national' party, the SLPIM), about 1956. The leaders of the SLPIM were drawn from the younger members of the chiefly stratum of Kono society, largely from the non-diamond chiefdoms.[96] Although in social background they thus resembled the

SLPP leadership, their programme demanded reforms which would allow more participation by commoners in government, and as the licensing system's effects became apparent, a curbing of the chiefs' powers. They also demanded more land from the SLST for hand digging, control over SLST's private police force, and more social development which would benefit all the people of the region.[97] In the diamond area up to 1960, they operated an organisation as 'radical' by Sierra Leone standards as were their beliefs, setting up in effect a structure parallel to the chiefs and District Officer to handle complaints and to press for the redress of grievances.[98] But from 1960 onwards the leadership gradually slid back into the more normal Sierra Leone pattern of building support on the basis of chiefs or rival ruling house factions.[99]

Although the SLPIM won every election, district and national, in Kono from 1957 to 1963, the national government's harassment gradually took its toll. Chief Mbriwa was suspended in 1962, and deposed and banished in 1963; a few months later, three of the four SLPIM members of Parliament crossed to the SLPP, as did a majority of the District Councillors, an action which miraculously released substantial central government funds which had until then been withheld from the District Council.[100] At the grassroots level, the issuance of the residential permits required of all non-Konos in the district was made contingent on professing membership in the SLPP.[101] When Albert Margai became Prime Minister, the issue of permits was removed from the chiefs, thus alleviating a major source of discontent, but persecution of the remaining SLPIM members continued. In 1965, Chief Mbriwa's banishment was ended, he announced the dissolution of the SLPIM and his adherence to the SLPP, and a few weeks later was re-elected as Chief of Faiama chiefdom.[102]

The loss of its leaders however, did not end radicalism in Kono. The DPC was formed in July 1965 on an even stronger platform of redistribution of wealth to the Kono people as a whole[103] and indicated its somewhat less exclusively Kono outlook by immediately entering into a firm alliance with the APC. Even more than the SLPIM, it became a target for both the chiefs and the national SLPP leadership, but managed to hang on to a good deal of its support, eventually winning two out of four contested seats in the 1967 elections.[104]

The problems the Margais faced in Kono showed vividly the difficulties imposed on a leader by existing structures and commitments. To an even greater extent than in the north, Kono discontent stemmed from a condition of relative economic deprivation, which in theory could be alleviated by the government pouring development funds into the district to build roads, schools and other desired amenities. The fact that Kono comprised only about 8 per cent of Sierra Leone's area and population made such a redistribution of national resources economically feasible, if a leader was willing and able to override the clamour of other areas. There was the complication that part of the ordinary Kono's discontent arose from the behaviour of the chiefs in the diamond areas, but if Dr Margai had been prepared to exercise as much coercion against these chiefs as he allowed against the SLPIM, they could have been compelled quite easily to meet the SLPIM's demands. But because Dr Margai appeared unwilling to discipline the Kono chiefs and other long-standing SLPP supporters, these in turn were able to freeze out the SLPIM men who were coerced into coming across in 1963.[105] By the time Albert Margai succeeded in getting a formal dissolution of the SLPIM in 1965, he was forced back into dependence on the chiefs by the rise of the DPC, and thus could not afford, as his brother could have done, to abandon these reactionary allies. Making the SLPP national leadership acceptable in Kono would never have been an easy task; but the best chance for it would have been in 1963-4, when the SLPIM was in confusion, and more important, the chiefs could have been disciplined without the risk of a radical opposition taking advantage of this action. It was a situation which called for bold initiatives, against the chiefs and SLST, and towards a reconciliation with the SLPIM. Dr Margai, I suspect, simply would not have entertained the idea of such actions, while his brother's weakness was a lack of sufficient farsightedness to see the possibility of resolving 'the Kono problem' for a very long time.

(d) The Lebanese

The Lebanese occupy a somewhat anomalous place in Sierra Leone society.[106] On the one hand, in the eyes of most Sierra Leoneans they fall outside any putative Sierra Leone 'community'; they are as clearly 'foreign' as the British. On the other hand, most of the 3,000-odd Lebanese in Sierra Leone have known no other home; although they may have retained family ties with Lebanon, may think of retiring there, and (largely because of Sierra Leone's citizenship laws) hold Lebanese passports, they are more a part of the Sierra Leone community than of any other. Furthermore, their position differs from that of the expatriate businessmen from Europe or Japan in a crucial respect; they have no powerful government behind them ready to come to their defence if they run into difficulties. It is for this reason that I have decided to deal with them in this section on ethnic divisions rather than under the otherwise more appropriate heading of external business influences.

As foreigners, and at that a close-knit social group who kept themselves largely apart from the Sierra Leoneans (though there were a number of cases of Lebanese men marrying Sierra Leone women), the Lebanese did not participate to any significant extent in Sierra Leonean society outside the economic sphere. Here their impact was highly concentrated, with the great majority engaged in retail trade and diamond dealing, activities which brought them into much closer contact with the ordinary Sierra Leonean than did the occupations of European businessmen. They dominated the retail trade in Sierra Leone; outside half a dozen of the largest towns there were no European-owned retail stores while African traders' shops were comparatively tiny affairs, with very limited capital, stocks and credit facilities for their customers. The major stores in every sizable town, and also in those rural villages where the rice and palm oil trade was considerable, were invariably Lebanese, normally run by a single family, with Africans rarely being given any positions of responsibility. On the other hand, the Lebanese traders frequently spoke the local language fluently and were willing to provide credit when European business men would not and Africans could not.[107] Their reputation among both the African intelligentsia and among Europeans was poor; they were generally regarded as the schemers behind much of the illicit diamond mining and smuggling,[108] as well as the profiteering in rice and palm oil during periods of scarcity. SLST's concern over Lebanese involvement in diamond stealing was such that SLST employees were forbidden to enter Lebanese shops in Koidu, and entry to the SLST compound was forbidden to all Lebanese.

Among ordinary Sierra Leoneans attitudes towards the Lebanese seemed somewhat less hostile. During the northern riots, there was at least one reported incident where a Lebanese trader's goods were carefully removed to safety before his shop, owned by a hated chief, was burned to the ground.[109] Dawson's study of group attitudes in the north found that while Africans avoided intimacy with the Lebanese, they generally regarded them favourably, citing the Lebanese propensity to learn local languages, marry African women, provide financial assistance, and build fine buildings.[110] Conversely, asked which groups 'cause trouble', only three of a sample of thirty-nine cited the Lebanese; Temnes and Mendes seemed much more inclined to cite each other than this group of outsiders. It seems that there was not a great deal of potential for using the Lebanese as scapegoats, as General Amin was to use the Asians in Uganda, although it is possible that they could be pushed into this role.[111]

A number of government actions after Independence suggested some hostility towards the Lebanese, and to some degree also suggested a government desire to meet popular aspirations for Africanisation. First came the retroactive restriction of automatic citizenship to persons of 'negro African descent', abridging the original provision at independence that any resident of Sierra Leone became a citizen automatically if one of his parents or grandparents had been born in the territory (itself a provision which eliminated most Lebanese adults, since relatively few were of the second generation to be born in Sierra Leone).[112] Then came a ban in 1963 on any non-Africans trading in rice[113] and after Albert Margai had taken over, a series of restrictions on non-citizens' participation in such fields as goods transportation, sand and gravel haulage, baking, and 'any other business as the Minister may from time to time stipulate'.[114] Although these bills gave the appearance of opening up more opportunities to Africans, since there were few Africans available to take advantage of the opportunities, and it was possible to circumvent the new restrictions by setting up dummy African 'owners', little was changed. The Lebanese continued to trade quietly in their principal spheres, even though they could foresee the possibility of more stringent controls being applied in the future; and they continued to offer discreet support to the government of the day, as well as the occasional personal sweetener to an individual minister or civil servant, to be allowed to carry on as before. But beyond the indirect effect of encouraging an attitude of cynicism towards laws and probity by their willingness to engage in illicit diamond dealing and bribery of officials, their effect on Sierra Leone politics was limited. Certainly their free-enterprising approach would make them unsympathetic to a 'socialist reconstruction of society' on, say, the Tanzanian post-Arusha model, and they could offer considerable inducements to political leaders to stop such dangerous thoughts from being expressed in the political arena. But they had to be discreet in their approach, because with no powerful government behind them, their position was extremely vulnerable if a government did decide to look for an economic scapegoat.

Milton Margai and Ethnic Conflict: The Limits of Benign Neglect

Dr Margai's conservative restraint in dealing with social changes had mixed effects in the field of ethnic relations. In dealing with the Creoles, whose strong self-consciousness precluded any overarching or assimilative strategy, he pursued a successful balancing strategy, within the limits of a basic *laissez-faire* approach. But with the Northerners, whose early lack of self-consciousness led him to use the overarching appeals of unity among all 'countrymen' and loyalty to the chiefs, his reluctance to undertake more than minimal action to alleviate discontent led to a hardening of ethnic and regional identities that ultimately toppled his successor. Although the luck of his coming to office at a time when no group other than the Creoles had linked their ethnic self-consciousness to political conflicts meant that he could survive without a great deal of ethnic balancing, his lack of clear conciliatory measures towards disaffected regions allowed regional opposition to build to the point where the range of options for his successor was drastically reduced.

Dr Margai's first major attack on the Creoles, his 'handful of foreigners' speech in the Protectorate Assembly in September 1950,[115] came after it had been made clear that no accommodation could be reached between the Creoles and the educated Protectorate elite, and several of his subsequent actions attempted to heal the breach. Following the 1951 elections, the only two SLPP supporters from Colony seats, M.S. Mustapha and A.G. Randle (the latter an old friend and half Mende), were given portfolios, although Dr Margai made quite clear that even though they were SLPP members, they were not part of 'our majority'.[116] Dr Margai may have considered it prudent to show a conciliatory face for the benefit of the British as well as for the Creole supporters of the SLPP, since his subsequent actions and words continued to show an ambivalence towards the Creoles, with conciliatory gestures being almost invariably followed by further appeals to anti-Creole sentiment. Thus in the 1957 election, while a rule was made and largely adhered to that all SLPP candidates in the Colony were to be Creoles,[117] at the same time Dr Margai was quite prepared to appeal to 'Protectorate solidarity' against the Creoles.[118] In 1960 no less than three Creoles from opposition parties were given places in the United Front.[119] Yet a year later, following criticism from a Creole member of the cost of Independence celebrations, the Prime Minister referred sourly to 'you disgruntled people in Freetown' and went on:

> I only feel sorry I was unable to take the fun fair to the provinces – perhaps my people would have thanked me better.[120]

Again in 1962 a major conciliatory action was joined with a remark suggesting the same 'we-they' division; in redistributing seats prior to the 1962 election, the Prime Minister used a population quota of 50,000 for the provinces but less than 15,000 for the Western Area, justifying this imbalance with the comment

> If we had applied that to the Western Area, it would have been disastrous, but we do not want to take advantage of minorities. We want our colleagues in the Western Area to feel we still have the good-will for them.

and later, closing the debate, observed, 'When we started, we began with only fourteen seats and the Colony had seven.'[121]

On the whole, the Prime Minister treated the Creoles well in their area of greatest weakness, the political arena. From 1957 onwards there were never less than two Creoles in the Cabinet, and from the United Front onwards, never less than five, by far the greatest over-representation of any ethnic group. Further evidence of his consideration for the Creoles' weak political position was his willingness to allow the Western Area continued over-representation in the legislature,[122] coupled with the continued nomination of Creoles as SLPP candidates in most Western Area seats.

However, Dr Margai appeared to balance these concessions to Creoles in the 'political' field with efforts to restrain their pending predominance in the bureaucracy, the judiciary and the educational fields. He was more subtle than Sir Amadu Bello in Northern Nigeria, who explicitly chose to retain British officials rather than allow southern Nigerians to fill northern administrative posts;[123] Dr Margai simply slowed down as far as possible the pace of all Africanisation,[124] despite the combined clamour of the Creoles and the younger and more impatient provincial men. But since most of the qualified Africans for these posts were Creoles, the effect was primarily to slow down Creole ascendancy in these fields. He could not be too thoroughgoing in this, however; if it appeared to the Creoles that they were being kept out simply in order to preserve places for up-coming provincial men, they were already strongly enough entrenched to have seriously sabotaged the governmental machinery. Then too, Dr Margai believed strongly enough in a natural order of things that he would be reluctant to put younger men, whether Creole or provincial, over older ones. His policy could be described in brief as slowing down, but not resisting, the movement of Creoles into the range of positions in which they were specifically qualified to replace expatriates.

The rather generous balancing policy Dr Margai pursued towards the Creoles could only operate under a particular set of conditions. First, in their areas of strength, the Creoles' takeover of jobs was not at the expense of provincial men; there were no provincials available. Second, in the area of weakness for the Creoles, the political arena, they were a fairly small minority, and even though their over-representation implied the under-representation of other groups, these other groups were not too severely disadvantaged. However, some areas, notably the north, *were* disadvantaged; but this brings us to a third condition, namely that the disadvantaged group was not in a position to articulate its grievances. The first generation of northern leaders had been brought into the political system on the basis of 'Protectorate solidarity' against the Creoles, and it took time before some of them came to see this solidarity as benefiting the Mendes more than themselves. Further, the SLPP's northern politicians worked almost entirely through the chiefs, and from the 1955-6 riots onwards the chiefs (and indeed the whole chiefly establishment) depended rather too heavily on government favours to make vigorous representations on behalf of their region. While this combination of factors lasted, the cost to Dr Margai of extending special favours to the Creoles was lower than any alternative strategy. However, as the first and third conditions weakened, the costs of this strategy began to mount, although it was left to Albert Margai to pay the bill.

While the northern tribes remained disadvantaged compared to Mendeland throughout the 1950s, their first generation of national spokesmen were well taken care of within the SLPP. Nearly all held positions of prominence within the SLPP after 1951, and after 1957 most received Cabinet posts or equivalent positions elsewhere.[125] These individuals, we should note, were all closely related to the chiefs.

Two other emergent groups of northern leaders, each with their own set of reasons for opposing the current local rulers, were less successful in finding places within the SLPP. One group was the locally-oriented leaders of opposition factions within individual chiefdoms (Yolla Bangura of Samu is an example) whose opposition to their chief widened gradually, but by no means inevitably, into support for a party which spoke for northerners. Such leaders, tied up as they were with the dominant local institutions, were neither particularly radical nor particularly concerned with the national operations of the APC, but they were an essential link in its lines to the grassroots. The second group, much more conspicuous nationally and more influential in proclaiming the official policies of the APC, was based on the 'second generation' of nationally conscious northerners, those who had become politically aware during the 1950s when the chiefs' treatment of their people deteriorated so sharply. One of the most serious weaknesses of Dr Margai's SLPP was that it offered few opportunities for these younger men to be co-opted, especially in the north.[126] To some extent this was a circular process, as Simpson's comparisons of local elites imply; because the APC offered an outlet for the younger men to play leading political roles they were less likely to struggle for such opportunities through the SLPP, and thus the older generation's hold on the SLPP could remain more complete than in the south.[127]

Dr Margai's failure to accommodate this second group of dissident northerners can be attributed more to his reluctance to advance the younger generation than to any bias against northerners *per se.* It is hard to find any evidence that he consciously favoured the south, or southerners, and there are some indications against such an argument. The United Front made some Temnes supect that Dr Margai had embarked on a policy of favouring Mendes and 'driving the Temnes away'.[128] But he did not have a great deal of choice within the Parliamentary system; it was hard to see any northern MPs who were tolerably qualified and yet had been left out of the post-1960 Ministry. The problem lay in the fact that there had been few northerners of any stature elected to the 1957 legislature, and this in turn reflected the shortage of talented and educated northerners. It is true that Dr Margai could have found some way of bringing Siaka Stevens into the United Front, thus removing the most likely focus around which northern discontents could be organised. But his failure to do so can be attributed, I believe, to personal and ideological animosities rather than regional or ethnic ones.

As evidence of overt acts which reflected a tribal bias by Dr Margai, one can only cite such facts as the retention of Bonthe Town's gross over-representation in the legislature through its two seats which on a population basis had no justification.[129] Although one prominent Temne SLPP member claimed to me that the retention of these 'rotten boroughs' in Mende territory was an illustration of Dr Margai's Mende bias, I suspect it was more an illustration of 'letting things be', in this case because Bonthe Town had historically been treated as part of the Colony and when the other Colony seats were split in two, it was natural to treat Bonthe in the same way. Certainly there was no clear pattern of active government support for the development of the south, least of all Dr Margai's own Bonthe district, as opposed to the north; such development as did take place in each area was largely outside the government framework, and largely on an *ad hoc* basis.

We could summarise by suggesting that a *laissez-faire* attitude, rather than any explicit ethnic bias, determined Dr Margai's behaviour towards various ethnic groups. Where the effect of letting events take their 'natural' course was to give a group such advantages that it might feel well-treated and reconciled, as in the case of the Creoles and the bureaucracy, the effect was relatively harmonious. Where the effect was to encourage suspicions and the perpetuation of existing disadvantages, as in the case of northern representation in the political elite, the result was to arouse latent conflicts, even though Dr Margai had no conscious intention of stimulating such conflicts.

Albert Margai: The Miscast Tribalist?

Among the many ironies of Albert Margai's brief span of leadership were his contributions to ethnic discord. His career had brought him into closer and more cordial contact with Creoles than had his brother's, and yet by 1967 Creoledom was more solidly aligned against him than it had ever been against Sir Milton. He made more efforts to bring economic development to the north than ever his brother had, yet came to be reviled by northerners as the arch-tribalist, the man who sought to subordinate them permanently to the Mendes. How, in three short years, did he manage to so thoroughly antagonise these major groups in the Sierra Leone polity?

Part of Albert Margai's difficulties must be attributed to a disastrous lack of Machiavelli's *fortuna*. In dealing with the Creoles, Albert Margai was suspected of wishing to supplant them by Mendes at every turn; yet most of the appointments which gave rise to this suspicion had been made before he became Prime Minister. In the north, the airfields at Bonthe and Gbangbatoke became symbols of the government's intention to channel all development into Mende areas; yet in the humbler facets of development such as water supplies and roads, the north fared as well as the south. Then, too, the fact that he came to power *after* a regionally based party was firmly established in the north meant that many actions which he regarded as totally innocent of regional or ethnic connotations would be interpreted in these lights by his opponents.[130]

But Albert Margai's lack of a coherent ideology in the face of strongly held and conflicting regional and ethnic identities was the major factor in establishing his reputation as an arch-tribalist. Without the convictions necessary to develop a plausible overarching strategy, the Prime Minister had to seek to balance the competing claims of different ethnic groups; but to do this successfully, he had to be aware of the range of situations that each group considered to have a bearing upon its position as an ethnic group. His difficulties arose largely from his failure to realise that actions he took to enhance his personal position were open to 'tribalist' interpretations, even though no such considerations occurred to him.

While the major motives behind many of his actions were personal greed and insecurity, Creoles and northerners gave more weight to a possible ethnic interpretation, and were able to polarise Sierra Leone politics around this interpretation.

During his years in Sierra Leone politics, Albert Margai had developed what for a provincial politician was a relatively close relationship with Creoles. His legal practice in Freetown had early brought him into close professional contact with many Creoles, and even though there had been considerable ill-feeling on both sides when in 1950 he had challenged the Creoles to elect him as a Freetown City Councillor[131] by 1958 the Peoples National Party included several Creoles, and the party's paper strongly defended the Creoles from the attacks of the SLPP.[132] From this period stemmed his close relationship with several Creole lawyers, notably Berthan Macauley, later as Attorney-General the man primarily responsible for persuading the Governor-General to call Albert Margai to form a government, and Gershon Collier, the *eminence grise* of Albert's regime.

When he took over as Prime Minister, Albert Margai's first gestures were reassuring to the Creole community, and particularly to its professional and administrative members. To the Bar Association he affirmed his commitment to a competitive party system,[133] and he told civil servants they would be free from political interference, and that advancement would depend on non-partisan merit.[134] Since this approach would secure the Creole position, civil servants initially appeared ready to give the new Prime Minister their support.

But a blunder attributable to the Prime Minister's failure to think through the potential costs of actions soon cast a shadow of distrust on these relations. In September 1964 a successful APC challenge to the legality of the Freetown Council gave the government an opportunity to reform the council's structure.[135] Rashly, the government increased the elected members from twelve to eighteen, cut the number of appointed members from six to three, and provided that the whole council should be elected at one time, from six wards based on the national constituencies.

As steps to provide democratic party control over the capital's government, these actions were laudable. But from the point of view of strengthening government control over Freetown, they were ill-advised, given the fact that 70 per cent of Freetown's population was Creole or northern, and that APC candidates generally out-polled SLPP ones in three wards, and were likely to break through in the three others. The Prime Minister evidently intended the elections to provide a demonstration of his electoral appeal; at any rate, he personally led the SLPP's campaign. But the APC won eleven of the eighteen elective seats, thus gaining control of the council and the power to elect the Mayor of Freetown.[136] The result was hardly a repudiation of the SLPP; the party's candidates polled their highest vote ever, and their share of the total votes was only 2 per cent less than the SLPP's average over the previous four years.[137] Nor could it be taken as a 'Creole' vote against Albert Margai; the SLPP's biggest gains came in an area of Creole concentration, and its biggest losses in the heavily northern east end. But the Prime Minister's distrust of 'Freetown people', and his resulting efforts to consolidate an up-country base, began after the election. And it was his efforts to build a secure base up-country, stimulated by the realisation that his electoral hold was weak, that led to his greatest disaster, the drive for a one-party state.

Since the drive for a one-party state played the major role in creating both Creole and northern distrust of Albert Margai, we should consider briefly what it was that each of these groups feared about such a regime brought about under Margai's and the SLPP's auspices. The Creoles' opposition rested on both normative and pragmatic grounds. Normatively, many Creoles, especially among the professional elite, regarded an 'open' political system in which different parties could organise and compete for office, a pluralist social order with certain spheres 'off limits' to political interference, and a 'rule of law' binding on government as much as any private citizen, as essential parts of Sierra Leone's political heritage. Given their political position, Creoles could find a practical value in these principles; but they also seemed in many cases to value them on normative grounds, to a degree comparable to their counterparts in, say, Britain or Canada.[138] On pragmatic grounds, of course, their position as a small minority with specialised skills in the law and positions requiring formal education gave a solid base of self-interest to their adherence to pluralism and the rule of law. Politically, they might play a 'swing' role in the likely event that north and south lined up against each other. But more important was their concern to keep areas such as the bureaucracy and higher education as far 'off limits' as possible to direct political control. In a one-party state under provincial leadership, especially of the Mendes with their growing number of educated men, it would become easier for the government to use its powers to advance countrymen's claims in these areas.

The northerners' concerns were somwhat different. Their backwardness, to whose political implications they were becoming increasingly sensitive, seemed perpetuated by Mende dominance in the national government; and at the same time Margai's use of the northern chiefs to strengthen his position against the APC was making the chiefs appear increasingly like stooges for the 'Mendemen's party'. The one-party state, in northern eyes, would not only remove the ordinary man's means of protesting against his chief by voting APC, but would also perpetuate Mende dominance and thus northern backwardness. It was not so much a one-party state as such, but a one-party state controlled by Mendes and chiefs, that aroused northerners' fears.

With these concerns in mind, we can better appreciate the impact that specific actions of the Prime Minister had on each of these groups. The Creoles' anxieties were focused largely upon Sir Albert's attitudes towards the judicial system.

In early 1965 an article in the APC newspaper *We Yone* by a former Produce Marketing Board employee, claimed that the Prime Minister had wanted to hush up a tale of managerial corruption in the PMB.[139] The government responded by charging the editor of *We Yone* with sedition and defamatory libel, charges on which a Freetown jury was quick to find the editor not guilty. Asked at his next news conference to comment, the Prime Minister replied that the jury's decision was 'shameful'.[140] A few months later the government introduced an amendment to the Criminal Procedure Act restoring the colonial government's method of avoiding the partiality of the predominantly Creole Freetown juries, trial by judge alone at the request of the Attorney General. This provision was used in a spate of libel prosecutions against opposition newspapers. But the Bench, also solidly Creole, was equally resistant to government pressure, and few of the prosecutions succeeded.[141] In late 1965 came a further act by Sir Albert which angered most members of the Bar and Bench. The Chief Justice, Sir Samuel Bankole-Jones, who had been particularly resistant to Sir Albert's attempts at getting the opposition silenced, suddenly found himself forced to accept a 'promotion' to the post of President of the Court of Appeal, a position which he had earlier recommended should be abolished as superfluous.[142] This blatant attack on the judiciary, coming as it did in the midst of the drive for a one-party state, intensified the conviction of many Creoles that Sir Albert's goal would involve the destruction of the 'rule of law' upon which their personal wellbeing, and possibly their physical safety, depended. Though by this time all the damage that could be done to Sir Albert's relations with the judiciary had been accomplished, further incidents kept the animosities high. In June 1966 Mr Justice Cole handed down an injunction restraining a committee the Prime Minister had set up to examine the one-party state from meeting, and a furious Prime Minister was barely restrained from forcing the committee to meet in defiance of the injunction.[143] Finally, in January 1967, the Prime Minister appointed his confidant Gershon Collier to the post of Chief Justice, an act of defiance towards the legal profession which outraged almost all its members.[144]

The escalation of animosities was mutual. In their opposition to Sir Albert, many Creole civil servants began to leak information about the government's plans, as well as the more questionable actions of Sir Albert and his Ministers, to the APC, which gleefully seized on them.[145] Sir Albert's reaction to this covert opposition was to rely even more heavily upon his inner circle of PNP associates, largely Mendes, and to intensify his distrust of the Creoles.

But while his bad relations with Creoles might be attributed to the incompatibility of their goals and his, Sir Albert's relations with northerners were largely attributable to blundering insensitivity. While he could do nothing about northern resentment over the fact that he rather than a northerner had succeeded Sir Milton, his purge of two Northern Ministers (and a Ministerial Secretary) and his failure to replace them was an avoidable mistake.[146] Initially he won support in the north by his policy of putting pressure on chiefs to curb their rapacity and obey the laws; but after the Freetown elections he fell back on a policy of stamping out the APC through the chiefs, the only instruments available for this task. Many chiefs were happy enough to attempt this on their own, since the APC was quick to fan local factional quarrels, as well as to attack individual chiefs for their misconduct. But when Sir Albert began using the chiefs as his agents to curb the APC, the effect was to intensify northern suspicions of a 'Mende' government which for its own sinister purposes was intimidating the 'northern man's party', and to leave the northern chiefs in the position of discredited agents of this government. If Sir Albert had been able to curb the chiefs' abuses at the same time as he was persecuting the APC, he might have succeeded in winning a majority of the northern electorate over to the SLPP, or he might have been able to forgo persecuting the APC entirely. But since the chiefs were his only means of weakening the APC's electoral threat, he could not curb them. Alternatively, he might simply have held aloof from the local persecutions of APC members, letting the chiefs do this work out of their own self-interest, while he sought to establish himself as the disinterested 'father' of all his people. There would be a risk in this approach that too many chiefs in the north would decide to come to terms with the APC, thus allowing it to grow to a much more menacing opposition, especially when coupled with the internal opposition to Sir Albert within the SLPP.[147] It is a moot point whether this would have been a greater risk than pushing the chiefs into persecuting the APC. All we can say is that the cost of the strategy he did pursue (and 'strategy' is probably a misleading term for what was essentially a reflex response to the 1965 situation) was so high as to produce political bankruptcy, while recognising that the alternative of letting the chiefs do the work alone might have been equally costly.

Northern suspicions of the new Prime Minister were further aggravated by the apparent 'Mendeisation' of the key posts in the civil service and other governmental bodies. It was true, as the Prime Minister told Parliament in September 1965, that most senior civil service posts were still going to Creoles, and that in the previous two and a half years ten of these appointments had gone to men from the Northern Province, against only eight from the Southern and Eastern Provinces.[148] He noted that of the eight appointments made on his advice (rather than that of the Public Service Commission) since he became Prime Minister, four were from the Western Area, three were from the Northern Province, and only one was from the south.[149] But it was equally true that the three most important posts in the civil service – the Secretary to the Prime Minister, who was also Head of the Civil Service, the Financial Secretary, and the Establishment Secretary, who handled internal promotions and discipline – were all firmly in Mende hands.[150] However, it should be noted, first, that these appointments had been made under Sir Milton, and second, that in seniority and levels of training these individuals merited their appointments. Other important positions filled by Mendes under Sir Albert included Commanding Officer of the Royal Sierra Leone Military Force, General Manager of the Produce Marketing Board, with its extensive control over agricultural development and jobs, and Chief Elections Officer, who played a key role in any general election arrangements.[151] While these jobs, and a sprinkling of others, comprised only a small minority of the high-level government positions, they were both vitally important and extremely visible, with the latter quality attracting a good deal of northern attention.[152] Two of these appointments, ironically, hurt Albert in unexpected ways. The Produce Marketing Board's management became so involved in corruption and bungling that by 1967 it was unable to pay farmers cash for their produce, with a consequent weakening of support for Albert even in Mende areas, while Brigadier David Lansana's appointment was not widely appreciated by his officers, and his unpopularity may have contributed to the 1967 military coup which saw him arrested by his own officers, thus forestalling his attempts to restore Sir Albert to office.

In the economic sphere, Sir Albert was frequently accused of directing all development towards the south, but it is hard to substantiate this charge. It is more plausible to argue that some of the more extravagant projects were for the benefit of the Prime Minister and a handful of other influential citizens, who were more often from the south than the north. The most dramatic of these elite projects were the two airstrips rushed to completion in 1965-6 at the Prime Minister's home towns of Gbangbatoke and Bonthe, while Kabala, somewhat further from Freetown in travelling time,[153] remained without one, in direct contradiction of the recommendation of a transportation survey commissioned by the government in 1963 that Kabala should have an airfield but that there was no economic justification for new fields in the south.[154] However, with the Prime Minister and his brother having a strong interest in Bonthe and Gbangbatoke, whereas Koinadugu district was represented only by two amiable but not influential Ministerial Secretaries, the result was not necessarily attributable to ethnic prejudice.

The building of roads was a form of development with a much wider social impact, thanks to the ubiquitous 'mammy lorries' which provided cheap transportation from all villages near them. Here there was a division of responsibility, with the District Councils and chiefdoms responsible for the minor and 'feeder' roads, often little more than tracks scraped through the bush and capable of taking only limited volumes of traffic, while the national government was responsible for trunk roads with heavy gravel bases or even tarmac, and helped District Councils with secondary roads where these formed a part of the national road network. In the opening of new feeder roads and secondary roads, there is no evidence to suggest that Albert Margai's regime discriminated against the north. As for national road-building, there was if anything a bias in favour of the north, with the major project initiated under Sir Albert being the heavy-duty tarmac Tonkolili-Kono road, while the roads from Mano to Bumpe, and from Bo to Kenema, remained unpaved, and consequently quagmires during the rainy season. Overall, we could argue that the road-building programme was extravagant in places [155] but not that it reflected a bias towards Mende areas.

We have already noted the comparatively backward state of northern agriculture,[156] largely using data compiled midway through Albert Margai's period of leadership. Here certain projects by the Produce Marketing Board did seem to be planned for the south on questionable grounds: a proposed fibre-making factory at Bonthe and an animal foodstuffs factory in Moyamba could have been just as well located in the north.[157] Twice as much oil palm plantation acreage went to the south as to the north.[158] However, other projects seemed to be shared out on a reasonably equitable basis; an attempted rubber plantation in the south was matched by a cashew plantation in Port Loko district, while the ploughing of Bonthe's swamp ricelands by government-owned tractors was matched by similar activity in the Makeni grasslands.[159] On the whole, it seems difficult to sustain any charge of systematic bias in favour of the south in this area of activity.

In education, if there was any bias, it was towards the North. Primary school enrolment increased at twice the rate in the north than it did in the two southern provinces from 1962-3 to 1967-8, even though this still left the north considerably behind in enrolment per 1,000 population.[160] Though we cannot determine whether the stimulus for this increase came from above, or from a desire on the part of northerners to 'catch up' educationally, since the funds came from the central government it clearly was not placing obstacles in the way of northern self-assertion.

One final element in Albert Margai's contribution to ethnic conflict needs mentioning. Although a leader's personal predilection for self-enrichment would seem to have little to do with his ethnic identity, the fact that the Prime Minister and those around him who were getting rich through a number of government-favoured enterprises[161] were largely Mendes, added an ethnic dimension to the ordinary northerner's sense of exploitation. The 'Kabala cows' episode, the enrichment of Produce Marketing Board officials through misuse of funds, and the choice jobs going to PNP men, all involved exploitation of ordinary farmers by an elite, but they also seemed from a northerner's perspective to involve Mendes enriching themselves at the expense of the North.

While the fact that a number of Mendes were selected for key posts suggested a *prima facie* case for tribal bias, there were many Mendes whom the Prime Minister distrusted, and who in their turn had no great regard for him. Many of the Prime Minister's allegedly 'tribalist' actions were in fact attributable to much more personal considerations, notably the desire for security which led him into the one-party state venture, and the desire to provide an abundant personal life for himself, which led him to lavish development expenditures and to bring his own gains to his home districts.

In pursuing these goals, he progressively undermined his position with different ethnic groups, while seemingly unable to anticipate the reactions each new step would provoke. The possibility of a relatively fluid pattern of alliance was gradually reduced for him, as one group after another came to regard him as the arch-enemy who had to be replaced. The alliance he created against himself, however, was not an enduring one; the interests of Creoles, the different northern tribes and the Konos could be served together in an anti-Margai coalition, but common dislike of Albert Margai was hardly strong enough to bind them irrevocably. Nor were ethnic identities necessarily activated in a fixed and rigid form; the northerners who felt aggravated at Albert's alleged biases could see that Temnes, Limbas, Susu, Koranko and Kono as well were all sharing a common deprivation of expected benefits, and likewise the Creoles' concerns over his threats to individual liberty were ones which could be shared by all 'right-thinking' men, regardless of tribal identity. In fact, we could argue that by bringing different groups to see their common grievances, Albert Margai helped replace a potential suprarational 'tribalism' with a more diffuse, and more rational, feeling of regional identification, and beyond this, with a feeling of co-operation between regions.[162] His perceived 'tribalism', in short, did not lead to any irresolvable ethnic conflict, but simply to new alignments based largely on the ethnic units comprising Sierra Leone, alignments which could just as eaily fall apart as soon as a new basis for conflict developed.[163]

Conclusions

It is clear that during the period under examination, the salience[164] of various subnational identities to the political process shifted dramatically. At the beginning of the Margai era, an ethnic identity, Creoles, was opposed to a regional one, the Protectorate. By Independence, the Creole identity, while not quiescent, was no longer highly salient to the political alignments then developing, but a new division combining ethnic and regional elements,Mendes versus the northerners, was taking shape, while another 'ethnoregional' identity, Kono, had already entrenched itself as the basis for an autonomous political force. By the time of Albert Margai's defeat in the 1967 elections, the ethnic element in the Mende identity had clearly become uppermost[165] while the Creoles had been realigned into a near-solid block opposed to Albert Margai and the SLPP, in alliance with a broad regional coalition embracing nearly all northerners plus the Kono.[166] The questions for this study to consider are, what effects did the national political leaders' behaviour have on the nature of the subnational identities that developed, and conversely, what constraints did the development of various subnational identities impose on the two leaders?

In considering how national leaders could deal with these subnational identities, I would stress that these identities were not intractable. Two characteristics contributed to this: their *defensive* nature and their *rational* content. By their 'defensive' nature I am referring to the fact that all the politically salient identities considered in Sierra Leone were called into being as responses to perceived deprivations or threats of deprivation. The Temnes, for example, saw their tribe as losing status (and members) to the 'purer' Muslim tribes in Freetown, and later saw their home areas as being denied a 'fair' share of economic development and their members apparently being excluded from a share of political power. The Creoles in the 1950s and later in 1965-7 saw their entire culture in danger of being overwhelmed by the up-country hordes, while one could even argue that the Mendes in the 1967 election stayed largely loyal to Albert Margai in order to protect themselves against the threat of northern domination.[167] By 'rational' content I mean first that these identities were based on features that could be perceived by non-possessors as well as their possessors and second, in so far as these identities embodied claims upon the rest of the polity, those claims were capable of being met. To be more specific, the Creoles' identity was based upon their possession of cultural attributes such as education and an orientation towards work which they regarded as entitling them to a special role in the running of the Sierra Leone polity. The up-country leaders were not prepared to accept this claim, but they could only deny it on the grounds that other bases for claims against the polity should be given more weight; they could not deny that there was a valid basis for the Creoles' claim. To use a different illustration, the Temnes (and other northerners) came to feel by the time of Independence that other parts of the country were receiving a disproportionate share of economic benefits, and more important, that their spokesmen were being denied an equitable share of political power. Again, Mendes might well disagree with the Temnes on what constituted 'equity' but the basis for the Temnes' case was one which had to be acknowledged.

To put the problem in a different way, the identities in question were *not* based upon any suprarational belief, any vision of the group concerned as being a 'chosen people' or having some non-arguable right to special treatment. There was no assertion that a particular group should be a 'master race' or even that it should be left alone because of some non-definable characteristics beyond the comprehension of outsiders. Nor were the boundaries of the groups concerned necessarily ethnic; while all Creoles and all Konos enjoyed a common culture and a common language, with the ease of communication that this implies, northerners were a very mixed group linguistically and culturally, which served as a strong moderating influence on their ability to expand their claims beyond specific demands for the end of felt deprivations.

While a substantial element in the sense of deprivation creating these subnational identities was economic, this was not their most important component. The major issue at stake was the use of political power, and I think it not unreasonable to see the alignment as one of oppressors and oppressed (using these terms to describe an asymmetrical power relationship in which the subordinated group perceives its position as unjust). Even if Albert Margai had poured all development funds into the north, Mendes would still have held the power to decide where these funds should go in future. It is because there was a high concentration of power in the political elite, and more specifically in the hands of the Prime Minister and Cabinet, that the Creoles remained perpetually uneasy despite their success in retaining control of many key areas. It was the fact that political power was perceived as being used for the advantage of some and the disadvantage of other ethnic and regional groups that made ethnic and regional identities the most salient for the polity. But equally important, it was the fact that the uses of political power were perceived in rational terms that made it possible for ethnic and regional alignments to remain fluid, and thus to maintain the possibility of change in the system. Two illustrations of this are, first, the breakaway of the northern tribes from their 'Protectorate' alignment with the Mendes and their eventual alliance with the Creoles for the 1967 elections, and second, following the coming to power of this coalition of Temnes, Limbas, Creoles and other non-Mende groups, the formation in 1970 of a new predominantly Temne opposition party, with some Mende support.[168]

But where does political leadership enter into this emergence and submergence of ethnic and regional identities? I would suggest that a leader's actions, both those intended to have an effect in this area and those taken out of entirely separate concerns, can have a considerable effect in stimulating identities that are quiescent or conversely in subduing identities that had been activated, but that they cannot create an identity from nothing. Thus Dr Margai by his generous treatment of the Creoles was able to turn their active hostility into wary neutrality. By his lack of a vigorous development policy he allowed the north to remain a backward area and thus contributed to the creation among northerners of the common bond of economic deprivation, although his policy here was only one contributing factor to a long-standing condition. Albert Margai started under a northern cloud of suspicion and the range of inept actions he took served to reinforce this suspicion. With the Creoles, by contrast, he managed to reactivate hostilities which his brother had fairly well damped down, although again we are considering only an activation of latent attitudes rather than a reversal. A somewhat different illustration of the limits to a leader's power to change attitudes is the fact that Mende areas in the 1967 election voted as strongly as they had done in 1962 for SLPP, and more important, against APC candidates. Even though many Mendes were unhappy with Albert Margai, and a number of candidates running as Independents repudiated him, none of these Independents was prepared to ally openly with the APC, and no APC candidate made a strong showing among Mendes.[169]

Given each leader's personal predilections, the choice of strategies open to each which might have overcome these problems was limited. Given his conservative inclinations, Dr Margai's choice was between a balancing strategy with a strong bias towards those groups contented with the status quo and an overarching strategy extolling tradition and the chiefs: he could hardly be expected to crusade for a major reform of existing institutions. His efforts to conciliate the Creoles through a balancing strategy were reasonably successful, though whether it would have continued to remain an acceptable strategy as the number of provincial claimants for high-level jobs and northern awareness of their legislative under-representation both increased, is open to doubt. His attempts at an overarching strategy with the northerners was less successful, partly because northern selfconsciousness was awakened through events beyond his control, partly because the chiefs were a major contributing cause to northern discontent. But if he had been prepared to act more forcefully to alleviate northern discontent, what could Dr Margai have done? To have attempted a balancing strategy solely by pumping more resources into northern development would probably have intensified ordinary northerners' discontent with their chiefs, since many of the benefits would have been channelled off to the latter's use. But to expect Dr Margai to take the further necessary steps of reforming chieftaincy was to expect too much from someone of his views working through the political structure he had built. His conservative approach might have worked for several more years, though at the cost of increasing repression. But it did nothing to allay the growth of strong regional disaffection, or the likelihood that political movements based on this disaffection would develop increasing strength.

When Albert Margai came to office, there was a slight possibility that one strategy open to him might have prevented the spread of ethnic and regional opposition to his rule. While he could do nothing about the two severe handicaps of being a Mende and the former Prime Minister's brother, he might just have been able to succeed with an overarching strategy of appealing to all those who wanted major changes in chieftaincy and in the symbolic field of foreign relations. While most members in the SLPP, in Parliament as well as at the local level, would have been unhappy about such changes, he might have been able to offset this opposition by offering generous terms of alliance to the APC's national cadres, and counting on Prime Ministerial powers of patronage and punishment to prevent his conservative critics from forming an effective alliance against him. Such a strategy would have been risky, and to assess the risks would have needed a high level of self-confidence and enough consistency to give the impression that the Prime Minister was embarking on changes in the direction sought by the APC's (and some of the SLPP's) national activists. This was probably asking for an unrealistic level of foresight from a national leader. But the balancing strategy which was the only feasible alternative was very hard to work when northerners felt the balance needed to be redressed in their favour in *all* areas.

The constraints that ethnic and regional attitudes imposed on a leader's range of choices should be fairly evident. In the formation of the SLPP in 1951, the fact of Creole hostility made it nearly inevitable that the SLPP leaders should align themselves with the chiefs, with all the consequences that flowed from that action. When Albert Margai sought a one-party state to secure his position, the fact of Creole hostility precluded his use of the administrative and judicial apparatus to suppress opponents, and thus made possible the survival of an organised opposition and the holding of a fair election. After 1960, Temne and Limba suspicions of the Margais' aims faced both leaders with a choice of either providing resources for the north on such a scale as to risk serious disaffection elsewhere, or writing off the area and relying on the narrow majority that could be built up over the rest of the country.

The growth of ethnic and regional animosities was not entirely harmful to the two leaders, however. The fact that both regimes offered a disproportionate share of benefits for a privileged class, the 'traditio-modern elites', held open the risk that some counter-elite might seek to unite all those who did not reap these benefits, as in fact the APC sought to do. One way of keeping such an opposition from growing too strong was to try to limit its appeal to particular ethnic groups, or more precisely to ensure that among sufficient of the governing party's supporters the opposition was identified as a party of 'strangers'.[170]

This approach was fairly successful against the APC in Mende country, although by 1967 the groups excluded from Albert Margai's regime were too numerous for the tactic to win elections.

Notes

1. 'Common culture' and 'self-sufficiency' are admittedly elusive concepts. If, for example, we suggest that religion is an essential part of any 'common culture' we have thereby divided the Germans, the Dutch and the English into several separate groups. This illustration underlines the point that it is the salience of particular attributes to the persons concerned that determines whether they comprise a part of the culture that unites the group and at the same time helps differentiate it from other groups. 'Self-sufficiency' I use in the Aristotelian sense of a group large and diverse enough to provide without outside resources those social and economic features that lift human society above mere survival, and allow it to develop a distinctive way of life.
2. This is the definition used in Walker Connor's excellent article, 'The Politics of Ethnonationalism', *Journal of International Affairs*, 27, 1, July 1973, p. 2.
3. 'Tribe' and 'tribalism' as used by anthropologists denote a group linked by their descent from a common ancestor. Unfortunately, the term has come in popular usage to refer to any self-conscious ethnic group, regardless of its basis of descent, and has also acquired rather pejorative connotations. On the rare occasions when I employ the term 'tribalism' I will use it in this popular sense.
4. Connor, 'Politics of Ethnonationalism', p. 1, notes that of the world's 135 states, 'all but fourteen . . . contain at least one significant minority'.
5. Cf. the four stages – coexistence, contact, compromise and coalescence – outlined by Ali Maxrui in his article, 'Pluralism and National Integration', in Leo Kuper and M.G. Smith (eds.), *Pluralism in Africa*, Berkeley and Los Angeles, University of California Press, 1969, p. 334.
6. Norman Miller's phrase is a very useful reminder of the limits imposed on individuals' consciousness by this physical barrier. See his 'Political Mobility and the Pedestrian Society', *Canadian Journal of African Studies*, IV, 1, Winter 1970, pp. 17-31.
7. See M.M. Green, *Igbo Village Affairs*, London, Cass, 1964, p. 7.
8. For the Ibos, see Richard Sklar, *Nigerian Political Parties*, Princeton, N.J., Princeton University Press, 1963, p. 65. For a striking illustration, the creation of the 'Bangala' out of a potpourri of groups, see Charles Anderson, Fred von der Mehden and Crawford Young, *Issues of Political Development*, Englewood Cliffs, N.J., Prentice Hall, 1967, pp. 31-3.
9. Some Vai did continue to identify themselves as a group distinct from the Mendes, and a good number termed themselves 'Vai Mende'.
10. Merran McCulloch, *Peoples of Sierra Leone*, London, International African Institute, 1950, pp. 50-1.
11. Pollock, *Influence, Authority and Economic Opportunity*, p.49.
12. Leo Kuper has described this pattern of alignment of perceptions along a particular dimension such as ethnicity as an 'encompassing principle'. See his 'Theories of Revolution and Race Relations', *Comparative Studies in Society and History*, 13, 1, Jan. 1971, pp. 99-101.

13. See, for the Bangala, Anderson, *Issues of Political Development*, pp. 31-3.
14. The setting up of 'bilingual districts' under the federal Official Languages Act and the offer in some provinces of French-language schools may slow down the trend to assimilation, but it seems likely that most Francophones will continue to succumb to the immense economic and social pressures to work and live in English.
15. The Tutsi approach of massacring the Hutu elite seems to have worked in the short run, but one wonders how much of a heritage of bitterness has built up. The Amhara approach of selective assimilation and careful neglect of most other groups, coupled with the build-up of the Emperor as a symbol of unity, seems more likely to work over the long run.
16. This illustration is taken from Kuper, 'Theories of Revolution', p. 92. For a more general study of the factors producing ethnic conflicts see Donald Horowitz, 'Multi-Racial Politics in the New States: Toward a Theory of Conflict', Michael Stein and Robert Jackson (eds.), *Issues in Comparative Politics*, New York, St Martin's, 1971, pp. 164-80.
17. The explanation I am following here is basically that of Clifford Geertz, in his 'The Integrative Revolution', in *Old Societies and New States*, New York, Free Press, 1963, pp. 109-11. I do quibble, however, over his use of the term 'primordial' to describe these attachments. Those attachments which unite the whole ethnic group rather than a group of blood relatives are not necessarily any more 'natural' than, say, a sense of 'mateship' or worker solidarity; it is just that there are more of these links.
18. Or at least preferred by them to any other, although they may acknowledge that others can prefer a different way. Malays, for example, admit that Chinese are better businessmen, but consider their success makes them crude and uncivilised. See Horowitz, 'Multi-Racial Politics', p. 170.
19. The list could be extended indefinitely, and could embrace every continent. We might, for example, cite manifestations of this attitude in Israel, Japan, and Germany among independent states, and within Canada, Belgium and Cyprus among groups which do not enjoy political autonomy.
20. The United Progressive Grand Alliance in Nigeria in 1964, and to some degree Milton Obote's Uganda Peoples' Congress in Uganda in its early years, represented alliances of threatened groups against an antagonist more powerful than any of the individual groups in the alliance.
21. I have been told, for example, that few ordinary Ashanti objected to Krobo Edusei's wife's purchase of a golden bed; it showed that one of their own had 'made good'.
22. See Gavin Kitching, 'The Concept of Class and the Study of Africa', *African Review* 2, 3, 1972, p. 347.
23. See Immanuel Wallerstein, 'Ethnicity and National Integration in West Africa', *Cahiers d'Etudes Africaines*, 3, Oct. 1960, pp. 129-39.
24. See Mazrui's observation that an African Minister 'mixes on terms of equality with more humble citizens only if these come from his own tribe'. Cited in R.H. Jackson, 'Political Stratification in Tropical Africa', *Canadian Journal of African Studies* 7, 3, 1973, p. 396.
25. That many ordinary men do not want this kind of society even if an elite were willing to work for it is persuasively argued by Robert Lane; see 'The Fear of Equality', in *Political Ideology*, New York, Free Press, 1962, pp. 57-81.
26. The cases of English-speaking Canada, the Protestants in Northern Ireland and the Greeks in Cyprus show various degrees of commitment by a majority to getting its own way. As Robert Dahl has argued, even an 'apathetic majority' which does not feel strongly on an issue can still override a minority's interests if it acts as a majority. See *A Preface to Democratic Theory*, Chicago, University of Chicago Press, 1956, ch. 5.

27. For example, appeals to 'appointment by merit' in the civil service (with merit meaning quality of education) leads to an advantage for the group enjoying superior educational qualifications.
28. The Habsburgs' use of the monarchy as an overarching symbol of unity for the entire Austro-Hungarian empire, or Haile Selassie's similar use of his own position in Ethiopia, were characteristic approaches of conservative ideologues.
29. For example, Archbishop Makarios of Cyprus was never able to gain the confidence of the Turkish minority following the polarisation over the 'Enosis' struggle in the 1950s.
30. 'Nnamdi Azikiwe and Jomo Kenyatta illustrate this ambivalent status of leaders who were both 'Father of their Country' and at the same time involved in partisan acts on behalf of a particular group within the state.
31. See Sandbrook, 'Patrons, Clients and Factions', p. 118.
32. It will be recalled that Mendes and Temnes each comprised about 30 per cent of the population, with no other tribe comprising more than 8 per cent. See note 14, p. 53.
33. See Cartwright, *Politics in Sierra Leone*, p. 54.
34. See Hayward, 'A Radical Political Organisation', pp. 10-11.
35. I have taken as evidence of ability to control a seat the fact that a group comprises more than half the population in that seat. In 1957 Mendes controlled 18 of 43 seats; in 1962, 32 of 74; and in 1967, 33 of 78.
36. John Sinclair 'Perceptions of Social Stratification Among Sub-Elites of Sierra Leone', unpublished paper presented at the Sierra Leone Symposium, University of Western Ontario, May 1971.
37. James Littlejohn notes that Temnes trading with each other or involved in a 'palaver' would use Krio rather than Temne, presumably to avoid too intense a personal interaction (personal communication).
38. Cf. Ali Mazrui's argument that concern over Ganda dominance brought the non-Ganda tribes of Uganda closer together. 'Privilege and Protest as Integrative Factors: The Case of Buganda's Status in Uganda', in Robert Rotberg and Ali Mazrui (eds.), *Protest and Power in Black Africa*, New York, Oxford, 1970, pp. 1072-87.
39. See Kenneth Little, 'Structural Change', pp. 225-31.
40. Although there were some clashes in Mendeland between Mendes and northerners in 1968 these were less intense than, say, the confrontations between Ashanti and the CPP in Ghana in 1965-7, let alone the conflicts in Nigeria, Rwanda, Burundi, or Zaire, to name only some of the more conspicuous ethnic battles.
41. See Porter, *Creoledom*, pp. 63-4.
42. Richardson and Collins, in their *Economic and Social Survey*, noted that even in the Rural Area nearly all the Creoles sent their children to school, while less than a fifth of the tribal people did so (p. 411).
43. Gaynor Cohen, 'Recruitment to the Professional Class in Sierra Leone', unpublished paper given at Sierra Leone Symposium, University of Western Ontario, May 1971.
44. This problem has been a popular theme with African novelists; see, for example, James Ngugi, *The River Between*, London, Heinemann, 1965, and Chinua Achebe, *No Longer at Ease*, London, Heinemann, 1963.
45. Gaynor Cohen, 'Recruitment to the Professional Class', p. 14.
46. Abner Cohen, The Creole Way of Death', unpublished paper at Sierra Leone Symposium, University of Western Ontario, May 1971, pp. 19-20.
47. For a detailed discussion of the role of the Masonic Lodges in Creoledom, see Abner Cohen, 'The Politics of Ritual Secrecy', *Man*, 6, 3, Sept. 1971, pp. 427-48.

48. Porter, *Creoledom*, pp. 12-13.
49. See Paul Hair's excellent review article of Fyfe's *History of Sierra Leone*, in *Sierra Leone Studies*, N.S. No. 17, June 1963, pp. 291-3.
50. Ibid., and Fyfe, *History*, pp. 615-19.
51. Some of the Creoles, notably Laminah Sankoh, the leader of the Peoples Party which gave its name to the SLPP in 1951, probably were primarily concerned to bring about a unity of all Africans. But most Creoles were aware that if the SLPP could be the party of all the people, still Creole skills would ensure that they occupied a disproportionate share of its higher echelons.
52. The price of survival for a privileged group would appear to be the appearance of abandoning its distinctiveness, a selective absorption of the hitherto excluded groups. See for a not entirely successful example of this, Digby Baltzell's *The Protestant Establishment*, New York, Random House, 1967.
53. Henry Gaffney, *Administration and the Administrative Service in Sierra Leone*, Ph.D thesis, Columbia University, as cited in Robert Jordan, 'The Creoles and the Civil Service in Sierra Leone', unpublished paper from Sierra Leone Symposium, UWO, p. 18.
54. These two were expatriates.
55. The one exception was a Kono. My data here are based on an inspection of names in the 1964 *Staff List;* it is possible that in the Ministry of Education I have mistaken one or two up-country people for Creoles, but such an error would not significantly affect the findings.
56. See Cohen, 'The Creole Way of Death', pp. 12-15.
57. This had been first formally stated in The Protectorate Land Ordinance No. 16 of 1927, which began: 'Whereas all land in the Protectorate is vested in the tribal authorities. . . .'
58. The threat from the Lebanese was curbed in 1962 by the Land Development (Protection) Act No. 61 of 1962, which banned non-citizens buying land in the Western Area.
59. The Census recorded 17,331 'African non-natives' out of a total population of 64,576. Although a few of these 'non-natives' would have been Africans from other territories, the great majority would have been Creoles. It is possible that a number of Creoles declined to be identified as 'non-natives', though in view of the developing polarisation between Creoles and 'natives' at the time, this seems unlikely.
60. The letter addressed to Dr Margai as Leader and Albert Margai as National Chairman, and dated 29 January 1957, claimed that it had been agreed that with the exception of Kande Bureh, 'candidates for both the municipal and the general elections . . . should be persons of expressly Colony origin'. But now, it claimed, Dr Bankole-Bright's recent prediction that Creoles were only being used as pawns for the SLPP and would never be put up as candidates at the forthcoming general election seemed to be well founded, since Creoles were being excluded from candidacies. I am grateful to H.E.B. John for showing me this letter.
61. Out of twelve seats in the Western Area, Creoles held the SLPP symbol for eleven in 1957, nine in 1962, and eight in 1967.
62. *Legislative Council Debates*, 1951-2, 31 Jan. 1952, p. 271.
63. See *Unity*, 5, 12 and 26 Feb. and 2 Apr. 1966, for various attacks on 'the Settlers'.
64. While the question of whether such discrimination actually existed is a difficult one to resolve, what is significant is that many of my up-country students were firmly convinced that it did exist.
65. Jordan, 'The Creoles and the Civil Service', p. 27.

66. Statement by Albert Margai in Parliament, *House of Representatives Debates*, 1965-6, 8 Sept. 1965, col. 164. One of the persons from the Western Area was a northerner in origin, but the rest were Creoles.
67. Although his study of intergroup relations suggested that the Creoles were relatively well regarded and were not as 'socially distant' as several other ethnic groups, Dawson did record some criticism of their attitude that 'they are better', though how far this represented a latent resentment that could be fanned is not known. See Dawson, 'Race and Intergroup Relations', Part II, pp. 220-30.
68. See Banton, *West African City*, p. 165, for an account of Bureh's role in the reassertion of Temne identity.
69. Bai Farima Tass was deposed in 1956 as a result of the northern riots.
70. See above, pp. 41-42.
71. See Enid Forde, 'Regionalisation of Economic Development in Sierra Leone', *Sierra Leone Geographical Journal*, 11, 1967, pp. 43-50.
72. R.J. Mutti et al., *Marketing Staple Food Crops in Sierra Leone*, Njala, The University College, 1967, p. 52, Table 3-4.
73. Sierra Leone, *Agricultural Statistical Survey*, 1965-6.
74. The average size in the north was 3.6 acres; in the Southern Province, 3.7 acres; and in the Eastern Province, 4.6 acres. Ibid., p. 7.
75. Only a third of the northern farmers, against more than hâlf those in the two southern districts, employed labourers, Ibid., p. 9.
76. Only 55 per cent of the farms in the north, against 80 per cent in the southern provinces, were on newly cleared land. Ibid., p. 12.
77. Mutti, *Marketing Staple Crops*, p. 92, Table 4-5.
78. Calculated from *1963 Census*, Vol. III, Table 7.
79. In the south in the same period, primary school enrolment rose from 11,446 to 52,997 students. Figures for 1948 are from the *Annual Report of the Education Department for 1948*, and for 1963, from the *Sleight Report*, p. 3.
80. Calculated from *1963 Census*, Vol. II, Table 9.
81. The Mines and Labour sections of Karefa-Smart's Lands, Mines and Labour portfolio were given to A.J. Demby, a Mende, though Karefa-Smart was given special responsibility for Defence and External Affairs (he became Minister of External Affairs on the attainment of Independence). Bureh's Works and Housing Ministry was split, leaving him with Works only, while Cyril Rogers-Wright was given Housing and Country Planning.
82. Cf. the creation of a 'Nyasa' identity among the different tribes coming from Nyasaland to work in the Copperbelt . See A.L. Epstein, *Politics in an Urban African Community*, Manchester, Manchester University Press for Rhodes-Livingstone Institute, 1958, p. 236.
83. This question of whether Northern voters were locally or regionally oriented has been argued in some detail between Victor Minkin and myself. See John Cartwright, 'Party Competition in a Developing Nation: The Basis of Support for an Opposition in Sierra Leone', *Journal of Commonwealth Political Studies*, X, 1, Mar. 1972, pp. 71-90; A.V. Minikin, 'Some Comments on "Party Competition in a Developing Nation" ', ibid., XI, 3, Nov. 1973, pp. 265-71; Cartwright, 'A Rejoinder,' ibid., pp. 271-8; and Minikin, 'Indirect Political Participation in Two African Chiefdoms', *Journal of Modern African Studies*, XI, 1, Mar. 1973, pp. 129-35.
84. The 1968 survey found that ten of eighteen northerners who claimed to have voted for the APC symbol in 1962 also claimed that they had chosen their candidate on personal or local rather than party criteria. See Cartwright, 'Party Competition', p. 75.
85. Ibid., pp. 83-4.

86. See above, p. 163.
87. Cartwright, 'Party Competition', pp. 79-82.
88. In addition, Chief Yumkella of Kambia district, was one of the two chiefs in the Cabinet as Ministers without Portfolio. It had been the practice from 1959 onwards to have one northern and one southern chief in the Cabinet.
89. See Barrows, *Grassroots Politics,* pp. 86-7.
90. For example, in 1964, it ranked sixth of the twelve district in popualtion per hospital bed, and eighth in the number of government health centres, dispensaries and treatment centres, and in 1963 it ranked ninth in the number of secondary school places per 1,000 population. More important for purposes of comparison, it ranked below the two adjacent districts of Kailahun and Kenema in all three areas. See Clarke, *Sierra Leone in Maps,* pp. 66, 68. (Interestingly, however, it ranked third among the districts in primary school places per 1,000 population, which may have contributed to the cadres of unemployed young men who eventually supported the DPC.)
91. Kono had representation in the Cabinet for only two brief intervals: in 1957 for two months after the elections, when Paul Dunbar held the Health portfolio, until he was unseated on an election petition, and from October 1963 to April 1964, when S.L. Matturi held the post of Resident Minister, Eastern Province, until Albert Margai came to power.
92. In the six 'diamond chiefdoms' of Kono taken together, no less than 43 per cent of the total population in 1963 were 'strangers' of other ethnic groups. In Nimi Yema, Gbense and Kamara chiefdoms, 'strangers' comprised 56, 54 and 52 per cent of the population respectively. In the diamond areas outside Kono, only one Kenema chiefdom (Wando) had more than 50 per cent 'strangers' (in the case of Bo and Kenema districts, non-Mendes), only one other chiefdom (Gorama Mende) exceeded 40 per cent 'strangers', and only seven exceeded 30 per cent. The impact of 'strangers' in Kono society was clearly greater than it was in the Mende areas.
93. See Minikin, *Local Politics in Kono District, Sierra Leone, 1945-70,* p. 183. I have found Minikin's work very useful in reconsidering some of my own earlier conclusions regarding Kono.
94. Ibid., p. 89.
95. Ibid., p. 214.
96. Ibid., pp. 337-9. See also Hayward, 'A Radical Political Organisation', p. 9.
97. Hayward, pp. 9-11.
98. Minikin, p. 242.
99. Ibid., pp. 243-4.
100. See Cartwright, *Politics in Sierra Leone,* p. 172.
101. See the complaints by the SLPIM's members of Parliament about mass arrests and political uses of residential permits, *Daily Mail,* 4 June, 1962; also the General Secretary's comment on the APC's decision to end its alliance, ibid., 31 July 1963.
102. For the announcement of the dissolution of the SLPIM see *Daily Mail,* 9 Mar. 1965; for the chief's re-election ibid., 4 May 1965.
103. See *We Yone,* 17 July 1965.
104. Hayward, who spent some time in Kono during the 1967 election campaign, suggests that in a fair election the DPC would have won four of the five Kono seats. 'A Radical Political Organisation', p. 20.
105. Ibid., pp. 25-6.
106. A detailed study of their economic role in Sierra Leone is H.L. van der Laan *The Lebanese Traders in Sierra Leone,* The Hague, Mouton, 1975. For a general account of the Lebanese, see R.B. Winder, 'The Lebanese in West Africa', *Comparative Studies in Society and History,* IV, 1961-2, pp. 296-333.

107. See Stanley, 'The Lebanese', pp. 160-1.
108. A belief given credence by the frequent arrests of Lebanese with illicit diamonds, and occasional more spectacular episodes such as the trial of Henneh Shamal, a major Kono area dealer, on charges of conspiracy, following a daylight holdup of an SLST shipment at Hastings airport. He was later acquitted. See *West Africa,* 22 Nov. 1969, p. 1422; 27 Dec. 1969, p. 1592; and 7 Mar. 1970, p. 271.
109. *Cox Report,* p.63.
110. Dawson, 'Race and Inter-group Relations', pp. 218-19.
111. On the other hand, we should note some of the harsher criticisms voiced by the African elite. See for example, the criticism by L.A.M. Brewah and K.I. Kai-Samba of Lebanese dominance in trade, *House of Representatives Debates,* 1962-3, vol. II, cols. 634-5, 639.
112. The Constitutional Amendment (No. 2) Act No. 12 of 1962.
113. *Sierra Leone Gazette,* XCIV, 48, 20 June 1963, p. 615.
114. The Non-Citizens (Restriction of Trade or Business) Act 1965, section 4 (f).
115. Protectorate Assembly, *Proceedings of the Seventh Meeting,* 26 Sept. 1950, pp. 28-31.
116. His words were: 'We would have made a vital mistake if we had decided to rest just on our majority and select only Protectorate people. But we decided as the position was almost two to one . . . that the only two colony members who were on our side should be brought in.' *Legislative Council Debates,* 1951-2, 31 Jan. 1952.
117. See above, p. 174.
118. See Scott, 'The Sierra Leone Election of 1957', pp. 210-11; also the protests of Creoles throughout this period, such as Sarif Easmon's letter, 'I ask You, What Harm Have the Creoles Done?', *Daily Mail,* 22 Nov. 1956, and the debate on a petition and demonstration attacking (Creole) judges in March 1958, *House of Representatives Debates,* 1958-9, I, 25 Aug. 1958, pp. 88-105.
119. Cyril Rogers-Wright and Gideon Dickson-Thomas became Ministers, and John Nelson-Williams a Ministerial Secretary.
120. *House of Representatives Debates* (mimeo), 26 July 1961, p. 44.
121. Ibid., vol. V, 17 Jan. 1962, pp. 138, 147.
122. On a strict apportionment according to population, the Rural Area should have had two and Freetown four seats.
123. I. Nicholson, 'The Machinery of the Federal and Regional Government', in John P. Mackintosh, *Nigerian Government and Politics,* London, Allen & Unwin, 1966, p. 184.
124. A conspicuous illustration was his delay in appointing a Creole as head of the Electricity Board. The Creole in question, A.P. Bruno-Gaston, had been acting head since September 1957. But a year later, before appointing him to the permanent post, the government brought out an Englishman to look at the job. See *Daily Mail,* 13 Sept. and 30 Oct. 1958.
125. Dr Karefa-Smart, I.B. Taylor-Kamara and Y.D. Sesay were all in the Cabinet; Banja Tejan-Sie, who failed to win a Parliamentary seat, was appointed a Magistrate; Alex Cotay, formerly editor of Dr Margai's *Bo Observer,* became Sierra Leone government representative in London, and after having to withdraw from that position, was Dr Margai's unsuccessful nominee for the post of party secretary, against a Mende advanced by Albert Margai.
126. In the south it did seem somewhat easier for younger men to force their way into the national arena and to be accepted by the national SLPP leaders. Maigore Kallon and M.J. Kamanda-Bongay after 1957, and L.A.M. Brewah, Kutubu Kai-Samba and Salia Jusu-Sheriff after 1962, were in temperament

at least more akin to the APC's northern representatives than to their elders in the SLPP from both south and north, and had few counterparts among the northern SLPP representatives.

127. Dick Simpson, 'The Generation Gap in Two Provincial Sierra Leonean Towns', *Pan-African Journal,* II, 1, Winter 1969, pp. 15-25. Simpson makes an implied reference to this tendency, although he does not note it explicitly.
128. The comment of one APC leader explaining why he had helped form the Elections Before Independence Movement and the APC.
129. Bonthe Town had a population of 6,894 and the Bonthe district 73,245. Even dividing the population of the two town and two district seats more evenly would have left the area over-represented, with an average of 20,035 persons per seat, compared to the national average of 35,167 per ordinary member's seat.
130. A parallel may be drawn here with the relationship between the Canadian Prime Minister, Pierre Elliott Trudeau, and Western Canada. Trudeau's apparent lack of interest in the wheat farmers' difficulties – epitomised by his rhetorical query before a farm audience, 'Why should I sell your wheat?' – was transmuted by the opposition parties into an alleged 'tribal' bias in favour of Quebec, which contributed greatly to Western alienation from the national Canadian government.
131. He eventually withdrew his candidacy before the election.
132. An editorial in *Liberty,* 18 Sept. 1959, stated: 'The SLPP . . . has spent much time wickedly and unashamedly preaching tribalism and having the effrontery to allow prominent persons in the party to publicly cast aspersions on the Creoles, an important section of the community.'
133. *Daily Mail,* 1 May 1964.
134. The speech is published as Sierra Leone, *Directives to Civil Servants and All Foreign Missions Abroad,* by the Honourable, the Prime Minister, A.M. Margai, Freetown, Government Printer, 1964.
135. See Cartwright, *Politics in Sierra Leone,* pp. 189-91, for a more detailed account of this episode.
136. The APC resolved potential problems of conflict within its ranks by electing Siaka Stevens (who was not a member of the Council) to the office of Mayor.
137. Across the city, the SLPP's candidates had averaged 5,495 votes per candidate in the elections from 1960 to the spring of 1964; in the October 1964 election they averaged 10,126 votes. APC candidates had averaged 5,662 votes from 1960 to 1964, and 11,423 in October, 1964.
138. One aspect of this, the independence of the Bar, was illustrated by Berthan Macauley, later to become Attorney-General, when he defended the APC leaders in 1961 against charges of sedition and incitement. In a letter replying to a columnist's remarks in the *Daily Mail,* he reminded the paper that a barrister was obliged to act on behalf of any client, regardless of whether he agreed with the client's views, to the best of his ability. See *Daily Mail,* 13 Apr. 1961.
139. See M.E. Yanni, 'My Dialogue with the Prime Minister', *We Yone,* 9 Jan. 1965.
140. Notes by the writer from the broadcast of the Prime Minister's monthly press conference, 30 Mar. 1965.
141. On this period of strained relations between the Government and the Bench, see the interesting paper by the then Chief Justice of Sierra Leone, Sir Samuel Bankole-Jones, 'The Judiciary and the State: The West African Experience', presented to the Second Commonwealth Chief Justices Conference, Port-of-Spain, Trinidad, 17-20 Apr. 1968, esp. pp. 23-5.

142. Ibid., pp. 32-3.
143. Cartwright, *Politics in Sierra Leone*, p. 225.
144. It provoked the extraordinary spectacle of two lawyers representing the Sierra Leone Bar Association bringing an action against the Attorney-General alleging that the appointment of Mr Collier to the post of Acting Chief Justice was unconstitutional.
145. From late 1965 to 1967, *We Yone* regaled its readers with a steady stream of generally accurate accounts of Ministers' (mis)behaviour based on information which clearly came from sources inside the senior administration.
146. He could have purged only Karefa-Smart, leaving Y.D. Sesay in the Cabinet, which might also have helped limit the possible threat that other Bo School Old Boys might rally round Sesay. Alternatively, he might have promoted one of the three rather mediocre SLPP northern backbenchers into the Cabinet.
147. See next chapter, pp. 230-3.
148. *House of Representatives Debates*, 1965-6, 8 Sept. 1965, col. 164.
149. Ibid., col. 165.
150. Peter Tucker, first Establishments Secretary and later Secretary to the Prime Minister, was actually Sherbro, but with Mende family connections.
151. This last post was filled, following the removal of an expatriate, by a man who was not only a Mende, but a relative of Sir Albert's.
152. Several of my northern students at Fourah Bay College were discouraged about their chances of getting civil service positions, claiming that Mendes were getting preference. Whether or not this was in fact true, the belief itself was significant.
153. At that time, a trip from Freetown to Kabala took at least six hours' hard driving along rough roads, whereas the trip to Gbangbatoke took less than half that time along roads which were largely paved, and even the trip to Bonthe could be made in three hours' drive plus an hour by fast launch, even though the normal boat trip from Mattru took four hours.
154. Transportation Consultants, Inc., 'Transportation Survey of Sierra Leone, March 1963', Washington, D.C., 1963, pp. 114-15. This report did suggest that Bonthe's field might be justified to facilitate government contact, although it was not justifiable on commercial grounds, whereas a field for Kabala was justified on economic, social and political grounds.
155. The Lunsar-Mile 47 road and the Pendembu-Nyandehun road, built at a cost of £37,667 and £23,498 a mile respectively through contractor pre-financing, were both high-quality roads which would make a long-lasting contribution to a basic road network, but their traffic load in their early years was far below the level necessary to justify this expenditure.
156. See above, pp. 175-6.
157. An oil-crushing factory at Bo, an instant coffee factory at Kenema, and a soap factory at Bo could all be justified on the basis of proximity to supplies and good transportation.
158. See F.M.B. Sawi, 'The Sierra Leone Produce Marketing Board, 1949-1969', unpublished M.A. dissertation, University of Birmingham 1972, p. 44. I am grateful to Peter Mitchell for this reference.
159. The mechanical ploughing scheme had been started in 1949, and Bonthe had always had more land ploughed than the Bombali district. Taking all the southern and all the northern circles together, we find that both regions increased their acreage ploughed to peaks in 1965 of 11,604 and 9,942 acres respectively, and that both rose and fell at approximately the same rate. I am indebted to Ken Swindell of the University of Birmingham for this information.

160. Enrolment in the north increased from 24,034 in 1962-3 to 37,878 in 1967-8, an increase of 57 per cent; in the southern and eastern provinces, it increased from 52,997 to 64,594, an increase of 24 per cent. This left the places per 1,000 population at 4.2 for the north, 5.7 for the east, and 6.0 for the south. The 1962-3 figures are from the *Sleight Report*, p. 3 and the 1967-8 figures are from the *Annual Report of the Department of Education, 1969.*
161. See below, pp. 256-7.
162. Cf. Ali Mazrui's argument that Ganda dominance in Uganda helped to bring Uganda's other tribes closer to each other in their anti-Baganda feelings; see above, note 38.
163. In this connection, it was striking that the strongest challenge to the APC government came not from the SLPP, but from a breakaway movement of Temnes in 1970. This party, the United Democratic Party, seems to have gained much of its support (which was never tested; the party was banned within days of its formation by Prime Minister Stevens) on the grounds that Temnes had not received a fair share of jobs and other benefits under the APC. See Cartwright and Cox, 'Left Turn for Sierra Leone?'.
164. I use 'salience' here in the sense that possession of a particular subnational identity implied holding a particular political affiliation. For example, to be a 'provincial' in Sierra Leone in the 1950s was to be an SLPP supporter, to be Temne in the 1960s was to be APC, just as in, say, the United States to be Jewish or black was to be a Democrat.
165. It is perhaps significant in this context that the only seat the APC won in the Southern Province in 1967 was one in which Sherbros and Temnes rather than Mendes predominated. The APC winner was a long-time Sherbro politician, Valecius Neale-Caulker, and one of the major chiefdoms in his constituency was that of Paramount Chief Honoria Bailor-Caulker, a Sherbro who refused to allow people to address her in Mende.
166. The Fula, largely based in Koinadugu, stayed strongly behind the SLPP (cf. their behaviour in Guinea in the 1950s) but all the other northern tribes seem to have swung heavily to the APC.
167. The alleged appeal by Albert Margai to Mende solidarity, that if Mendes did not stick together the northerners 'would cut the Mende man's throat', and most of the other appeals to Mende tribal sentiment, had more of a ring of fear than of boasting about them.
168. See Cartwright and Cox, 'Left Turn for Sierra Leone?'; Christopher Clapham, 'Sierra Leone: Civilian rule and the new republic', *World Today,* 28 Feb. 1972, pp. 88-9.
169. I have argued elsewhere that the 1967 results strongly suggest that the APC's support in the south could be almost entirely accounted for by northerners present in those constituencies where it was able to run candidates. See Cartwright, *Politics in Sierra Leone,* p. 250. I should add, however, that once the APC formed the government and was able to use the weight of central power to dispense rewards and punishments within Mende chiefdoms, it was able to achieve considerable success in a series of by-elections, winning nine out of eighteen seats in Mende areas, largely by taking in dissident factions in the numerous intrachiefdom disputes and being willing to nominate prominent ex-SLPP men who happened to have been on the 'out' side in 1967. See Barrows, *Local-Level Politics,* pp. 293-300, for further discussion of the effect of factionalism in Mende chiefdoms on the APC's ascendancy.
170. This parallels John Mackintosh's findings in Nigeria in 1959 that the three major Nigerian parties outside their home regions were identified as the parties of 'strangers', and thus beyond the pale of serious consideration as alternative rulers for other regions. See Mackintosh, *Nigerian Government and Politics,* pp. 304-6, 329-30 and 351-2.

7 THE PACE OF SOCIAL CHANGE AS A SOURCE OF CONFLICT

We have now examined two major types of conflict as they set constraints upon the range of choices open to a national leader. The conflicts involving regions and ethnic groups provided fairly clear-cut alignments; an individual was either a Creole or a 'countryman', a Mende or a Temne, and once such an identity became salient there was little difficulty for the individual or for anyone else in determining where he stood. Because of their polarising tendency and the high emotional charge they could carry, these conflicts were potentially extremely divisive, and a leader had to devote considerable effort to preventing their becoming salient. Conflicts within the individual chiefdoms posed considerably less danger to the maintenance of the national polity, both because they were fought in a smaller arena and because the cross-cutting ties of their participants prevented such a complete polarisation. This was particularly true of factional alignments between rival groups of patrons and clients, but even the less frequent 'class' alignments of ordinary farmers against the chiefly 'Establishment' were largely perceived in local terms and moderated by kinship links across class lines.

A third type of conflict could be perceived, though much more dimly, in Sierra Leone. This conflict was much less likely to create polarisations than the two already examined, because most individuals were far more ambivalent about their position in it, and it scarcely ever entered the political arena as a conflict between different groups. Nevertheless, it underlay many of the more particular clashes that took place. I refer here to the conflict over the desirability of the cluster of social changes set in train by the several facets of colonial rule, a cluster of changes to which I apply the term 'modernisation'.

I use the term 'modernisation' here advisedly, as a shorthand for a range of phenomena which lack sufficient underlying unity to be treated as a single concept, yet generally tend to occur together. While I would concur with the view that the term's very comprehensiveness has rendered it unusable as a concept[1] still we do have the undeniable fact that a range of changes have occurred together in many parts of the world, and have been of major significance within the societies in which they occurred. These changes can be seen at three levels: changes in individual attitudes, particularly attitudes to change itself and to the possibility of controlling man's fate; changes in patterns of relationships, including both the degree of fixity of the social order and the comprehensiveness of positions within it; and technological changes, specifically man's abilities to alter his environment. These changes are not necessarily 'eurhythmic'[2] in the sense that (say) men who learn to operate diesel locomotives must inevitably extend this 'rational' outlook to the question of why they should obey their Paramount Chief, or that men who accept new ways of farming must also accept the abandonment of a sacred ritual. But a good many of these changes *do* seem to support each other; men who become literate, or who travel to a city or mine to work, do tend to be less unquestioning in their obedience to traditional authorities, and farmers willing to alter their crop-growing techniques do tend to be less concerned with obeying traditional *mores* than do the stay-at-homes or the non-innovators. While there is no necessary connection between many of these changes, a change in one area often seems to offer encouragement to change in another unrelated area.

The key to making sense of this situation seems to me to lie in treating 'modernisation' as the process by which men seek to explain an increasingly comprehensive range of phenomena in secular terms.[3] This expansion of secular or 'rational' explanation seems to be the common thread linking the various changes that appear to cohere together. Thus in the area of man's control over inanimate objects, as well as over other living creatures, the spread of rational understanding (or the 'demystification' of phenomena) made possible the systematic exploration of new avenues for innovation.[4] Once it had been observed that water could turn a wheel, it could then be asked what tasks might be performed by the power from a continuously turning shaft; once it was accepted that electricity was a 'natural' phenomenon, and could be produced by turning a coil, it was a fairly straightforward matter to move to hyro-electric generators. At the same time the spread of rationality removed many suprarational sanctions against innovations,[5] thus clearing the way for the Industrial Revolution.

In its effects on social relationships, the spread of rationality was equally revolutionary. As men came to see that their relationships with the non-animate world were governed by comprehensible laws, rather than by the mysterious ways of divine forces, it was hardly surprising that some should seek to explain human relations in the same light. Also from the fifteenth century onwards technological innovations were given rise to new social groups more rapidly than these could be assimilated into a system of fixed ranks. Under this combination of pressures it was hardly surprising to find the system of fixed ranks in European societies breaking down. At the same time the spread of rationality forced rulers to create a new basis for their authority. No longer could they base their legitimacy solely upon suprarational or 'traditional' grounds. Inexorably, the perception that men could now expect rational explanations of why their polity was as it was led to the ruler being forced to justify his position in terms of the perceived interests of his subjects, and thus put obedience to the ruler on a much more self-interested basis than before.

The spread in the acceptance of secular explanations for phenomena was both a gradual and an uneven process. While we could say that it was fairly widely diffused throughout Western Europe and North America by the beginning of the nineteenth century, and had been largely taken up by the political and economic elites of all the world's major societies by the mid-twentieth century, still it was a state of mind which might for a given individual be much less developed in one area of existence than in another, or might even be excluded completely from certain areas. Thus we can find, for example, a British shipyard worker explaining the seaworthiness of ships solely in terms of the quality of their welding, location of ballast tanks and other 'rational' attributes, but accepting the political leader of his country on the basis that he is of a class of 'natural rulers'.[6] Similarly, an African academic may explain social patterns in his country entirely in 'rational' terms, yet feel compelled to obey the advice of an illiterate elder brother on family matters.[7] The fact that this way of looking at the world could manifest itself in different areas for different individuals, and could be totally excluded from certain areas, made its manifestations appear 'dysrhythmic'[8] but there does seem to be enough of an underlying common basis that we can use the term 'modernisation' to cover all the range of processes based upon the spread of secular explanation.

In Sierra Leone, 'modernisation' manifested itself in numerous ways, and the conflicts that arose from its spread called up varied and changing alignments. In the economic sphere it underlay the spread of new technologies and new roles: the growth of cash-crop agriculture and the use of new farming methods, the appearance of traders and wage workers, the mines and the services attached to these forms of economic growth, such as roads and lorries. Here both the dysrhythmic aspects of modernisation, and the conflicts engendered by its differential acceptance came into sharp relief. Many chiefs, for example, quite happily expanded their farms in order to enter the cash-crop market, while at the same time continuing to call for the traditional free labour for these farms from subjects who themselves were occupied with producing their own surpluses for sale in competition with the chief. Not unnaturally, many farmers came to feel that the chiefs' claims to labour were no longer sanctioned by custom, and this difference over the legitimacy of the chiefs' juxtaposition of the innovation of commercial farming with customary claims for assistance was one of the major underlying factors in the 1955-6 riots.[9]

The conflict also arose more directly in both local and national political arenas. For example, we might argue that underlying the struggle to remove the Paramount Chiefs from the judicial process lay two concepts of the chief's role which differed essentially in the degree to which they saw the chief as a mortal limited only by secular considerations. The argument for leaving the chief as head of the NA Court rested ultimately on his role as 'father' of his people, a role presupposing that he was inhibited by non-rational considerations from acting to the detriment of his 'children'. The contrary argument that a separate individual should be head of the court presupposed that the chief would act on the same prejudices and calculations of personal advantage as other men, and that the restraints on his behaviour were of no greater efficacy than the prudential kind that would limit other men similarly placed. The 'coming of politics' to the chiefdoms in the 1950s, and more broadly the appearance of new intermediaries competing with the chief for the clientage of the ordinary farmers in their dealings with national leaders,[10] was in part a process of infusing relationships with a larger component of 'modernity' into the chiefdom arenas. The Members of Parliament, candidates for office, and wealthy traders sought support on a much more explicit *quid pro quo* basis than the chiefs, and at the same time were less constrained by customary taboos in the performance of their functions. The constraints upon them were legal and prudential, not traditional, and thus in their encouragement of the development of an attachment based on a rational calculation of interests, we could term them 'modernisers' and the growth of their following in relation to the chief's an indication of the spread of 'modern' attitudes.

In the national arena also we can see evidence of a conflict over the extent to which the diffusion of modern attitudes should be encouraged. Whereas at the local level there were instances of quite explicit opposition to manifestations of modernisation,[11] politicians acting at the national level tended to resist more subtly. Thus no one openly objected to removing the chiefs from the judicial process; it just took a rather long time. It is difficult in fact to pinpoint specific situations in which this conflict was uppermost, in part because the question was invariably one of 'more' or 'less' rather than 'yes' or 'no', but also because it was generally thoroughly intermixed with questions of power, class and other considerations. Thus we can see in the prolonged struggle between Dr Margai and his brother the underlying issue of how rapidly change was to be forced by the government; but there was also the more practical question of who was to hold political power, in the resolution of which each combatant took allies wherever he could find them.

An important factor moderating the struggle within the SLPP was the close-knit nature of the up-country elite in the 1950s. If we take all the non-chief up-country members of Dr Margai's Cabinets from 1957 to his death as embracing most of this elite, we can see a number of factors making for cohesion, even if their beliefs and temperaments were quite varied. Considering first the 'objective' indicators of cohesion, fourteen of the eighteen in this group were members of ruling families, and eight had attended Bo School, most at a time when it was reserved for the sons and nominees of chiefs. Most of them had known each other in pre-SLPP days; six had been teachers, seven others had been in various forms of government service which took them into contact with each other around the provinces, and seven had been involved in the SLPP's forerunner, the Sierra Leone Organisation Society. On a more personal level, at least six of the Ministers were linked to other Ministers by marriage; Doyle Sumner's wife was a Margai, one of the Massallys was married to a Demby, and Jusu-Sheriff's mother was a Ngobeh. One might suggest that Sumner's survival in Albert Margai's Cabinet, or Jusu-Sheriff's support for the rather unprogressive chief Alpha Ngobeh, showed the strength of these family ties. The more general point to be stressed here is simply that these personal and social links did cut across, and often outweighed, 'ideological' ones.

It may be that the close-knit nature of the SLPP elite contributed to the growth of a politically viable opposition. As young men from a greater diversity of backgrounds moved and began to seek roles in the political arena, they often found difficulty in getting the opportunities they sought through the SLPP. In many respects this could be considered a 'modern versus traditional' clash, in that the criteria by which the younger men felt they should be judged were essentially those based on their individual training and skills, whereas the SLPP leadership in most constituencies tended to look more to acceptable social backgrounds. In any case, opposition parties, first the UPP and then the APC, offered to ambitious 'outsiders' more promising opportunities for political advancement than the SLPP. The very fact of their being 'outsiders' in turn widened the gulf between the SLPP and the opposition, helping intensify political conflict.

A Conflict over the Pace of Change in the SLPP: The 1957 Leadership Struggle

We have noted throughout this study that the SLPP was heavily skewed in favour of the more 'traditionally-minded' elements in the Sierra Leone polity, notably the Paramount Chiefs. Conflicts over the spread of 'modern' attitudes therefore were likely to be somewhat inhibited, with the 'modernisers' within the SLPP constrained both by their weakness within the party and by their personal ambivalence. Nevertheless, one major conflict did take place between those who wished to force the pace of change towards a more 'modern' society and those who wished to safeguard the existing ways. This was the struggle for the leadership of the party between the two Margais, which reached its climax in 1957.

Differences between the two brothers over educational policy, Africanisation of the administration, diamond policy and other issues had been apparent for some time before 1957. At the 1956 SLPP convention the Bo branch, which had earlier spearheaded demands for a more open diamond mining policy,[12] managed to have a new post of Party Chairman created, and then elected Albert Margai to fill it.[13] Dr Margai, however, remained Leader of the party. In 1957 the new electoral rules brought a great influx of non-chiefs into the SLPP Parliamentary group,[14] the body which chose the party leader. On 19 May 1957, this party caucus voted by twenty-two votes to twenty-one to replace Dr Margai as party leader by his younger brother. Within a few hours, however, Albert Margai announced that he was stepping down from the post that he had just won, so that his brother should become Sierra Leone's first Prime Minister.[15] That there was more to the episode than this was indicated by the next few weeks' developments, in which various groups in the party attempted to work out an agreement between the two brothers over whose supporters should get what portfolios. While Albert took a rather intransigent stand, Dr Margai offered appointments to some of his brother's less firmly committed supporters,[16] and meanwhile a series of election petitions removed six of Albert's followers from the legislature.[17] On 4 July 1957 a reconciliation committee announced that Albert Margai 'shall enjoy full Ministerial status as soon as practicable', but fourteen months went by in which three more ministerial-level posts were filled before

Albert finally announced that he was forming the Peoples National Party. By this time, however, his support within the SLPP had dwindled to the point where only four other SLPP members[18] followed him into opposition.

What brought about this dramatic challenge and equally dramatic turnabout? To some extent the differences between the Margai brothers were differences of personality and temperament, and Albert's challenge was based on personal ambition, while his failure could be attributed in part to his relative lack of skill. But there were also marked differences between the two men's supporters, differences which reflected varying commitments to hastening change.

The caucus elected to the legislature in 1957 was quite a different body than the SLPP group in the old legislative council. Only eleven out of forty-three, or 25.5 per cent were Paramount Chiefs, as compared to eight out of sixteen, or 50 per cent, in the old Council. No less than twelve, or 28 per cent had some post-secondary education, and seven were under age forty. It was the younger members, and to a lesser extent the more educated, who favoured replacing Dr Margai with his brother.[19] The grounds they gave, both at the time and retrospectively, were relatively short-term and programmatic; they thought Albert Margai would press more vigorously for independence, would hasten the Africanisation of the civil service, and would listen more to Sierra Leoneans and less to expatriates.[20] But in seeking these goals, they seemed prepared to trample on a basic African belief, that a younger brother should not seek to push aside his elder. Albert Margai's relationship with the Doctor, it will be recalled, was almost a filial one; Dr Margai had been instrumental in securing for Albert the PEPU scholarship which enabled him to study law in England, and as head of the family had been generally concerned with Albert's welfare. While most of those who opposed Albert would have resisted his becoming leader simply on the grounds that they did not trust his policies or beheaviour, the manner of his attempted takeover gave added strength of their objections, and on the other side weakened the resolve of his supporters to hand on.[21]

Both Albert Margai and his young supporters, then, were to some degree inhibited by the pull of traditional claims upon their behaviour. Although the fact that he had made the challenge suggested that traditional sanctions had little meaning for him, Albert's vacillation when he had won was at least partially attributable to his doubts over whether his challenge had been justified. It is true that straight power considerations probably played a larger role. A number of chiefs and other supporters of Dr Margai would have sought constantly to overthrow him if he had become Premier, and there was even some question about whether Governor Dorman would have allowed Dr Margai to try to form a new government, regardless of his removal from the leadership of the SLPP.[22] But if Albert had held on to the leadership, he could have consolidated his position by judicious offers of Ministerial posts to waverers, and thus put himself in a position where it would have been very hard to refuse him the Premiership. Lack of political skill and lack of nerve undoubtedly were major factors leading to his stepping down; but so also was his uncertainty over the rightness of his action in challenging his older brother.

But restraining the desire for change of the 'young men' of the SLPP was a relatively easy matter, in view of their close relationship with the established order. Nearly all of Albert Margai's supporters in Parliament, like those of Dr Margai, were the children or close relatives of chiefs, frequently themselves aspired to chiefship, and in nearly all cases relied on the chiefs' or other 'traditional' figures' hold over the ordinary voters for their own election. A strong element of self-interest, in short, led them to restrain their efforts at undermining the mystery buttressing the chief's authority, and more indirectly, to refrain from pushing too vigorously for changes that would upset the local 'Establishment'. We will find a greater tendency to support sweeping changes among the 'young men' who formed the cadres of opposition parties, which we shall examine in the next section.

Changed Outlooks and the Growth of Opposition Parties

We have already discussed specific events such as the diamond rush and the growth of cash-crop farming as factors bearing on political relationships, and have touched more briefly on patterns of formal education. We have also considered the most proximate factors in producing political organisations opposed to the hegemony of the Sierra Leone Peoples Party, namely 'class' and regional antagonisms. But there is a dimension to the question of why these antagonisms developed that we have not yet considered, namely the extent to which new patterns of interpersonal relationships created by the colonial experience contributed to their growth. The relationships I consider significant in this context are the functionally specific and limited ones arising out of the separation of men's activities into discrete spheres. The development of these relationships produced increased autonomy for the individual from hierarchical and peer pressure both by leaving interstices between different functions where such pressures would be exercised, and by allowing him to choose to some degree what hierarchies and peers he would associate himself with. The fisherman living in an isolated coastal village, for example, had little choice but to exchange his catch with other members of the village, to work with a limited choice of co-fishers, and to take part in all the appropriate rituals and ceremonies. But when he entered the wage economy, he could choose the ship on which he could work, sell his catch wherever the market seemed best, and make his own choice of appropriate ritual observances.[23] The price of this autonomy, however, was the loss of any comprehensive moral solidarity binding the individual into a community. While being one's brother's keeper (or vice versa) was a powerful commitment, being one's workmate's keeper was somewhat less so (especially if in his non-occupational cultural traits he was different), and beyond work, one's own family, and the self-selected circle of intimate friends, the degree of solidarity was slight indeed under normal circumstances.

From a leader's point of view, there were both gains and losses in this changing relationship. As men's specific interdependences increased, there developed an increased number of points at which the leader could exercise control over specific aspects of their behaviour; for example, he could extract a share of a farmer's crops much more readily through an export tax or duties on the products the farmer bought than through demanding part of what the farmer had kept for his own family use. But at the same time the substitution of the cash nexus for the more all-embracing notion of fealty to a superior made it easier for men to view any transaction with any leader as a short-term, self-interested act rather than an expression of moral solidarity.[24] His ability to set standards of behaviour, to call for support simply by virtue of the fact that he embodied the general interest of the community, was greatly weakened.

I am not arguing here that either the pattern of social relationships in pre-colonial Sierra Leone was entirely based upon this comprehensive notion of attachment, nor that all relationships developing out of the new occupational roles introduced through colonial rule were necessarily based on self-interest, or lacking a sense of moral solidarity. In fact, I would agree with the late Professor Titmuss's argument that even in the highly fragmented and depersonalised relationships of an advanced industrial society, one can find certain areas in which the commitment to help a stranger simply because he belongs to one's society has resisted the spread of the cash nexus.[25] But I would contend that the general tendency as functions in different spheres of activity become separated, as the range of roles proliferates and the roles themselves change more readily, as the number of personal contacts expands and as a growing proportion of these contacts are based on the cash nexus rather than on a more embracing moral relationship, is to develop a much more 'self-regarding' basis for one's relationship with the social order as a whole.

At the core of this shift in relationships within Sierra Leone lay the process known as Western formal education. In this term I include all those hierarchically-organised formal training programmes which are supposed to teach the young the methods developed in European civilisation for analysing the problems they are expected to encounter in life, and particularly those problems connected with the economic sphere, or 'the working world'. Western education differed from the more customary Sierra Leonean forms (for example, the Poro and Bundu societies) in its emphasis on 'rationality', the process of building an entire structure of understanding from a few basic assumptions relying entirely on secular or 'natural' (as opposed to supernatural) explanations. Literacy is a fundamental part of this 'rational' approach; in fact it has been argued that the critical questioning that led men to adopt an anlytical, reasoning approach was forced on them by the inconsistencies in past explanations made apparent by the maintenance of written records.[26] Certainly it seems plausible to accept the view of Harold Innis and his successors that literacy, with its constant recombining of discrete fragment units, produces a bias towards an analytical mode of thinking.[27]

The political implications of the spread of this anlytical mode of thinking are manifested at a number of levels. At the most general level, education introduced a more questioning attitude towards all forms of authority, from that of the head of the family to the national leader. The degree of obedience was not necessarily reduced thereby; but the justification for accepting leadership had to be made more 'rational', and the mystique of leadership was lessened. This weakening of the mystique of authority could be seen in a number of situations; for example, in the postwar attacks of the Protectorate educated men on the right of the British to continue to rule them, and equally dramatically, in the 1955-6 uprising against the hitherto generally sacred right of the Temne chiefs to demand such tributes as they desired. While the riots had far wider support than the educated men alone, there seems little doubt that the questioning of the chiefs' exactions which led to the uprisings was in part inspired by the influx of educated men into the chiefdoms.

A less direct but equally significant effect of education was the establishment of powerful new roles beyond the control of the political leader. Two examples of these new roles, and the power they could exert, were the legal profession and the lorry drivers.

The legal profession in Sierra Leone was modelled largely on the British pattern, and as we have noted, led the struggle to introduce an integrated court system which would have gradually submerged Sierra Leone customary law beneath British common and Sierra Leone statute law.[28] Entry into the profession was controlled by the Sierra Leone Bar Association, a self-regulating body operating under statutory authority from the government. All members of the judiciary, as well as such key figures in the administration as the Attorney-General and the Solicitor-General, had to be drawn from the membership of the profession. Although the government in theory retained the power to change the statutory rules under which the Bar Association operated, as well as to remove the restrictions on its choice of judges, to attempt such an action would be to arouse strong opposition even from nominal supporters in the legal profession on the grounds that the government was attempting to undermine the basic ethos of the profession. A clash of this sort in fact did develop during Sir Albert Margai's attempts to bring about the one-party state, first over his 'promotion' of the Chief Justice to the Court of Appeal,[29] second over an injunction restraining the one-party state committee from meeting,[30] and third over the appointment of Albert Margai's friend Gershon Collier as Chief Justice in 1967.[31] In all these cases, even lawyers sympathetic to Albert Margai found themselves joining with the larger body of his critics in protesting against his actions, and though they lost two of these encounters, each of these events contributed to the growth of opposition to the Prime Minister. The Bar Association's opposition was significant in two ways: first, because its members, especially the judges hearing trials of opponents of the Prime Minister, came to be imbued with a feeling that they had to lean over backwards against him as a counterweight to governmental pressure, and second, because in the eyes of a large number of people the Bar and Bench (or at least the Bench) were 'respectable' and, even more important, generally fair-minded people trying to uphold rules perceived as beneficial to all.

The lorry drivers' status in society was considerably lower than that of the legal profession, but like the lawyers their position gave them both influence and autonomy. On the face of it, lorry drivers were highly dependent upon both their government and their employers. They needed government action to provide motorable roads, and government permission to hold licences, to import vehicles and spare parts, and to allow them to organise a trade union. They generally needed capital from non-Sierra Leoneans to provide them with vehicles. But effectively none of these points of dependence worked to curtail their autonomy. The government could hardly refuse to maintain roads, or ban the importation of vehicles to punish lorry drivers; their service was too important to too many people. Nor could the vehicle owners effectively control them, short of taking over the driving themselves.[32] Now after 1960 many lorry drivers came to support the APC on both class and regional grounds; and the fact that they were too mobile to be controlled by the chiefs whose chiefdoms they passed through, and too important to the functioning of the economy[33] to be curbed by the national government, made them very valuable to the APC organisation, for which they could convey messages and party propaganda to almost any village without fear of persecution. Again, a new role created by technological developments created a significant area of autonomy, making possible political activities against the government which would not otherwise have been possible.

Enough has been said by now to suggest the ramifications of the new situation opened up by the spread of Western technology, education and the pattern of relationships associated with them. The one further point that should be made before considering its specific relationship to political activities is that these manifestations of 'modernisation' spread from central nodes in the *national* arena,[34] imposing themselves from outside on most local arenas. This meant that there was a severe imbalance between the proportions of individuals tending to 'modern' attitudes at the centre and in the local arenas; such attitudes were far more likely to be found among the pool of skills and backgrounds in an urban capital than in any of the rural villages where the bulk of the populace lived. It was dangerously easy for any organisation basing its strength upon urban cadres to get the impression that it might successfully advocate spreading 'modern' attitudes throughout the country, and might make political headway by coming down on the 'modern' side of a 'modern-traditional' alignment. Such a belief was deceptive. While individuals in rural areas might enhance their status by showing their connections with the national arena, or by possessing such attributes of 'modernity' as literacy or skilled technical training, they would also have to keep abreast of local factional alignments and maintain their standing in organisations such as Poro. A man who was not a 'son of the soil' was under an almost insuperable handicap in the local arena when he sought support on a political matter. In short, a party espousing 'modernising' attitudes could expect to win little rural support on the strength of these attitudes. If it could seek to get its way solely within the confines of the major urban centres it might fare satisfactorily; but if it were engaged in a nationwide competition for electoral support, it would have to win rural votes.

It might under certain conditions be possible for a party to put on one face in urban areas, and a different one for rural electorates, counting on a lack of knowledge among the rural electors to prevent their finding out what it really stood for. However, such information as we have concerning the diffusion of knowledge of political events in Sierra Leone suggests that a rather wide cross-section of individuals were aware of what happens outside their own chiefdom. Even Dorjahn's poll,[35] in which he argued that literates are considerably better informed on local as well as national affairs than are non-literates, indicated that a substantial minority of the non-literates in his Magburaka sample could identify figures having no ties with the local community. The 1968 survey, which asked twelve questions concerning such events as the 1957 struggle in the SLPP, the coming to power of Albert Margai and the recent depositions of two chiefs, produced a considerably stronger indication that non-literates, and even those who spoke no Krio, were aware of what had happened in qüite a number of these situations (Table 7. 1).

Table 7. 1: Awareness of Events in Sierra Leone (cumulative response)

Languages spoken	Responses providing some accurate detail	Other Responses	Total
Vernaculars only (N=39)	30%	70%	468
Krio (N=51)	33%	67%	612
English (literate) (N=49)	43%	57%	588

While those who were literate not surprisingly were best informed, the non-literates were certainly not as far behind as one might expect. We can suggest that awareness of major political events in Sierra Leone seems fairly well diffused throughout the population, and to the extent that those who are not literate are more strongly committed to 'traditional' institutions such as chieftaincy, leaders who would impose change can expect to encounter widespread grassroots resistance. A political conflict over 'modernisation' would not just involve a struggle at the centre, but would permeate throughout the polity, and we have already noted[36] that key institutions such as chieftaincy could command widespread popular support.

The Peoples National Party formed by Albert Margai and others in 1958 provided the best illustration in Sierra Leone of a political conflict along the dimension of 'modernisation'. In all the other parties whose conflicts with the SLPP illustrated this dimension to some degree – the UPP, the APC, the SLPIM and DPC – other conflicts along regional and class lines heavily overshadowed the 'modernisation' dimension. In the PNP-SLPP conflict these other structural dimensions were far less salient, as can be seen from an examination of the personnel, supporters and policies of the PNP.

The most striking feature of the PNP's national executive, which I shall take as its 'elite', was its high level of formal education. Seven of its thirteen members were lawyers, and two others were university graduates, whereas at this time (1958) only five of the fifteen members of the SLPP Ministry had university training. The PNP group was also much younger; eight of its members were under forty, as compared with two of the SLPP group. In so far as both formal education and youth tended at this time to be associated with 'modernising' tendencies, the PNP leadership showed a greater likelihood of being 'modern'. But against this we must set the fact that like the SLPP elite, they had strong ties to the 'traditional' *status quo;* six of their nine up-country members, like nine of the twelve up-country members in the SLPP Ministry, were members of ruling families.

This similarity of social background, besides serving as a possible inhibitor of 'modernising' tendencies among the PNP elite, served to restrict drastically the possibility that they would seek to fight the SLPP on 'class' grounds. The UPP's Creole leadership, and to a lesser extent the APC and DPC, could feel free to carry on that kind of campaign but the PNP's ties to the chiefs were too strong. Regional and tribal differentiation between them and the SLPP were also insignificant; both parties' elites showed similar patterns of Mende predominance, strong Creole representation, and a rather substantial under-representation of Temnes and other northerners. The PNP did make more effort to make the Creoles feel an integral part of the party than did the SLPP, and more generally attacked the SLPP for using divisive sectional appeals[37] but in terms of their inherent appeal to different regional and ethnic groups, there was little to choose between the two parties.

The base of electoral support for the PNP is not easy to determine, in part because the only elections held during its brief existence were local ones in which intimidation of both candidates and voters meant that preferences were quite unclear. The only indicators we have are very crude and rather unreliable, namely the seats won in the 1959 District Council and Bo Town Council elections, and the votes for the PNP in Freetown's relatively fair elections of the same year. The PNP's greatest electoral success came in the Bo Town Council elections in May 1959 when it won all three seats against SLPP candidates.[38] But in the countrywide District Council elections six months later it fared much worse, winning only twenty-nine out of 309 seats,[39] a fate which suggested that outside the main towns its appeal was not sufficient to offset the intimidation that the chiefs could bring to bear against it. In Freetown too its appeal seemed limited; in the city council elections its candidates finished last in all three wards, winning only 10 per cent of the vote.[40] Perhaps its weakness among northerners and the UPP's much stronger appeal to the Creoles contributed to this result.

In trying to specify the ways in which the PNP was more 'modernising' than the SLPP, we are forced to extrapolate from a very limited number of programmatic indications. The PNP leaders, despite their professions of sympathy for Sekou Touré and other 'radical' Pan-African leaders,[41] articulated no generalised philosophy or statement of aims comparable to that of the PDG or other 'radical' parties; they confined themselves almost exclusively to criticisms of specific government actions, and even in these there was a marked lack of consistency. Thus they condemned the government's slowness in Africanising the civil service and moving towards independence[42] but gave no indication of what kind of society they might try to build after independence was achieved. On the position of chieftaincy in society, they waffled; at times they condemned chiefs for 'retarding progress',[43] at other times they wanted the chiefs in a separate Upper House[44] for their own preservation, while at other times, they claimed that chieftaincy 'will continue to have a most important place in our national development for a very long time', and that it was the SLPP which was undermining the chiefs both by forcing them to work for it in inter-party struggles, and by such actions as abolishing the second speaker.[45] It seems probable, judging by the personal views expressed in interviews by ex-PNP men, that the more pro-chief statements were essentially a prudent recognition of the strength of pro-chief sentiment, and that the PNP leaders were on the whole rather impatient with the chiefs' commitment to tradition, as well as opposed to the way in which the chiefs worked against them on behalf of the SLPP.

The impatience with the slow pace towards Africanisation and independence, the frequent references to the need for 'progress' and 'development', and the criticism of the chiefs, all suggested an underlying desire to reshape society in a more 'modern' pattern, even if the PNP did not see fit to articulate this as a coherent philosophical goal. One could argue that the lack of a coherent underlying set of beliefs betrayed a purely personal basis for conflict, that Albert Margai and his PNP supporters were in opposition only because they saw this as a better path to success than working through the SLPP. Undoubtedly personal ambition did play a role in Albert Margai's decision to leave the SLPP, and probably also in the adherence of some of its other members. But they knew when they formed the PNP that it would be a long uphill struggle to power; and though we can suggest that they probably miscalculated badly the degree of that difficulty, it seems implausible that they should have seen working through the PNP as an easier route than staying inside the SLPP. Further, there was too much of a common temperament, an impatience with the slowness of change, shared by all the PNP leadership, to be able to say they were held together by nothing more than a desire for office. They wanted power in order to bring about some changes in the Sierra Leone social system, even though they never articulated clearly just what those changes were.

The All Peoples Congress is an even less clearcut case of a party in conflict with the SLPP along the 'modernising' dimension, despite its rather more radical orientation. 'Radicalism', in the sense of a commitment to greater equality in social relationships, has of course no necessary connection with modernisation, even though most 'radical' parties in the Third World have advocated widespread education, industrialisation and other measures which lead to a 'modern' society.[46] While the APC's Constitution envisaged 'a high degree of industrialisation and agricultural productivity' as its ultimate goal[47] it was no more explicit than its predecessor about how this goal would be brought about. In its attitude towards the chiefs it was more explicit, although again not clearly 'modernising'. Thus, while it repeatedly attacked the Tribal Authority system as 'feudal', its concern seemed principally to make the office of chief an elective one solely within the gift of the people of the chiefdom, rather than being subject to central government control.[48] Like the PNP it wanted the chiefs removed to a separate House and kept out of party politics, an understandable view while it remained in opposition.[49] But a generalised desire for 'progress', while underlying these specific attitudes was overshadowed as it had not been in the PNP by both a feeling of class antagonism towards the chiefs' privileges and a demand for regional equity. In their personnel also, the APC were not by most 'objective' indicators more 'modern' than the SLPP. They were less well educated; none of the APC founder members had university education, whereas a third of the SLPP Ministry had. The APC group were decidedly younger than the SLPP, with a median age of thirty-five in 1960 against fifty-three for the SLPP Ministry, and were less closely connected with chieftaincy, only four out of seven being members of ruling families.[50] While these differences were substantial, they suggested a greater likelihood of conflict along a 'class' dimension than along the 'modernising' dimension.

As for the APC's base of support, there is little evidence to suggest that it was drawn disproportionately from 'modernising' elements. An examination of social characteristics and APC voting for all Sierra Leone constituencies reveals only a slight positive correlation between APC support and indicators which might indicate a predisposition towards 'modernising' attitudes, while if we confine our examination to the four northern districts which supported the APC in 1962, we find the correlation between APC support and 'modernising' indicators is negative. (Table 7. 2).

Table 7.2: Spearman Rank-Order Correlations between APC Vote (as percentage of population) and Social Characteristics, by Constituencies.

	All Sierra Leone		North only
	1962	1967	
Urbanisation (percentage of population in towns of more than 1,000)	0.2911	0.1738	0.1033
Persons born outside district (in-migration)	0.1694	–0.300	–0.1604
Persons in non-agricultural occupations (towns of 2,000 or more only)	0.3401	0.1773	–0.1209

Aggregate data of this sort cannot, of course, offer conclusive support for any hypothesis on individual attitudes, but we can also find some direct evidence which at least renders improbable any hypothesis that APC supporters held more 'modernising' attitudes than SLPP supporters. The 1968 survey indicated that northerners supporting the APC in 1962 were no more inclined to look for leaders who favoured social change, or to regard as irrelevant 'traditional' characteristics among leaders, than were SLPP supporters.[51] APC supporters were exercised about the Prime Ministers' tribal biasses, of their chiefs and these Tribal Authorities, but not about a lack of 'modernising' activities in Sierra Leone.

In their rhetoric the two successive Kono opposition parties, the SLPIM and the DPC, resembled the APC in that both demanded an equalising redistribution of wealth to lower-status individuals and to 'have-not' areas. Underlying these 'class' and areal concerns there was a substratum of 'modernising' attitudes, at least in the negative sense that they sought an end to the preponderant power of the chiefs. In a more fundamental sense also the DPC in particular could be considered 'modern' in that it saw the possibility of changing the existing order of things by concerted social action. But while these 'modernising' orientations were certainly present, they were rendered nearly invisible by the overwhelming 'class' elements in the conflict between the SLPP and each of its opponents. Many of the leading SLPP men were just as aware of their opponents of the rational basis for the existing distribution of wealth, and the possibilities of changing this distribution. It was not so much a difference in degree of 'modernity' as a difference in interests that put Paul Dunbar, S.A. Sinah and others firmly into the SLPP camp, while George Mani, S.G. Fania and others turned up in the opposition ranks. Sometimes, as in the cases of Chief Mbriwa and K.J. Gamanja, personal rivalries or ideological convictions contrary to their 'class' interests might enter in, but again these were quite different dimensions than 'modernisation'.

Modernisation and Political Leadership

What were the effects of the conflicts among the 'modernisation' dimension on the two Margais as leaders? While disentangling this element from others will probably induce some dangerously oversimplified arguments, it will at least provide some indications of a significant difference hetween the two men, and will lead to a clearer understanding of the effects of the SLPP as a structural limitation on leadership.

The effects of this conflict on Dr Margai can be considered in two main areas: within the Cabinet, civil service, party executive and other national policy-making organs, and in his relations with more autonomous units, notably the chiefs and the opposition parties. In the first of these areas Dr Margai had to weigh and balance the predominant pressure of the educated men in his Ministry, the party and above all, the civil service, in favour of 'modernising' social relationships against the desire of many of his supporters, and above all the chiefs, to keep things as they were. In this balancing task he had to consider the second area, and particularly the questions of how far the chiefs would go in accepting change, what changes they would have to make to keep the support of their people, and how far opposition groups would be able to make inroads among the mass of ordinary voters.

For a leader whose main supporters were at one end of the 'modernisation' continuum, while his own inclinations were slightly more towards the centre and the chief opposition elements tended towards the other extreme, an optimal strategy would be to force his supporters to accept the changes he wanted made by warning them of the far less desirable changes in store for them if they failed to support him. In essence, this was Dr Margai's approach. On questions such as the deposition of chiefs after the 1955-6 riots, the introduction of Court Presidents, the expansion of educational facilities, and the use of chiefs as SLPP agents, the chiefs had little choice as long as Dr Margai's policies appeared preferable to those of the successive opposition parties. The relationship was not a one-sided one, however; once a substantial opposition had developed, beginning with the PNP, Dr Margai was forced to rely on the chiefs to help safeguard his own electoral position, and thus the situation became one of mutual support for survival. There was of course some risk in this situation, stemming from the possibility that a growing number of ordinary farmers would become independent participants in the political arena, rather than following the lead of their chiefs. If this were to happen, whether through the farmers' becoming desirous of a faster rate of change than the chiefs, or for some extraneous reason, the leader could find himself isolated at one extreme of the continuum with only a handful of supporters, while the bulk of the electorate had gone to the opposition.

The movement of a substantial segment of the 'modernising' elements into the PNP, and the subsequent adherence of many of these to the APC, did build up difficulties in the SLPP by forcing its national leaders into an increasing reliance on the chiefs. As long as the leader and the chiefs were not too far apart in their goals, and as long as the chiefs could deliver electoral majorities, this situation was acceptable to leader and chiefs alike. But if a new leader sought to introduce new goals which made him appear less clearly differentiated from the opposition, or if the chiefs could no longer be relied on to provide a majority, thus forcing a leader to seek a new basis for his power, then problems would arise. Both these conditions arose under Albert Margai's leadership.

The re-entry of the Mende elements in the PNP into the SLPP had not been received with unanimous enthusiasm by the 'old guard' SLPP members, since it implied distributing the benefits of office more widely and also because the PNP activists often seemed to hold values differing widely from those dominant in the SLPP. When Margai became Prime Minister, and PNP men began to appear as a sort of inner circle around him, many chiefs and other 'traditionalists' began a programme of covert resistance. This could be seen in the re-election of Sanusi Mustapha as Party Treasurer at Makeni in 1964,[52] in the defeat of the proposals for greater centralisation of the party at Bo in 1965, and in the apparent 'sitting out' of the 1966 District Council elections by a number of chiefs. Other factors, particularly personal and regional, were more important here, but the distrust of Albert Margai's commitment to social change underlay the other doubts. On the other hand, Albert Margai made a strongly favourable initial impression on many 'modernisers', notably among the civil service, and managed to attract into active participation a number of younger men who had been rather restless under Sir Milton.[53] This shift, if other factors had not interfered, would have brought a realignment with Albert Margai scooping in many of the 'modernisers' who had previously supported the APC and SLPIM, while leaving the chiefs and other traditionalists with the difficult task of setting up their own new opposition party.

But other factors precluded this development. The APC held on to its members on a combination of regional and class grounds[54] and as its emphasis shifted gradually towards concern over regional grievances, even some of the northern chiefs began to lean towards it. The civil service meanwhile became disillusioned with the Prime Minister through a combination of ethnic concern, anger over its politicisation, and disenchantment over corruption. The undoubted interest of the Prime Minister in promoting rapid 'modernisation' through the spread of education, better communications, industrial development and other means was simply not enough to offset the negative attributes of his relationship with many individuals who might have supported him on 'modernising' grounds alone.

These other conflicts, notably the ethnic alignments, made unlikely a much more drastic method by which the Prime Minister might overcome his difficulties. To hasten social change, and remove the drag of his conservative rural-based supporters, Sir Albert might have considered scrapping the parliamentary and party structures altogether and ruling through the civil service backed by the army. But apart from his own scruples against such a step, too many of the civil servants would have covertly resisted such a regime, however much they might have sympathised with its 'modernising' objectives. As for the army, its willingness to support Sir Albert in a drastic shake-up of the social structure had to be questioned. Although the Prime Minister managed after 1965 to weed out most of the non-Mendes and other potential APC supporters from the officer corps, the officers were as closely tied to the chiefs as were the SLPP elite. Despite his having replaced an expatriate with a Mende commanding officer, and despite the 'demonstration effect' of coups elsewhere it seemed unlikely during Sir Albert's period in office that the military would try to oust the civilian government.[55] But it was possible that if he took actions which were seen as contrary to the interests of the chiefly structure of privilege, the family ties of the officers might overcome their reluctance to intervene. Furthermore, the Prime Minister was constrained by the probability that if he did have to coerce his opponents beyond the bounds of legality in order to consolidate his personal position, the army might not be willing to carry out his orders.

Albert Margai thus found himself trapped by the configuration of his party's supporters and opponents. His path to changing Sierra Leone through picking up support from modernisers and ignoring the traditionalists of his own party was blocked by the fact that many of the modernisers refused on other grounds to give up their commitment to opposition parties. Thus while facing this challenge from a 'left' opposition, he was forced to work through a body of nominal supporters, the SLPP, who provided a considerable resistance to change from the 'right'. At the centre of the national government, where he had power to act directly through selecting personnel, providing patronage, and punishing deviants, he could override opposition from within the SLPP. But when he had to reach the electorate in the constituencies, he had to work through intermediaries, and here his choice was sharply restricted. Using the civil service as intermediaries was precluded because he could not trust them sufficiently for this purpose; building an organisation of centrally controlled party functionaries was blocked partly by the fact that additional 'free-floating' resources (personnel as well as funds for patronage) were just not available, and partly by the fact that the established members of the SLPP in the local arenas were not prepared to tolerate the formation of a rival structure, as they made clear at Bo in 1965.[56] Party organisers who could give their loyalty to the Prime Minister would have had to be 'strangers' in the constituencies to which they were sent, or they would have been too strongly cross-pressured by commitments to the local elites, of which they would generally have been a part.[57] But 'strangers' would have had a very difficult time influencing the local electorates unless they could act with the approval of the chief or other prominent members of the local elite behind them, even if they had patronage to dispense on a lavish scale; and members of the local elite were hardly going to bestow approval on 'strangers' seeking to advance Albert Margai's ends, if these were antithetical to their own. There was, in short, no way to avoid working through the chiefs, or at least though persons who supported chieftaincy as the dominant political institution in the local arena.

This created a double dilemma. First, of course, chieftaincy was one of the institutions posing a key obstacle to 'modernisation', since even where it did not depend to some degree upon suprarational belief, it did provide a focus for an integrated, holistic view of leadership, and by implication of all personal relationships. On a more practical level, many chiefs offered some resistance to the spread of education and other 'modernising' influences, and less directly, employed for their personal use resources that might have been used to further 'modernising' developments.[58] To rely on the chiefs for support, therefore, was to give hostages to precisely those elements in Sierra Leone society which were most capable of offering organised resistance to change. Second, to break away from this dependence on the chiefs required winning over 'modernisers' currently in opposition to the SLPP. But to show the 'modernisers' that his strength was such that they had no choice but to come to terms with him, Margai had to suppress the opposition parties, the APC and DPC – and to do this he had to use the chiefs, whose mistreatment of their people was a major factor in sustaining support for the opposition. In short, the harder he struggled to create a position for himself from which he could bring change, the more the Prime Minister was forced into relying on those elements in society which were best placed to frustrate his proposed changes.

Notes

1. The best critique of the concept of 'modernisation' that I am aware of is Dean C. Tipps,'Modernisation Theory and the Comparative Study of Societies: A Critical Perspective', *Comparative Studies in Society and History*, XV, 2, Mar. 1973, pp. 199-226. See also Henry Bernstein, 'Modernisation Theory and the Sociological Study of Development', *Journal of Development Studies*, VII, 2, 1971, pp. 141-60; C.S. Whitaker, 'A Dysrhythmic Process of Political Change', *World Politics*, XIX, 2, Jan. 1967, pp. 190-217; and Reinhard Bendix, 'Tradition and Modernity Reconsidered', *Comparative Studies in Society and History*, IX, 3, 1966-7, pp. 292-346.
2. See Whitaker, 'A Dysrhythmic Process', p. 192.
3. Cf. David Apter's use of the term in *The Politics of Modernisation*, Chicago, University of Chicago Press, 1965, pp. 9-11. Although Apter stresses 'choice' rather than 'rationality' as the key component of modernity, I see his formulation as being similar to my own. I would argue, however, that if 'rationality' is the hallmark of 'modernity', then no society can ever be completely 'modern'; it simply could not hold together without some suprarational beliefs.

4. It may be salutary to regard Daedalus and Icarus as the prototypes of 'rational' technological man; rather than accepting man's earthbound state as the will of the gods, they considered how birds flew, developed an innovative technology to achieve flight, and were successful – up to a point.
5. Perhaps the best example of this is the abandonment of sacred sanctions against usury, which by the end of the Middle Ages had made possible the productive use of capital which came to finance the revolutionary technological developments of the succeeding epoch.
6. See Robert McKenzie and Allan Silver, *Angels in Marble*, London, Heinemann, 1968, esp. pp. 167-70, 175, 177-8.
7. Cf. the reaction of Chinua Achebe's university-educated hero in *No Longer At Ease*, on discovering that his girl was *osu*.
8. One aspect of Whitaker's 'eurhythmic-dysrhythmic' dichotomy that bothers me is the problem of deciding at what point a change in one area has in fact brought changes in other areas. Consider, for example, an expansion of cash-crop farming brought about by the opening of a new road to markets. This need not necessarily weaken the chief's position; he may be able to collect more tributes, and have more resources to bind men to him, as a result of this increased prosperity. He can also count on continued obedience from his subjects as long as he controls the allocation of farmland. The change to cash crops thus would appear to be 'dysrhythmic', but is it really? Is his role of chief still the same when he has entered into more commercial relationships and when the basis of obedience to him has changed? I am not asserting that the role has changed, but I am suggesting that we must remember that we are dealing with a 'more-or-less' situation rather than an 'either-or' one.
9. See *Cox Report*, pp. 156-60, for illustration of this conflict.
10. Barrows, *Grassroots Politics*, p. 111, makes the point that the phrase 'the coming of politics' refers to the entry of national actors into chiefdom affairs, in the course of discussing the growth of competitors to the chief. See also Pollock, *Influence, Authority and Opportunity*, esp. pp. 203-16, for a discussion of the role of non-chiefly intermediaries.
11. For example, in the hearings on extending the franchise held by the Keith-Lucas Commission in 1954, one elderly and illiterate Kailahun chief perceptively opposed a taxpayer franchise because it would mean 'all men are equals'. Keith-Lucas Commission, *Transcript of Evidence*(typescript), 11 Aug. 1954.
12. For this episode, see Minikin, *Local Politics in Kono*, p. 214; also Bo *Observer*, 15 May 1954.
13. For an account of the convention, see *Daily Mail*, 28 Mar. 1956.
14. For a detailed description of the election, see D.J.R. Scott, 'The Sierra Leone Election of May 1957', in W.J.M. Mackenzie and Kenneth Robinson, *Five Elections in Tropical Africa*, London, Oxford University Press, 1960.
15. *Vanguard*, 21 May 1957.
16. He first offered Albert the Works and Housing Portfolio, and gave I.B. Taylor-Kamara Trade and Industry, while excluding Siaka Stevens and all the rest of Albert's supporters from any posts. (*Daily Mail*, 24 May 1957.) When Albert rejected this, he went much further, offering Albert Internal Affairs, with its control over the chiefs, and promising to find a post for Stevens. (Ibid., 28 May.) But Albert now insisted that his brother step down from the SLPP leadership (ibid., 29 May)and Dr Margai lost no time in withdrawing the offer. Several weeks later, Y.D. Sesay received

Information and Broadcasting, and still later Maigore Kallon, A.J. Massally, S.T. Navo and M.J. Kamanda-Bongay were given appointments. Only Kallon and Navo, of all those mentioned, followed Albert into the PNP.

17. A total of seven petitions brought by the UPP leader, Cyril Rogers-Wright, succeeded in dislodging SLPP members. While Rogers-Wright had his own interests in trying to throw the SLPP into turmoil, it is not impossible that he may have been given some encouragement in his targets by the Premier. At the very least, Dr Margai could take some cheer from a most fortuitous set of actions that undermined his intraparty opposition.
18. One, Maigore Kallon, was at the time a Ministerial Secretary; the others were backbenchers.
19. As nearly as I was able to ascertain from interviews several years after the event and from contemporary newspaper accounts, all the under-forties in the party caucus at that time supported Albert Margai. Of the eight members with university or legal training, apart from the Margais themselves, three backed Milton, including the only other medical doctor, and five backed Albert, including all three other lawyers.
20. See *Vanguard,* 21 May 1957. In my interviews, only one person suggested a broader 'traditionalists versus modernisers' theme, and he was a supporter of Dr Margai.
21. One of Albert Margai's supporters commented that 'it was most embarrassing for us' because all the Doctor's supporters were older men.
22. Sir Maurice has stated there was 'no question' about his accepting as Premier whoever the SLPP caucus selected as its leader. Interview, 20 Mar. 1973. However, if Albert and his supporters *believed* there was a possibility of this happening, then the belief would act to influence their actions. Furthermore, I have been told that other British officials did exert considerable pro-Milton pressure.
23. If not solely on the basis of his own preferences, at least by selecting workmates whose rituals were compatible with his own.
24. See F.G. Bailey, *Strategems and Spoils,* ch. 3, esp. pp. 42-4; also for African illustrations of these links, Pollock, 'The Organisation of Patronage', and Richard Sandbrook, 'Patrons, Clients and Factions: New Dimensions of Conflict Analysis in Africa', *Canadian Journal of Political Science,* V, I, Mar. 1972, esp. pp. 115-19.
25. See Richard M. Titmuss, *The Gift Relationship : From Human Blood to Social Policy,* London, Allen & Unwin, 1970. However, I would also agree with his contention that the principle of voluntary support for an activity which in a large-scale society necessarily involves impersonal relationships is easily undermined by the intrusion of a commercial system alongside it. See esp. pp. 156-72, 180-2.
26. See Jack Goody and Ian Watt, 'The Consequences of Literacy', *Comparative Studies in Society and History,* V, 1962-3, pp. 304-45.
27. See Harold Innis, *The Bias of Communication,* Toronto, University of Toronto Press, 1951, Marshall McLuhan, *The Gutenberg Galaxy,* Toronto, University of Toronto Press, 1962.
28. See above, p. 143.
29. See above, p. 192.
30. See Cartwright, *Politics in Sierra Leone,* p. 225.
31. See above, p. 193.
32. See S.M. Sesay, 'Drivers in the Transport Industry: A Case Study of Road Transport in Sierra Leone', *Sierra Leone Studies,* New Series, 19, July 1966, p. 88.

33. Besides the conventional economic functions of conveying goods and passengers, we might note their very important role in providing a communications network considerably more effective than either the post office or the telephone system. It was generally possible to get a letter from Freetown lorry park to any town in Sierra Leone in twenty-four hours by sending it with a lorry driver; through the Post Office, it might take a week or more. However, 1968 a direct-dial trunk telephone service between major towns was installed. This made it possible for the first time for the political and economic elites to communicate more efficiently with each other than could lower-status individuals who had to rely on the lorry service for communication.
34. For a discussion of the dispersion of some types of 'modernisation' see J. Barry Riddell, *The Spatial Dynamics of Modernisation in Sierra Leone,* Evanston, Northwestern University Press, 1970. Riddell does make the point that one indicator of 'modernisation', the growth of marketing co-operatives, shows a pattern of diffusion by example from one chiefdom to neighbouring ones, rather than being imposed from above. See pp. 70-9.
35. Vernon Dorjahn 'The Extent and Nature of Political Knowledge in a Sierra Leone Town', *Journal of Asian and African Studies,* III, 3-4, July-Oct. 1968, pp. 203-15. Non-literates did best (and came closest to literates) in naming the Prime Minister, with 83 per cent (against 100 per cent of literates) correct. But 36.5 per cent (against 81 per cent of the literates) correctly identified a Freetown Muslim religious leader (who was, admittedly, a Temne) recently jailed for fraudulent conversion, and 21 per cent correctly identified the recently deposed Chief Mbriwa (as did 62 per cent of the literates).
36. See above, pp. 130-2.
37. See, for example, *Liberty* (the PNP paper) 18 Sept. 1958, and *Daily Mail,* 15 Sept. 1958.
38. *Daily Mail,* 24 May 1959.
39. Independents, some of whom were PNP sympathisers afraid to run under its elephant symbol, won 59 seats; SLPP candidates won 219. See *Vanguard,* 28 Oct. 1959.
40. *Sierra Leone Gazette,* 12 Nov. 1959, p. 859.
41. Just after Guinea's independence, a PNP delegation made a goodwill visit to Conakry, in conspicuous contrast to Dr Margai's studied indifference to the PDG's success. See *Daily Mail,* 21 Oct. 1958.
42. See, for example, the report of Maigore Kallon's speech, ibid., 18 Oct. 1958, and the PNP's statement of policy, ibid., 18 Jan. 1960.
43. Ibid., 18 Oct. 1958.
44. See *Vanguard,* 20 Jan. 1960, and *Liberty,* 8 Aug. 1959.
45. *Liberty,* 8 Aug. 1959.
46. One conflict in which a relatively 'radical' party supported traditional values, while its 'conservative' opponent supported 'modernising' ones, was that in Ceylon in the 1950s. See Marshall Singer, *The Emerging Elite: A Study of Political Leadership in Ceylon,* Cambridge, Mass., MIT Press, 1964.
47. All Peoples Congress, *Constitution,* Part I, Sec. 3(v).
48. All Peoples Congress, '1962 General Election Manifesto'.
49. See for example its statement of policy at its 1963 convention, cited in *Daily Mail,* 19 Apr. 1963. After it came to power in 1968, no more was heard about putting the chiefs in a separate House or keeping them out of politics
50. See Cartwright, *Politics in Sierra Leone,* pp. 130, 132, for further details.

51. See Cartwright, 'Party Competition', pp. 78-9.
52. See Cartwright, *Politics in Sierra Leone*, p. 189.
53. For example, Kutubu Kai-Samba, an extremely able young lawyer who had refused to serve under Sir Milton, joined Margai's Cabinet almost immediately.
54. Cartwright, 'Party Competition', p. 85.
55. But we must recall the alleged plot in February 1967; see above p. 80.
56. See above, p. 231.
57. It was likely that any person with sufficient education and sophistication to be an effective organiser would have been a member of a ruling family. Nor would the possibility that the person appointed came from a rival faction to the chief help the Prime Minister, since such an organiser would probably use his central connections to help his local faction rather than the other way round.
58. For a particularly strong statement on this latter problem see Kilson, *Political Change in a West African State*, pp. 197-216.

8 ECONOMIC DEVELOPMENT AND POLITICAL LEADERSHIP

The most important of all the constraints upon the two Margais has as yet barely been alluded to. This contraint was the pressure for 'development' stemming from, first, the fact that Sierra Leoneans possessed a level of goods and services far lower than that of the industrialised countries, and second, that increasing numbers of them were becoming aware of this fact. This perception that Sierra Leone had a low 'standard of living' raised squarely for the Margais (as for almost every leader of a Third World country)[1] the question of what, if anything, could be done to alter the situation. The 'revolution of rising expectations' may have been a cliche, but it was no less real for that; growing numbers of people both wanted and felt it was possible to have more food, better housing, improved transport, safer drinking water and a growing range of consumer goods.

This notion that human action could alter the lack of material affluence that had been the lot of most people in most countries throughout history was a facet of 'modernisation' as I described it in the previous chapter. It grew out of the spread of Western influence around the world, partly as a byproduct of the generalised spread of 'rationality' and partly as a more specific awareness that the 'industrialised nations' had attained a high level of material affluence, and thus offered a model for emulation. The political leaders of nearly all Third World countries, supported by substantial segments of their people, set for their countries the goal of 'catching up' to the affluence and the technoloigcal capabilities of the industrialised states, even though they differed sharply on appropriate paths to this goal.[2]

Since the problem facing Third World leaders was essentially one of growing awareness of deprivation, rather than the actual lack of material goods itself, the range of possible ways of handling the problem was fairly broad. At one extreme, a leader might try to damp down the growth of aspirations for a better life, either by keeping his people in ignorance of the possibilities or by persuading them that the existing order's supernatural sanctions were sufficiently strong that they would be wise to shun the proposed new values. This strategy, which in different forms seemed to underlie the actions of such a disparate group of leaders as Haile Selassie of Ethiopia, General Alfredo Stroessner of

Paraguay, the late François Duvalier of Haiti and General Ne Win of Burma, was basically defensive and probably not tenable over a long period. There were just too many ways in which the examples of Western-style 'development' might penetrate a polity.

At a nearby point on the circle of possibilities lay the strategy of trying to focus popular attention on a goal other than the accumulation of personal material possessions. This strategy was not a denial of the possibility of a better life; rather, it was an attempt to suggest that the values comprising a 'better life' were not predominantly material, or that in the field of material improvements emphasis should be upon goods which could be produced locally and enjoyed collectively. We could describe the Chinese approach essentially in these terms; and a similar strategy could be seen in Tanzania after the Arusha Declaration, and in Cuba under Castro.

But most Third World leaders accepted as their goal the creation of an industrial economy, with its transformation of raw materials into manufactured goods, specialisation of functions, and wage labour. Where they differed was over who should control this industrial economy, and over what its links should be with the rest of the world. Was the government to use its power to press for indigenisation of key posts in industries, for retention of profits within the country, and for a share of ownership to be vested in local hands, or was it to accept foreign investment with no strings? Was it to seek industries which would export their products, or should it pursue a policy of manufacturing for domestic markets? And how far should it press investors to process raw materials within the country, or to concentrate on the production of goods that were socially useful?[3] Underlying the divergent answers to these questions were widely different concepts of 'development' and theories about how it might be brought about.

When leaders of Third World countries spoke of 'developing' their countries, their understanding of 'development' encompassed the notion of economic growth, an increase in the various indicators of economic wellbeing such as per capita income or energy consumption, and value added through processing raw materials. This growth ultimately can be attributed to an increase in the output of goods and services for a given input of labour, or in other words, increased productivity. While this increased productivity is a necessary condition for economic development, 'development' involves further changes in the structure of economic relationships: greater specialisation of labour, broader and more complex patterns of interdependence, and increased integration of the entire territory into a single economic unit.[4]

'Industrialisation', the creation of a capacity to transform raw materials into manufactured products, is the most commonly sought form of 'economic development', although other forms are possible.

The creation of a capacity to process raw materials was seen by many leaders as the means to a further end, which they also tended to subsume under the general notion of 'development'. This end might be described as an increase in the ability of a country to control and direct the economic changes affecting it. Increased productivity or the possession of sophisticated techniques for processing a product were of little use to a country if the market for its product suddenly vanished because of decisions made beyond its borders. The desire to reduce their 'vulnerability',[5] to build their economies in such a way that they could deal on a more nearly equal basis with the industrial states, was as important a part of 'development' for many leaders as was any increase in material wellbeing.

In analysing their situation and seeking ways to improve it, the leaders of Third World countries could draw upon two sharply contrasting intellectual schools. The 'modernisation' school, predominantly American and heavily funded by United States foundations, argued that economic development in the 'developing' countries grew out of major changes in cultural and personal attitudes within the countries. Either the development of a single key attitude[6] or the interaction of a complex combination of shifts[7] would unleash new patterns of behaviour which would bring about economic change. The distinguishing feature of the 'modernisation' school was its contention that change was essentially an internal problem for societies. The external environment, and specifically the Western states, were generally neutral or benevolent forces, offering benign support for the modernisers within each new state as the latter struggled to spread their attitudes into a resistant 'traditional' or 'residual' sector, but not having any major effect upon the new states beyond the force of example.

The 'neo-Marxist' school,[8] more heterogeneous in background, far less well financed but no less dogmatic, was slowly beginning to emerge by the late 1950s.[9] Focusing primarily upon economic relationships between the industrial capitalist states and their (former) colonies, and secondarily upon the emerging relations within the erstwhile colonies, they contended that political decolonisation did not alter the fundamental relationship of exploitation between imperial power and colony. Far from promoting economic development, the capitalist states were tying their former colonies ever more tightly into a peripheral relationship in which the ex-colonies' continuing export of raw materials in exchange for manufactured goods would preclude their ever developing an independent industrial capability. This unequal exchange, which left the ex-colonies at the mercy of capitalist price-fixing cartels, was abetted by the emergent colonial bourgeoisie, which ensured itself a comfortable position by taking its small share from the exploitation of its fellow nationals. This process, 'the development of underdevelopment', was inexorably widening the gap between the poor non-industrialised states and the rich industrialised ones. And while they paid lip service to 'aid', the political leaders of the capitalist states knew full well what they were doing, and continued to organise the 'pillage' of the Third World because it was to their benefit to do so. Third World leaders, therefore, could only escape from 'underdevelopment' by severing their links with the Western capitalist states.

Before considering how far developments in different sectors of the Sierra Leone economy support either of these theories, we should recall the period we are considering, since this has a considerable effect upon leaders' perceptions of their possible options. At the time of Sir Milton's death the African states had just gained their political independence, and had had little time to test the effect of this independence upon the range of economic choices open to them. Latin America and Asia, where longer periods of political independence had had little effect in producing economic development as African leaders conceived it, were too far away from most leaders' concerns for Africa to draw lessons from. Furthermore, information about these areas (and indeed, about practically all areas outside their own countres) was still provided through the metropolitan powers' channels, and even where this did not reflect the biases of the dominant business interests[10] its concerns were not those of the Africans.[11] The academic neo-Marxist critiques were just beginning to appear, and since these indicted the ex-colonies' leaders as well as the metropolitan powers, the former tended to dismiss them.[12] There was as yet little doubt concerning the fundamental benevolence of the Western states – after all, they had just granted independence to the colonies – and conversely there was in many states considerable doubt about the desirability of regimes such as those of Nkrumah, Touré, Modibo Keita and Ahmed Ben Bella.[13] In such an atmosphere the prevailing view was that economic development could be brought about by co-operation between the new states and the Western powers, with the only question being what were the most effective means to this agreed end.

More than in most African states, the elites of 'loyal Sierra Leone' were inclined to accept a close relationship with Western states, and particularly with Britain. Their relationship with Britain was a peripheral one not just in the economic sense put forward in studies of economic dependency[14] but in the more encompassing sense of affirming the values promoted from a 'centre' to which they were nevertheless 'outsiders'.[15] Being a 'periphery' in Shils' sense implies, of course, a *voluntary* commitment; if a group or a society ceases to accept the values of their 'centre' then they are no longer its 'periphery'. Throughout the period under review, few Sierra Leoneans questioned such key elements of the 'centre's' value system as formal academic education, a market economy, social gradations based on educational or economic achievement, or for that matter, the desirability of maintaining close links with the 'centre'. In such a situation, the range of 'thinkable' choices for a leader in the economic sphere was necessarily smaller than if the values of the 'centre' were being called into question.

The economy of Sierra Leone at Independence could not produce a high material standard of living for many of its people, and at the same time incorporated many obstacles to improving that standard of living. It contained three productive sectors: an agricultural sector marked by low per capita outputs and low returns; an 'enclave' mining sector operated by large foreign corporations; and an indigenous mining sector providing many economic opportunities for Sierra Leonean entrepreneurs, but at a high social cost. I will examine each of these sectors from the perspectives of four questions: what contribution was the sector making to economic development at the time of Independence; what changes had to be made in order to improve its contribution to development; what changes were possible, given the constraints we have already examined; and to what extent could a leader affect the changes that might come about?

Agriculture, primarily to provide domestic food supplies but also to fill a sizable export market, was Sierra Leone's most widespread economic activity, with three-quarters of those gainfully employed, some 700,000 persons, engaged in it.[16] Farms were generally small (the average size was four acres), and while three-fifths of all farmers sold some cash crops, considerably fewer were primarily dependent upon growing crops for sale.[17] This was probably just as well for most farmers, since neither export nor domestic sales offered the farmer a good return. From 1951 to 1964 the price of palm kernels, long Sierra Leone's dominant agricultural export, had dropped by nearly a quarter, and the price of cocoa, at one time regarded as a promising field for agricultural expansion,[18] had dropped by two-thirds. Ginger and piassava, two other long-standing products, fetched the same price in 1964 as in 1951, leaving kola and coffee as the only significant agricultural products that had increased in value.[19] Probably it was largely in response to the lack of price incentives that the overall tonnage of agricultural produce dropped by 28 per cent in this period; at any rate, its value dropped even more, by 37 per cent,[20] leaving agricultural exports contributing some £4.8 million, or less than a sixth of Sierra Leone's total exports, by 1964.[21]

Farming for the domestic market was no more attractive financially. If we consider the position of a farmer growing the staple food crop, rice, on an average sized Sierra Leonean farm, we can make some rough calculations of his financial position. A farm of four to six acres of upland rice will yield about 500-600 lbs of rice per acre; if planted in the less tasty swamp rice, it may yield as much as 1,800 lbs, but probably nearer 1,400.[22] At the Rice Corporation price in the 1960s of £37.50 a (long) ton, this would mean that the farmer would receive a *gross* annual income of between £33 and £180, more often nearer the former. Other crops offered little better return if grown on the same sized acreages. By comparison, labourers in Kenema and Makeni in 1968 were earning £100-£120 a year, tailors and seamstresses £90 and street sellers £150-£175.[23] In such circumstances, more enterprising or innovative individuals were likely to move to the towns rather than to seek ways of improving farming.[24]

To provide better returns for the individual farmer would require one of three things: a spectacular increase in the price he received for his products relative to the goods he purchased; substantially increased yields per acre; or much larger individual farms. The first of these possibilities was clearly not feasible for domestically marketed crops, and highly improbable for export ones. Increased yields per acre could probably be achieved within the existing framework of shifting cultivation or equivalent methods of fallowing by the use of high-yield seeds and fertilisers. There were a number of risks, however, both biological and economic. Biologically, dependence upon a genetically limited range of high-yield seeds increased the risk of massive crop failures, while fertilisers, irrigation and insecticides could all have deleterious side effects.[25] Economically, reliance upon fertilisers or other imported technology could result in any financial gains being siphoned off by the fertiliser manufacturer rather than improving the farmer's standard of living. For export crops, there were the additional risks that, first, several 'underdeveloped' countries might simultaneously be rushing to fill a fairly static demand, with the result that prices would drop, and second, if they did succeed in raising the price of their product, manufacturers in the 'developed' countries would turn to substitutes. Increased productivity for export markets, in short, was likely to be self-defeating, with farmers producing a considerably larger crop for a smaller gross return.

Increased food production for the domestic market was economically more promising. In Sierra Leone, the finite capacity of the human stomach was far from being reached, and Sierra Leoneans might thus either obtain a greater variety of health-giving foods, or might obtain their food more cheaply, thus making it possible for them to devote more of their incomes to the purchase of other domestic goods and thus stimulate other sectors of the domestic economy. There was, of course, the risk that gains in food production would be squandered on imported consumer goods, a problem to which I shall return later; but we can say that increased agricultural productivity created a possibility of further economic growth.

Increasing the size of farms rather than productivity per acre raised rather more serious problems. Four to six acres was all the land that a Sierra Leone farmer and his family could handle with existing technology; larger farms would require either hired labour or mechanisation. Hiring labourers to do what they had already been doing as independent farmers would leave these people worse off than before; it might benefit those who gained possession of the larger farms, but not the bulk of the population. Mechanisation would raise the awkward question of what to do with the dispossessed small farmers, since there was no great amount of unused land suitable for farming.[26] The two methods used in the industrialised states for disposing of surplus rural population could both be ruled out; there was no new land for mass emigration, and no African government had sufficiently strong control over its people to force people off the land into factories in the ruthless manner of (say) the British aristocracy or the Russian Communists.

The one possibility in agriculture, then, was to increase the yields of crops for domestic consumption, and to attempt to ensure that the savings realised through this were channelled into domestic industries. Such a programme would require a government capable of persuading farmers to accept new methods, persuading the populace as consumers to expand their use of domestic rather than imported goods, and inducing entrepreneurs to meet these increased demands. The first of these steps would call for a government with strong links with the rural populace;[27] the second would require either a strong appeal to nationalist sentiments or the ability to cut off access to imported goods; while the third would entail the ability to get either domestic or foreign entrepreneurs to undertake the manufacture of consumer goods, utilising domestic resources.

The foreign mining operations involved far less people than did agriculture, but they contributed somewhat more to government revenues, and far more in export earnings. The two dominant mining corporations in Sierra Leone were the Sierra Leone Selection Trust, exporting between £4.5 and £9.5 million worth of diamonds in the early 1960s, and the Sierra Leone Development Corporation, exporting about £5 million worth of iron ore.[28] A chrome mine had closed in 1963, and a bauxite mine and rutile producer started exporting in 1965 and 1967 respectively, but their contributions were all negligible, none of their exports approaching £½ million value a year.

We shall consider the effects of this mining on Sierra Leone's economic development under four heads: revenue produced for the government, the build-up of capital investment in Sierra Leone, the development of skills among Sierra Leoneans, and the stimulation of other parts of the economy.

Sierra Leone's main revenue from the mining companies was a tax on company profits. For SLST, taxes in 1961 and 1962 ran at about £1½ million;[29] I have no figures for Delco, but its contribution would have been roughly of the same order of magnitude.[30] In addition, there were taxes of an undetermined amount on the incomes of employees of these companies, and duties on the goods which they imported, although these probably did not exceed £200,000-300,000.[31]

A second contribution to Sierra Leone's development is the building up of capital equipment in the country. Van der Laan estimated SLST's capital assets in 1962 (excluding such difficult areas as the value of its prospecting) at £6 million.[32] Delco's assets, which included a 52-mile railway built with a low-interest Sierra Leone government loan in the 1930s, as well as ore loading docks and pelletising and concentrating equipment, were given a book value in 1972 of £12.25 million.[33] However, most of the capital equipment of these two companies was quite specific to their own operations. If the mining companies abandoned operations in Sierra Leone, or were taken over, the capital investment they left in Sierra Leone would be of little use to anyone else.

A more lasting contribution was the development of skills among Sierra Leoneans, including many of wide application, in the maintenance and servicing of mechanical equipment, and later accountancy, engineering and other professional training. SLST had been apprenticing twenty men a year since 1956 in the electrical and mechanical trades, and by 1972 had 120 Sierra Leoneans on their 'senior staff', mostly in specialised technical mining operations.[34] About a quarter of the tradesmen eventually filtered into other jobs in the Sierra Leone economy, although among the professional group turnover was negligible, in part because of the specialised nature of their skills.

The final area in which the mining companies may have aided development was in the stimulation of other parts of the Sierra Leone economy. Certainly in their own relatively backward districts, their payrolls had a marked impact in providing opportunities for petty traders, artisans and others able to provide the goods and services sought by men on full-time wage employment. These effects were most obvious in agriculture, where they stimulated cash sales of palm oil, rice, fish and other Sierra Leone staples.

But the effect of the forward linkages was somewhat limited by the fact that those gaining steady wage employment appeared to have a propensity to increase their consumption largely in the area of imported goods; from gourds of palm wine they moved up to beer in which the main Sierra Leonean ingredient was water (though in fairness, the Sierra Leone Brewery did in turn provide additional employment, as well as a reasonably palatable product), or to imports such as transistor radios, watches or bicycles. Since foreign suppliers were able to shape many of these demands by well-financed advertising campaigns, would-be Sierra Leonean entrepreneurs faced a difficult struggle to enter the growing markets.

As for the backward linkages produced by the mining firms, these were virtually nil. A few Sierra Leoneans managed to get contracting jobs for transport and construction, some furnishings were locally made, and more indirectly awareness of the possibility of employment with SLST and Delco encouraged youths to gain educational qualifications they might not have sought otherwise. But given the fact that Sierra Leone produced very few of the items needed by a modern mining company, it was hardly surprising that most of the supplies for both SLST and Delco were brought in from European centres.

In summary, we could say that both SLST and Delco were typical 'enclave' operations.[35] They brought employment to a handful of men, who in turn provided a limited demand for goods and services from other Sierra Leoneans. Their main benefit to the country in economic terms was their tax revenues, which provided the government with

20-25 per cent of its revenues. Against this would have to be put certain costs to Sierra Leone, which in SLST's case would certainly include a substantial share of the £650,000 budget of the Royal Sierra Leone Military Force,[36] which was needed on several occasions to quell illicit mining on the SLST leases in Kono. In addition, an undeterminable portion of infrastructural costs such as roads would not have been needed had the mining industries not been there, and less directly, there would have been fewer models for emulation in the consumption of imported goods, from automobiles to liquor.

In order to maximise its benefits from these extractive mining operations, Sierra Leone had either to use these operations as the starting points for a chain of integrated economic activities entailing capabilities for creating new goods,[37] or to extract sufficient revenue from mining to finance the development of such creative operations in other sectors.[38] Both of these courses faced severe obstacles. The 'obvious' starting point in developing forward and backward linkages from any mining activity was to process the minerals within the country. But Sierra Leone's biggest export, raw diamonds, could only be 'processed' for the gem and industrial trade by skilled cutters, with little capital equipment.[39] Such an industry would likely become another expatriate enclave, providing few further linkages with the rest of the economy. Bauxite and rutile also were poor candidates for processing, the former because it required vast quantities of cheap electric power which Sierra Leone lacked, the latter both because its transformation into titanium required specialised technological skills and also because its markets were specialised and integrated ones.

An iron and steel industry, which provides the greatest total linkage effect of any industrial activity,[40] held more promise for using Sierra Leonean minerals as the basis of industrialisation. But Delco's output was firmly committed to established steelmakers, while any replacement firm with the skills and capital could find dozens of less unrewarding sites for locating a steel industry. Sierra Leone's lack of coal was no problem, but the lack of indigenous capital and technological skills would have stopped any attempt by the government to found such an industry itself.

Extracting more revenue from the mining industry for indigenous development thus seemed by default to be the only path which lay open to Sierra Leone's leaders. This might involve raising taxes while leaving all decisions on production in the hands of the company, taking a share of control in the company, or outright nationalisation. In considering these possibilities we must not forget the great difference between the period 1950-65 and the present in what we may term the 'world climate of opinion' concerning the possibility of Third World countries asserting control over their resources. While President Nasser had successfully nationalised the Suez Canal, the fates of Dr Mossadeq of Iran and Senor Arbenz of Guatemala suggested that tackling a giant corporation was a very risky business. The mystique of omnipotence surrounding mining as well as oil companies only began to fade in Africa after the Congo's half-successful takeover of Union Miniere in 1967 and Zambia's takeover of its copper industry in 1969. Both the Margais seem to have accepted the belief that expropriation of foreign firms would lead to a curtailment of further private investment, as well as jeopardising aid from Western governments and Western agencies such as the International Development Bank.

Beyond this state of mind, there were more practical obstacles to gaining greater wealth from the mining companies. Sierra Leone's iron and bauxite ores were each only one source among many in the world, and could only be extracted by capital-intensive, technologically advanced methods. If the Sierra Leone government demanded a share of ownership, or even what the companies considered too high a tax rate, the companies could argue that world market conditions did not permit higher taxes, and could as a last resort abandon their Sierra Leonean operations, leaving Sierra Leone with literally mountains of iron or bauxite ore. The only mining company whose production Sierra Leone could have handled without outside help was SLST, since diamonds could be extracted either by its capital-intensive methods or by hand excavation. When the APC government eventually did take a 51 per cent share in SLST's operations in 1971, its motive was basically to capture control of the industry most symbolising foreign economic domination in Sierra Leone. But it did have a powerful (though costly) ultimate bargaining weapon. If SLST had refused to accept the government's terms, the government might have found it 'impossible' to stop illicit miners from overrunning and destroying SLST's property, even though this would also have entailed a severe tax loss to the government. But it held no such bargaining lever in dealing with Delco or Sieromoco (the bauxite mining company). While SLST's symbolic position was undoubtedly the most important factor, and the less attractive financial position of the other companies had also to be borne in mind, the lack of any comparable leverage may have also contributed to the government's decision in 1973 to abandon its plans to take majority shareholdings in the remaining mining companies.[41]

Using the corporate mining sector to develop Sierra Leone, then, first required a leader who could make an accurate assessment of just how far he could squeeze the various companies successfully, and second, the development by the government of a long-range plan for industrialisation. The first step would entail a level of information which would be hard to obtain while the second would involve fighting off demands for current expenditures in many areas in order to make long-term investments in trained manpower and capital goods, and quite possibly would magnify regional disparities. It was not an easy strategy, but the alternative was to enjoy the good life for the decade or two while minerals lasted, and then to face the problem of declining living standards.

The indigenous small-scale diamond mining sector had a far greater impact on Sierra Leone's economy than did the mining companies, although its potential benefits were probably less. We have already referred to the magnitude of the 'diamond rush',[42] which at its illegal peak involved probably some 75,000 men, and after the licensing scheme stabilised at about 45,000 diggers per year.[43] The legal recorded exports from this alluvial mining were running at about £10 million a year in the early 1960s,[44] and some 75-80 per cent of the proceeds were going to the Sierra Leonean claimholders.[45] Even if we subtract from this figure as opportunity costs the greatest drops in rice and palm kernel production, at a maximum costing Sierra Leone £2.25 million, we are left with a net gain to the Sierra Leone economy of more than £5 million.[46]

The question, however, is how much of this additional income was invested for further economic growth. Van der Laan, warning that the question has not been well studied, concluded 'the proportion (invested) has been small'.[47] Undoubtedly most of the diggers, those who received only a few pounds a year for their efforts, spent all their earnings on consumption, the great bulk of it for imported goods. Those who 'struck it rich' also seem to have put a great deal into consumer goods, if the rise in imports of cars, materials for more luxurious houses, and other consumables is any indicator. However, quite a number did invest in more productive goods such as lorries,[48] as well as more intangible 'goods' such as higher education for their children. Certainly a large number of the small contractors, traders and other indigenous entrepreneurs who by the 1960s were springing up in most provincial towns had obtained at least part of their working capital from participation in the alluvial diamond mining scheme. The Lebanese, both as diamond dealers and as general suppliers to the increased trade resulting from the diamond boom, also acquired substantial sums. While it seems likely that a considerable part of their profit was repatriated against eventual retirement to the Lebanon[49] some was invested in productive enterprises in Sierra Leone such as the footwear, tyre retreading and paint factories which offered some alternative to imports.

Even the substantial proportion of diamond income that went to imported consumer goods indirectly supported productive investment, both through enriching traders who might reinvest their earnings, and through providing a substantial share for the government in the form of import duties. Since import duties averaged over 20 per cent on all imports,[50] the government could be said to have benefited to the tune of at least £1 million a year from import duties alone on the additional wealth produced by diamond mining. It is true that most of this money went into recurrent expenditure rather than earmarked 'development' projects, but to some extent it at least made it possible for Sierra Leone to sustain a higher level of maintenance of infrastructure and long-term investment in education than would otherwise have been the case.

We can conclude that small-scale indigenous diamond mining probably made a more substantial contribution to Sierra Leone's development than foreign mining, through its diversity of channels. It contributed nearly as much wealth to government coffers as did the comparable value of 'enclave' diamond mining, and considerably more to the private section through its more widespread diffusion of wealth into the hands of diggers, some of whom invested a portion of it productively in other areas. In the more intangible area of developing skills, alluvial mining made a considerably less sophisticated contribution than did either SLST or Delco; on the other hand, such skills as were developed were far more widely diffused, and because they were less sophisticated, were probably more widely usable in other endeavours. Finally, there was the intangible but probably considerable psychological benefit that such success as Sierra Leoneans enjoyed in mining was owed not to the benevolence of expatriate firms, but to the use of their own abilities, and thus bolstered their self-confidence.

I do not want to leave the impression that indigenous diamond digging was an unalloyed blessing for Sierra Leone. Its social effects had serious negative implications for economic development. Most conspicuously, it led to a great deal of contempt for the authority of both the chiefs and the central government, and while the Kono chiefs probably deserved this contempt, a central government which sought to win acceptance for its concept of a 'public good' embracing all Sierra Leoneans would be severely handicapped if sizable social groups felt its edicts were to be resisted at every turn. Less directly, the accessibility of diamonds also undermined government authority, through making possible illicit dealing, smuggling of diamonds, and bribing of government officials to tolerate this state of affairs. While we can accept the argument that bribery was a means of rectifying an imbalance between political and economic power,[51] especially in the case of the Lebanese who were its most conspicuous users, still it represents an extreme form of self-regarding behaviour. The attitudes that were engendered by the diamond rush, then, undermined the ability of the government to make any overarching appeal to all Sierra Leoneans to seek a collective long-run good at the cost of forgoing short-term personal gains. What I have in mind here is the possibility of a government seeking to pursue a form of 'self-reliance', for example by forcing a policy of import substitution in order to gain the range of 'spin-offs' in other fields, even though this policy would make life more costly for many people in the short run. Such a call for sacrifice might succeed where the political culture inculcated attitudes of concern for the good of the society as a whole; but it would scarcely have a chance in a society where the prevailing attitude was that everyone was entitled to pursue by whatever means were available his personal interest.

Linked to this self-regarding attitude we should also note the encouragement the diamond rush gave to a 'get-rich-quick' attitude, with its consequent emphasis on heavy use of imported consumer goods. Possibly the propensity to consume rather than invest would have been as great even when wealth was acquired more slowly; but it seems likely that the unpredictable nature of alluvial mining, where a man might suddenly 'strike it rich', was peculiarly conducive to consuming a high proportion of the increased wealth.

While despite these drawbacks indigenous mining probably still contributed more to the economic development of Sierra Leone than any other sector, its potential to contribute was already nearly maximised. Any attempt by government to extract a higher proportion of the revenue from diamonds at either the digging or the dealer level would simply lead to further diamond smuggling, an activity which was nearly impossible to control. Efforts to achieve a better recovery rate on diamonds through more thorough sifting of the gravel were also unlikely to meet with much success, since small-scale operators were already using the techniques they considered most profitable. Encouraging larger-scale operations by driving out small diggers would have done nothing but increase the number of illegal diggings, which skimmed off the best diamonds and increased the difficulty of recovering the others. The indigenous system, in short, was already making its maximum possible contribution to the Sierra Leone economy.

Nor could any political leader have done much to affect the situation. We noted earlier that the government in 1956 was forced to make legal an activity which would have continued regardless[52] and that all it managed to do was to channel and regulate both digging and dealing to a limited extent through licensing schemes. Beyond this, it could take the step that Albert Margai took in 1964 of removing ancillary powers from the corrupt local authorities,[53] and might have gone further in efforts to eradicate corruption at the national level.[54] But all the government could do was to channel and regulate diamond digging, and that to a very limited extent; it could neither inspire nor dissuade people in this activity.

The way in which each of the three economic sectors developed created its own set of vested interests, who would resist any attempt by a political leader to alter the status quo. Some of these interests were direct and obvious; for example, the mining companies would clearly oppose any attempt by government to take over their properties,[55] and Lebanese diamond dealers judiciously contributed to both the SLPP and the APC.[56] Other interests were slightly less direct, but equally obvious; the importers (again mostly Lebanese) who depended upon continued mining and agricultural prosperity to finance the purchase of the goods they imported, and the civil servants, teachers and others who enjoyed these Western consumer goods, both had strong commitments to existing arrangements. Two further groups, however, benefited from the *status quo* in ways that were neither direct nor obvious: the chiefs and the politicians.

The chiefs' major concern was to minimise the number of wealthy entrepreneurs who might offer alternative forms of patronage to their own. An 'enclave' mining operation, whose diffusion both of cash and entrepreneurial Sierra Leone personnel was minimal, was from their viewpoint much to be preferred to either alluvial mining or large-scale cash-crop agriculture.[57] The number of new political intermediaries who did in fact appear as a result of the diamond rush[58] showed what could happen if a major trend towards industrial development began. Both from the viewpoint of the national leaders and of the chiefs, an enclave system in which the foreign mining companies paid revenue directly to the central government but otherwise did not create much disturbance was preferable to the uncertainties and challenges posed by the growth of an indigenous entrepreneurial class with autonomous financial resources and bases of operation beyond the chief's control. Cash-crop agriculture was in this context somewhat less threatening; while successful farmers could enjoy some financial security, they were still living under the legal authority of their own chief, and were dependent on him for new land allocations as they expanded operations. It was industrial development, under which men would not longer be beholden to the chiefs for any of the necessities of life, that posed the major threat.

Most chiefs were not openly opposed to indigenous economic development. Many did not even see its implications, and the more sophisticated ones saw that prosperity in the chiefdom reflected favourably upon the chief as its 'father' and that they could generally secure through taxes and tributes as well as through their own entrepreneurship a share of whatever development did take place. But they did have some interest *qua* chiefs in seeing that development threw up as few challengers to their authority as possible, and this often dampened their enthusiasm for the process.

The final group who had some interest in the existing state of affairs was the politicians. Now most politicians, both because of their often bitter personal encounters with Europeans and because of the weakness of their country's position, felt some sympathy for nationalistic demands that a greater share of the national economy be brought under Sierra Leonean control.[59] But working against this feeling, at least in relation to Sierra Leone's major mining companies, was the mystique of omnipotence, and more practically, the realisation that there was very little that any Sierra Leone government could do to alter its existing state of dependence on the companies' revenues and the supplies of 'aid' and skilled personnel provided by their home governments. Among the results of this situation were a corrupting relationship of dependence on the major corporations, a displacement of economic nationalism against the Lebanese, a susceptibility to 'development' proposals emanating from outside the major established firms, and ultimately a falling back upon the 'sweets of office'.

The creation of a dependent relationship between the politicians and the foreign companies was perhaps the most serious effect of the latter's entrenchment in the economy. Some aspects of this dependence were quite open, and caused scarcely any concern within Sierra Leone. Thus a 3½ per cent ten-year loan of £1 million by the Diamond Corporation in 1961, an interest-free five-year loan of £280,000 by SLST in 1963, and a 6 per cent six-year loan of £1,100,000 by Delco in 1964 were all gratefully accepted by the Sierra Leone government.[60]

More personal were the hospitality suites in London and New York offered by the Diamond Corporation and other companies to Ministers travelling abroad. How much these relations too were taken for granted is suggested by this astonishing statement in the Forster Report's examination of Ministers' assets:

> Both Dicor London and Messrs. Tempelsman provide such hospitality to relieve Government of these burdens, and the result of their kind gesture is lost when recipients of hospitality retain allowances provided them by Government.[61]

Evidently the fact that these two companies depended on Sierra Leone legislation for their privileged position over rough diamond purchasing and diamond cutting respectively within the country did not unduly disturb the Commissioners.[62] But to me the line between this 'hospitality' and donations of money or materials to a political party,[63] and the outright 'gift' or bribe to an individual politician in consideration for favours rendered or expected seems a rather difficult one to draw. In fact, it may be that such gifts as the scholarship provided by Philips Telecommunications for the son of Kande Bureh, the Minister of Communications, *after* Philips had been awarded a £168,000 contract to provide transistor radios for resale to the public, create considerably less binding obligations by Sierra Leone to the company than did Dicor's and Delco's loans.

This relationship was not entirely a one-sided one. In some cases the companies appear to have been squeezed in order to provide 'sweets of office' for a Minister,[64] while in others they were compelled to help the government against opposition parties. Thus in 1965 when the SLPP needed a one-vote change in Freetown Council to be able to elect their candidate as Mayor, the Lebanese-owned Intrabank miraculously offered to an APC councillor working for them a scholarship which would take him abroad just before the crucial mayoral vote.[65] During the bitter 1967 election, an APC opponent of the Prime Minister's brother was trying in vain to hire a boat to take him to the nominating office. An official of Sherbro Minerals Limited lent him a company boat, with the result that he arrived in time to submit his nomination papers. (He was subsequently disqualified on the technicality that two of his nominators had made slight errors in signing their names.) The unfortunate official found himself deported a few weeks later.[66]

But these minor gestures did not alter the basic balance of power between the companies and the Sierra Leone government. While the major companies had given 'hostages' in the form of their large fixed investments in Sierra Leone, the Sierra Leone government needed their economic contributions at least as badly as they needed Sierra Leone's resources. Furthermore, in any dispute on the principle of unrestricted private operation, they would be backed not only by most other foreign investors in Sierra Leone, but by the British and American governments and their acolytes in the World Bank and the International Monetary Fund as well. The 'sweets of office' they provided for politicians were an extra investment against nationalist (or from the companies' viewpoint, 'irrational') acts against the companies' rights, but they were probably not essential to the companies' continued operations in Sierra Leone.

The Lebanese traders, with no major overseas base nor a powerful government behind them, were in a much more vulnerable position, and while as individuals they were not intensely disliked by most Sierra Leoneans,[67] their dominance of retail trade throughout Sierra Leone made them a highly visible group against whom attacks could be made with relative impunity. Although European enterprises were also objects of suspicion, it was most often the Lebanese who were singled out by more 'nationalistic' members of the Sierra Leone elite as parasites draining away the country's wealth.[68] Lebanese accordingly were the main targets of a series of restrictive laws first tightening the requirements for citizenship so as to remove the automatic right of any Lebanese born in Sierra Leone to claim citizenship,[69] then prohibiting non-citizens from buying land[70] and dealing in rice.[71] and later, under Albert Margai, from dealing in a whole range of commodities and activities, including cement blocks, bakeries, mineral water and lorry transport.[72] Since Ministerial discretion was involved in these prohibitions, and Lebanese were nearly indispensable in some of them, it is difficult to be certain whether such legislation was a genuine manifestation of nationalist feelings, or simply a device to extort money from the Lebanese businessmen in exchange for 'tolerance'. While the legislation had some symbolic value, its practical effect in creating openings for Sierra Leone entrepreneurs was limited.

A somewhat different way of asserting economic 'independence', which again left fundamental problems unresolved, was to look for new channels for trade and development, rather than looking solely to those companies whose contacts had been built during the colonial regime. While in principle this was an excellent idea, it did help to heighten the susceptibility of Ministers to fast-talking businessmen who seemed able to offer glowing visions of grandiose industralising schemes. While the main factor in Ministers' accepting bad economic deals was probably plain, old-fashioned greed, we should not overlook the more favourable predisposition some of them had towards seeking economic relationship with companies other than the established British ones and their almost desperate eagerness to get new factories established at almost any cost.[73] Since most of these deals involved government members, and such records as they left were well concealed in government files, we can do little more than illustrate two of the commonest ways in which foreign entrepreneurs took money from Sierra Leone.[74]

The commonest means by which promoters enriched themselves at the expense of Sierra Leone was through the sale of unsuitable goods or services, relying on a degree of naivete or cupidity on the part of the buying official.[75] A well-known example in Sierra Leone was the case of the fifty Willys Jeeps bought from an Israeli importing firm in 1961 at the behest of the then Minister of Communications, Kande Bureh.[76] The Department of Road Transport in 1961 was on the point of standardising the government's general purpose transport fleet of Land Rovers when the General Manager of Dizengoff (SL) Limited, Joseph Eiger, offered Israeli-assembled Willys Jeeps as an alternative. Since the Jeeps were an almost unknown quantity in Sierra Leone, with no spare parts, several technical shortcomings, and a price slightly higher than the Land Rover tender, all the (expatriate) civil servants in the Ministry recommended against the purchase of a large order; at most, they suggested, then should be tried, and if these were satisfactory then future purchases could be expanded. Nevertheless, the Minister overruled his advisers and had an order for fifty Jeeps placed. The results confirmed all the experts' fears, with most of the Jeeps experiencing serious problems, and Dizengoff failing almost totally to honour the commitment that it had been forced to make to provide adequate spares as a condition of receiving the order. Nevertheless, the government never gained compensation from the company even for those shortcomings which could clearly be laid at its door.

The other pattern is for the entrepreneur to induce the host government to share the financial risk of his enterprise, while he skims off a guaranteed reward through management fees, sales from other enterprises, or other means. A number of joint projects were entered into by the Margai governments in the 1960s, most of them desirable in principle, but with no careful cost analysis or competitive tendering.[77] An example was the Sierra Leone Cement Works, formed in 1963 with the Sierra Leone government holding 8,000 of its initial 15,000 shares, and bolstered by being given a monopoly on cement sales in the country, a move which led to severe shortages and a price increase of some 25 per cent in the cost of cement.[78] As the firm's financial difficulties (for which it was paying an outside organisation a management fee based on the value of its transactions) increased, the government raised its holdings to £51,000, and by 1969 was guaranteeing nearly £¾ million worth of debts. In 1970 the APC government finally closed it down.

The motives of the politicians in entering such deals were mixed. To some extent they were genuinely eager to be able to show their constituents signs that the country was 'developing'. To some extent also, they needed the personal 'kickbacks' from the award of contracts, and the 'jobs for the boys' new industries could provide, to maintain their personal political machines. But in many cases there was no apparent electoral imperative, and no convincing economic case, for a particular contract; the motive seems to have been personal greed on the part of the politician. Now venality among politicians is hardly unique to Sierra Leone; the exposes since 1973 of the Nixon Administration in the United States, to cite only a conspicuous recent example, show exchanges of favours for cash on a far grander scale. The important feature to note here is that the political system tended to become enmeshed in a web of corruption. Politicians in office became increasingly loth to risk losing the pleasures they could enjoy, and had an increasing incentive to avoid an unsympathetic government raking up their past behaviour. Equally important, many of the 'public' tended to grow cynical about all politicians,[79] thus both making it difficult for any new leader to appeal to the altruism of his countrymen, and creating an atmosphere in which newcomers to office would be expected to enrich themselves at the expense of the public.

While the politicians and local businessmen were the chief beneficiaries of Sierra Leone's dependent relationship with the industrialised states, other segments of the populace also became committed to this relationship. The 'open economy',[80] which permitted the manufacturers of consumer goods in the industrialised states to use all their taste-creating powers on the Sierra Leone market, had a considerable seductive effect upon ordinary Sierra Leoneans. While the successful politician or administrator gloried in his Mercedes-Benz.[81] the labourer impressed his friends with imported ready-made clothes. Although some imported goods such as transistor radios and bicycles opened up new dimensions of existence, the replacement of palm wine by bottled beer and soft drinks (for which all the ingredients except the water were imported) served no 'developmental' purpose beyond conditioning people to look to Western technology for 'the good things of life'. As such attitudes became internalised they became increasingly hard to alter.

How much help is either the 'modernisation' or the 'neo-Marxist' paradigm in interpreting the features of Sierra Leone's economy that I have sketched above? While I do not wish to undertake an exhaustive analysis of their rival claims at this point, a few comments on the shortcomings of each seem appropriate.

The 'modernisation' model's postulation that internal attitudes influenced by the example of the industrialised states will enable Third World countries to replicate the features of those states seems to underrate the effect of one vital feature: the fact that the existing industrial states have brought into being a pattern of relationships that establishes them as the 'centre' sources of technological innovation and processors of raw materials, and the Third World countries as the 'peripheral' recipients of innovations and suppliers of processable materials. Internal attitudes favouring changes have certainly developed in Third World countries, but as we saw in Sierra Leone's case the changes sought by those groups possessing influence in the polity are likely to be the ones strengthening the country's peripheral position. While nationalist, racial or other non-economic factors may induce the political elites of Third World countries to try to alter this relationship, the strong vested economic interest many of them have in maintaining it works against their seeking to follow the harder path towards creating their own industrial capacity.

This is not to say that the neo-Marxist model provides a satisfactory explanation of the Third World's situation, although it does seem to come somewhat closer to the heart of the problem. I doubt, however, that there is a significant element of the conscious conspiracy that is often implied by the Marxists to exist among the governments and major corporations of the industrial states. There are enough instances of sharp differences and rivalries both between corporations and governments to suggest that a more plausible explanation of these organisations' behaviour is simply their pursuit of their perceived self-interest.[82] Furthermore, it is not just a group of bourgeois leaders who bind the Third World countries into a dependent relationship with the Western states; fairly substantial segments of the population have come to see the goods provided through this relationship as desirable, and would undoubtedly offer stiff resistance to any ascetic leader who tried to persuade them to take up less materialistic values. In other words, while the people of the Third World countries may often feel that they are being exploited in a particular relationship, they far less often feel that the entire pattern of relations is oppressive, and without such a feeling they are hardly likely to turn *en masse* to revolutionary collective solutions. Finally, it is not at all clear that the 'centre-periphery' relationship must inevitably widen the gap between the two types of economy, or whether the peripheries haltingly and slowly may be able to add bits of industrial capacity to their economies; not at a rate which will allow them to 'catch up' to the 'developed' countries, to be sure, but at least as fast as they would advance in this direction under any other social order.

In the specific case of Sierra Leone, the neo-Marxist approach offers considerable insight, yet seems to lack appreciation for some important elements of the Sierra Leone reality. Its contention that export-oriented economic activity, as epitomised by SLST's mining and the marketing of coffee, cocoa and other agricultural crops, created both a dependent relationship with the industrialised states, and a Sierra Leonean 'bourgeoisie' who benefited from this relationship, seems a reasonable general statement of the situation. But in three significant areas it seems deficient. First, its implicit assumption that the rest of the populace would remain poor and potentially revolutionary seems doubtful; substantial numbers of people became better off, and also became more capable of improving their own position through acquiring more education and skills during the period under study. While this might not dampen revolutionary ardour, it did give them some stake in the system. Second, the assumption that the bourgeoisie would accept their 'comprador' position in the world capitalist system seens questionable; even Albert Margai made sporadic efforts to break away from this system, and his failure to do so seems attributable more to the limits of his skill and the net of constraints than to a lack of will. Third, neo-Marxist analyses have no place for ethnic and regional conflicts; yet these exercised a significant influence in inhibiting class cohesion both among the bourgeoisie and among potential radical challengers. Any Sierra Leonean leader was caught in a complex net of constraints, of which those imposed by the country's dependent place in the world economy were among the most important; but self-induced psychological and ideological limitations as well as the independent effects of regionalism and localism were also important.

Political Leadership and Economic Dependence

What possibilities were open to a political leader in an 'underdeveloped' country, given the features we have noted? In examining what a leader might consider his possible range of choices, we can go back to the internal constraints discussed earlier; the leader's ideology, his policies and his style.[83] What I described as the 'radical ideologue', the 'conservative ideologue' and the 'non-ideologue' will see the limits to their range of choices quite differently, even though each may fail to take full advantage of the possibilities within those limits. In judging the degree to which each does take advantage of the possibilities he can perceive, we must bear in mind that any leader's knowledge and time are both finite, and that he is likely to settle for what he considers a 'best available' rather than a 'best possible' solution (the latter generally being perceived only through hindsight).[84]

The 'radical ideologue' is the most likely to try to alter the peripheral status of his country, since he alone is likely to raise the question of whether his country should continue to be a dependent periphery. An ideology which proposes a major transformation of the society along lines which lead to a strengthening of that country's exchange position in relation to the industrialised states[85] will necessarily entail a wide range of innovative policies to break out of existing patterns. It will also necessarily involve a creative style, again because existing alignments and ways of viewing problems tend to lock the polity into a dependent relationship.

To gather support for this approach, a leader will need to inspire people to support him on a non-material basis, either through a shared commitment to goals or through a charismatic attachment. Since his attempts at economic restructuring, whether through a form of autarky or through introducing increasing elements of manufacturing into his country's trading commodities, will almost certainly run foul of most foreign companies in his country and probably of their governments as well, he is in any case unlikely to be able to obtain many resources suitable for maintaining support through material payoffs. While the hair shirt may not have quite the same status appeal as the Mercedes it is possible that the leader's (and his supporters') conspicuous use of the garment may offer the necessary inspiration to ordinary people to support him, at least if not too much prosperity has been trickling down to them up to this time. Relatively privileged groups such as the armed forces present a more difficult problem if it can be done; a rebuilding of the armed forces from scratch with thorough ideological indoctrination may offer some security, although even this is by no means a certain safeguard.[86]

Assuming he can develop a sufficient power base to maintain office, the next question would be how the radical ideologue might use his powers. The line between fixity of purpose and fanaticism is alarmingly thin, and there is a strong possibility that a leader determined to make changes would not be too greatly concerned about the human costs of the means he chose to achieve these ends, especially if many people were only lukewarm towards his vision of Utopia. Whether there is any formula by which a small state can make radical changes towards a less 'vulnerable' condition at any level beyond local self-sufficiency is not yet clear; certainly the example of Guinea, Sierra Leone's nearest neighbour, offered little encouragement.[87] Since the prospects under which such a leader might emerge in Sierra Leone were among the most adverse conceivable, the chances of a change to a less dependent status bringing a better life to most people were not good.[88]

A 'conservative ideologue' was unlikely to see any need for drastic restructuring of his society, unless it was in order to return to a previous, more desirable state. His goal would normally be to slow down the rate of social change, or at least to temper specific changes so that they affected the narrowest possible range of men's lives. In Sierra Leone's case, for example, a conservative such as Dr Margai sought to hive mining activities off into isolated enclaves, or if that were not possible, to bring alluvial digging under as much social control as possible. He sought to avoid any major shift in agriculture to, say, individual land tenure, which would drastically alter the power relations between a chief and his people, and he sought to utilise existing structures such as chiefdoms for new functions, rather than create new structures which would require new personnel. The specific policies he followed to implement these goals were, of course, 'conservative', and he generally used a 'brokerage' style, though with a strong bias towards those sectors sharing his views.

Because he was generally building upon long-established habits and customs, the conservative ideologue could usually manage to retain most of the support he needed through non-material appeals. The sort of system in which appeals to maintain traditions would continue to be effective would inevitably be one in which men's aspirations had not yet begun to outrun the possibilities of satisfying them; while most voters expected their chief and MP to provide some material improvements for their villages, their felt needs could be satisfied with a fairly modest outlay of material benefits. As changes disrupting established relationships spread through the society, however, the conservative ideologue's non-material appeal would weaken, and generally at the same time a rising level of aspirations and spread of participation would increase dramatically the amounts of material payoff needed. If other men besides the chief became intermediaries, they too would need financial sweeteners; and if people wanted a hospital rather than a dispensary or a paved road rather than a track, this would raise the outlay required by the leader. Thus the conservative ideologue faced the danger that if changes were forced on his society despite his best efforts to contain them, his own position would be undermined. Since the country's relationship with the industrialised states as a supplier of agricultural and mineral products and a recipient of manufactured goods generally involved increasing alterations in the social structure to provide these goods and markets, the conservative ideologue was in the ironic position that his unwillingness to see the need for any major change was the main contributing factor to the weakening of his position. In Sierra Leone, Dr Margai's 'Open Door' policy allowed a tremendous range of inducements to plunge Sierra Leoneans deeply into the cash economy, even to the most remote village store with its bottles of Guinness and its imported tomato paste. But to get the money to pay for these goods, men either had to sell more cash crops or go off diamond mining; and both these activities gave them more independence from their chiefs and thus of the system Dr Margai had built.[89] In such cases, the best the conservative could do would be to carry on a rearguard action, knowing that the content of his conservativism would have to undergo steady modification if he were to survive.

The non-ideologue is the least likely of the three types of leader to question the *status quo,* in that he lacks benchmarks by which to judge it. He may well introduce specific innovative policies, as Albert Margai did in seeking to improve relations with the Communist states, and with Guinea and Ghana, but without ideological guidelines these policies may run at cross-purposes to each other or be vitiated by other actions, as Albert's gestures towards northern development were vitiated by his channelling resources into his personal interests.[90] He is likely to follow a brokerage style, but may become creative if he sees this as the way to implement a particular policy; however, he is unlikely to use a creative style to achieve a long-term goal. The non-ideologue's greatest strength is his freedom to adjust his behaviour to new situations as these are thrust upon him; but the lack of a personal commitment which gives him this freedom also gives rise to his greatest weakness, his inability to build a strong following based upon non-material commitments.

A leader like Albert Margai, who cannot rally sufficient support on the basis of some dominating appeal, must necessarily try to build that support through the more personal links of patron-client relations if he is to survive. If, as in Albert's case, he is trying to bring in new groups to offset opposition within the structure he has inherited, he has an even greater need for the resources to provide material payoffs, since he will still have to keep what he can of the existing structure behind him, or at least neutral. Albert's situation was a particularly difficult one; not only was the SLPP built almost entirely upon personalised local power bases which could only be maintained by patronage, but the cost of maintaining patronage links in each area was increasing as more participants entered the political arena. Since the Prime Minister was trying to build up a new party structure independent of the principal local patrons, the chiefs, yet was unable to dispense with the chiefs' support, he had an urgent need for financial resources on a scale not previously known in Sierra Leone.

While personal acquisitiveness certainly contributed to his behaviour, a much more compelling factor was his need for cash to finance his personal machine. The need for large sums seems to have given the Prime Minister an incentive to plunge his government into such costly 'development' projects as the Produce Marketing Board's instant coffee factory (when Sierra Leone's coffee production was already committed elsewhere), and the contractor-financed hotel at Lumley Beach.[91] Some of the most dubious projects, such as the SLPMB's palm kernel oil mill[92] were entered into by Albert Margai before he became Prime Minister, but the major push for economic expansion, financed largely by external short-term contractors' credits and by the use of accumulated cash balances and bank credit, began in late 1964. The results, in the studiously neutral words of an International Monetary Fund study, were that:

> exports declined, imports increased and the balance of payments deficit, which had been Le 0.6 million in 1964, rose to a record Le 11.6 million in 1965. The total official foreign exchange reserves . . . declined from Le 29.2 million at the end of 1964 to Le 17.6 million at the end of 1965 . . . the budget estimates (for 1966/67) . . . showed an uncovered deficit of Le 19.3 million. In these estimates, the Government budgeted for an increase of almost 100 per cent in its development expenditures. The SLPMB, which had committed its liquid assets to long-term projects, was unable to meet current liabilities to the buying agents of approximately Le 3.0 million and did not have the financial resources needed to purchase product for export. At the same time, large repayments were falling due on external suppliers: credits, and it was anticipated that the balance of payments would deteriorate further. [3]

What this meant in human terms was that farmers were being given credit slips instead of cash for their sales of export produce to the SLPMB, civil servants' and teachers' salaries were being paid several weeks late because of the government's shortage of cash, and there were numbers of layoffs from development projects. While the scale of Sierra Leone's development expenditures in this period was such that even a modest levy on each contract would give the Prime Minister resources in the order of hundreds of thousands of pounds, far more than he could realise by petty extractions from the chiefs, Lebanese and others,[94] the non-monetary costs, both in terms of loss of confidence and anger against the Prime Minister's apparent self-enrichment while ordinary people were experiencing hard times, may well have outweighed the political benefits of ample funds.

It was not the corruption of Albert Margai's regime *per se* that created so much disillusionment; while most Sierra Leoneans could perceive that what he was doing was morally wrong, their moral sensibilities would probably have been blunted if they had felt that the Margai regime was giving them some rewards too, or even if he had given them a vision of a better life in the future.[95] But when he could offer neither a material nor a spiritual payoff, his corruption became one more item in the list of grievances against him.

Conclusions: Can a Leader Change the Economy?

While the economic problems which contributed to Albert Margai's downfall were in part brought on by his particular approach to leadership, still many of the obstacles to development in Sierra Leone seemed impervious to any form of political leadership. Static agricultural export crop prices, the reluctance of foreign capital to invest in manufacturing, and the fact that iron and diamonds were diminishing resources[96] were 'contradevelopmental' factors beyond the power of any type of leader to change. Any realistic appraisal of Sierra Leone's economic prospects had to ask how much hope *any* approach could offer; the choice might not be between the alternatives posed by Sekou Touré, 'poverty in freedom or riches in servitude', but of poverty with either freedom or servitude.

Sierra Leone's features were such that a continued peripheral relationship with the West was most unlikely to provide much economic growth, let alone the structural alterations we might term 'development'. The existing and any prospective sources of agricultural export earnings were all under the constraint that if the price rose, either other producers would flood the markets or the 'developed' countries would turn to substitutes. Iron and diamonds were wasting resources, and the former was far too abundant throughout the world and the latter's marketing was too tightly controlled by the De Beers cartel for Sierra Leone to alter prices by its own decision. Foreign investors were not interested in Sierra Leone's small market either for processing its own raw materials or for import substitution industries, and if Sierra Leone decided to process its own raw materials and then sought export markets, it could be fairly sure that the processors in the 'developed' countries would do their best to prevent its products gaining access to their markets.[97] Nor could it expect more than a pittance in 'aid' from the rich countries for the purposes of developing its industrial potential either for self-sufficiency or for export markets, again largely because of opposition from the rich countries' domestic interests as well as through indifference. None of the major links with the 'developed' countries offered good prospects of improving Sierra Leone's position. I should stress that this was not a deliberate conspiracy against the Third World; rather, it was simply the working out of the different corporations' and governments' pursuit of their self-interest. But since the self-interest of most corporations and of most rich states did not include the development of the poorer countries, the effect was the same.

Over the long run, the prospect that the Third World might 'catch up' with the rich states is probably illusory in any case. Even if one accepts the critics of the Club of Rome[98] who contend that natural resources will last for many years yet,[99] even the most optimistic projections regarding the availability of such non-renewable resources as oil do not try to contemplate how long reserves would last if the 'underdeveloped' countries began manufacturing on a scale sufficient to provide them with the quantities of material goods enjoyed by the 'developed' countries.[100] Even if the underdeveloped countries could go part way in 'catching up', they would at best turn into poorer versions of the 'developed' countries, a form of 'development' which would probably produce an ever more embittering 'peripheral' status.

Assuming, then, that the one prospect for 'development' may be the creation of a society based on a radical new set of values, and making the very risky assumption that such a set of values can in fact be realised, what are the prospects for a radical change? The major problems are of expectations, both about what people desire and how politicians will behave. In Sierra Leone, any radical leader coming to power would have to face the fact that many people had grown accustomed to a way of life based upon certain standards of consumption. Senior administrators enjoyed their cars, their whisky and their trips abroad; skilled workers enjoyed their bottled beer and transistor radios; and even the farmer in the bush sought a corrugated iron roof as a sign of status.[101] To curtail some of these imports, even the less useful ones, would lead to an erosion of the leader's support, and of willingness to work for the goals he was putting forward. At the same time, the effects of the Margais' style of politics had accustomed most people to thinking that politicians were out primarily for their own good, that professions of altruism were to be treated sceptically. Politics was a source of material payoffs, not of sacrifices. If a leader sought to rally people on a call of 'Self-reliance through sacrifice' he would have to alter some deep-rooted convictions about the nature and purpose of politics in Sierra Leone. It could be done, but it would require a much more thorough re-education of the populace than would have been the case if altruism had held a stronger position from the time a national political culture began.[102]

This discussion has dealt with the problems of Sierra Leone's economy in isolation from the factors discussed in previous chapters. We have not considered the extent to which local structures, ethnic conflicts or other factors have affected the choices open to a leader in the economic sphere, although clearly there is some interaction. In the concluding chapter we will consider some of the ways in which these factors interact, and then see what general lessons Sierra Leone's experience holds for political leaders elsewhere.

Notes

1. For simplicity, I am lumping the world's states into three groups: the 'Western states', 'capitalist states', or 'Western industrialised states', comprising North America, Western Europe, Japan, South Africa, Australia and New Zealand, all of which possess a substantial industrial capability, predominantly under the control of a limited number of private individuals or organisations; the 'Communist states', comprising the states of Eastern Europe (including Yugoslavia), the Soviet Union, China, North Korea, North Vietnam and Cuba; and the 'Third World', comprising all the remaining independent states. Obviously there are anomalies here; Cuba's economic problems are much closer to Bolivia's or to Costa Rica's than to Czechoslovakia's; the asymmetry of Canada's relations with the United States makes them resemble those between say, the Ivory Coast and France more than they resemble the relations between France and Germany; and Trinidad's level of economic development is much closer to that of Portugal or Bulgaria than it is to that of Upper Volta. Yet broadly speaking, these categories do offer groupings as cohesive as any other reasonably simple categorisation.
2. Those two long-standing neighbours and antagonists, Kwame Nkrumah and Felix Houphouet-Boigny, offer as sharply contrasting paths to an agreed

end as we can find anywhere. See Woronoff, *West African Wager,* for an account of their divergencies; also Elliott Berg, 'Structural Transformation versus Gradualism' and R.H. Green, 'Reflections on Economic Strategy', both in Philip Foster and Aristide Zolberg (eds.), *Ghana and the Ivory Coast,* Chicago, University of Chicago Press, 1971.

3. A recent article in *West Africa* 18 Mar. 1974, p. 297 noted that malnutrition and death among babies was resulting from the promotion by milk manufacturers of bottle-feeding among African mothers. Evidently Coca-Cola and other purveyors of 'coloured sugar water' (as Ivan Illich terms soft drinks) are not the only producers of goods of dubious social value.
4. That one can have increased productivity without necessarily achieving the structural changes that are also a part of 'development' is well brought out in the study of Liberia by Robert Clower et.al., *Growth without Development: An Economic Survey of Liberia,* Evanston, Northwestern University Press, 1966.
5. The term is Denis Goulet's. See his *The Cruel Choice,* New York, Atheneum, 1971, pp. 38-49.
6. Such as David McClelland's 'desire for achievement', or Daniel Lerner's 'empathy'. See McClelland, *The Achieving Society,* Princeton, Van Nostrand, 1961 and Lerner, *The Passing of Traditional Society,* Glencoe, Free Press, 1958.
7. For example, see Everett Hagen, *On the Theory of Social Change: How Economic Growth Begins,* Homewood, Illinois, Dorsey, 1962, or John H. Kunkel, *Society and Economic Growth,* New York, Oxford, 1970.
8. I use the prefix 'neo' primarily to distinguish the academically respectable scholarship of writers such as Baran, Jalee, and Frank from the 'vulgar Marxism' peddled by Soviet academicians, who insisted on seeing class formation and motivation strictly in terms of European industrial societies. For an excellent summary of the 'school' see Colin Leys, *Underdevelopment in Kenya.* Berkeley and Los Angeles, University of California Press, 1974, ch. 1.
9. Paul Baran's *The Political Economy of Growth,* which influenced many of this school, first appeared in 1957. Pierre Jalee's *The Pillage of the Third World* first appeared in 1965 and Frantz Fanon's *Damnées de la Terre,* whose critique was close enough to the Marxists' that we can consider him as falling within this 'school', appeared in 1963. Most of the empirical work in this area, such as Gunder Frank's *Capitalism and Underdevelopment in Latin America,* Harmondsworth, Penguin, 1971, did not appear until the late 1960s.
10. Best illustrated in recent years by the massive distortions of what Allende's regime in Chile was doing, which were presented by the American newspapers and spread by the Associated Press throughout the English-speaking world. For a comment on this distortion, see James Taylor, 'The Chilean Experiment: We're Getting a Distorted View', Toronto *Star,* 12 Sept. 1973, p. B4.
11. To take some illustrations from Britain, journals such as the *New Statesman* and the *New Left Review* contained only a smattering of articles on matters of concern to the Third World, and scarcely any written from a non-European perspective. The Fabian Society's *Venture* was one of the few periodicals concerned largely with the Third World and presenting a few of its perspectives, but the number of African political leaders it reached was very, very small.
12. Fanon's condemnation of the 'dictatorship of the bourgeoisie' hit sensitive nerves in nearly every new African state. Even Sekou Touré came in for

attack as a 'neo-colonialist stooge', in B. Ameillon, *La Guinée, bilan d'une independence,* Paris, François Maspero, 1964.

13. Siaka Stevens, who later was to call upon Guinea to protect his regime, once expostulated to me on the evils of Touré's regime, with its severe suppression of personal liberty and failure to provide a good life for its people. Interview, 31 Dec. 1965.
14. For example, as used in the excellent theoretical formulation of 'centre-periphery' relationships by Johan Galtung, 'A Structural Theory of Imperialism', *African Review,* I, 4 Apr. 1972, pp. 92-138.
15. This conception of 'centre' and 'periphery' is drawn from Edward A. Shils, 'Centre and Periphery', in *The Logic of Personal Knowledge: Essays Presented to Michael Polanyi,* Glencoe, Free Press, 1961, pp. 117-30.
16. *1963 Census,* Vol. III, Table 7.
17. Mutti, *Marketing Staple Food Crops,* p. 52, claims that 22 per cent of farmers grew rice primarily for sale, basing his claim upon agricultural census data concerning farmers' 'usual practices'.
18. See the report by the Chief Commissioner for the Provinces, H. Childs, *A Plan of Economic Development for Sierra Leone,* Freetown, Government Printer, 1949, p. 22 (the *Childs Report*).
19. I have calculated these changes from data in Ralph Saylor, *The Economic System of Sierra Leone,* Durham, N.C., Duke University Press, 1967, p. 38.
20. Ibid., p. 40.
21. Calculated from *Quarterly Statistical Bulletin,* No. 5, Dec. 1965, Table 14.
22. See Ken Swindell, 'Rice', in Clarke, *Sierra Leone in Maps,* p. 76, and Saylor, *The Economic System,* p. 43. Julian Pollock, who actually worked a farm in the Northern swamplands as a 'participant observer', has reported yields of 750 lb per acre. Pollock, *Influence, Authority and Economic Opportunity,* pp. 310-11.
23. Central Statistics Office, *Household Survey of the Northern Province,* 1968-9, Table 16, and *Household Survey of the Eastern Provinces,* Table 16.
24. Cf. Caroline Hutton's observations on the attitudes of school leavers in Uganda towards farming: 'The majority of school leavers' . . . lack of enthusiasm towards agriculture appeared to derive from the level of income which they perceived to be associated with it . . . The problem is the low incomes to be got from cultivation, and the lack of any prospect of any real improvement for those cultivating small plots without capital or expertise.' 'Unemployment in Kampala and Jinja, Uganda', *Canadian Journal of African Studies,* 3, 2, Summer 1969, p. 439.
25. Of the many books recently published in this general area, perhaps the most comprehensive is Paul and Anne Erlich, *Population, Resources, Environment,* San Francisco, W.H. Freeman, 1970. Another relevant to the biological hazards of innovation is M.T. Farvar and J.P. Milton, *The Careless Technology,* Garden City, New York, Natural History Press, 1972. A balanced article dealing with both biological and economic problems is Clifford Wharton, 'The Green Revolution: Cornucopia or Pandora's Box', *Foreign Affairs,* XLVII, 3 Apr. 1969, pp. 464-76.
26. Since most land is farmed on a long-term rotation, the most likely outcome of some farmers acquiring most of the accessible land would be that those left with less available land would give their areas less fallowing time, with a resulting increase in erosion and the formation of hard 'pan', and a loss in fertility.
27. For a description of how one attempt at bringing agricultural change failed, see Nicholas Hopkins' study of a Malian village, 'Socialism and Rural Change in Mali', *Journal of Modern African Studies,* 7, 3, 1969, p. 466.

28. Figures from *Quarterly Statistical Bulletin,* No. 5, Tables 29 and 30.
29. Van der Laan, *The Sierra Leone Diamonds,* p. 60.
30. Delco claimed in 1961 that it had paid £10.4 million in taxes over the previous nine years. Sierra Leone Development Company Limited, 'Iron Ore from Marampa', pamphlet, n.d. [1961].
31. Delco, in ibid., claimed a payroll in 1960 of £320,000. An SLST official has told me that in 1967-8 SLST's African payroll was £800,000. If we assume in the early 1960s the two companies were paying out £1 million a year, an estimate that a fifth of this went to the government through taxes and import duties would be fairly generous.
32. Van der Laan, p. 61.
33. Cited in *West Africa,* 8 Aug. 1972, p. 1031.
34. John Morten, former SLST General Manager, interview, 20 Mar. 1973.
35. After writing this section, I discovered a more sophisticated general argument along similar lines written by Charles E. Rollins in 1956, but making the additional point that most 'underdeveloped' economies lack the mechanisms for investing such receipts as they do gain into productive capital works. 'Mineral Development and Economic Growth', in Robert Rhodes (ed.), *Imperialism and Underdevelopment,* New York, Monthly Review Press, 1970, pp. 181-204.
36. Sierra Leone, *Estimates of Revenue and Expenditure,* 1965-6, p. 71.
37. Cf. Albert Hirschman's concept of 'forward and backward linkages', in *The Strategy of Economic Development,* New Haven, Yale University Press, 1958. Galtung, 'Structural Theory of Imperialism', pp. 100-6, makes a similar point with his argument that the 'gap in processing levels' between a nation that merely ships out a raw material and one that manufacturers goods from this material has significant 'spin-off' effects in such diverse fields as education, research, communications and military capabilities.
38. The plans of Iran and other oil producers after the 1973 oil 'crisis' to use their increased revenues for industrialisation suggest what might be done along these lines – if all the producers of an essential commodity can act in concert to increase their prices.
39. Van der Laan notes (p. 88) that diamond cutting may not require quite such a long apprenticeship as is generally believed, since Israel seems to have trained new cutters fairly rapidly. Be that as it may, the only attempt to establish a diamond cutting factory in Sierra Leone, jointly financed by the Sierra Leone government and Leon Tempelsman, a large American dealer, seemed to be as much a means of obtaining extra rough diamonds for the American market as a training ground for Sierra Leonean diamond cutters. It did employ sixty Sierra Leonean cutters, but because it needed considerable expatriate staff, did not make money.
40. See Hirschman, *The Strategy of Economic Development,* p. 108.
41. See *West Africa,* 5 Mar. 1973, pp. 303-4.
42. See above, p. 62.
43. Ken Swindell, 'Monthly Employment of Native Diamond Mining Workers', in Clarke, *Sierra Leone in Maps,* p. 96, cites a peak of 42,174 in February, 1963.
44. *Quarterly Statistical Bulletin,* No. 5, Table 29, yields an average value for recorded exports from 1960 to 1964 of £9.8 million.
45. See van der Laan, p. 192, at which he cites figures of £8.8 and £9 million for the claimholders' receipts for 1960 and 1961 respectively.
46. The peak imports of rice into Sierra Leone, which until 1954 had been self-sufficient in the commodity, were 38,000 tons in 1956 and 43,000 tons in 1959. At a Rice Department price of £37.50 a ton, this would

indicate at most a foregone income of about £1.5 million for those rice producers who went diamond digging, assuming these were ones capable of marketing rice. Similarly, palm kernel production dropped from 76,000 tons in 1952 to 52,000 tons in 1963. At the producer price of £30 a ton, this drop represented just under £¾ million worth of sales.

47. Van der Laan, p. 192. See also his comments on pp. 179-80 and more generally in Ch. 13.
48. D.T. Jack, *Economic Survey of Sierra Leone,* Freetown, Government Printer, 1958, pp. 8-9 shows that while overall imports tripled from 1951 to 1956, capital goods such as cement and lorries only doubled.
49. See Stanley, 'The Lebanese', pp. 162, 172.
50. Calculated from data on value of imports and import duties in *Quarterly Statistical Bulletin,* No. 1, Tables 3 and 13.
51. See, for example, James C. Scott, *Comparative Political Corruption,* Englewood Cliffs, N.J., Prentice Hall, 1972, esp. pp. 29-34.
52. See above, p. 62.
53. He took the issuing of residence permits out of the hands of the chiefs, who had turned this power into a very lucrative source of personal revenue, and put it in the hands of the District Officer.
54. Though it would have been rather difficult to do much at the national level when the Prime Minister himself appeared to be involved in corrupt dealings. See especially *We Yone,* 6 Aug. 1966, and Sierra Leone, *Report of the Forster Commission of Enquiry on Assets of Ex-Ministers and Ex-Deputy Ministers,* Freetown, Government Printer, 1968, pp. 59-66, (hereafter *Forster Report*).
55. Both SLST and the Diamond Corporation channelled political contributions exclusively to the SLPP. A Diamond Corporation official was also found following the 1968 'sergeants' coup' trying to induce the soldiers not to allow Siaka Stevens and the APC to form the government. Stevens's desire to bring the diamond industry under Sierra Leonean control had been well known for many years.
56. See Neil Leighton, 'The Lebanese Community in Sierra Leone: The Role of an Alien Trading Minority in Political Development', paper presented at the American African Studies Association annual meeting 1972, p. 23.
57. We should recall the chiefs' opposition to alluvial mining, noted above, p. 64.
58. See above, pp. 125-6.
59. Recall Dr Margai's comment that 'If I were to indulge my personal feelings, I would push out all Europeans today', see above, p. 99.
60. Cited in Sierra Leone, *A Progress Report on Economic and Social Development,* 27 Apri. 1961-31 Mar. 1965, p. 86. We should note that the APC did express some concern about this indebtedness to companies operating in the country.
61. *Forster Report,* p. 22.
62. In fairness, it should be noted that the Commission did record as unlawful 'sweets of office' similar hospitality to other Ministers. See, for example, ibid., pp. 42-3, where it criticised ten-day trips to Sweden by the Minister of Trade and Industry and his wife which were paid for by a Swedish engineering firm.
63. Apart from cash donations, the Diamond Corporation is alleged to have allowed Dr Margai to use its company plane after the 1962 elections to contact the Independents, and thus ensure a majority for himself.
64. For example. Bureh apparently asked for the scholarship from Philips for his son. *Forster Report,* p. 41.

65. Intrabank at the time had been open for less than a year, and may genuinely have only then decided to send the Sierra Leonean abroad. But the coincidence was suspiciously neat.
66. See testimony of the APC candidate, Dr S.H. Pratt, and of Sam Margai before the Dove-Edwin Commission, in *Daily Mail,* 11 July and 1 Aug. 1967.
67. John Dawson, 'Race and Inter-Group Relations in Sierra Leone', Part II, *Race,* VI, 3 Jan. 1965, p. 218.
68. For some evidence of the strength of anti-Lebanese feelings among MPs, see *Daily Mail,* 19 Dec. 1962; also *House of Representatives Debates,* Session 1962-3, Volume II, 17 Dec. 1962, cols. 630-54.
69. The Constitution Amendment (No. 2) Act No. 12 of 1962, amending Section I (1) of the Constitution, restricted automatic citizenship to persons whose father or grandfather was 'of negro African descent'.
70. The Land Development (Protection) Act 1962, No. 61 of 1962, Section 3.
71. Government Notice 649, *Sierra Leone Gazette,* XCIV, 48, 20 June 1963, p. 615.
72. The Non-Citizens (Restriction of Trade or Business) Act 1965, Section 4.
73. This belief in the overwhelming importance of obtaining almost any kind of industrial activity for an economically backward area, coupled with a belief that private entrepreneurs from outside possess talents unavailable within their jurisdiction, have led many other political leaders into disastrous ventures. For example, the governments of several 'underdeveloped' Canadian provinces, which could have drawn on considerably more trustworthy 'expert' advice than was available to the Sierra Leone government, were nevertheless badly fleeced in the 1960s by dubious promotions. See Philip Mathias, *Forced Growth,* Toronto, James Lewis & Samuel, 1971, for accounts of Prince Edward Island's fish plant, Nova Scotia's heavy water plant, and Manitoba's notorious Churchill Forest Industries, in which Manitoba taxpayers shelled out $92 million to an unknown set of dummy corporations hiding behind Swiss company law.
74. For a discussion in general terms of this problem, see Sayre. P. Schatz, 'Crude Private Neo-Imperialism: A New Pattern in Africa', *Journal of Modern African Studies,* VII, 4, Dec. 1969, pp. 677-88.
75. Ibid., pp. 679-80. See also D.L. Cohen and M.A. Tribe, 'Suppliers' Credits in Ghana and Uganda – an Aspect of the Imperialist System', *Journal of Modern African Studies* X, 4, 1972, pp. 525-41.
76. This account is a summary of the findings reported in the *Report of the Commission . . . on the matters contained in the Director of Audit's Report . . . For the Year 1960-1,* pp. 25-52 (the *Cole Report*).
77. See the 'Broadcast Talk' by Prime Minister Stevens, 28 Mar. 1969 (printed by Government Printer, Freetown), in which he described the problems of a shoe factory, oil refinery, hotel, cement factory and metal door factory, none capable of producing at competitive prices, and together involving the government in debts of more than £5 million.
78. See *House of Representatives Debates,* Session 1965-6, Vol. II, 18, cols. 12, 83, 212.
79. The 1968 survey's question, 'What do you think of politicians generally?' drew sixty negative responses, including thirty-six specifically alleging dishonesty; and only sixteen positive responses. Two further questions, 'Are they interested in the good of the constituency?', 'Are they interested in the good of the country?', drew almost as many negative as positive responses. Only the question, 'Are they interested in benefiting themselves?' produced near unanimity.
80. In the sense used by Dudley Seers in his article, 'The Stages of Economic

Growth of a Primary Producer in the Middle of the Twentieth Century', in Rhodes, *Imperialism and Underdevelopment*, pp. 164-7.

81. Mercedes-Benz' success in supplanting the Jaguar as the success symbol of the elite in British West Africa can, I suppose, be interpreted as a symbolic gesture by the elite against the 'colonial mentality' rather than as a comment on the relative efficacy of British and German salesmanship.
82. The willingness of ENI, the Italian state oil company, to break the united front of corporations against the Middle Eastern and North African Producers in the 1950s, illustrates how different organisations' self-interest may diverge. See Michael Tanzer, *The Political Economy of International Oil and the Underdeveloped Countries*, Boston, Beacon, 1969, pp. 28-9. For another revealing account of commercial rivalries, this time between the French and the Americans, see Charles Darlington, *African Betrayal*, New York, McKay, 1968.
83. See above, pp. 24-6.
84. See above, p. 89.
85. I use 'exchange' here in a very broad, non-economic sense to cover the transfer of ideas as well as commodities. If, for example, persons from the industrialised states came to perceive that they might learn something from the African states in (say) delivery of health care or other social services, this would indicate that the African states were becoming less 'peripheral' and were moving towards greater equality. It is of course quite possible to have transformations of the society which simply reinforce its peripheral position by inducing it to look increasingly towards the centre, not just for its commodities and technology, but for all its values.
86. The survival of Sekou Touré, and of Julius Nyerere after the 1964 Tanganyika mutiny, suggest that an ideologically controlled army may be a safe one. Certainly it seems a more promising approach than the efforts made in Ghana, Mali and Cyprus to balance a politically unreliable army with a counterweight organisation more firmly committed to the leader, since none of these counterweights succeeded in resisting a military coup.
87. Whether Tanzania will succeed in its efforts to develop through 'self-reliance' is still an open question. Two possible successes, at least from an economic perspective, might be North Korea and North Vietnam; although both started from considerably stronger bases than did any African states, the devastation the American air force wrought on both made their subsequent recovery and later performance impressive.
88. See below, pp. 265-6.
89. While a cash-crop farmer still needed to obtain fresh land for expansion of his farm through the chief, he could rent or 'lease' long-term access to land from other villagers. Also, the very fact of his having more cash available gave him more leverage in relation to his chief.
90. The airfields at Gbangbatoke and Bonthe were among the more conspicious examples of this. See above, p.195
91. For details of the instant coffee factory, see the *Report of the Beoku-Betts Commission of Enquiry into the Sierra Leone Produce Marketing Board*, Freetown, Government Printer, 1968, pp. 34-6, 53-7, (hereafter *Beoku-Betts Report*).
92. For details of the palm kernel mill, see *Beoku-Betts Report*, pp. 4-31. The mill was at first to cost £391,000, but on Albert Margai's instructions the chairman of the PMB signed a contract for £658,000, a figure far higher than the value of such a mill should have been.
93. Rattan J. Bhatia, Gyorgy Szapary and Brian Quinn, 'Stabilisation Programme in Sierra Leone', *IMF Staff Papers*, XVI, 3 Nov. 1969, p. 505.

94. See above, p. 147. for levies on the chiefs.
95. One of the more notorious examples of corruption in a leader of an 'underdeveloped' country was the case of Sir Richard Squires, Premier of Newfoundland from 1919 to 1923, and again from 1928 to 1932 -- his victory in 1928 occurring despite a damning Report by a Royal Commissioner on gross financial malfeasance undertaken with the Premier's full knowledge and complicity. But Squires was able to offset this liability with his appeal to Newfoundlanders' hopes of achieving new prosperity. See S.J.R. Noel, *Politics in Newfoundland,* Toronto, University of Toronto Press, 1971, pp. 151-87.
96. Estimates of the date by which the economically worthwhile supplies of diamonds would be exhausted rarely ranged later than 1985, while the Marampa iron ore deposits were expected to run out even earlier.
97. For example, in the early 1960s Brazil began to process its low-grade coffee beans, which it never exported, into instant coffee. As this instant coffee began to gain markets in the United States and the Soviet Union, American processors persuaded Washington to put pressure on Brazil to give American processors equal access to the cheap Brazilian beans and to impose an export tax on its instant coffee. The Brazilians at first refused on the grounds that such steps would destroy its fledgling industry, but eventually were forced to grant the Americans equal access to their beans. See Toronto *Globe and Mail,* 18 Nov. 1967, and United States Department of State *Bulletin* 60, 3 May 1971, pp. 590-1.
98. The best-known publication of the Club of Rome is the short summary by Dennis Meadows et al., *The Limits to Growth,* New York, Universe Books, 1972.
99. See the article by William Page, 'The Non-Renewable Resources Subsystem', in H.D.S. Cole et al., *Thinking About the Future: A Critique of 'The Limits to Growth',* London, Chatto & Windus for Sussex University Press, 1973.
100. Robert Heilbroner, in a brilliant review article of the Erlichs' *Population, Resources, Environment,* New York Review, XIV, 8, 23 Apr. 1970, pp. 3-9, has flatly stated: 'The underdeveloped countries can never hope to achieve parity with the developed countries.'
101. This, like so many other signs of economic development, had unforseen ecological side effects. The replacement of thatch by metal roofing increased the life-span of farmers' houses from five to more than ten years, with the result that farming villages were relocated less frequently. The soil in consequence was more heavily used, and thus tended more frequently to turn to unusable hard ironstone pan.
102. Tanzania, which has had more success in developing a political culture along the lines I have in mind than most other states, had the advantage that it started with few people habituated to a competing set of individualist and materialist values.

9 CONCLUSIONS

We have now examined in some detail the attitudes of two political leaders and their behaviour in dealing with the problems generated by their polity. Their own attitudes and the various fields within which they operated imposed a wide range of constraints upon Milton and Albert Margai, both as discrete variables and also through their interactions. In this chapter I should like, first, to summarise in general terms the argument I have made in the specific case of Sierra Leone; second, to consider the ways in which various fields interact with each other to put limits to a leader's range of choices; and third, to consider the prospects for leaders wishing to change their countries' situations, particularly in Africa, but more generally in the 'underdeveloped' states.

I have argued that the limits to what a leader can do are set by the interaction of his own attributes with the patterns of relationships established between him and other actors in the polity. Specifically, the leader operates within the internalised constraints imposed by his 'world view' (radical ideology, conservative ideology or non-ideological), the specific policies he finds acceptable (conservative or innovative), and the style in which he seeks to implement his policies (brokerage or creative). In his relations with others he is constrained by his basis of legitimacy (whether adherence to him as an individual or to his role, and whether 'material' or 'spiritual'), and the nature of his links to the populace (whether 'direct' through loyal intermediaries or 'indirect' through strong ones). In a multi-ethnic state he must also consider whether he must use a balancing strategy or can try an overarching one, and must weigh the distribution and strength of those wanting and those opposed to various forms of social change. In the economic sphere he may have the choice of trying to slow down the integration of his people into large-scale interdependent units, of trying to divert their desires from individual consumer products to more social or less materialist goals, or of accepting conventional notions of economic 'development' and of pursuing them either through an industrialising 'structural transformation' approach, or through a raw material-exporting 'incrementalist' approach.[1]

Each of these variables represents a constraint on the range within which other variables can operate. A conservative ideologue like Dr Margai was most unlikely, for example, to try to change Sierra Leone's pattern of strong intermediaries, to deal with ethnic relations by an 'overarching' strategy which might undermine existing institutions, or to seek economic change through either an appeal to non-material attitudes or through structural transformations, both of which required the creation of new values. A non-ideologue like Albert Margai would find it impossible to build legitimacy for himself on the basis of a personal, non-material appeal, which would need a consistency of approach obtainable only through an ideology. Without this consistency, he might also find it difficult to employ a creative political style, and would certainly have difficulty in attracting loyal intermediaries on any enduring basis even if he did wish to establish direct links with the populace. He would also find it hard to make a credible appeal that would override ethnic differences, and would be most unlikely to possess a strong enough vision of an economic Utopia to press for any strategy other than an 'incrementalist' one.

The patterns that emerged in each of the political arenas – international, national and local – in their own turn each set limits upon the range of policies and styles open to a leader. Three limitations which appeared in Sierra Leone seem to have particularly wide relevance. First, once a pattern of strong intermediaries had been established as the links between the leader and the populace, no leader could impose radical transformations from the top down without breaking the power of this group of intermediaries and setting up a new group of more loyal ones. Second, once several ethnic groups possessing sufficient numbers or skills to disrupt the state had developed strong identities, any leader had to concern himself with maintaining a balance among their conflicting claims; a conservative or radical ideologue seeking to override these identities would need a singularly propitious set of circumstances to succeed. Third, as the range of interests benefiting from the export of raw materials and the import of consumer goods increased, it became increasingly difficult for a leader to consider either a non-consumerist or an industrialising strategy, both of which required the populace to forego individual material satisfactions.

Each of these three features made the prospects for a radical ideologue seeking a major social transformation seem extremely dim. The persistence of strong intermediaries seemed to preclude even a non-ideologue using a creative style for more limited changes, while the conservative ideologue as well as the radical would be blocked from using any national unifying appeal by the strength of ethnic differences. The one possibility for a leader to override ethnic differences by a unifying appeal was to find a situation in which all groups could equally perceive an external force as a threat; but the chances of finding such a situation seemed slight.[2] Albert Margai could not turn the SLPP into a centralised party loyal to himself; what he (or any other leader wishing to dispense with the chiefs) would have had to do was to create entirely new structures. It might also be possible to rally the large portion of the populace who received little benefit from the existing distribution of wealth in support of a programme of sacrifice for the future; but such an appeal would have had to overcome resistance from the substantial number of strategically located traders, lorry owners, civil servants and others who benefited from the *status quo.*

Each of these features of the Sierra Leone political system by itself posed a formidable obstacle to any major structural changes. But each also served to reinforce the others, thus leaving any leader who tried to work through the existing structures 'locked in' to an essentially non-ideological (or conservative ideologue's) approach of limited incremental change in social, economic and political structures, of continued balancing between different ethnic and regional claims, and of continuing 'vulnerability' in external relations. It is instructive to note the range of ways in which ethnic conflicts, the position of the chiefs, and the maintenance of the colonial era's economic relationships each affected other areas, thus curtailing dramatically the range of possible courses open to a leader.

The major ethnic conflicts, first between Creoles and countrymen and later between Mendes and northerners, had ramifications in all the political arenas in Sierra Leone. The Creole-countryman conflict's most obvious effect was to ensure that the Paramount Chiefs retained a commanding role in their local arenas, and gained considerable power through the SLPP in the national arena, with consequences to be examined below. But the relegation of the Creoles to a largely oppositional role in national politics had other more direct effects in constraining the leaders' range of choices. The weakness of the achievement-oriented Creoles' position in the councils of the governing party meant that pressure for 'change from above' was not as strong as it was in other countries where the Westernised elite was ethnically a part of the same societies as the bulk of the population. At the same time, given the widespread expectation that an end to British rule required the Africanisation of institutions whose roles required formal Western education, the Creoles came to dominate the higher civil service, the professions and the educational establishment. Thus they were in a position to make their demands felt, but in the form of a conflict between the politicians on the one side, and the civil service and other 'non-political' elites on the other. Not only did this restrict the Prime Minister's ability to consolidate his personal hold on the country, but it increased his reliance on the chiefs by rendering the civil service suspect as an instrument of communication and control. Although Creole civil servants were not likely to work against the interests of Sierra Leone in the international arena, here too the Creole-countryman conflict may have contributed to the consummation of some of the less savoury international financial deals since Ministers may have down graded the advice of their Creole civil service advisers.

The Mende-northerner conflict too had repercussions outside the national arena. In the local arenas it helped retard the development of a 'class' alignment by inducing chiefs and commoners to support the same political party as an expression of ethnic solidarity.[3] In the international arena, it put some extra pressure on the government to seek any kind of development in order to provide better opportunities for the north, and it is possible that the sight of a strong ethnically based opposition party may have made Sierra Leone seem that much less stable and thus marginally less attractive to foreign investors.[4]

The strong position of the Paramount Chiefs in the SLPP was the root of even more widespread consequences than ethnic conflict. First, because the chiefs were locally based, 'strong' intermediaries rather than 'loyal' ones, the SLPP remained a loose, decentralised structure. This meant that a national leader could not exercise much power over local events through the party, and since the implementation of any innovative national policies depended ultimately upon the extent to which they could be brought down to the 'grassroots', the leader's ability to promote such policies was seriously impaired. Second, and reinforcing this structural weakness, the lack of 'loyal' intermediaries to proselytise on behalf of the leader's views, and the indifference of the chiefs to 'national' questions except in so far as these affected their local position, led to a lack of any unifying set of beliefs among the SLPP's main supporters. Since a coherent ideology was necessary to implement an 'innovative' programme in any field, the absence of this ideological coherence served as a powerful support for the *status quo*. 'Radical' or 'nationalist' goals in economic policy, or in Sierra Leone's internal social relationships, would need to align a considerable body of Sierra Leoneans in their support to overcome entrenched opposition to them, and the SLPP simply did not provide any basis for undertaking such an alignment. Again, a national leader wishing to bring change was hamstrung.

The structural and ideological weaknesses of the SLPP also combined to help perpetuate Sierra Leone's vulnerability to external forces. If Sierra Leone was to reduce its dependence upon the manufactured goods of the industrialised states, the government had to either redirect peoples' desires away from these goods or else mobilise sufficient domestic investment to undertake a programme of industrialisation under indigenous control. But since either of these programmes would require both a strong and ideologically coherent leadership and committed cadres through which this leadership could educate the populace to support it in these efforts, there was no chance of their being realised through the SLPP.

The maintenance of Sierra Leone's colonial economic relationships, with raw material exports being exchanged for manufactured imports, also had its effects suffused across the national and local arenas. The fact that on the one hand its contribution to the development of skills and funds for domestic investment was minimal, while on the other hand its contribution to the growth of an unlimited desire for imported material goods was under no such restraint, put Sierra Leone's government (and indeed, all the governments of 'underdeveloped' countries) under a pressure of expectations that it could not hope to meet.[5] This inability to meet the expectations of a wide range of its citizens must have made some contribution to the widespread cynicism about 'politics' which is such a common feature of Sierra Leone, and indeed of most African states. In this respect Sierra Leone was probably luckier than several other African states, in that its population had had somewhat lower expectations than most about the blessings that independence would bring.[6] But even scepticism about the benefits of political action, while less corrosive than hope turned to cynisicm, was a poor foundation on which to build a commitment to a 'good society' embracing all Sierra Leoneans.

At a more practical level, limited economic development meant limited revenues available for the political leadership. In the absence of any ideological cement, material payoffs were necessary both to maintain the commitment of individuals to the leader, and of subnational units to both the leader and the polity. But at the regional level, even part from the fact that the chiefs as the main distribution channel would have hampered any attempt at equity, there certainly were not the resources available to the national government to undertake a programme of helping the Northern Province to 'catch up' with the south. Even the Kono district, whose smaller size at least made a programme of 'catching up' feasible, never received enough in special grants to allay its discontent, at least in part because meetings its demands would have required the government to ignore the equally vociferous demands of other more favoured regions.

At the personal level, payoffs appeared easier to obtain. Sometimes non-material rewards, such as support for a Court President's post or a job with the Produce Marketing Board, would bind an individual to the leader, and might even lead to increased additional revenue for him, which he could use in turn to make other kinds of payoff.[7] But in considering the long-term maintenance of the leader's position, these payoffs might prove costly. For example, because a number of the appointees to the Produce Marketing Board, including the General Manager, collaborated with the Prime Minister in squandering the Board's funds on uneconomic projects, the Board was unable to pay farmers for their produce in cash,with the result that many farmers became quite antagonistic towards Albert Margai and the SLPP.[8] While for the most part, the resources available appeared sufficient to satisfy those seeking them, the hidden costs built up widespread dissatisfaction. In a more dynamic economy, these costs would not have weighed so heavily; but given the slowness of Sierra Leone's economic growth, it was not surprising to find a lack of resources for political payoffs becoming a serious problem by 1967.

My argument so far can be summarised in two general points: first, that developments in any one part of a leader's environment have effects in all the other parts, and second, that the different developments appear to form mutually reinforcing patterns. Thus a leader who is non-ideological or who uses a brokerage style tends to draw out strong intermediaries; with these intermediaries comes a heightening of ethnic awareness because no steps are taken to dampen it down, and also an obstacle is built to the creation of a society not oriented to material consumption through the fact that each of these intermediaries pursues his own calculated interests. At the same time growing ethnic awareness and a desire for more material payoffs both work against the development of a common ideological commitment among intermediaries. The result, then, is that initial tendencies both in a leader's behaviour and in the structures around him strengthen each other and thus make it increasingly difficult for him or for a succeeding leader to break out of these patterns without a revolutionary upheaval.

Lest this sound too determinist, it should be stressed that these interacting constraints are not fixed for all time, nor do they constitute a closed system involving only the leader and those with whom he interacts directly. Rather, these constraints are all ongoing processes, and form parts of a web linking not just the leader, but all actors in the local, national and international arenas in varying degrees. But in order to evaluate political leadership, we can look at the pattern of constraints at a given time, and ask what would have been the effects of a change in leaders' ideologies, policies, styles and bases of legitimacy at that time. In this way we may be able to get some idea of the point at which leaders get 'locked in' to a particular pattern (or conversely, for how long they still have some opportunity to pursue alternative courses) and the significance of the different components of leadership. Let us look, then, at the leadership possibilities open at two separate times in Sierra Leone's recent history: in 1953, just after the Creole-Protectorate battle had been resolved and before the diamond rush had started; and in 1964, when Albert Margai succeeded his brother.

Any leader taking office in 1953 would have had to face several constraints; the suspicion of the Creoles, the largest portion of the formally educated elite; an electoral system almost entirely under the control of the chiefs, and sending a substantial bloc of chiefs to the legislature; and a colonial bureaucracy with little interest in changing established routines and few funds to implement new programmes. He also faced a largely quiescent farming population, showing little concern about their identities as Mendes, Temnes or Limba, some concern but no concerted opposition to the exactions of their chiefs, and having a generally low standard both of living and of economic aspirations.

A conservative ideologue with a Protectorate base, such as Dr Margai, could work quite happily within these constraints. The existing pattern of relations between chiefs and commoners, with its 'right to rule' on one side and deference on the other, seemed a stable one. The colonial bureaucracy might be pressing its political and administrative reforms at the chiefdom level too quickly for some chiefs' taste, but its readiness to leave most economic development to private entrepreneurs ensured that in this sphere changes would not come with unseemly haste. He could be content, too, that no passionate ethnic claims to self-assertion (other than those of the outnumbered Creoles) intruded in the national arena, sparing him the need for overriding or balancing such claims.

Had a leader with no ideological commitments come to office in 1953, he would probably not have acted very differently from Dr Margai, although he might have followed the tides of educated African opinion in pressing for greater reform in chiefdom government and for more rapid economic development. For reasons of personal security he might also have made some effort as Dr Margai conspicuously did not, to develop a party organisation less reliant upon the chiefs. But without a strong ideological commitment, such a leader would probably have followed a path of least resistance, and such a path led towards the chiefs and the British bureaucrats.

A radical ideologue whose views were known probably could not have gained office in 1953, at least if his 'radicalism' extended to include reducing the position of chiefs, or confrontations with the British. Even if he were able to gain office, he would have had a difficult time building up the cadres of committed supporters necessary to implement such changes as increased popular participation in local government, or programmes of economic improvement such as Guinea's 'human investment'.[9] It might have been possible for a Protectorate leader to gain support as the Protectorate's defender against even more drastic threats of change by the Creoles, as Ben Bella was later to win support from Algerian traditionalists as the defender of the faith and traditions against urbanised opponents,[10] but only so long as he did not act directly against the chiefs' perceived interests. A more extreme strategy, which might have worked in the north, but was doubtful elsewhere, would be to appeal to the people against their chiefs; but without cadres or organisers such an appeal would be hard to launch.[11] A radical leader's best hope would be to pursue dissembling tactics, first by building up an autonomous party organisation ostensibly to deal with the Creoles and with the British, and then turning it against the chiefs. But although the chiefs' lack or organisation would help him, the lack of any broad popular awareness in the Protectorate until the diamond rush made rallying mass support for such a party a near impossible task. It was not until the massive social upheaval of the diamond rush that potential cadres were available for a radical leader, and even then they still required political education.

The same lack of potential cadres meant that any leader in 1953 would largely have to confine himself to a brokerage style; while there was plenty of grassroots discontent, as the 1955-6 riots were to show, it had not reached the level where spontaneous uprisings practically forced a leader to adopt a creative style, as was to happen later in parts of the Belgian Congo.[12] Since the cheap transistor radio had not yet arrived, the only way in which people could become aware that a leader was articulating popular discontent was by word of mouth; without an organisation to spread the word, and the grassroots response it provided, it was hard for a leader to do more than mediate among those interests which were articulated.

The legitimacy of a leader in 1953 could derive from a number of sources. A leader acceptable to the chiefs could enjoy their still strong hold on their people, and he would also enjoy such legitimacy as the British colonial regime possessed as long as he co-operated with it. If he were to undertake a radical attack upon either of these institutions, he would have to find some other basis of legitimation; since he would probably not enjoy much access to funds,[13] and lack the cadres necessary to build a machine, he would have to rely upon a personal charismatic appeal, as Touré, Kenyatta and to a lesser extent Nkrumah did in their early days. But without widespread discontent over the *status quo,* and without an effective system of mass communication, the success of such an appeal was problematic.

If the choice up to 1953 was between a conservative ideologue and a non-ideologue as national political leader, how much difference did the leadership of one rather than the other make? What differences might have occurred in the political patterns that developed up to 1964 if a less conservative leader has held office? In undertaking such speculations, we need to be aware of two hazards: first, the unforseen effects of any action may be as little evident to an analyst employing hindsight as they were to a leader at the time his actions were taken; and second, out of the complex web of circumstances generating a particular pattern, there is inevitably some arbitrariness in deciding what portion of influence can be assigned to a political leader. Nevertheless, we can indicate some probable differences in developments which will in turn suggest the extent to which a particular leader can shape events.

The area in which Dr Margai's personal prejudices were most significant was the position of chieftaincy. His strong pro-chief leanings allowed him to maintain the colonial regime's protection of chiefs against intrigues from below, while at the same time he greatly reduced the controls from above, and allowed the chiefs to entrench themselves both in the government and the ruling party. His use of the chiefs as conduits for such central government privileges as mining licences and building loans also contributed to maintaining their position against the intrusion of new 'patrons', to some extent offsetting the incursions of such new rivals as Court Presidents and Members of Parliament. This bias in favour of the chiefs contributed greatly to first the 1955-6 riots and then the establishment of a somewhat class-conscious opposition in the north, and to the even more class-conscious opposition in Kono; and even in Mende country it built up a body of dissatisfied younger men inside the SLPP.

A leader with a less conservative bias might not have avoided a substantial dependence upon the chiefs, but at least he might have reduced their privileged position and their opportunities for abuse of their people, thus making it less likely that persons resenting those privileges would have to form opposition movements to try to end them. At the same time, since reducing the chiefs' voice in the national government would have given greater scope for 'modernisers' seeking more rapid economic development and a more 'meritocratic' society, the national government might well have become much more remote from ordinary people, and less attuned to their demands.[14] The major social cleavage, in other words, would have probably been between an urban centre and a rural periphery, rather than being carried down to each chiefdom.

Dr Margai's failure to attempt to alleviate regional disparities[15] was a rather more indirect aspect of his conservatism, but was a direct cause of the awakening of ethnic consciousness among the Konos and the Temne, Limba and other northern tribes. Again, a less conservative individual might have been more willing to work to alleviate disparities in order to head off ethnic discontent, although it is doubtful that enough resources were available for the 'backward' areas to prevent their feeling discriminated against. The only strategy that had a reasonable chance of success in averting the growth of ethnic consciousness was the radical one of distracting attention from economic disparities by appeals to other common interests.

The diamond rush, whose uprooting effects permanently changed the political face of Sierra Leone, was beyond the control of any political leader, at least in its aspects as a mass search for personal wealth. A conservative could seek to contain it through traditional structures, a non-ideologue could try to come to terms with the desires and new orientations brought about by it, but neither was likely to make any creative use of the energies unleashed by it. It is just possible that a radical leader with a creative style could have channelled the new sense of self-reliance and questioning of old institutions engendered by the diamond rush into a political movement seeking a major reconstruction of the society, but probably the taste for increased consumption developed in the boom would have precluded any development strategy based on either internally generated investment or a non-material orientation. The diamond rush's most critical effect, then, even more than its calling into question the existing social structures, was its encouragement of heightened material consumption among ordinary Sierra Leoneans, which tied Sierra Leone more firmly into a peripheral position in relation to the industrialised states.

In the field of economic development, Dr Margai's conservatism probably benefited Sierra Leone. It was not until his own grip had weakened and Albert Margai took control of the Finance portfolio that Sierra Leone entered into the large number of disastrous arrangements with contractors which most countries anxious to develop seem prey to.[16] In general, Sierra Leone seems to have kept pace with other West African states of roughly comparable endowments, while in areas where the leader's choices were decisive, such as the building of presidential palaces, his regime had nothing to compare with the edifices of Tubman, Houphouet-Boigny or even Hubert Maga of Dahomey.[17] While Dr Margai's 'Open Door' policy did nothing to break Sierra Leone out of its dependent relationship with the industrialised states, he at least did not do much to increase that dependence.

In judging the effects of Dr Margai's leadership, we need to consider also the contribution of his brokerage style. Dr Margai's willingness to take opponents into his government might appear to indicate a willingness to compromise[18] but it was not. The leaders of opposition groups were given places, to be sure, but on Dr Margai's terms. In this ability to co-opt opponents into his entourage, Dr Margai resembled the Emperor of Ethiopia,[19] or to some extent Léopold Senghor of Senegal, who shared with him the absence of any personal royal legitimacy. This ability to remove opponents without modifying the system removed the articulators of discontent, but left the potentially dangerous situation of increasing dissatisfaction with no outlets.

The effects of Dr Margai's beliefs and style, then, could be summarised as follows: his conservative ideology, by maintaining the chiefs' position, helped push critics of chieftaincy into the opposition parties, but at the same time delayed the development of a sharp cleavage between a privileged urban educated elite and the countryside. The same conservatism slowed the pace of economic development, including its more costly manifestations. His brokerage style absorbed opponents in the political elite but did little to alleviate regional discontents, and nothing to guide the newly mobilised diamond diggers into support for the regime. His attitudes and behaviour thus left a wide opening for an opposition party to capitalise on a range of growing discontents.

By 1964, the social changes that had taken place in Sierra Leone under Dr Margai's leadership had modified considerably the range of possible choices for a leader. Among the major changes that had occurred, the following seemed most significant.

First, the number of persons whose situation could lead them to question the privileges of the chiefs had greatly increased. The substantial increase in the population of the cities and towns, the opening up of more widespread contact for rural dwellers through new roads and the transistor radio, and above all the massive participation in the diamond rush, all contributed to a more fluid situation. In the north and Kono opposition parties were translating this potential into actual discontent with the chiefs, while elsewhere the introduction of rival roles, notably the Court President, the Member of Parliament, wealthy diamond dealers, and less directly, central government officers, all challenged the chief's pre-eminent position. All these developments contributed to reducing the deferential grip of the chiefs, and replacing it with a more materialist patron-client attachment. Such an attachment, to be sure, was equally conservative[20] but there was a somewhat greater possibility that it in turn might break down rapidly, if the supply of material inducements became inadequate, or other considerations entered men's consciousness.

Second, there was now a strong ethnic awareness among most tribes, rather than a pan-Protectorate identity among those who transcended purely local awareness. Northerners and Konos felt strongly that they were disadvantaged, while Mendes were becoming aware that they enjoyed a relatively privileged position, and thus needed to take defensive precautions to safeguard it. The Creoles too, while not so passionately aroused as they had been in the early 1950s, were still warily guarding their civil service and educational strongholds. No Prime Minister, least of all a Mende, could expect to override this range of ethnic concerns without a great deal of preparatory work, and the bargaining nature of the governing party made massive shifts of resources to the disadvantaged groups improbable.

Third, the relative prosperity diffused over the countryside by the diamond rush had built up a widespread commitment to the enjoyment of a 'consumerist' society.[21] While Tanzania and neighbouring Guinea had never had a sufficiently prosperous body of Africans to build up much consumer demand for luxuries, and thus could accept the calls for continued sacrifice which Julius Nyerere and Sekou Touré made, Sierra Leone's position was closer to that of Ghana, where Nkrumah's attempts to impose austerity programmes met with bitter resistance from a widespread sector of society which had become accustomed to these goods.[22] Whatever else a political leader might try to do, he would have a hard time curbing the importation of manufactured consumer goods into Sierra Leone.

Taken singly, each of these constraints might be worked around by a wide range of leadership approaches; but in combination, they left open only very restricted possibilities. In dealing with the chiefs, Dr

Margai's conservative approach was becoming increasingly untenable. Not only were growing numbers of persons finding the chiefs' role irrelevant to their lives, and new rivals assuming many of their functions, but the chiefs' own behaviour was weakening their support. While their hold on ordinary rural dwellers was still strong, and thus their role as intermediaries was viable, the fact that criticism of them was concentrated in the more articulate and urban sectors of the society meant that a leader holding firm in their support would find himself increasingly isolated from those able to exert most influence over the whole polity. A less committed, more balanced approach such as that promised by Albert Margai was more likely to keep some support from both the chiefs and their detractors, though because of the chiefs' role in containing organised opposition, such an approach would inevitably be somewhat skewed in their favour. A more radical approach, replacing the chiefs by more loyal intermediaries, might have been sustainable by this time if a leader could find sufficient time and resources to maintain these intermediaries. But even the All Peoples Congress, which had started on a basis of anti-chiefism, found after 1968 that its path of least resistance to the grassroots was through the chiefs. In 1968 Prime Minister Stevens made it clear to his supporters that his government would support chieftaincy,[23] and by 1973, after purging the diehard SLPP supporters, the APC was making as full use of the chiefs as ever the SLPP had.

By 1964, 'tribal' and regional identities had hardened to the point where only a 'balancing' strategy among the different groups might be acceptable; a conservative's overarching appeal to chieftaincy and traditional values would seem irrelevant, and a radical's only chance would be to find an external force which all could view as a serious threat.[24] But a leader from the group suspected by all the others of trying to establish its hegemony would inevitably have to tilt the balance a long way in favour of the disadvantaged groups, even as he sought simultaneously to damp down any 'tribal' manifestations; and as we noted earlier[25] there just were not sufficient material resources available to allow the north to 'catch up' with Mendeland for a long, long time. Some leaders, it is true, were more skilful than Albert Margai in pursuing a 'balancing' strategy; Milton Obote, for example, who had the advantage of coming from one of Uganda's 'backward' areas, had managed to damp down a good deal of Uganda's 'tribal' discontent and was on the verge of reducing it further through his ingenious cross-regional electoral system, when he was overthrown by General Amin.[26] Félix Houphouet-Boigny, aided by the rising prosperity which washed over most of the Ivory Coast, managed to contain Ivorien tribalism by a mixture of developmental projects and elite appointments. But across Africa, the record of containing ethnic differences was not an impressive one. That an overarching appeal might not work in Sierra Leone was graphically demonstrated in 1970, when the APC government was confronted with a menacing new opposition party rising out of its own ethnic core, the Temnes. Temne expectations had been dashed at two levels; among the elite, where the 'jobs for the boys' expected in the civil service had been taken instead by more 'qualified' Creoles and at the local level, where a lack of finance prevented the massive 'catching up' programme in schools, dispensaries, feeder roads and other developments that had been expected.[27] The APC quickly banned the new party, but its appearance had been a sharp reminder that once ethnic consciousness was aroused, the resources for coping with it had to be substantial.[28]

In the economic sphere, the search for any kind of foreign investment that could be obtained was pursued under Albert Margai with far less restraint than had marked his brother's approach. This eagerness for tangible signs of economic activity, coupled with the Prime Minister's need for funds for his machine, left him vulnerable to the various manipulations of contractor financing and other often questionable promotions, and probably on balance left Sierra Leoneans economically worse off than if no such 'developments' had taken place. But since a more restrained approach would have appeared to flout the desires of 'modernising' elements, at least until the bills came in some years later, it would have been politically very risky. A 'radical' approach which in any way threatened the liberty of foreign investors to come and go as they pleased would also have been politically costly; not only would it have reduced the political elite's access to the finances necessary for a political organisation, but it would have alienated the wide range of traders, lorry driver, service personnel and others who directly benefitted from the import of foreign capital and goods.[29]

The system Albert Margai inherited in 1964 faced serious difficulties. Because of the growth of regional discontent, he was trapped into supporting the chiefs; to placate his anti-chief supporters, and to finance them, he had to seek substantial foreign investment, which precluded heavier demands on the existing mining enterprises. A consistent 'conservative' approach would simply have allowed these conflicts to accumulate; an overt 'radical' would find it nearly impossible to find an appeal that would overcome both ethnic suspicions and economic vested interests. A non-ideologue or a conservative prepared to modify his beliefs for the sake of maintaining a balance among existing demands might succeed in protecting his own position for a considerable time, although he would always be vulnerable to the risk that some group capable of disrupting the polity would refuse to accept the rules, or that different claims might be irreconcilable.[30] But his range of actions would be extremely circumscribed, and he would need a considerable element of luck as well as substantial resources to maintain his position.

Sierra Leone by 1964 offered no clear way in which a leader of the incumbent party could ensure his own survival, let alone offer a better life to his people. Neither radical nor conservative ideologies held much hope if implemented by an SLPP leader, while a non-ideologue was likely to simply let problems accumulate. Divisions within the polity had grown too deep for a creative style to override them, while a brokerage approach was hamstrung by too scarce resources. The very legitimacy of the leader might be undermined by the strength of ethnic feelings. One possible escape from this impasse seemed to be to change the whole elite in power, to give a new group a chance to make a fresh start. But even a new group, as the APC was to learn, had to work within the same constraints of ethnic antagonisms, unreliable intermediaries, domestic desires that outran resources, and foreign interests which were often at cross purposes with those of any Sierra Leone government.

The Limits to Choice

What general lessons can this study provide about the ability of leaders to affect events? It is striking to observe how far-reaching are the consequences of any action or inaction on the part of a leader, both in the breadth of fields affected and in the length of time over which they linger. But equally striking is the fact that many of the 'actions' which have far-reaching consequences are not consciously chosen, but rather develop slowly over time so that a pattern is firmly established before the leader perceives that a choice was possible. Studies of 'decision-making' which imply that the decision-makers have considered the range of choices open to them, and are aware of the consequences of their choice, seriously distort this reality.

The breadth of fields over which an action has repercussions has frequently been noted.[31] Vinogradov and Waterbury note a recurring pattern in Morocco whereby a ruler's actions in suppressing his opponents reduces the country's available wealth, and thus the resources which the ruler needs to maintain his support against further opponents.[32] James Bill has observed that in Iran a land reform programme intended to rally the peasants to the Shah's support against the educated middle class created expectations among the peasants for further change that could only be met by calling upon the skills of this selfsame middle class.[33] In Sierra Leone, the SLPP's reliance on the chiefs meant that a Prime Minister could not reallocate funds to less prosperous regions, and thus had to face growing 'tribal' disaffection. Sometimes the action causing wide repercussions is almost fortuitous, as was the assassination of Tom Mboya in Kenya in 1969. The killing of their leading spokesman in the government heightened Luo fears of Kikuyu domination just at the time when a government policy of wooing Oginga Odinga's Luo-based Kenya Peoples Union seemed on the point of succeeding. The resurgence of Luo ethnic consciousness staved off the peaceful absorption of the KPU, and Kenyatta instead had to ban it a year later, with the result that Luo suspicions were further inflamed.[34]

The time over which consequences persist, by creating patterns from which a leader later finds himself unable to escape, is also significant in imposing limits on leadership.[35] In Sierra Leone the Creole-countryman division in 1948-51 allowed the establishment of a chief-oriented non-nationalistic governing party, which throughout its tenure of office proved resistant to any attempts at a major social transformation in the countryside. We can find many examples of equally significant turning points elsewhere. Thus the decision of Northern Nigeria's moderates such as Abubakar Tafawa Balewa to side with the Emirs rather than with the 'radicals' in 1951 entrenched in power a class which could not afford a sufficiently open political system to prevent the breakdown of the first Nigerian Republic.[36] The fact that Guinea was a neglected backwater unsuitable for coffee or other crops that would have supported a planter bourgeoisie made it possible for Sekou Touré to build a successful radical movement.[37] Decades of concern over 'security' as the most vital goal of Moroccan politics served, when a radical party finally challenged the King directly, 'to drive many Moroccans from active politics altogether. . . . Caution as usual seemed the best policy'.[38] In all these and many more cases, a leader seeking to pursue a course of action found his way open or barred by patterns laid down years before.

In the Sierra Leone case, as I suggested above, certain 'critical' developments occurred in such a way that the leaders were not only unaware of their long-term consequences, but scarcely showed any signs of trying to influence them. They were most certainly not 'decisions' in the sense of conscious choices beteen competing values; yet they were 'critical' developments in the sense that alternative possibilities were open, and the course followed had a substantial impact upon the range of choices open to a leader in subsequent situations.[39] The four events I would designate as 'most critical' in Sierra Leone's political history from 1947 to 1967 are: the estrangement of the Creoles from the Protectorate people, the building of the SLPP around the chiefs, the 'Open Door' policy for economic development, and the failure of both the Margais to meet the regional grievances of the North.

The estrangement of most Creoles from the Protectorate following the 1947 constitutional proposals had its roots deep in Sierra Leone's history. The generations of social (though not political) superiority they had enjoyed over the 'aborigines' made any political arrangement in which the latter's numbers would be given greater political weight than the Creoles' cultural advantages hard for the Creoles to accept. It was possible, in view of the chiefs' unwillingness to share power with the educated Protectorate men, that an alliance of the latter with the Creoles might have been constituted, in which the Creoles' greater sophistication would have offset their lack of a numerically significant base. But two factors foreclosed this possibility: the Creoles' intransigence towards the Protectorate's educated elite was at least as great as that of the chiefs, and the Protectorate elite, again through a cumulative process of small advantages, nearly all had blood connections with the chiefs, which served to moderate their differences of interest. It would be most misleading to pinpoint any of the specifc acts by leaders of the Creole community, such as Otto During's motion in 1948 to recommit the constitutional proposals, or Wallace-Johnson's attacks in 1950 on Albert Margai, as being 'critical' in the sense that if they had not occurred, Creole-countryman relations would have been substantially different; these minor actions had a cumulative effect, but the Creoles' approach grew in such a way that no one act could be said to have been decisive.

Yet clearly this Creole-countryman split was a 'critical' turning-point. If the Creoles had been fully involved in a 'nationalist' movement, it is unlikely that Dr Margai would have been Prime Minister, that the governing party would have relied so heavily upon the chiefs, or that its relations with the mining companies would have been quite so circumspect. While we cannot say what form Sierra Leone's subsequent history would have taken, we can be fairly confident that it would have been quite different.

If the Creole-countryman split was the result of a long historical development, the symbiosis between the SLPP leaders and the chiefs was in its later stages partly fortuitous. Up to the widening of the franchise for the 1957 general election, it was hard for the SLPP leaders to avoid a considerable reliance on the chiefs, both because of the importance of the chiefs as a bloc in the legislature and, more important, because they controlled the selection of *all* Protectorate representatives to the legislature through the Tribal Authorities and District Councils. Nevertheless, even before 1957 it would have been possible for the SLPP leaders to put some effort into building up an extra-Parliamentary organisation in anticipation of the extension of the franchise, an effort they conspicuously failed to make.

After the 1957 election, when the SLPP's educated elite were nearly all in the legislature through direct election, and the chiefs no longer had a stranglehold on the electoral process, a reshaping of the SLPP to reduce its dependence on the chiefs was at last possible. Whether the younger and more eager 'modernisers' would have overcome their family ties with the chiefs and the force of inertia sufficiently to force such a reshaping of the party is problematic, even if the SLPP had continued to unite all Protectorate men against Creole opposition parties. But the split between the Margai brothers which culminated in 1958 with the breakaway of some of the 'modernisers' into the PNP, tipped the balance decisively against any reorganisation, both by weakening the internal pressures for change in the SLPP leadership and by forcing it to rely more heavily than before on the chiefs to put down a potentially menacing opposition party. I suggest this development was fortuitous in so far as the structure of the SLPP is concerned, in that to a large extent conflicts between individual personalities led to the PNP breakaway. If Dr Margai and his brother, or perhaps more important, those advising the two men, had been somewhat less antagonistic towards each other, the attempted reconciliation in 1957 might have succeeded. Again, however, it is not possible to point to one specific act which committed the SLPP to the path or reliance on the chiefs for its local support; the 'decision' was a cumulation of minor actions, and more frequently non-actions, which ultimately left both the Margais with no choice. Yet again the consequences were of major significance; if the SLPP had not relied so heavily upon the chiefs, it might well have been able to contain or even eliminate the APC, and Albert Margai might well have succeeded in establishing his personal position beyond challenge. Less directly, the SLPP might have been able to deal more effectively with the problem of northern regionalism, which also contributed to the downfall of the party as well as of Albert Margai.

The 'Open Door' economic policy for development was essentially a continuation of the colonial pattern of drifting and assuming that somehow *laissez-faire* would produce results. One might suggest that to some extent the 'Open Door' was pressed upon Sierra Leone by the British, although under colonial rule it was only British firms which received a welcome. The choices at Independence, however, were between the 'Open Door' for Western investment and some form of priority planning in which such investments would only be permitted under specific conditions. These conditions might include any of: restrictions on the types of activity open to foreign investment, restrictions on the share of control the foreign investor might exercise over the venture, or restrictions on the extent to which profits from the venture could be repatriated. Given Sierra Leone's somewhat weak position in competing with more than thirty other African states, imposing any such conditions might appear to be simply a way of refusing any investment at all. In other words, the 'Open Door' policy was scarcely a choice once the government had decided that economic development had to be sought, a decision which itself hardly appeared to allow debate.

Yet the 'Open Door' implied a considerable stepping up of Sierra Leoneans' aspirations, with the further implication that these would tend to outrun the country's capabilities. While this problem would have arisen in any case, the decision to continue an economic system in which all desires were judged as equally valid, where one man's desire for a Mercedes was measured by the same standard as another's need for rice, meant that existing inequities in the country would remain, and that in consequence it would be difficult to rally people in pursuit of any brave new world. Further, it ensured that the tastes cultivated among Sierra Leoneans were directed towards the use of private consumer goods, that they would seek health through drinking a bottle of Guinness rather than through enclosing the village well. And by building up Sierra Leoneans' desire for consumer goods, it ensured that their position as peripheral consumers of the manufacturing states' goods was strengthened. Again, however, this was a gradual process; no one could point to a single incident or time and say that it was the point at which Sierra Leone had embarked irrevocably on this course.

Northern discontent, too, developed gradually. It could be argued that its roots lay in the fact that the missions established more schools in the south, or that the south was the location of Sierra Leone's diamonds. More proximately, since northern discontent was not politically articulated until after the 1960 United Front, one could argue that the chiefs' hold on the SLPP, by making it a brokerage party and thus responsive to demands in proportion to their articulation, ensured that no special effort would be made to help the north 'catch up' until its spokesmen began to protest loudly enough for their demands to be heeded. One could even cite Albert Margai's blunders such as sacking northern members of the Cabinet, or carting off the cows from Kabala. But no one of these factors is a sufficient explanation; each certainly contributed, and it is plausible to suggest that even after 1960 some vigorous steps by Sir Milton might have allayed northern anxieties, but we cannot cite any clear point beyond which northern opposition to the SLPP was irreversible. Once again, the leaders drifted into this situation, being warned from time to time that it was developing, but because of various unrelated constraints being unable to act to prevent it.

In all four of these cases, then, while the events themselves were 'critical' in that they opened up certain long chains of consequences and precluded others, we simply cannot pinpoint the time at which this division came. Rather than using the metaphor of coming to a fork in a path, we might better picture the political leaders as scrambling through a trackless forest, seldom able to see more than a short way ahead, and often scarcely aware that they are drifting towards one outcome rather than another. In picking one's way through a trackless forest, one tends to follow a line of least resistance, sometimes even when one can see unpleasant consequences from continuing in this direction; there is, after all, always the possibility that the unforeseen consequences of following other routes might be even worse, or more likely that some unexpected opening will appear before the problem ahead become insuperable. Optimism for the future has been one of the great hallmarks of the past two centuries, and in the case of the 'developing' states it is fortified by the knowledge that others have accomplished what they are trying to do. Whether their optimism is justified is a question to which I will return in a moment.

Is there any particular approach to leadership that offers more hope than others of finding a route through this forest of difficulties to some plateau of a better life? At first glance, we might expect the leader with a radical ideology encompassing ways of bringing about a reconciliation of local, regional and ethnic interests, and of satisfying economic aspirations, to have the best chance of accomplishing this,[40] since he at least has the benefit of a map which should help him maintain a consistent direction. But when we look at the record of the few surviving 'radical' regimes in Africa[41] the record has not been particularly impressive. In some cases, such as Algeria and Zambia, the attempts at a radical transformation have been bogged down under the pressure of privileged bureaucracies, or of ethnic conflicts.[42] In others, such as Guinea, the initial radical transforming thrust seems to have been replaced by rather desperate attempts to protect the regime's position by purges and terror, while the economy moves back towards local self-sufficiency at a subsistence level.[43] While it did accomplish the vital task of making most Ghanaians identify with the country, Nkrumah's regime was no glowing testament to the efficacy of 'radical' measures.[44] Nyerere's regime, while it seems to be having some success in developing an altruistic concept of the 'new Tanzanian man' among the elite,[45] still has not shown convincingly that it can imbed such attitudes firmly in the evolving Tanzanian political culture.[46] At best, we can say that under particularly favourable circumstances the radical approach may work, but that there is a considerable risk that it can lead to a repressive regime no longer concerned with the interests of the people, or that it will be overthrown by a combination of internal and external enemies.

A non-ideologue seeking to steer a conciliatory course among the competing claims within the state can survive under favourable conditions, but his ability to build a better society is more problematic. Clearly, in order to balance claims he cannot allow these to become irreconcilable. It also seems important that he should have to deal with only one crisis at a time, in order to reduce the risk that all his viable options in dealing with one problem are not blocked by a different problem. Milton Obote, for example, succeeded in resolving the Buganda problem, first by his alliance with the Kabaka Yekka and then by ousting Mutesa II, before he attempted to tackle the problem of privileged elites through the 'Common Man's Charter'.[47]

Successful 'non-ideologues' may in fact have a very clear idea of the changes they want to accomplish, but may simply be careful to disguise the fact that the specific 'incremental' changes they make when the occasion seems auspicious add up to fairly sweeping social transformations.[48] Félix Houphouet-Boigny, so frequently regarded as either a 'conservative' or at least as a non-ideologue, in retrospect appears to be one African example of such a disguised radical.[49] Although it is still an open question whether the Ivory Coast's 'economic miracle' will ultimately bring about structural changes that will reduce the country's 'vulnerability' and its peripheral relationship with the industrialised states, it seems clear that Houphouet-Boigny has succeeded in accomplishing a major socio-economic change, the establishment of a dominant African bourgeoisie, and the ascendancy of its values over more 'traditional' ones.[50] Without a clear idea of where he is going, a leader is unlikely to accomplish such a transformation; there is too great a likelihood that he will take expedient actions that foreclose courses he would later like to follow.[51]

The conservative ideologue, I suggested earlier, tends to be fighting rearguard actions against changes introduced from outside the society. Sometimes, like Haile Selassie or King Hassan of Morocco, he has a deep reservoir of personal and institutional legitimacy on which he can draw to sustain himself against attacks by those impatient for change.[52] At other times, he has built a position as the 'Father of his Country', a leader possessing the advantages of age and experience over his lieutenants, whom he generally allows to carry out the routine tasks of government, while he intervenes primarily in crises. Kenyatta is the obvious illustration of this type of leader.[53] The conservative's resistance to change for its own sake does offer some barrier to the destabilising effects of rapid upheavals,[54] although as long as changes can still be thrust on the polity from outside, he risks allowing grievances to accumulate until they explode. The other area in which the conservative's approach seems unsatisfactory in a former colonial territory is in dealing with the new state's dependent relationship with the industrialised states. Whether or not one accepts the thesis that the industrialised states are determined to prevent the Third World from building its own industrial capabilities, it seems fairly clear that the present raw materials for manufactured consumer goods exchange is not going to make the people of the raw material producing countries any better off.[55] The conservative's tendency to allow this pattern to harden may well leave his polity locked into this condition beyond any reasonable hope of breaking out.

There seems to be no magic approach to leadership, then, that guarantees that a leader will either be able to achieve satisfying goals for his polity or even to assure his own survival. While it is not inevitable that he will lead his country over the spectacular precipices of national bankruptcy or a breakdown of government control, or into the more extensive morass of stagnation and corruption which seems to lie in wait for most small peripheral countries, the chances of avoiding these outcomes do not seem good. The combination of foresight, skill, existing circumstances and plain luck necessary to carry a polity around these obstacles seem sufficiently uncommon that few leaders of African or other Third World countries are likely to succeed in bettering their peoples' lives.

This broad barrier to hope is joined by more specific factors to produce a peculiarly corrupting effect upon African leaders, a strong pressure to seek what they can for themselves rather than working to better their countries. Internally, the weakness of mechanisms both for channelling innovations downwards and popular attitudes upwards have left the major effective influences on the leader those of persons concentrated in the capital, notably the civil servants, the military, and business, professional and other formally educated groups. Outside the country, few persons possessing any power care how a leader runs his state. African leaders, with the noteworthy exceptions of Nyerere and Kaunda, have eschewed any attempts to apply moral pressure even to the most brutal regimes.[56] While the media in the industrialised states have frequently drawn gory pictures of 'primordial' savagery, neither their governments nor their major corporations have shown any squeamishness in seeking advantageous economic arrangements; while chaos which might endanger their executives' lives is bad for business, a regime which efficiently kills off its opponents is not.[57] Any attempt by a leader to reduce his state's dependence upon the industrialised states will bring attacks from both foreign corporations and from domestic vested interests. It is very easy under such circumstances for a leader to abandon whatever dreams he may have had of bettering his country, and to concentrate on bettering his own position, while making just enough effort as a leader to keep the state from collapsing.

Probably no national political leader's motivations can bear such a simplistic interpretation as that they sought only their own good; Albert Margai, Fulbert Youlou of Congo-Brazzaville, and Maurice Yameogo of Upper Volta all had visions of what they would do for their countries, just as surely as did, say, Sir Richard Squires of Newfoundland or Richard Nixon of the United States, even though all tended to see the good of the country and their own good as inextricably intertwined. But there is no reason to expect African leaders to be more idealistic or altruistic than politicians elsewhere; and while countries like France or the United States have sufficient structural and cultural restraints built into their political systems that they can force a Chaban-Delmas or a Nixon from office, such restraints are very much weaker in Africa. The result is that it is considerably easier for a leader in Africa than for a leader elsewhere to pursue personal satisfactions free from any restraints other than his own conscience, while it remains comparatively difficult for him to pursue goals that will make significant changes in his country.

The problems facing African leaders, then, are daunting ones, and they cannot be sure that any course they may follow will lead them to a desirable goal for their country. I hope that studies like this, by showing the constraints within which leaders must operate, can help dispel both the unrealistic expectations that surrounded most leaders at independence, and the harsh judgements that were later made about both their competence and their motivations.[58] It may be, too, that as leaders become sensitive both to the time and to the breadth of areas over which their actions have ramifications, they may be able to avoid at least some of the pitfalls that lie ahead. Certainly no one can feel any great assurance that somehow 'things will come out all right'; but as long as there are some possible courses of action that may improve their countries' situations, we need not totally despair.

Notes

1. An 'incrementalist' approach can produce some industrialisation in a country, as Elliott Berg has argued. See 'Structural Transformation versus Gradualism', in Foster and Zolberg, *Ghana and the Ivory Coast*, pp. 215-17.
2. Even an attempt by the colonial power to halt the movement towards independence, which in most African territories would have served to unite all the African groups in protest, would in Sierra Leone probably have had considerable support among Creoles, and possibly among many ordinary people up-country as well.
3. How far this went can be seen from the fact that in the 1968 survey, the northern members of the 'Establishment' in the sample – Tribal Authorities and members of ruling families – claimed to have voted solidly for the APC in 1967, whereas in 1962 most had voted SLPP.
4. In the debate on the one-party state, Albert Margai claimed that opposition accusations of corruption were keeping foreign investors away. I am inclined to think that the opposite might be the case, that investors would prefer government leaders who could be bought to those who might have a fanatical commitment to principles.
5. Of critical importance in creating this pressure of expectations is the simple fact that the Western nations already were industrialised when Africans became aware of the possibilities of industrialisation. See on this Michael Lofchie (ed.), *The State of the Nations*, Berkeley and Los Angeles, University of California Press, 1971, pp. 9-18.
6. See Cartwright, *Politics in Sierra Leone*, pp. 128-9, for some details of the lack of expectations about benefits deriving from Independence.
7. The appointment of Gershon Collier as Ambassador to the United States, from which position he helped Albert Margai in his overseas investments, is one of the more striking illustrations of this.
8. See above, pp. 263-4.
9. For the rise and fall of this attempt by the Guinea government to mobilise manpower for local improvements, see David Hapgood, *Africa: From Independence to Tomorrow*, New York, Atheneum, 1965, pp. 148-50. Hapgood suggests that the main reason for the failure of this programme was that from its initial orientation towards creating facilities that would be of use to the people of the area, such as feeder roads, schools and hospitals, it gradually shifted towards providing facilities such as office buildings and rest houses for the political elite.
10. P.J. Vatikiotis claims that despite his desire to reshape Algerian society,

which formed the basis of his appeal to city-dwellers, Ben Bella at the same time managed to appear to rural traditionalists as the devout Moslem who would protect their ways against his more 'Westernised' colleagues. 'Tradition and Political Leadership', ***Middle Eastern Studies,*** 2, 4, 1966, pp. 330-66.

11. The inability of the Northern Elements Progressive Union of Northern Nigeria, perhaps the best example in Africa of a purely 'class' party, to win more than a minority of the *talakawa* to its support, is indicative of the magnitude of these difficulties. As Post points out, to ask the ordinary farmer to vote against the Emir's expressed wishes was asking him to vote against not just all his social 'betters', but against the entire natural order of things and even against God. K.W.J. Post, *The Nigerian Federal Election of 1959,* London, Oxford University Press, 1963, p. 423.
12. In the Congo, Weiss has noted that the leaders of the Parti Solidaire Africaine were forced to incorporate far more members than they had anticipated and to adopt a more radical posture as a result of spontaneous local protests which went far beyond their original intentions. Herbert Weiss, *Political Protest in the Congo,* Princeton, N.J., Princeton University Press, 1967, pp. 192-208.
13. The CPP in Ghana did manage fairly early to turn the Cocoa Purchasing Commission into a useful source of funds for a party machine, as the Jibowu Commission revealed; but by this time (1956) it had reached an accommodation with the British colonial administration, and was not pressing an anti-chief stand strongly. See Austin, *Politics in Ghana,* pp. 341-2.
14. Julian Pollock has noted that government officials in the Bombali district left themselves disadvantaged in their influence over ordinary people as compared to traders and chiefs by their custom of living in separated residential areas. *Influence, Authority and Opportunity,* pp. 161-2. Cf. Norman Miller's comment that Tanzanian administrators have adopted European norms of conduct, keeping their distance from ordinary people. 'The Political Survival of Traditional Leadership', *Journal of Modern African Studies,* VI, 2, Aug. 1968, pp. 192-3.
15. That this was not solely attributable to a lack of resources was suggested by the fact that he did appoint a special Kono Development Officer and establish a special Kono Development Fund in 1958, when agitation had reached a peak. Within two years both the fund and the officer had quietly faded away.
16. See Cohen and Tribe, 'Suppliers' Credits in Ghana and Uganda', and Schatz, 'Crude Private Neo-Imperialism' for illustrations from other parts of Africa.
17. Maga's palace, though valued at a mere $3 million, was perhaps more of an extravagance than those of Tubman or Houphouet-Boigny, since Dahomey could not even balance its operational budget at the time without a French subsidy.
18. Cf. Ali Mazrui's interesting article on Milton Obote, in which he argues that Obote's skill lay in his style as a 'reconciling' leader able to bring together opposing viewpoints, yet keeping in mind his own long-term goals. 'Leadership in Africa: Obote of Uganda', *International Journal* (Toronto), XXV, 3, Summer 1970, pp. 538-64.
19. For a discussion of Haile Selassie's approach, and its limits, see Christopher Clapham, 'Imperial Leadership in Ethiopia', *African Affairs,* 68, Apr. 1969, esp. pp. 116-17.

20. Two of the characteristics cited by James Scott as contributing to the inherent conservatism of political machines seem particularly appropriate in the African setting, namely their emphasis on short-run gains at the expense of long-run transformations, and their fostering of inter-class collaboration rather than class conflict. See his 'Corruption, Machine Politics and Political Change', *American Political Science Reveiw,* LXIII, 4, Dec. 1969, pp. 1154-5.
21. I am using here the distinction made by Alan Wells in his study *Picture-Tube Imperialism? The Impact of U.S. Television on Latin America,* Maryknoll, N.Y., Orbis Books, 1972. Wells argues that there are two distinct elements in attitudes towards economic development: 'consumerism', the 'increase in the consumption of the material culture of the developed countries' (p. 43), and 'producerism', the 'mobilisation of a society's population to work . . . in the non-consumerist sector of the economy' (p. 45). While over-simplified, Wells's work does make it clear that the growing desire among sectors of the Third World to emulate the consumer products and tastes of the industrialised states is not necessarily accompanied by a desire to create one's own products or even to acquire the skills necessary to reproduce the developed countries' material culture for oneself, and that this predominance of 'consumerism' over 'producerism' will inevitably maintain these countries in their 'peripheral' status.
22. While there were other elements in the antagonism towards Nkrumah's policies manifested among small businessmen, prosperous farmers and wage labourers (not least resentment over corruption which benefited only the elite), the imposition of the austerity programmes had a substantial effect in undermining his regime. For two different perspectives, see St Clair Drake and L.A. Lacy, 'Government versus the Unions: The Sekondi-Takoradi Strike, 1961', in Gwendolen Carter (ed.), *Politics in Africa; Seven Cases,* New York, Harcourt Brace, 1966, pp. 67-118, and Barbara Callaway and Emily Card, 'Political Constraints on Economic Development in Ghana', in Lofchie, *State of the Nations,* pp. 82-7.
23. See 'Machet's Diary', *West Africa,* 14 Dec. 1968, p. 1463.
24. Albert Margai did make a half-hearted attempt to reunite all 'countrymen' against the Creoles in 1966, but found little response in the north. Sekou Touré has continuously sought to unite all Guineans against the threat of foreign 'imperialists', but how effective this appeal remains is uncertain.
25. See above, pp. 41-2, 175-6.
26. See Mazrui, 'Leadership in Africa', pp. 555-64. The electoral system Obote proposed to institute would have required that a candidate win electoral support in all four of the country's regions to be elected to the legislature. See Michael Twaddle, 'The Amin Coup', *Journal of Commonwealth Political Studies,* X, 2, July 1972, p. 102. It bore some resemblance to the electoral system of Lebanon, whre candidates must be drawn proportionately from specific religious groups, but all candidates must be elected by all the electorate.
27. See Cartwright and Cox, 'Left Turn for Sierra Leone?'.
28. In fact, it seems likely that many improvements serve to whet appetites for further ones. James Bill notes that in Iran 'villages with wells were demanding electricity; those with wells and electricity asked for grade schools; those with wells, electricity and grade schools pleaded for high schools; those with wells, electricity, grade schools and high schools requested girls' schools; and Kazirun, with all these facilities, was demanding a technical college'. *The Politics of Iran,* Columbus, Ohio, Merrill, 1972, p. 154.

29. In Ghana, Nkrumah's radicalism was apparently curbed by the need for massive foreign financing for the Volta River project; he allegedly felt that 'deference to the West and playing the role of a compromising pragmatist was a necessary price to pay to assure the success of the programme'. Barbara Callaway and Emily Card. 'Political Constraints on Economic Development in Ghana', in Lofchie, *State of the Nations*, p.79.
30. A parallel argument that a conservative balancing strategy reaches its limits when a group arises that will not accept these rules is made by Waterbury in his study of Morocco. He suggests that while the existing elites play by the rules of a system based on royal favours and shifting alliances, a body of educated youth has come into being who are likely to reject the whole system, since they gain nothing from it. See John Waterbury, *The Commander of The Faithful*, New York, Columbia University Press, 1970, esp. pp. 300-15.
31. For some general comments on this, see Taketsugu Tsurutani, *The Politics of National Development*, New York, Chandler, 1973, pp. 154-6; also Albert Hirschman, *Journeys Toward Progress*, New York, Twentieth Century Fund, 1963, p. 269.
32. A. Vinogradov and J. Waterbury, 'Situations of Contested Legitimacy in Morocco: An Alternative Framework', *Comparative Studies in Society and History*, 13, 1, Jan. 1971, p. 56.
33. Bill, *Politics in Iran*, pp. 153-5. This strategy of calling in the peasants to act as a conservative counterweight to 'modernising' urban demands is one advocated by Samuel Huntington in *Political Order in Changing Societies* (pp. 435-8, 443-60); Bill's study suggests, however, that this strategy is a very risky one, since it may well unleash a range of demands from the peasantry that a conservative leader is incapable of meeting.
34. See Donald Savage, 'Kenyatta and the Development of African Nationalism in Kenya', *International Journal*, XXV, 3, Summer 1970, pp. 528-31.
35. Tsurutani, *Politics of National Development*, pp. 154-6, is as much concerned with the time dimension as with the breadth of effects.
36. For a discussion of the events producing this alignment, see Richard Sklar, *Nigerian Political Parties*, Princeton, N.J., Princeton University Press, 1963, pp. 91-6.
37. Virginia Thompson and Richard Adloff's comprehensive work on the 1950s, *French West Africa*, New York, Greenwood, 1969, notes that Guinea's sudden upsurge at that time was entirely due to mining (pp. 136-9); African farmers' production of cash crops for export was less not only than Senegal's on the Ivory Coasts, but even than Dahomey's (pp. 313-30). The rural sector simply did not undergo an 'embourgeoisement' comparable to Sierra Leone's.
38. Vinogradov and Waterbury, 'Contested Legitimacy in Morocco', p. 55.
39. I am using 'critical' here in the sense of those decisions which are most general in their scope, and thus subsume the widest range of consequent decisions. For example, the decision by a developing country that it wants to undertake economic 'development' is a fairly general decision subsuming more specific decisions to admit foreign mining companies, which in turn subsume even more specific decisions concerning the number of expatriate employees each company will be allowed, the rate of tax on their operations, and so on. This is the 'decision-making tree' model originally developed by public administration theorists, but more recently adapted for use in studies of leadership and power. See McFarland, *Power and Leadership in Pluralist Systems*, ch. 6, for a full discussion.

40. Although the reference to 'economic aspirations' implies that a 'better life' means one with improved material conditions, the same argument would apply to a leader whose 'better life' consisted of increasing his peoples' autonomy or self-reliance or pride in their identity.
41. That 'radical' regimes have had a rather poorer survival record in Africa and elsewhere than have more 'conservative' ones can be attributed in large measure to the fact that they tend to be much more heavily subjected to external attempts to undermine them, and to some degree also to the relatively high degree of sympathy their opponents within the country can command. The French ousting of Djibo Bakary of Niger, the open rejoicing by the British government at Obote's overthrow by General Amin, the constant carping in the West at Nkrumah's and Touré's handling of their political opponents while equally severe handling by less radical regimes was ignored, all form part of the extra burden which such governments in Africa and elsewhere in the Third World must bear. While there has been no campaign by foreign powers against a 'radical' African leader as concerted as that which eventually brought about the murder of Salvador Allende and hundreds of his followers, the attitudes of the Western states towards such regimes as Nkrumah's and Sekou Touré's could scarcely be called sympathetic.
42. For a discussion of the bureaucratic undermining of Algeria's 'revolution', see David and Marina Ottaway, *Algeria: The Politics of a Socialist Revolution*, Berkely and Los Angeles, University of California Press, 1970. For a sympathetic discussion of how 'tribalism' broke down a balancing strategy in Zambia, and undermined the implementation of President Kaunda's 'Humanism', see Richard Hall, 'Zambia's Search for Political Stability', *World Today* XXV, Nov. 1969, pp. 488-95. For a much more critical account stressing corruption, abuses of power and a high level of dependence on expatriates as factors bogging down the Zambian economy, see James R. Hooker, 'Zambia since Independence', *American Universities Field Staff Reports*, Central and Southern Africa Series, XV, 12.
43. For a discussion of the plots and purges in Guinea since 1960, and Touré's increasing perception of them as originating with external enemies, see Claude Rivière, 'Purges et complots au sein du Parti Democratique de Guinée', *Revue française d'études politiques africaines* 95, Nov. 1973, pp. 31-45. For a sympathetic overview which nevertheless stresses the strangling effects of economic and bureaucratic bungling, see Ladipo Adamolekun, 'Some Reflections on Sekou Touré's Guinea', *West Africa*, 19 Mar. 1973, pp. 371-2; 26 March, pp. 403-4; 2 April, pp. 434-5; and 9 April, pp. 464-6.
44. One criticism of Ghana, of course, was that it was not truly 'radical' in its measures. See Robert Fitch and Mary Oppenheimer, *Ghana: End of an Illusion*, New York, Monthly Review Press, 1966. R.H. Green makes an attempt to argue that Ghana's record is really better than its critics suggest, but even he has to acknowledge that the record was less than satisfactory. 'Reflections on Economic Strategy', in Foster and Zolberg, *Ghana and the Ivory Coast*, esp. pp. 249-51.
45. Raymond Hopkins's study, although unfortunately completed before the Arusha Declaration gave altruism much more of a cutting edge, provides a good deal of evidence that the younger members of the educated elite at least professed Nyerere's values. See Raymond F. Hopkins, *Political Roles in a New State*, New Haven, Yale University Press, 1971, esp. pp. 133-9.
46. David Feldman's article on the growth of self-seeking among the more effective farmers in a *ujaama* village offers a salutary warning of the

difficulty of creating new values. 'Rural Socialism in Tanzania', in Colin Leys (ed.), *Politics and Change in Developing Countries,* London, Cambridge University Press, 1969.

47. See Mazrui, 'Leadership in Africa.' Mazrui makes the point that the Charter's title was much more radical than its contents (p. 555) which suggests that it was more an attempt to keep everyone happy than a genuine commitment to change.

48. Tsurutani's article 'Political Leadership' on the success of the Meiji reform leaders in Japan makes the point that while the reformers were prepared to mediate and to consolidate their achievements from time to time, they always kept their eyes on an ultimate goal. See also Huntington's discussion of the use of 'Fabian' and 'blitzkrieg' strategies and tactics, in *Political Order in Changing Societies,* pp. 344-58.

49. See the interpretation by Aristide Zolberg, 'Political Development in the Ivory Coast', in Foster and Zolberg, *Ghana and the Ivory Coast,* pp. 12-15. We might also note his refusal to appeal to historical antecedents in seeking to create an Ivorian identity: see Zolberg's 'Patterns of National Integration', *Journal of Modern African Studies,* V, 4, Dec. 1967, p. 464.

50. See the articles by Elliot Berg and Alain Levasseur in Foster and Zolberg, op.cit., for discussion of some of the structural changes that Houphouet-Boigny's policies have brought about.

51. If, for example, Houphouet-Boigny had reacted to French repression in the period 1948-51 by espousing a militant anti-French nationalism, as did his lieutenant in the RDA, Sekou Toure, it seems unlikely that the Ivory Coast would have been favoured with the sustained French investment and consequent economic prosperity which it enjoyed from the mid-1950s onwards.

52. The months the military in Ethiopia took during 1974 to strip the Emperor of his powers before daring to attack him directly indicates the strength of his hold on the populace. It is not only conservative leaders who can build up such a position; the military in Indonesia similarly spent months cutting away Sukarno's powers before completely removing him from office.

53. See Mazrui, 'Leadership in Africa', pp. 539-41; also Savage, 'Kenyatta and the Development of African Nationalism.'

54. I would be inclined to expand Mancur Olson's argument about the destabilising effect of rapid economic growth to cover all forms of rapid social change that alter significant existing social relations. See his 'Rapid Growth as a Destabilising Force', *Journal of Economic History,* XXVII, Dec. 1963, pp. 529-52.

55. In this I concur with Galtung's argument about the relative spin-off effects of raw material production and of processing. See 'A Structural Theory of Imperialism', pp. 100-4.

56. Their silence, both individually and collectively, on the slaughter of Hutu leaders in Burundi, and on the carnage wrought by General Amin's soldiers against all his suspected enemies., is eloquent on this point.

57. For one illustration of this 'business-as-usual' attitude, see Roger Morris, 'The United States and Burundi; Genocide, Nickel and "Normalisation" ', *The Progressive,* Apr. 1974, pp. 27-9.

58. Among the works which most emphatically argue that African leaders are motivated primarily by personal lusts for power or riches, see especially Sir Arthur Lewis, *Politics in West Africa,* London, Allen & Unwin, 1965, Stanislav Andreski, *The African Predicament,* London, Michael Joseph, 1969, and Henry Bretton, *Power and Politics in Africa,* Chicago, Aldine, 1973.

METHODOLOGICAL APPENDIX
THE 1968 QUESTIONNAIRE REGARDING LEADERSHIP IN SIERRA LEONE

In 1968, the writer and Professor Jordan decided to supplement our own observations on political leadership with a sampling of the opinions of ordinary Sierra Leoneans. Since we made this decision after I had obtained my research grant, we were hampered by lack of time and money; however, we thought that shaky as the data collected might be, they would at least offer some indication of prevailing attitudes.

The questionnaire was administered to a stratified sample of 139 adult male Sierra Leoneans, all native to the localities in which they were interviewed. The interviewers were fourteen students from Fourah Bay College, most of them former students of the writers, and drawn from different ethnic groups (five Mende, four Temne, two Limba, one Koranko, and two Kono). Each interviewer was to find ten respondents of his own language group selected so that the total group met certain quotas based on age, literacy, occupation, status, participation in local government, and size of residential location, and to interview these respondents in their own vernacular language, with the responses being translated into English by the interviewer and written down by him. The responses were all coded by the writer for computer analysis.

Such a loose procedure is filled with pitfalls, most of which unfortunately were unavoidable. Since prevailing social attitudes in Sierra Leone dictate an attitude of wariness towards 'strangers', especially educated strangers asking questions about politics, and since at the time of the survey a new government installed by a military coup was just beginning to assert its power, it seemed necessary that the interviewers should confine their questioning to respondents who knew them personally. Although there were dangers that the interviewers' status as educated men as well as their connections with 'big men' in the area and the high value placed on consensus in most communities might all bias respondents' replies, the experience of other researchers in interviewing strangers suggested that personal acquaintance might be the less of two evils. Since relying on personal acquaintance as a means of gaining access to respondents also undermined any 'randomness' in the sample, it was also decided to work through a stratified quota system.

The ideal interviewing system of arming each interviewer with a tape recorder and having someone else translate the interview transcript into English was unfortunately ruled out by both cost and availability of possible translators. This left the responses open to substantial possibilities of diverse translations, as well as to the risk that interviewers may have put words into their respondents' mouths; the only real safeguard against this was the likelihood that different interviewers' biases would cancel each other out. Although I did check most interviewers' accounts of their interviews, there appeared to be a few cases where the interviewers' views prevailed. Finally, the questionnaire turned out to be much too long, and this may have led to distorted or misleading responses in the latter part out of boredom.

Despite these weaknesses, there seemed to be enough material of interest in the responses to justify using them as indications of probable attitudes, provided they were used only as an additional line of confirmation for arguments substantiated through other means. I do not consider the questionnaire results reliable enough that they could be used to build a case for which no other convincing evidence existed; but when they confirm from a different direction attitudes for which other evidence already exists, I consider them useful as supplementary material, and have used them as such.

INDEX

Africanisation 99; *see also* Civil service
agriculture 195-6, 242-2; northern lag in 175-6. *See also* Farmers Aku (Muslim) Creoles 171
alliances: in 1948-51 45-6; against Albert Margai 197
All Peoples Congress (APC) 73-4, 230; bases of support 177-9, 216, 223; relations with chiefs 147-8, 193, 227, 286; with Dr Margai 94, 97; with Albert Margai 102, 192; views on one-party state 78; on intermediaries 187-8; on modernisation 227-8; alliance with DPC 181. *See also* opposition, Stevens, Siaka
army: alleged coup 80-1; Mende CO 194-5; as barrier to change 231-2

Bai Koblo Pathbana, Paramount Chief 77, 94, 175
Bankole-Bright, Dr Herbert 44, 60, 95, 172
Bankole-Jones, Sir Samuel 192
Bo School 43, 146, 210n, 216
bourgeois values, 104-5

cabinet: imbalance between North and south 176-7; Creoles in 186
centre-periphery relations 242
chiefdoms 37
chiefdom clerk 124, 126
chiefdom speaker 124
chiefs: traditional roles 37, 44-5, 95-6, 131, 215; changes in position 123-32, 137-40, 214-5, 221; in Kono 180, 182; attitude to northern riots 69; to law reform 141, 142-3; to economic development 252-3; position in national government 48, 50; in SLPP 60, 61, 146-8, 218; leaders' strategies toward 132-6; Dr Margai's relations with 91-4, 230; Albert Margai's relations with 103, 105, 106, 143-8, 181, 231, 232-3; PNP and 225-6; APC and 147-8, 193, 227, 286
choices, leaders' 89; in 1953 280-2; by 1964 284-8
citizenship 184
civil service: as intermediaries 118; British officials in 48; Creole role 173-4, 186; Albert Margai's relations with 79, 102, 190, 193, 194, 231. *See also* Africanisation
class consciousness 67, 119, 163, 165; as threat to chieftaincy 127-9; and SLPIM 72; and APC 177-8, 227-8
clientage 120-7; and party competition 149; and modernisation 215; costs to Albert Margai 263-4
climate of opinion; and economic control 241
Cole, Mr. Justice COE 192
Cole Report 98
Collier, Gershon 190, 193
communication. *See* Intermediaries
Colonial Office: as source of pressure on Dr Margai 138
colonial government: structure 36
conflict. *See* class consciousness; ethnic conflict; modernisation
conservatism: Dr Margai's 92, 93-5, 98-9, 109, 140, 143; effects 284; and 'strong' intermediaries 150, 277; and economic change 261-2; and ethnic awareness 283
constitutional advance 46-9; and northern riots 69-70, 138; facilitates Dr Margai's emergence 92
constitution (Sierra Leone) 48-51; proposed republican 80
corruption, governmental 98, 194, 196, 254, 255, 256-7; costs to leaders 251, 264; as factor in northern riots 67-8; Lebanese role in 184
'countrymen': as basis for political solidarity 170-5
court messengers 137
court presidents: and chiefs 124, 125, 139, 141-3; and Prime Minister 106, 144-5
Cox Report 93, 137

Creoles 36, 39-40, 170-5; values 170-1, 191, 192; position in government structures 173, 174, 192; attitudes toward Protectorate 44, 59-60, 171-2; relations with Dr Margai 185-7; with Albert Margai 77, 79, 190, 191-3
'critical' developments 289-93

Democratic Peoples Congress (DPC) 181-2, 228-9
dependence 252-8, 259-64, 275, 278-9. *See also* economic development
diamond rush 34, 61-5; economic and social effects 65-6, 177, 180, 149-51; differences between Dr Margai and Albert Margai 63-4. *See also* mobilisation: Sierra Leone Selection Trust
Diamond Corporation (Dicor) 253, 254
district councils 124
Dorman, Sir Maurice 138, 219

economic development: defined 239-40; 'modernisation' model 240, 258; neo-Marxist model 240-1, 258-9; effects on chieftaincy 106, 125-7, 136; in north 41, 195-6; in Kono 181-2; role of Lebanese 183-4. *See also* agriculture; dependence; modernisation
economic policies 74-5, 255-7, 262; alternative strategies 238-9, 247-9
economy 34-5. *See also* agriculture; economic development; mining
education 39; effects 221; Creole position in educational system 40, 174; northern position 42, 176, 196; in Kono 180; levels of among party elites 225, 227
elections; rules for 81-2, 97-8; Freetown Council 190-1. *See also* franchise
elites 42-4, 134; dependence on foreign investors 253-7; factors for cohesion 216. *See also* Creoles; Protectorate intelligentsia
entrepreneurs, Sierra Leonean 105, 249-50
ethnic conflict 160, 162-3, 164; effects of on chieftaincy 277-8; Creoles against Protectorate 170-5; Mendes against north, 176-9; Konos against Mendes 179-80
ethnic groups 35, 53n, 159, 168
ethnic identities 119, 159-69, 178, 275; strategies for dealing with 165-8. *See also* 'countrymen'; Creoles; Kono; Mende; north; regionalism
ethnicity. *See* ethnic groups
Executive Council 46
export crops 242-3

farmers: numbers 128-9
forced labour 94, 139
foreign corporations 18, 253-7; and chiefs 134, 252-3; political donations 82
franchise 46, 48, 174
Freetown 36; 1955 riots 66-7, 96; 1964 council election 190-1

Gulama, Paramount Chief Julius 101

ideologue, 25, 30n
ideology, 25, 30n, 89, 93, 110, 150-1
information: diffusion among populace 224
intermediaries, role of 117-9, 135-6, 275; in APC 187-8

John, H.E.B. 44, 172
joint enterprise 256-7
judiciary 49; Albert Margai's conflict with 192-3
Jusu-Sheriff, Salia 216

Kai-Samba, Kutubu 146
Karefa-Smart, Dr John 76, 175
Kono identity 65, 179-82
Kono Progressive Movement. *See* Sierra Leone Progressive Independence Movement
Krio (language) 170. *See* Creoles

land ownership: as Creole grievance 44-5, 173
Lansana, Brigadier David 80, 81, 83
law, English and native: separation 142; integrated 143
lawyers: views on local courts 142; automony 222
leadership 11-12; elements: legitimacy 18-21; policies 22-3, 25-6; style 23-4; external constraints on leader 15-8; internal constraints 89-91 types of leader 25-6; relations with local leaders 121-2;

with chiefs 132-6; and ethnic strategies 167-8; and strategies in agriculture 244-5; and economic growth 259-63; possibilities for different types of leader in 1953 280-2; in 1964 284-8
Lebanese, 53n 182-4; economic activity 105, 249-50, 252, 255; political donations 82; Sierra Leonean attitudes toward 68, 183-4
Legislative Council 46, 47, 101
legitimacy 12-13, 17-19, 214; types of 19-21; Dr Margai's basis of 93-6. Albert Margai's basis of 106-7
libel charges: as weapon against opposition 192
linkages, economic: from mining companies 246; from alluvial diamond digging 249-50
literacy 38-9; among chiefs 124. *See also* Information
Local Courts Act (1963) 106
local courts 140-3, 147, 215
lorry drivers 222-3

Macauley, Berthan 76, 190
Margai, Albert 26, 32, 61, 67, 69, 71, 76, 77, 82, 96, 98, 290; character and career 100-8; contrast with Dr Margai 109-10; attitudes toward local government and chiefs 60, 141, 143-8; handling ethnic conflicts 179, 189-96; conflict with brother 217-9; economic dilemmas 262-4
Margai, Dr Milton 26, 32; character and career 91-100; handling ethnic conflicts 184-9; relations with chiefs 60, 69, 137-40, 230; treatment of opposition 72-3; conflict with brother 101, 217-9; contrasts with Albert Margai 109-10
Masonic lodge 171
Mbriwa, Paramount Chief T.S. 72, 77, 94, 181, 229
Member of Parliament: as rival to chief 126
Mendes: education 42; in Cabinet 87n; in civil service 102, 194-6; over-representation in Parliament 188
military. *See* army
mining: contribution to Sierra Leone economy 34-5, 245-7. *See also* diamond rush
mobilisation 18, 38-9, 71; differences between north and south 41-2
'modern' sector 17, 106
modernisation 212-5, 230-1
'modernisation' model. *See* Economic development
moral community: and cash nexus 220
Mustapha, M.S. 67, 185, 231

nationalism 159, 253
neo-Marxist model. *See* economic development
Nongowa chiefdom, 145-6
north: development of regional discontent 175-9; Dr Margai's handling of 187-8; Albert Margai's handling of 193-6; opposition to one-party state 79, 191-2, 193-4
northern riots (1955-56) 67-9, 137-8, 177, 183

one-party state 77-80; and chiefs' involvement 147-8; Creole opposition to 191; northern opposition 191-2, 193-4
opposition 70, 71, 73, 116-7; produced by SLPP's nature, 149, 216-7; basis in new roles 222-3. *See also* specific parties

paramount chiefs. *See* Chiefs
patronage 97, 106, 142-5, 175
Peoples National Party (PNP) 71-3, 101, 190, 193, 218, 224-7, 230-1
'periphery' status 242
personal links among elite 216
pluralism 16, 119, 191; supported by electoral system 51; by social change 221-3
political arena 13-4; interplay of national and local 106, 116-22, 126-7, 143-8
political efficacy: national and local compared 131
political elite. *See* elites
political participation. *See* clientage; elites; intermediaries; northern riots; populism
political structures; and pluralism 51; and regionalism 178-9; and ethnic concerns 199; and economic dependence 278
populism 125; obstacles to 129-30
Poro Society 36-7; conflict between Mende and Kono 180

prime minister, 49-50, 76, 95-6, 179, 192-3
Produce Marketing Board (PMB) 192, 194, 279
professions: Creole predominance in 40
Protectorate Assembly 43, 92, 101
Protectorate Educational Progressive Union (PEPU) 43, 92, 100, 218
Protectorate intelligentsia 45-6, 59

radicalism 26; obstacles to 122, 251, 252-3; symbolic 106
Rationality 198-9, 213-4
Regionalism 41-2; defined, 159; in Kono 72, 179-82; in north 73, 76-7, 147-8, 175-9, 193-6; and one-party state 78. *See also* ethnic conflict; ethnic identities; north
resident ministers 96, 140
'residual' sector 16-7
rice. *See* agriculture
riots. *See* Freetown; northern riots
roads 35, 41, 195
Rogers-Wright, Cyril 70-1
'rule of law': Creole support for 191, 192

Sankoh, Laminah 172
scapegoats: Creoles as 174-5; Lebanese as 184
sedition trials 192
secularism. *See* modernisation
Sesay, Y.D. 175, 210n
Sierra Leone: physical and demographic features 32-5
Sierra Leone Cement Company 75, 256-7
Sierra Leone Development Company (Delco) 34, 245-6, 253
Sierra Leone Peoples Party (SLPP) 43; as 'Protectorate' party 60-1; and chiefs 77-8, 138, 146-8; lack of openings for 'young men' 187-8; changes in elite 218
Sierra Leone Organisation Society (SOS) 216
Sierra Leone Progressive Independence Movement (SLPIM) 72, 180-2, 228-9. *See also* ethnic conflict; Kono identity; regionalism
Sierra Leone Selection Trust (SLST) 34, 61, 180, 181, 183, 245-7, 248, 253
social mobilisation. *See* mobilisation
Stevens, Siaka 32, 60, 61, 62, 67, 73, 82-3, 175; relations with Dr Margai 97, 188; split with Albert Margai 101; attitude toward chiefs 69, 148
strategies: for dealing with chiefs 149-51; for containing ethnic conflict 200-1; for economic development 259-64; over-all 274-88
style. *See* leadership

Temne 36, 56n, 179, 183
traditional culture: as restraint on Albert Margai's challenge to brother 218-9
Tribal Authority (TA), 41, 42, 46, 123
tribes. *See* ethnic groups
'tribalism' 159. *See* ethnic identity

United Front 96-7
United Sierra Leone Progressive Party (UPP) 70-1, 138, 216

values: created by diamond rush 251

wage workers 128
Wallace-Johnson, I.T.A. 60, 172, 290
We Yone (APC newspaper) 79, 104, 192

'young men': and northern riots 137
Youth League 60

www.ingramcontent.com/pod-product-compliance
Lightning Source LLC
LaVergne TN
LVHW090805070826
844660LV00022B/1086

9781442638976